W9-BNN-028

IRVING BERLIN

IRVING BERLIN

American Troubadour

EDWARD JABLONSKI

HENRY HOLT AND COMPANY   NEW YORK

Henry Holt and Company, Inc.
Publishers since 1866
115 West 18th Street
New York, New York 10011

Henry Holt® is a registered trademark of Henry Holt and Company, Inc.

Published in Canada by Fitzhenry & Whiteside Ltd.,
195 Allstate Parkway, Markham, Ontario L3R 4T8.

Library of Congress Cataloging-in-Publication Data

Jablonski, Edward.
Irving Berlin: American troubadour / Edward Jablonski.
p.   cm.
Includes discography, filmography, bibliographical references, and index.
ISBN 0-8050-4077-3 (hb: alk. paper)
1. Berlin, Irving, 1888–   . 2. Composers—United States—
Biography.   I. Title.
ML410.B499J33   1999
782.42164'092—dc21   98-3058
[B]   CIP

Henry Holt books are available for special promotions and premiums.
For details contact: Director, Special Markets.

First Edition 1999

Designed by Kate Nichols

Printed in the United States of America
All first editions are printed on acid-free paper. ∞

1   3   5   7   9   10   8   6   4   2

FOR

MICHELLE JACQUELINE AHLBERG

Let me sing a simple song
That helps to jog the world along—
Along its weary way—
And I'll be glad today.

Let me mold a homely phrase
For those who sit through wintry days
Before a fireside
And I'll be satisfied.

Let me be a troubadour
And I will ask for nothing more
Than one short hour or so—
To sing my song and go.

IRVING BERLIN
1938

CONTENTS

CONTENTS

IRVING BERLIN

PRELUDE:

GOLDEN SHORE

A SLENDER LITTLE BOY of four or five, huddled in a blanket and clinging to his mother, stared wide-eyed at the flames. The night glared, darkened by smoke and redolent of burning wood. He heard laughter, shouting, and screams. He did not understand all of this, but he knew that the small wooden structure now engulfed by fire was the home he shared with his parents, his brother, and his four sisters. His name was Israel.

His father, Cantor Moses Beilin, did understand: this was an eruption of the pogroms, those destructive, murderous, often fatal raids on Jewish settlements in czarist Russia that usually occurred around the time of the Orthodox Russian Easter.

Moses remembered reading about the Easter Riots, and one of the most savage pogroms, some dozen years before, following the assassination of Czar Alexander II. Alexander, an enlightened ruler, had introduced major reforms into Russian life, including the emancipation of the serfs, the encouragement of education, and the reduction of the time that must be served by Jews conscripted into the Russian army (often as early as the age of eight) from twenty-five years to five. Those who survived their service—and many did not—were permitted to travel outside the Pale of Settlement, a 400,000-square-mile ghetto annexed from Poland late in the eighteenth century. Jews were confined to this area and could not leave it unless they fulfilled certain requirements: they must be either wealthy and traveling on business matters, or high school graduates (some Jews were permitted to be educated), or Cantonists, as veterans of army service were called.

Alexander II, during his reign, had also encouraged the modernization and expansion of the Russian railway system, a good work that was a critical element in Moses Beilin's future plans as he bitterly contemplated his torched home.

The czar's regime had come to a violent end in 1881, the same year the Beilins' middle son, Benjamin, was born. Alexander was killed by a terrorist bomb; within a month, six conspirators, all members of the revolutionary People's Will party, were seized. Five were hanged, but the sixth, Hessia Helfman, was spared because she was pregnant; she was also a Jew. After the hangings, at Eastertime, several pogroms erupted in Russia.

The shtetl in which Moses Beilin served as cantor had been spared then, but now its time had come. The seeds of this new outbreak had been planted with the succession of Alexander III, son of the assassinated czar, to the throne. He had proceeded to undo much of his father's work and had instituted a policy of political oppression. In 1882, on the advice of corrupt bureaucrats in his government, he had promulgated what he termed Temporary Rules to place further onerous restrictions on the Jews; "temporary" in this case would last for twenty-five years.

When the Beilin home was destroyed, Benjamin, who had been overlooked for military impressment, was thirteen. He had evaded the draft because his parents had lied about his age. Young Israel would be eligible to serve in another three or four years. The new czar was not a kindly prince, as his father had been characterized by the British-born Jewish statesman Disraeli. Life in the Pale was already bad enough; with Alexander III in power, it could only grow worse. As the last flames flickered and dawn lighted the smoldering shtetl, Moses Beilin resolved to find a new life in America.

"America was in everybody's mouth," recalled a young Russian, Mary Antin, writing around this same time.

> People who had relatives in the famous land went around reading their letters for the enlightenment of less fortunate folks. . . . Children played at emigrating; old folks shook their sage heads over the evening fire, and prophesied no good for those who braved the terrors of the sea. . . . All talked about it, but scarcely anyone knew one true fact about this magic land.

Magic to some, it was a *goldene medine,* or Golden Land, to others. Amid the charred waste of his and his family's lives, Moses Beilin dreamed of reaching that longed-for place.

The name of the town where the shtetl was burned is not known, nor is the precise date of the burning, though it was probably in April, at Easter-time. What is certain is that the Beilins, at some point in their exodus, found a temporary haven with relatives in the city of Tolochin, in Belorussia, about eighty miles southwest of Smolensk. Tolochin had earlier been the birthplace of some of the Beilin children, and the oldest son and a married daughter probably still lived there. When Moses proposed his plan, the latter two chose to remain behind. The daughter, named Ethel (no one recalls the son's name), eventually joined her family in New York.

The question was, when the time came, how could Moses get himself, his wife, Leah, nineteen-year-old Sarah, sixteen-year-old Sifre, thirteen-year-old Benjamin, eight-year-old Rebecca, six-year-old Chasse, and the last-born, Israel, safely out of Russia?

It is possible, but not certain, that the town from which they fled was Moses's own birthplace, Tyumen (also called Temun or Tumum), in Siberia. While it was hundreds of miles east of the Pale of Settlement, an educated, itinerant cantor might have been permitted to journey there, even under the heavily restrictive rule of Alexander III.

Israel, the couple's eighth child, was born to Moses and Leah Lipkin Beilin in the spring of 1888. For years his official birth date has been given as May 11. In 1888 the Old Style (or Julian) calendar was in use in Russia; there's a twelve-day difference between that and the Western calendar. Leah Beilin could only recall that Israel was born in the spring. The date may have been her guess and it remained. His father was then forty-one or so (all dates in the story of the Beilins are approximate and suspect), and his mother about thirty-nine. If Tyumen, in western Siberia, was in fact the site of the house burning, Moses and his family were confronted with a formidable journey. Russia is a land of vast distances: Tyumen lies more than a thousand miles east of Moscow, and Tolochin, their one known starting point, is another three hundred miles to the south (and these are straight-line approximations—airline miles—not the true, much longer distances the Beilins would have had to travel by wagon or rail).

If we take Tolochin as their point of departure, we can only wonder, how did the Beilins, with six children ranging in age from five to nineteen, and six pieces of luggage (including a featherbed and a samovar), manage to arrive in New York Harbor on September 13, 1893? Further, how did they reach Antwerp, Belgium, to board the *Rhynland* on September 2? What must they have endured? What must it have cost them physically, psycho-logically—even financially? Regrettably, no one kept a record of their epic journey.

Other families in similar circumstances did keep diaries, however, and it is possible to reconstruct the passage of the Beilins overland from Tolochin to Antwerp—a distance roughly equal to that from New York to Denver, in a time of primitive transportation and social malevolence. They would have followed a route already established by the Paris-based Alliance Israelite Universelle, a group founded by the Baron Maurice de Hirsch in 1860.

Initially, de Hirsch had funded an educational program in Galicia, the Austro-Hungarian part of Poland acquired in the Partitions, which shared a border with the Russian portion of the acquisition, the Pale of Settlement. But later, when the first great flood of refugees began to flow out of Russia during the pogroms in the wake of the assassination of Alexander II, branches of the Alliance were set up in Austria, Germany, and other parts of Europe. Meanwhile, in 1881, the Baron de Hirsch Fund was organized in New York to assist in the settling of Jewish refugees from Europe in the United States and Canada. When the Beilins fled their homeland, there was thus an escape route in place.

The first challenge of their trip consisted in getting out of Russia. With all their children and luggage, they would have boarded a train at Mogolev, the nearest major town, probably with other emigrants. The Alliance would have arranged for their transportation beforehand. The train would carry them across a hostile (to Jews) Belorussia, to the town of Dubno, near the Austrian border of Galicia. There they would leave the train and by wagon, by cart, or on foot, skirt the border city of Radzivil and cross stealthily into Brody, in Austria.

Once in Brody, the emigrants would be in the hands of the Alliance and out of Russian jurisdiction. While the Austrian government in 1893 was not strict about documents, the Russian frontier, with its guards and immigration officials, was frequently closed to anyone with a Jewish passport—though a bribe might help, depending on the whim of the inspectors.

In Brody the emigrants would be screened for the next phase of their journey; it was here that the heartbreak began. Poor health and age meant rejection. If an emigrant passed the physical tests in Brody but was refused entry at New York, the shipping company would be obliged to repatriate the unfortunate individual at its own expense. The shippers therefore insisted that the Alliance be cautious in selecting those who were to leave for America.

Appeals for vigilance also came from America itself. Manuel A. Kursheedt, of the Russian Emigrant Relief Committee, complained that the Alliance was sending too many "clerks or tradesmen [who] know no handicraft and wish to peddle. We are overrun with peddlers already, who have become a source of much annoyance to us."

Particularly irritating to the Jewish population already established in the United States was the influx of eastern European Jews. Rabbi Isaac Wise of the Relief Committee in Cincinnati, for one, objected to their "corrupt German-Hebrew-Slavonic excuse for a language [i.e., Yiddish]." And, too, in the words of historian Ronald Sanders, the Russian Jews were often "resolutely orthodox . . . [and] disconcertingly ethnocentric. And, perhaps worst of all, they tended to be poor." The penniless newcomers unwittingly taxed the resources, not to mention the sensibilities, of the Jewish charities in the United States. They arrived, having studied the enthusiastic letters sent by relatives who had preceded them, expecting to be greeted with open arms at a golden door giving onto streets of gold.

The Beilins passed scrutiny in Brody, where Moses judiciously stated as his occupation *"shomer"* (i.e., "overseer" in a kosher butcher shop). They were given some money for the next stage of their journey, along with a circular that, among other things, instructed them to acquire a shoulder bag containing three loaves of bread and a water flask. "The flask," it read, "can be refilled with fresh water at the various stations where there are long waits. It is further recommended to bring along some brandy, cheese, and other desirable foodstuffs, since no food or drink will be provided during the entire overland journey."

The fare, as arranged by the Alliance, was roughly fifteen dollars (or its ruble equivalent) for each adult, and probably half that for children. Counting Sarah and Sifre as adults, the total cost of transportation from Brody to Antwerp would amount to some ninety 1883 American dollars.

All tickets were held by an Alliance escort whose job it was to shepherd his charges through the vicissitudes of their long trip—including language problems, illnesses, confidence men practicing fraud en route, and various other obstacles that passengers unaccustomed to stations, cities, and strangers might encounter.

From Brody, the train would proceed to Lemberg (now Lvov), Poland, then to Kraków and Breslau (now Wroclaw). Crossing into Germany, the passengers would go on to Berlin, where they would be met by representatives of a local German-Jewish organization who would guide them through officialdom. Germany was a hotbed of anti-Semitism and, at the point when the Beilins passed through, had especially stringent medical regulations because of a cholera epidemic.

Their route would then take them across northern Germany, with probable stops and layovers to pick up more emigrants. There may even have been confusing changes of trains along the way, but nothing is definitely known about that. Finally, after what may have been several days, the travelers—by now tired, grimy, frightened, and disoriented—would arrive at their destination: Antwerp, Belgium.

The Alliance would meet the emigrants there and arrange for their passage to America, often chartering ships to transport them. The fare, as negotiated by the Alliance with the steamship company, was about thirty dollars per adult, and half fare for children. The Beilins would thus have paid about $270 total for their journey to the United States. In Antwerp they were advised that those who had no bedding should buy pillows, mattresses, and blankets "since only empty bunks have been provided on the ship." It was also suggested the emigrants purchase eating utensils. After they boarded the ship, they would be out of the hands of Alliance Israelite Universelle and at the mercy of the shipping line.

Once on board the *Rhynland,* the Beilins were on their own to suffer through the next, and most unpleasant, phase of the trip: steerage. Only the affluent could afford first- or second-class staterooms.

"In steerage [in the aft portion of the ship, belowdecks over the churning propellers]," notes Rita Giordano, writing about early immigration,

[the] immigrants faced two weeks to a month of rough seas, crammed together . . . giving birth, getting sick, dying in the same dank quarters. Often these quarters were filthy; lice and vermin were common, and the food, if it didn't run out, was hardly gourmet. . . . [The] crossing was a miserable ordeal of nausea, fear of what was to come, and seemingly endless days on the open sea.

"Crowds everywhere," observed Edward Steiner, an Iowa clergyman who crossed the Atlantic incognito to study conditions on such ships. "Ill smelling bunks, uninviting washrooms. The odors of scattered orange peelings, tobacco, garlic and disinfectants meeting but not blending. No lounge or chairs for comfort, and a continual babel of tongues—this is steerage."

But there was also a more distressing, and irremediable, affliction. The Beilins, like many of their fellow travelers landlocked all their lives, had never seen so much water—and the Atlantic could be rough. Even so, choppy waves were not a prerequisite for horrendous attacks of seasickness; a swaying of the ship and a tilted horizon were often sufficient. "Hundreds of people had vomiting fits," recalled Israel Kasovitch of his own crossing, with babies "throwing up even their mother's milk. As all were crossing the ocean for the first time, they thought their end had come. The confusion and the cries became unbearable."

The Beilins undoubtedly suffered along with the rest. On calm, clear days, many sought relief from the clamor and reek of steerage on the crowded deck. Of this trip young Israel Beilin would recall but one incident, in which a pocket knife dropped from a bunk above left him with a small scar on his forehead.

After eleven days at sea, the *Rhynland* approached New York Harbor and slipped past the recently installed colossus by French sculptor Frédéric-Auguste Bartholdi, *Liberty Enlightening the World* (more popularly known as the Statue of Liberty). The enormous figure of a woman, situated on Bedloe's Island in the Upper Bay, towered some three hundred feet above the water. The sight of this imposing statue and the skyline of Manhattan revived the travel-weary voyagers. Lining the ship's rail, they shouted, waved their caps, pointed. "The people were screaming," one thirteen-year-old Russian girl, Clara Larsen, would remember, "and some . . . were crying. It was all a kind of joyous feeling [of] coming to a land of freedom and a land of love."

No doubt a good deal of this joyousness consisted in the realization of most aboard that their miseries at sea were at last over. As for the land of freedom and love, they must first pass through a chamber of horrors along with the five thousand or so other apprehensive petitioners who landed each day.

Ellis Island comprised a group of buildings situated on a landfill north of Liberty Island, off the coast of New Jersey. Once an arsenal and fort, the structures had been converted into a federal immigration center in 1892, a year before the Beilins arrived, replacing the infamous New York State–run Castle Garden. By the end of the nineteenth century, New York was the major port of entry into the United States, the destination of most immigrants from Europe. There were other entry ports, including New Orleans, Boston, Philadelphia, and Baltimore, but by the 1890s New York was processing four-fifths of the total. The swelling ranks of immigrants—the great masses of refugees driven from eastern Europe by persecution and lured by the promise of the Golden Land—meant that Ellis Island became literally, as it was characterized by scholar Malwyn A. Jones, "a gigantic sieve, whose sole function was to keep out undesirables." It has been called a "cross between Devil's Island and Alcatraz."

The main building, as described by Ronald Sanders in *Shores of Refuge,* was a "ramshackle pavilion that looked like a drab and massive seaside resort hotel." The building was impressive, if ugly—about 400 feet wide and 150 deep. The immigrants were processed on its two floors, in a single miserable day if good fortune smiled.

As soon as the *Rhynland* docked in Manhattan, all those passengers who passed the preliminary port health inspection debarked. Cleared first- and second-class cabin passengers, once through Immigration, were free to leave; other cabin passengers, suspected of carrying contagious or infectious diseases, were detained and, along with all steerage passengers, ferried across the Hudson River with their luggage, wearing identity tags corresponding to a number on the ship's manifest. Once off the ferry, carrying bundles, often clenching their identity tags in their teeth, or with the children's pinned to their jackets, the immigrants were directed first into the main hall and then into penlike structures made of wire and pipe. The next step was the medical examination. In single file, they faced the scrutiny of two U.S. Public Health Service doctors, the first on the alert for physical or mental abnormalities, the second looking for signs of various diseases. All children over two had to proceed through alone.

If the first doctor detected some imperfection, he would make a chalk mark on the right shoulder of the individual's jacket. Infirmities ranging from mental illness (designated by an X) to goiter (G) and even hernia (K) were sufficient cause for detainment, additional physicals, and sometimes even repatriation. Likewise singled out were paupers, anyone suspected of "moral turpitude," and contract workers, who Immigration believed might be imported to lower wages or break strikes. It was a curious paradox: it was difficult to enter the country if you had no job, and even more so if you did have one.

The second physician was there to deny entry to anyone with infectious or contagious diseases such as tuberculosis, cholera, typhus, or, at the time of the Beilin immigration, trachoma, a very contagious form of conjunctivitis that could cause blindness.

The examination for this last condition was frightening for children and adults alike: briefly, but agonizingly, the examiner would evert each eyelid with an instrument that some were certain was a buttonhook. Youngsters of Israel's, Rebecca's, and Chasse's age often screamed during this procedure.

Just as critical, but less distressing, was the test for favus, a highly contagious scalp disease. If either trachoma or favus was found, the carrier was subjected to further examination. If treatable, he or she then underwent medical care in the island's hospital; if not, rejection and deportation were the inevitable result. All of the Beilins went through their physicals chalkless and moved on to a registration clerk, assisted by an interpreter, for further probings: name, nationality, destination—and do you have the money to get there? (At least thirty dollars was mandatory, though there was no law in force to that effect.) Other queries focused on character: Were you ever in prison or in an almshouse? Are you an anarchist? a polygamist? Who paid for your passage, and will you be met? If an immigrant's fare had been paid "by reason of any offer, solicitation, promise or agreement . . . to perform labor in the United States," he or she was sent back as a contract laborer.

On undergoing such interrogation, one fifteen-year-old British girl, Ellen Whaite, responded, "I thought we were coming to a free country." She was more fortunate than many other immigrants, especially the eastern European Jewish refugees: she could at least speak the language, and was therefore treated with less insensitivity and contempt.

"Our immigration officials have not been as humane as they might have been," admitted Commissioner Edward Corsi in a study considering conditions in the early years of Ellis Island. The staff was shorthanded, overworked, and underpaid, a situation that fostered poor paperwork (many who passed through Ellis Island arrived with one name and left with another), bribery, and abuse. "It was a constant grind," recalled Fiorello La Guardia, who as a young law student worked as an interpreter there. "The immigration laws were rigidly enforced and there were many heartbreaking scenes on Ellis Island." In those early years (and, in fact, even later), the New York port of entry was known as Heartbreak Island, or the Island of Tears.

The emotionally and physically drained, bewildered, and frightened immigrants were often herded like cattle by the guards. Their luggage was looted by baggage handlers, they were overcharged for food—and through it all, the din was almost unbearable. Guards shouted, children wailed, and screams indicated that an immigrant had been rejected. (There were many tragic sequels to such episodes: another study of Ellis Island's history revealed that in the years from its opening in 1892 up to 1932, about three thousand suicides occurred on that Island of Tears.)

Having survived the ordeal, the eight Balines (at Ellis Island the name Beilin became Baline) could now board a ferry weighed down with their (unlooted) luggage, cross the bay, and finally set foot in America in lower Manhattan's Battery Park. There they were met by a relative of Leah's, who inexplicably knew where and when to meet them, and taken by truck (according to one source; it was more probably a horse-drawn wagon) to an address on the Lower East Side, on Monroe Street. Somehow, again, there was a three-room basement apartment waiting for them. The Balines' exodus of several weeks or more was at last ended, and a new chapter in their lives was about to begin.

According to author Alexander Woollcott, who was not above a bit of hyperbole if it contributed to a good yarn, the Balines arrived at Monroe Street with "baggage [of] such odds and ends of clothing, furniture [*sic;* Woollcott also contrived the truck] and frying pans as had been hauled from the flames when the house was burned in Russia. Of course there was a featherbed into the depths of which a small boy could sink out of sight as into the East River."

As Woollcott blithely continued the tale, the Balines soon began "to adjust themselves to the economic scheme of things and the first wages were dribbling in[, so] they moved to a slightly airier tenement around the corner in Cherry Street"—330 Cherry, to be precise, above Radlow's Fancy Grocery. The key word in Woollcott's own airy sentence is *tenement.*

Tenements were not designed to provide comfort or salubrity or to please the eye; profit was the motivation. Many abandoned warehouses and factories were converted into warrenlike apartment buildings, but the tenements that were built especially for the exploitation of the newly arrived immigrants on the overpopulated Lower East Side were, if possible, even worse, at least until the passage of the Tenement House Law in 1901. The tenement into which the Balines moved was one of the "old law" houses, and Cherry Street, once fashionable, was by 1893 but an extension of the waterfront slum, a congeries of tenements, saloons, and brothels whose employees, as appraised in *Vices of a Big City,* published in 1890, were merely of "a little higher order" than the "very low" who flourished on Water Street, one block south of Cherry and several blocks to the west, between James and Catherine slips. The waterfront and the areas around Cherry, the Bowery, and Water were magnets for sailors seeking drink, a brawl, or a woman—and a poor setting for families with children. But families nonetheless swarmed there in appalling numbers.

In an effort—a futile one, as it turned out—to keep the Alliance Israelite Universelle from inundating the port of New York with immigrants, the harried secretary of the Russian Emigrant Relief Commission, Manuel A. Kursheedt, wrote to Paris describing a typical old-law tenement:

> a house built on a plot of ground usually twenty-five feet wide by a hundred feet deep, part of which is occupied by an open yard and outhouses; upon the small space left a tenement is built five or six stories (*étages*) in height, with about twelve small rooms on each floor. . . . There are frequently twenty-four families in one house; occasionally two or three families occupy the same room or rooms for sleeping, cooking, sitting and every possible purpose.

Ventilation, plumbing, heat, and light were minimal or nonexistent. Such conditions, Kursheedt warned, fostered demoralization, disease, and a high death rate. Those who did not peddle or work in the notorious sweatshops labored in their homes, where entire families, including children, would

> sit up half the night in their ill-ventilated rooms, trying to earn a living. Their food is of the poorest; consequently in a few years they break down [two of the Balines would soon suffer this fate]. Their complaints are usually of a pulmonary character, and they live a lingering existence for a few months or perhaps years, then die, leaving on our hands a widow already worn down with trouble, and a number of little children.

Kursheedt's letter was written ten years before the Balines settled into Cherry Street, but during the intervening decade, conditions had only worsened.

The apartment on the third floor of 330 Cherry Street consisted of four cramped rooms, small boxes in which eight people lived, worked, and slept. One of the rooms would be the kitchen, equipped with a wood-burning stove; water was drawn from a faucet in the hall. Outhouses were typically located in the courtyard at the rear of the tenement; overhead, the courtyard would be webbed by clotheslines, and the ground all around cluttered with carts, pails, and children at play.

If they were fortunate, the Balines may have had four beds spread out through their flat—ideally, but arguably, one for Moses and Leah, one for Sarah and Sifre, and another for Chasse and Rebecca (or perhaps all four girls slept in a single bed). Benjamin probably shared his cot with Israel. The Americanization of the Balines had begun. They brought a newly simplified name (not a rare practice) from Ellis Island. In time, other changes followed: Sifre became Sophie, Rebecca preferred Ruth, Chasse was altered into Gussie, and Israel would undergo the most drastic change of all.

The other three apartments on the floor were similarly crowded, airless, and dark. Nonetheless, Cherry Street, for the Balines, was an improvement over Monroe. Basement apartments were dank and sunless, and the air that came in from the street deposited dust and dirt. And since plumbing in tenements was primitive at best—one privy for every twenty tenants, either one to a floor in the hall, for the fortunate, or several in the courtyard—any backup in the system soon converted a basement apartment into a cesspool.

The rent on the Cherry Street apartment was nine dollars a month. One account has the Balines sharing their lodgings with a boarder to assist with the expense, a common practice that is unlikely, though possible, in this instance.

The world outside the tenement was as congested. New York's "teeming Lower East Side" was no mere cliché; in the words of novelist Leon Kobrin, it was a "gray, stone world . . . where even on the loveliest spring day there was not a blade of grass. . . . The air itself seems to have absorbed the unique Jewish sorrow and pain, an emanation of thousands of years of exile. The sun, gray and depressed; the men and women clustered around the pushcarts; the gray walls of the tenements—all looks sad."

The narrow downtown sidewalks were lined with small shops that competed with the numberless pushcarts and wagons in the street. Fruits and vegetables were displayed in their windows, as were brooms, clothing, and hats. The shops also sold kosher meats, kindling for stoves, and other necessities. One of the noisiest and most noisome markets was on Hester Street, near Ludlow; it was known as the Pig Market, though no pork could be found there. It was the place to buy secondhand, or thirdhand, overcoats (at fifty cents each), or eyeglasses, no prescription required, at thirty-five cents a pair—or even slightly damaged eggs. On Friday mornings, before the Sabbath began, Hester Street was crowded with shoppers, the air ringing with the street cries of peddlers and the shouts of children running through the market.

Moses Baline, according to Woollcott, found irregular work in the kosher meat markets, certifying the preparation of chickens for purchase according to the Law. He also sang in a local synagogue and led its choir, in which his son Israel sang. Woollcott intimated that Cantor Baline was ambitious on behalf of his son, "a boy who had a clear, true soprano voice—a plaintive voice tuned to the grieving of the shul."

The entire family, except for Israel and six-year-old Chasse, worked. Like many in the tenements, the Balines could do bead work (preparing ornamentation for the garment trades) at home; even the youngest children could assist by cutting away excess threads. Sarah and Sifre contributed to the family income, which Leah managed, by working in sweatshops (for ten hours a day) and later in the cigar industry. Benjamin eventually took the same path in a shirt factory; Israel and Chasse were spared by child-labor laws, which did not, however, apply to work done at home.

Before the advent of the unions, labor in the "needle" trades was harsh, often seven days a week. Signs placed in freight elevators read: "If you don't come in on Sunday, don't come in on Monday." The child-labor laws were subverted by concealing the underaged in tall wooden packing cases, and covering them with shirts, whenever an inspector was expected in the shop.

Life in the tenements, and work in these shops, deeply affected the family. There was minimal privacy; egos chafed, and staggered work hours caused even close families to grow estranged. Hillel Rogoff, editor of the *Jewish Forward,* was appalled by the "moral and spiritual anguish" such conditions wrought, noting that street life further alienated the young, whose "minds were often poisoned against their parents by the ridicule of the gutter." Non-Jewish street gangs, made up of the children of earlier immigrants, more assimilated and no longer "greenhorns"—primarily Germans from the north, above Houston, and Irish from the dock area in the south—crossed into the Jewish quarter to intimidate, vandalize, or pick fights with the newcomers.

Jewish elders were distressed at their children's evident abandonment of their faith and their language. The young were eager to blend into the American scene, to speak English, not Yiddish, to talk, look, and dress like their classmates. They put aside their dark Old World clothing and other symbols of orthodoxy—younger men shaving their beards and cutting their curled sidelocks—to escape "uptown" from the unspeakable environment of the tenement, sweatshop, and pushcart. Many demanded reforms in religious services, wanting to Americanize them, to modernize traditional ritual, to introduce mixed choirs, to replace the synagogue's women's gallery with family pews.

The Balines, for their part, remained aloof from the changes that the affluent uptown Jews brought to the shul. They chose not to "acculturate," not to adapt to the hard, strange ways of a fractious world where there was too much preoccupation with success and money and too little time for prayer and the synagogue. But there was no avoiding the fact that money was a major factor affecting their lives. Even under ordinary circumstances, it was always a struggle for new immigrants to get by, but in the year the Balines arrived, the United States was stricken by its worst depression since its founding. The panic of 1893 wreaked havoc on the railroads, instigating the deadly Pullman strikes in the Midwest; on the Lower East Side, the United Hebrew Charities opened soup kitchens in the streets to feed the unemployed and the poor.

Moses took whatever work he could get, and Ben continued in the sweatshop, where pieceworkers earned two cents per pair of pants. Speedy needlework might bring in as much as ten dollars a week, sufficient to pay the family's rent.

Sarah and Sifre fared better, rolling cigars for two dollars a day. At the time, a skilled bricklayer was paid five dollars a day, though few bricklayers emigrated from the Pale: it was an existence without a future. Still, some immigrants prospered, most of them refugees from Germany who had arrived a decade or more before. They succeeded either by birthright (as, for example, the Warburgs, in banking) or through ambition and hard work. Taking the latter route, Joseph Seligman began as a peddler, then became a clothing manufacturer before switching to banking; one of the later Seligmans in the firm, Jesse, was a patron of both the Metropolitan Museum of Art and the American Museum of Natural History. Then, too, there was the German-born banker Otto Kahn, who came to the United States in the same year as the Balines. When still in his midtwenties, he went into banking and railroads and became a major figure in the arts, especially as a member of the board of the Metropolitan Opera Company.

These uptown immigrants, while the Balines struggled on the Lower East Side, lived stylishly in Fifth Avenue mansions; Kahn's own, at East Ninety-first Street, fashioned after an Italian Renaissance villa, might have been light-years away from Cherry Street. But one day in the future, Israel and Otto would meet.

When Israel was about seven, Leah enrolled him in school on nearby Essex Street. After school he contributed a little to the household income by selling newspapers in Park Row, near City Hall. At P.S. 20, Israel is reputed to have been a poor student (as would be another East Side boy then named George Gershvin, who would follow him there five years later).

When Israel was nine, his sister Sifre died, at the age of twenty. The exact cause is unknown, but it was probably tuberculosis (the "White Plague," or, as it was best known, the "tailor's disease"). Cholera, typhus, and smallpox also took a heavy toll on the Lower East Side (as well as other sections of New York) in the late nineties and around the turn of the century.

Four years after Sifre's death, Moses Baline died; his age listed on the death certificate was fifty-three. He had been suffering for months with a severe chronic cough and shortness of breath. Added to this debilitating misery were sharp leg pains that made climbing the stairs at Cherry Street or at the synagogue at first difficult, then impossible. Distraught, Leah turned to a local charity for aid, and in July Moses was placed in a facility for the indigent and terminally ill. He died on July 19, 1901. The cause of death was recorded as chronic bronchitis and arteriosclerosis.

Leah Baline, fifty-two or fifty-three, with no skills and speaking no English, was thus left alone to watch over her family. Israel was a schoolboy (and newsboy) of thirteen; Ben, nineteen, was employed by a local shirt factory and now must be man of the house; Gussie (Chasse) was fourteen, Rebecca sixteen, and Sarah a woman of twenty-seven.

Only Israel, the youngest, was without a real job.

1

THE BOW'RY

OON AFTER his father's burial, Israel left P.S. 20 to work full-time selling the *Evening Journal,* William Randolph Hearst's contribution to yellow journalism. At one cent per copy, it was not a bountiful source of income (the cost to Israel was probably half that).

The newsboys, or "newsies," were an established workforce by the turn of the century. Most came from immigrant families and had been orphaned or abandoned; their ages ranged from about eleven to fifteen. Aggressive, loud, and tough kids, they were the best means of newspaper distribution in the era before newsstands. They worked the well-traveled sections of New York, including Times Square, City Hall, and the East River bridges.

Israel preferred being closer to home and plied his trade along the Bowery and adjacent streets. One of the earliest and most persistent anecdotes about his brief career as a newsie (another Woollcott tale that is undoubtedly true except in some of its colorful details—for example, its description of the "dirty little barefoot newsboy") had him standing on an East River pier observing the loading of a ship destined to sail for China. Having sold five *Journal*s, he took a little time off to watch the activity on deck, ignoring a nearby crane that was lifting carts into a coal barge. In one unobserved sweep, the crane propelled the boy, his unsold papers, and his five cents into the river. He appeared lifeless as his papers drifted away, much to the amusement of the dockhands. Then someone realized the boy might be drowning.

Finally, Woollcott reported, "an Irish wharf rat of no official standing . . . parted recklessly with his shoes and jumped in after the small merchant."

By the time the boy was brought back to the pier, an ambulance was waiting to take him to Gouverneur Hospital, where, according to one doctor, a great deal of the East River was pumped out of him before he revived. To the amazement of the nurses who placed him on a cot, the five pennies he had earned that day were still clenched in his fist.

When he arrived at Cherry Street that night, as was the custom, he no doubt tossed his earnings into his mother's apron as she sat in a kitchen chair. It often troubled him that his coins were copper, while those of the others, even Gussie, who was only a year older, were silver.

"I guess I never felt poverty," he would say years later, recalling the Cherry Street days, "because I guess I'd never known anything else. . . . In the summer some of us slept on the fire escape or the roof. I was a poor boy with poor parents, but I didn't starve. I wasn't cold or hungry; there was always bread and hot tea."

He remembered, too, selling pieces of the samovar in which their tea was brewed to a local junk man for five or ten cents each, until the prized possession was gone. Another boyhood memory concerned his first sight of a Christmas tree, at an Irish friend's home across the street. The decorations, the candles, and the candy dazzled him. There was little money at 330 Cherry for such luxuries.

In the summer, Israel's favorite form of recreation was swimming—in the East River. He was proud of his skill, small and thin but muscular as he was, and he frequently boasted of his escapades. At the foot of Montgomery Street he would doff his clothes and secrete them in a special niche under the pier—the parlor, he called it. Part of the game was managing to clamber up to the dock without being seen by the police, who regarded naked boys as indecent; from there he would jump into the river. His great feat was a round-trip swim in the murky waters to Brooklyn and back.

His aquatic ability, and his experience as a newsboy, reinforced his growing awareness of himself, and his self-assurance; he had become, in a term as yet uncoined, "street-smart." This, combined with his sense of shame at not contributing enough to Leah's apron, would soon compel him to leave home to lessen his mother's burden.

The decision was, to some degree, a curious one. The early stories present this drastic step as one Israel took on his own. A musical journalist, Henry O. Osgood, writing before Woollcott's biography appeared, had Izzy, as he called him, running away from school and home at fourteen "not because he was bad, not because of any quarrel, but because he felt his share of the common earnings had not increased proportionately with his strength." Woollcott himself, writing a year later, agreed, but added a significant detail: "Finally," he asserted, "in a miserable retreat from reproaches unspoken, he cleared out one evening after supper, vaguely bent on fending for himself or starving if he failed. In the idiom of his neighborhood, where the phenomenon was not uncommon, he went on the bum." Both writers got the boy's age wrong: he was only thirteen.

It is possible that his siblings made Israel feel uncomfortable about his smaller contribution. He could easily have given up his unprofitable career as a newsboy and followed his brother Ben into a sweatshop, but clearly he had no intention of doing that. That life was not for him, even though it would have increased his share of the common earnings. He had other plans.

The life he would seek was revealed to him while he peddled his papers along the Bowery. On his rounds he would sometimes take a chance and push his way through the swinging doors of a forbidden saloon, hoping to sell a few papers. (Saloons and gambling dens were stigmatized as malevolent by the Children's Aid Society.) Sales were scant in saloons, since few were there as readers, but Israel was impressed in some of these places to see youngsters, some of them his own age, making more than he did simply by bursting into song, preferably a current hit or a tear-jerking ballad. The drinkers, especially the more inebriated, would demonstrate their appreciation by tossing coins at the feet of the no-doubt-untutored vocalist.

Israel knew he could do better than some of the vocalists he encountered in the saloons and along the Bowery. When he left home that fateful evening, he turned to the left on Cherry Street, walked the ten or so blocks to Catherine, turned right, went five blocks uptown to Chatham Square, where Catherine crossed East Broadway, and found himself in another world.

Originally an old Indian trail in the seventeenth century, when Manhattan was known as New Amsterdam, what is now the Bowery later became the road to the farm (*bouwerij*) of the colony's director general, Peter Stuyvesant, situated near what is now Astor Place. In time it became part of the main route to Boston. By the next century it was an elegant broad street of fine homes, including that of inventor-politician-philanthropist Peter Cooper.

In Cooper's time it also had its share of taverns and oyster bars, and was the center of New York's theatrical life with its minstrel shows (on his way down, Stephen Foster lived at number 15 Bowery). The first blackface minstrel group made its debut at the Bowery Amphitheatre (number 37); others flourished both on the Bowery proper and on side streets, significantly moving west toward Broadway after the Civil War. Only a few blocks north on Broadway, at Spring Street, stood Niblo's Garden, where a hodgepodge of ballet, song, extravagant scenic effects, and scantily clad dancers entitled *The Black Crook* was presented in 1866; it has since been called the "first American musical," a doubtful designation, but probably close enough.

In the late 1890s an extraordinary Yiddish theater would blossom along the Bowery (at the Windsor, Thalia, and the People's) before moving to Second Avenue and uptown. To some extent, its flowering bolstered the decline that had set in on the Bowery, and some vaudeville houses remained in business for a while before deteriorating into burlesque.

By 1901 the theaters were gone, and the taverns had degenerated into saloons dispensing five-cent whiskey and, sometimes, knockout drops. Where there was no saloon there was instead a flophouse, or a dime museum featuring assorted human curiosities—bearded ladies, wild men of Borneo—and misproportioned fauna with extra heads or legs. Auction houses had sprung up in buildings abandoned by the businesses that had relocated uptown; these new establishments specialized in recently fabricated "antiques." The Bowery by the turn of the century was a magnet for the homeless, the aimless, and the shifty. Pawnshops flourished along the street, as did tattoo parlors, and barbershops where one could have a black eye cosmetically touched up.

When Israel Baline, thirteen-year-old runaway, arrived on the scene, the Bowery was the place to go for entertainment, inebriation, drugs, prostitutes, and colorful characters. In addition, it was the locus of fleecing, robbery, venereal diseases, even murder. It was, in short, an area that lured slumming tourists seeking the thrills of the tenderloin, in 1901 much the same disreputable place that had inspired Charles Hoyt's song of a decade before:

> *The Bow'ry, the Bow'ry!*
> *They say such things and they do strange things*
> *On the Bow'ry!*
> *The Bow'ry!*
> *I'll never go there anymore!*

A decade after Hoyt interpolated the song into an early hit musical, *A Trip to Chinatown,* the denizens of the Bowery persisted in saying and doing things that shocked, titillated, and beguiled the uptown, out-of-town, even foreign voyeurs for whom they put on such a good show. Some of those "things," it is true, were merely another part of the act; though less educated, the denizens were rather sharper than the wide-eyed slummers. Young Israel in time would come to realize that certain aspects of the Bowery were in fact staged sideshows, not nearly as risky as customers were led to believe. Nonetheless, it was a tough part of town, and he managed to experience its threats, amusements, and practical schooling without ever succumbing to its temptations. But he learned always to be wary, careful, and alert.

On that first day, he must first have had to consider the question of lodging, a problem readily solved by dropping into some bars along the street, bursting into song, and picking up the coins tossed into the sawdust on the floor. Ten cents would get him a cot in a nearby flophouse, and an additional five cents would provide privacy of a sort: a little cubicle, as he remembered, with a partial screen open at the top—low enough that "the next guy could reach over and take your clothes." The solution was to sleep on them and use your shoes as a pillow, though for another quarter a night you could also rent bedding.

An early confrontation in one of the flophouses was nearly fatal: Israel and another boy got into an argument that ended in a fistfight. "The kid stabbed me," he recalled, "and I was rushed to Bellevue [Hospital]." As soon as he recovered, he was back on the Bowery busking. Reasonably successful at this pursuit, he generally had a good night on Saturdays, singing at MacAlear's near the waterfront and earning a certain fifty cents. He lived for a year at a flop-hotel known as the Mascot, and would later remember that another of the places he slept in had once sheltered Stephen Foster.

Eventually he attached himself to a seasoned busker known only as Blind Sol, a respected figure in the area who, because of his disability, needed an assistant to lead him from bar to bar. Blind Sol, with assistant, could safely work even the most notorious neighborhoods and bars. According to Alexander Woollcott, streetwalkers often spelled young Izzy at his job, taking the "night off [from their own work to] establish a drawing account with Saint Peter by serving as a guide for the blind singer."

The ambitious Israel had no intention of remaining a Bowery busker for long. Before his fourteenth birthday, he auditioned for the chorus of a musical entitled *The Show Girl,* with songs by H. L. Heartz and R. A. Barnet (their second of the 1902 season). Production troubles during the show's out-of-town tryout resulted in songs being added and performers subtracted; in April, when *The Show Girl* arrived in Binghamton, New York, aspiring chorus boy Baline was fired for reasons unknown. (The show subsequently limped into New York, where it opened in May and closed in July.)

Undaunted, impressed with show business, and liking the idea of earning a regular salary and singing better songs (mediocre though they might be) than he did on the Bowery, Israel took a trip uptown to West Twenty-eighth Street when he returned to Manhattan. There he found the offices of the Harry von Tilzer Music Publishing Company. Twenty-eighth Street between Broadway and Sixth Avenue was then known as Tin Pan Alley, the name having moved up from Fourteenth Street with the industry when vaudeville and the theaters shifted northwest toward Broadway.

Harry von Tilzer was a successful songwriter as well as a publisher. His first hit was "My Old New Hampshire Home," a celebration of Admiral Dewey's victory at Manila Bay in 1898, which sold two million copies but earned him a mere five dollars—an experience that no doubt inspired him four years later to establish himself as a publisher, to protect his own wares. The Von Tilzer Company was a new firm when Israel turned up at its office in 1902. At the time, Harry von Tilzer's most popular song was "Bird in a Gilded Cage"; when not occupied with publishing, he continued to produce the occasional tune, including "Wait Till the Sun Shines, Nellie," "I Want a Girl (Just like the Girl That Married Dear Old Dad)," and "When My Baby Smiles at Me."

Now fourteen, Israel passed his vocal test and was hired to demonstrate von Tilzer songs, as a song plugger. That he could not read music was immaterial; neither could many songwriters in Tin Pan Alley (or even many pianists). He had a good ear and a good memory, and he quickly learned the songs he was hired to plug.

Von Tilzer, a friend of saloon impresario Tony Pastor, sent Israel to Pastor's Music Hall on Fourteenth Street to promote the company's songs at a salary of five dollars a week. Pastor himself had moved up from the Bowery, where he managed one of his "concert saloons." It was in one of these saloons that the great Lillian Russell got her start. Pastor, unhappy with the tone then prevalent in minstrel shows and burlesque on the Bowery, introduced a type of family entertainment that he called variety, later to be known as vaudeville (which he is credited with conceiving)—ladies invited.

The only memory that Israel retained of Pastor's was that on the bill when he appeared were the Three Keatons, whose youngest member, Buster, was tossed around the stage by his parents. Israel sang "The Mansion of Aching Hearts" by von Tilzer, rising from his seat in the balcony impulsively, as if he could not contain his admiration for the great song that accompanied the Keatons' antics.

It seemed that he was not destined for show business, however—or not yet, anyway. After a brief stay at Pastor's, Israel returned to busking on his customary rounds, alone or with Blind Sol. Curiously, nowhere in the documentation of Israel Baline's life at this time is there any indication that he ever saw his family, who lived and worked only a short walk away. Woollcott wrote that in the early weeks of Israel's vagrancy, having a bum in the family seemed a disgrace to the Balines and their friends; Leah Baline even ventured into the unsavory precincts of the Bowery hoping to get a glimpse of her wayward son, but to no avail.

Nor did Israel return to Cherry Street. His surrogate family, and his few friends, congregated on the Bowery. One of these was George Washington Connors, who preferred to be known as Chuck, the Mayor of Chinatown (which he was not, except through pure self-creation and with the help of a couple of reporters who wrote for the *World* and the *Sun;* Connors was, in any event, colorful enough without their fabrications).

Woollcott intimated that Chuck was of the Cockney persuasion, which role he came by honestly enough. Connors himself said that he had been born right there in Chinatown, on Mott Street, but he had in fact been brought there by his parents as a baby from Providence, Rhode Island, and grown up in those streets long before Israel came to the Bowery. Like Israel, Connors began as a newsboy, but he ended up as a clog dancer at the Gaiety Museum. Early in his life, he married and lived cleanly, at one point even operating a string of cars on the Third Avenue Elevated rail line. His wife taught him to read and write. Her death before the marriage could mature put Connors back on the streets, where he drank heavily.

On one occasion, while in a deep state of intoxication, Connors fell into the hands of a gang of "crimps" (Cherry Street was once a center for such groups) who preyed on drunks (most often sailors), drugging them and then robbing or shanghaiing them. When Connors came to, he was an unwilling crew member on a ship bound for London. While waiting for the vessel to sail back to New York, Connors wandered into Whitechapel, where he encountered London costermongers selling various items in the streets. What he admired most about them was their work clothes, elaborately decorated with large buttons ("pearlies"), embroidered jackets, and caps. When he returned to the Bowery, Connors arrived in style, wearing his costermonger uniform (he substituted a derby for the cap), to take his position as the mythical Mayor of Chinatown.

He found his true calling as a "lobbygow" (pidgen Chinese for tour guide), with the Bowery and Chinatown as his bailiwick. He spoke the language of the former fluently and that of the latter none too well, though well enough to fool tourists. In his early costermonger period, Connors escorted only celebrities through the perils of Chinatown, pointing out notorious tong hatchet men (more likely innocent proprietors of laundries and such) and women who, his guests were informed, were "slaves." The highlight of his tour was a visit to a hypothetical opium den in a tenement, where two of his own employees, a woman and a man, portrayed "dope fiends." Along the way, Connors led his charges into several selected saloons (part of whose take would be shared with the intrepid guide), which sojourns made him well known and popular along the Bowery.

Among Connors's more prominent patrons during this part of his career as Chinatown's mayor were such figures as Sir Thomas Lipton (of tea fame), French cabaret star Yvette Guilbert (from whom he gallantly declined to accept a tip since they were in the same profession—acting), and, in her pre-Ziegfeld phase, the beauteous Anna Held, with whom he appeared at Hammerstein's Victoria in 1896 in a vaudeville sketch entitled "From Broadway to the Bowery."

Connors would pursue his profession into the teens of this century, sporting his derby, pea jacket, and silk scarf, and always a smile. In the course of his work he came across a young busker, Izzy Baline, a nice, quiet kid with a good voice. Connors believed that the boy could improve himself, get off the streets, and find steady employment as a singing waiter. Sometime early in 1904, Connors took him to the recently opened Pelham Café on Pell Street. The building had once been the home of the Chinatown Music Hall; the proprietor was one Michael (presumably; he was called Mike) Salter. Like the now-fifteen-year-old Baline, Salter was a Russian-born Jew. The large window of the new café bore the legend "THE PELHAM," its address, "12," and below, to the right, "M. SALTER, PROP." Salter's sign painter seems to have had a special affinity for the full stop (there was one between THE and PELHAM) if not for the apostrophe: at the entrance, above the swinging doors, another sign read: "SALTERS CAFE."

Because of Salter's swarthy complexion, the place was invariably known as Nigger Mike's. Mike's was one of the regular stops for tour guide Connors (who is further supposed to have conceived the fox trot on its dance floor). The chief bartender was known only as Sulky; the backroom pianist was M. "Nick" Nicholson. "Blind Tom" also played that piano at times, often to accompany Blind Sol. It was on that same timeworn upright that Izzy Baline would teach himself to play the piano.

At the beginning of the twentieth century, the Bowery was known as the paradise of thieves. Reform mayor Seth Low closed down the dives after his election, but the corrupt administration that followed, headed by George McClellen, regarded the new incarnations that came after with a benign love for graft. Among these later dives were the Pelham and its rival Callahan's Dance Hall Saloon, on Doyers Street.

A number of underworld figures—among them "Kid Twist," "Big Jack" Zelig, and "Bald Jack" Rose—frequented the dives, and some even opened their own saloons. Like the sights on Connors's Chinatown excursions, their notoriety was exaggerated for the benefit of tourism: Connors steered only the best to Nigger Mike's. The Pelham, to uptown, to out-of-town, and evidently to British connoisseurs, was known as one of the most colorful of the low dives around the Bowery. As Woollcott phrased it, the saloon's "sagacious proprietor [Salter] rather encouraged the legend that his backroom was a sort of thieves' Algonquin, a pickpockets' round table, a Coffee House for the lawless."

Izzy Baline, for a consideration of seven dollars a week, took his place as a singing waiter at the Pelham from eight at night until six in the morning. In addition to his weekly stipend, he got to keep his share of the coins customers tossed onto the floor. After hours, or before, he would tinker on the piano in the back room. His was a unique approach in that he avoided the white keys and played only on the black, in the key of F sharp; before long, in this manner, he was picking out the melodies of current popular songs.

Other talents, equally primitive at first, were also revealed at the Pelham, where Izzy would regale patrons with parodies of those same popular songs. The elementary-school dropout thus became a lyricist, or, as he would prefer, a lyric writer. He and his fellow waiters frequently entertained their customers by singing then-politically correct songs in dialect, from which no ethnic group was immune—not the Irish, Italians, Jews, or blacks (who were lampooned in "coon songs"). The preferred fare was livelier dance numbers, though as the drinking continued and closing time approached, lugubrious ballads were found to encourage tearful tipping.

In his first year at Mike Salter's, young Baline may well have rendered the song he had first introduced at Pastor's, von Tilzer's "The Mansion of Aching Hearts," whose lyric by Arthur Lamb would have brought lumps to patrons' throats as Izzy sang with feeling:

> *She lives in a mansion of aching hearts,*
> *She's one of a restless throng;*
> *The diamonds that glitter around her throat,*
> *They speak both of sorrow and song;*
> *The smile on her face is only a mask*
> *And many's the tear that starts,*
> *For sadder it seems, when of mother she dreams,*
> *In the mansion of aching hearts.*

Such sentimentality was ripe for parody, as were many other, similar ditties memorializing mothers, fallen women (many of whom, when not working, frequented the Pelham, which despite its shady reputation was quite a safe place), and sons and fathers lost to drink.

Even more popular, however, were such sparkling tunes as Joseph Howard's "Goodbye, My Lady Love," and songs by a new young composer-lyricist and author, George M. Cohan, then appearing in his own show, *Little Johnny Jones,* at the Liberty. Two songs from that show were especially popular in 1904: "Yankee Doodle Boy" and "Give My Regards to Broadway." The musical was produced by Sam H. Harris, who, along with Cohan himself, would figure significantly in the later career of Israel Baline.

The life of a singing waiter was a physical grind, and the sleeping habits young Izzy formed at this time would affect him for the rest of his years: he invariably slept through the day and was active, even restless, during the night. Nonetheless, it was a reasonably good life; he enjoyed the singing and the enthusiastic reception accorded his parodies. His witty jibes were a popular feature at the Pelham, where he would stay for three years, until 1907, when his talent for lyric writing would reach an unexpected fruition and he would be fired by Mike Salter.

Near the end of 1905, now seventeen, he made the New York papers, or at least the columns of the *World.* The Pelham attracted some celebrated visitors, with an assist from Chuck Connors, and thrived on newsmen, entertainers, and society folk who wanted to mingle with gamblers and other toughs (pickpockets did particularly well in such places). One night late in November 1905 Connors brought a large party to the Pelham, the most illustrious of whom was Prince Louis of Battenberg, a rear admiral in the British Navy and husband of a granddaughter of Queen Victoria (a German prince, he would renounce his German title during the First World War and take the more properly British name Mountbatten).

The prince's visit to the United States garnered him plenty of press coverage, plus the protection of a couple of plainclothesmen. They were accompanied by August Belmont, of the banking family and the New York subway system, a Lady Susan Townley, and Mrs. John Drexel. Generous, but not to a fault, Mike Salter offered the entire party drinks on the house, but according to the *World* reporter, Belmont insisted on paying (no doubt to Salter's relief). One of the women then asked for a song from the singing waiters, and they were treated to a rendition of "Gee, but This Is a Lonesome Town," where "Everyone looks dreary/ Everyone looks weary." According to Woollcott, Izzy refused Prince Louis's tip, a gesture that made the front page of several papers. In fact, it was the royal visit itself that got the press; the singing waiters who serenaded the party were identified merely as "Izzy and Bullhead," hardly a publicity coup.

So much for fame, as Izzy continued serving drinks and vocalizing without further press interest either in him or in the café. Especially irritating to Salter was the fact that some of his business was being drained away to Callahan's around the corner, and for no better reason than that that saloon's "professor," pianist Al Piantadosi, and a waiter, "Big Jerry," had written a song entitled "My Mariucci Take a Steamboat" (clearly in Italian dialect), and everyone was deserting the Pelham to hear it performed at Callahan's. A wrathful Salter peremptorily ordered his own resident professor and the smart little Izzy, whose sometimes racy parodies seemed to amuse the customers, to write a song.

This they did. If an Italian song was bringing them into the rival saloon, they, too, would write Italian; originality was no virtue here. They worked at Nicholson's piano in the back room. Since Izzy was good with words, it is probable that he wrote the lyric first and then Nick, at the piano, with a change here and there, worked out the melody. Their repetitious laboring, according to Woollcott, annoyed the Pelham's patrons, who expressed their criticisms by tossing damp bar cloths at the struggling artisans.

Finally it was complete, with the title "Marie from Sunny Italy," a true ballad and not a parody. It was no masterwork, but it would nevertheless evolve into an important "first." There was a hindrance, however: neither of its authors could set down the music. Pianist Nicholson could read simple sheet music but felt insecure about attempting a manuscript; with the words written out on a sheet of paper, though, he had no trouble playing the song.

The lyric, two verses and a chorus, while not the handiwork of a major songwriter (at least not yet), reveals the hand of a young man well practiced in the form and content of popular song. There are some peculiar rhymes: "my queen" with "mandolin," for example, or "patiently" with "happy be," and then, in the second verse, this:

> Don't say "No," my sweet Italian beauty,
> There's not another maiden e'er could suit me.

It is a simple, sincere song, free of the ethnic slurs that were so common in the early years of Tin Pan Alley, but in it Izzy Baline displayed a familiarity with the conventions, and the clichés, of that song factory. The initial verse is quite polished for its time (excepting its final couplet):

Oh, Marie, 'neath the window I'm waiting,
Oh, Marie, please don't be so aggravating.
Can't you see my heart just yearns for you, dear,
With fond affection and love that's true, dear?
Meet me while the summer moon is beaming,
For you and me the little stars are gleaming.
Please come out tonight, my queen,
Can't you hear my mandolin?

The chorus goes:

My sweet Marie from sunny Italy
Oh, how I do love you.
Say that you'll love me, love me, too,
Forever more I will be true,
Just say the word and I will marry you
And then you'll merely be
My sweet Marie from sunny Italy.

Izzy and Nick were pleased with their work, but they still needed a copy on paper, so they sought out a Bowery cobbler (again, Woollcott is the source) known as Fiddler John, who spent his time away from his bench busking the bars. After he confessed that he could not write music, either, according to Woollcott, they found someone else who could, "a young violinist who shall remain unidentified . . . because he has since clothed himself in the grandeur of a Russian name and betaken himself to the concert platform with the air of a virtuoso just off the boat from Paris."

Whoever this figure was, he did the job, and Izzy and Nick had their song, which they took to Tin Pan Alley. According to Woollcott, "Marie from Sunny Italy" was "promptly accepted by Joseph Stern for publication." Jos. W. Stern & Co. was actually not in Tin Pan Alley proper, but ten blocks north, at 102–104 West Thirty-eighth Street, which may suggest that the Pelham team did some shopping around. In any event, three unquestioned facts are known about that publication: the writers split the advance of seventy-five cents; if it was a raging success at the café, there is no record of it; and there was a determining typographical error on the cover:

Words By
I. BERLIN

Now nineteen, with a published song to his credit, Izzy Baline had also acquired a more Americanized last name. For his first name he used an initial rather than either "Israel" (too formal) or "Izzy" (too common). The precise moment when he was transformed fully into Irving Berlin is unknown, but it must have been within the next two years: that is the name on all his published songs from 1909 on.

The year, 1907, when "Marie from Sunny Italy" was published was also Izzy's last with Mike Salter. He had made a few friends in Chinatown, one of them an aspiring pharmacist and fellow Russian immigrant named Joseph M. Schenck, who had emigrated in 1900. Schenck worked at number 6 Bowery, the Olliffe Pharmacy, then reputed to be the oldest drugstore in America (founded circa 1803). It was a reliable medical center on the Bowery, which Woollcott, in his usual vivid manner, represented as being an outlet for opium (in its raw form, as gum) for the Chinese, as well as a first-aid station for anyone injured in a brawl, and a place to wait until an ambulance arrived from Gouverneur Hospital.

Schenck was an older (at twenty-nine), friendly man whose pursuit of a degree from the College of Pharmacy was soon abandoned in favor of show business. A year after the slighted publication of "Marie from Sunny Italy," Schenck left number 6 and the college to build the Palisades amusement park in New Jersey with his brother Nicholas. Later they would go into the fairgrounds business, then expand into vaudeville and movie houses before finally moving on to Hollywood and moguldom.

Joe Schenck is reputed to have purchased the first copy of Izzy and Nick's newly minted song. It is possible, though debatable, that he was a patron of the Pelham; it seems equally likely that Izzy may have needed an occasional aspirin after a night of serving and singing at the café. In any event, frequent sightings in the street would have been inevitable. Precisely when the two actually met is not known, but the friendship born on the Bowery was to last a lifetime, and Schenck would play an important part in the future of I. Berlin.

So would another good friend, Max Winslow, once a cabaret singer and eventually another song plugger for Harry von Tilzer. Early one morning on his rounds, Winslow dropped in to hear the waiters at the Pelham. When the one called Izzy stood up to sing his parody of "Are Ye Comin' Out Tonight, Mary Anne?," Winslow listened raptly, for this was a von Tilzer publication. While Izzy's was definitely not the authorized version, Winslow was nonetheless struck by the talent, as lyric writer, of the skinny waiter with the shock of black hair and the large brown eyes. There was something about his presence that appealed to him. He also noted the reaction of the customers, who reportedly expressed their approval with laughter and pounding on tables.

Winslow spoke to von Tilzer the next day and recommended that the company hire the youngster as a staff lyricist at a modest salary of fifteen dollars a week; he may even have sung a few lines from Izzy's parody, which, while not printable, revealed an embryonic songwriter. Von Tilzer was neither amused nor impressed, and his answer was no. Izzy was disappointed, for he was tired of Salter's café, but he was grateful to Winslow and would never forget his effort on his behalf.

It remained only for Mike Salter to provide Izzy Baline (now Berlin) with the impetus to take the next step in his progress uptown. The setting was the bar of the Pelham, the time one morning soon after the failure of "Marie from Sunny Italy." Sulky the bartender went home at 6:00 A.M., and Salter left Izzy in charge until closing two hours later, at 8:00. (His stint as a waiter usually lasted from 8:00 P.M. until 6:00 A.M.; this particular shift would have been a twelve-hour stretch.) His duties were to sweep the back room, draw beers for the parched on their way to work, and keep an eye on the till. He failed in this last.

Having fallen asleep at the bar, Izzy was awakened by the strenuous shaking of Mike Salter, who pointed to the open cash register. The twenty-five dollars that had been there when Sulky left was now gone. Salter, ordinarily an affable man, but noted for his vile temper when drinking, castigated Berlin and ordered him out of the saloon, warning him never to return. A chastened and bewildered, formerly employed I. Berlin left what had been a haven for him, a home away from home, for more than three years. He was on the street again.

The incident would have a curious twist and a sequel. Sulky contradicted Salter's version of the tale, insisting that Salter himself had taken the money, a common practice for him; if inebriated, he may simply have forgotten doing it. In any case, he unconsciously did his young employee a favor. As for the sequel, fifteen years later, Mike Salter died destitute, leaving behind a widow and five children, the youngest only five years old. Few attended his funeral, but among them were Kenneth Sutherland, the Tammany boss of Coney Island, and Irving Berlin, by 1922 a most important figure.

Because of his onetime celebrity, Salter's funeral was covered by the newspapers. Berlin offered a kind of eulogy when he urged Walter Davenport of the *Herald*, "Treat him as kind as you can. He was no angel, maybe, but there are a lot of guys on the street today who would be in jail if it hadn't been for Nigger Mike."

The former Izzy, now Irving or Mr. Berlin, was no harborer of grudges, and despite the sometimes abusive treatment he had suffered at the hands of the alcoholic Salter, he still felt he owed him something. The odd reference to the petty (or not-so-petty) criminals Salter had kept out of jail harked back to Chinatown, where Mike had been an active politician and a ward heeler of the old school. Should one of his constituents be apprehended while plying his trade, picking pockets or entering a building through a second-story window, Salter would use his influence with the police, or with higher-ups, to get him freed. He would even employ bogus witnesses (usually weeping mothers) in his efforts.

It was known, too, that Mike Salter had been an enthusiastic voter: one election day, his zeal even carried him to several different polls to register his preferences. On this occasion he was found out, and it became necessary for him to manage the Pelham from a Canadian refuge until the grand jury lost interest in him.

Salter was at his most unangelic when he ejected Izzy from the café. Happily, the resilient singing waiter was not unemployed for long. He knew of a new place that had opened in Union Square, uptown; the proprietor was a former boxer, Jimmy Kelly, who had owned the Mandarin Club on Doyers Street, near the Pelham. Kelly had wisely set up his newest establishment closer to what had once been a major theatrical and fine-restaurant district. By 1907 or so its theaters featured mainly variety and vaudeville; some of the restaurants were gone, but Tony Pastor's and Luchow's remained on Fourteenth Street.

Kelly's, also on Fourteenth, was decidedly a move upward, within walking distance of the cluster of music publishers on Twenty-eighth Street and a gathering place for not only the usual drinkers and pleasure seekers but also vaudeville performers and people in the music business, among them Izzy's champion from von Tilzer's, Max Winslow. Soon after the missing-money incident at the Pelham, young I. Berlin was hired as a singing waiter by Jimmy Kelly, sometime in 1907.

At Kelly's, Izzy concentrated on his singing, though he did manage to write two minor songs during his first year there. With pianist Maurice Abrahams (or "Maurie Abrams"), down from Tin Pan Alley, he wrote "Queenie, My Own," a quickly forgotten ballad. (Abrahams eventually became a publisher and wrote what was called special material for vaudeville performers [that is, a song or skit written to match a performer's particular style and talent], including his wife, Belle Baker. He achieved some success with such songs as "He'd Have to Get Under (Get Out and Get Under to Fix Up His Automobile)" and "Ragtime Cowboy Joe." Five years later Berlin and Abrahams would collaborate again on "Pullman Porters on Parade." Because Izzy was by then under contract to another publisher, he used a pseudonym, "Ren G. May"—an anagram, curiously, of *Germany,* perhaps triggered by an association with *Berlin.*)

A more important though equally forgotten song was "The Best of Friends Must Part," an example of Izzy's greater ambition. For this number he created both words and music. These two added up to his total song output for the year 1908.

The following year would prove pivotal. A now-unknown song and dance man who heard Berlin sing something of his own one day in Kelly's commissioned him, for the promised fee of ten dollars, to write him some special material. He was singing at Tony Pastor's and wanted a "Wop" dialect song for his act. At the time much saloon talk was being devoted to the unhappy fate of an Italian named Pietro Dorando, who had lost the marathon in the 1908 London Olympics after a group of overly helpful sports fans rushed onto the track and appeared to assist him toward the finish line. He was disqualified for this aid, and the gold medal went to an American, John Joseph Hayes.

This story gave Izzy an idea: his lyric tells the sad tale of a patriotic Italian-American barber who bets his entire savings on Dorando and loses it all. But by the time the lyric was finished, the vaudevillian had changed his mind. It appeared that Izzy, too, had lost on "Dorando." Unwilling to let it go at that, however, he headed northward, finally ending up at the Ted Snyder Company on West Thirty-eighth Street. He recited his lyric to Snyder's office manager, the imposing, bluff, and blunt Henry Waterson.

Waterson approved of the words but wanted to hear the music, asking Izzy something like, "You've got a tune to this?" Anxious to make the sale, the young man lied and said he had.

Waterson then offered Izzy twenty-five dollars (ten in advance and the rest if it was a hit) for "Dorando" and sent him into a cubicle with a piano and the staff arranger, Bill Schultz, who would take down the melody. Shaken, Izzy nonetheless managed to improvise a tune on the spot; it was published soon after and became a popular song in vaudeville. This greatly pleased Waterson and Snyder, who listened intently when, later in 1909, Berlin and another active writer, Edgar Leslie, came in with a comic number inspired by the notoriety of Richard Strauss's controversial opera *Salome.* The previous November, Strauss's work had been the object of a protest in Philadelphia; its New York premiere, at the Metropolitan, was stopped in midrun due to outrage at the wicked Salome, the head of the saint on a platter, and, most especially, the Dance of the Seven Veils. The opera was also banned in Berlin and London.

Leslie came to Berlin with an idea about exploiting the anti-*Salome* fervor with a comic dialect number. The Sadie of their song is a burlesque dancer whose routine shocks her "sweetheart" Moses, who shouts from the audience, "Where is your clothes?" and implores her, "Sadie Salome, go home!" (née Sadie Cohen, she has taken a stage last name to rhyme with "home").

"Sadie Salome, Go Home" was an even bigger hit than "Dorando," enjoying a sale of some three hundred thousand copies of sheet music and being widely sung in vaudeville and in saloons such as Kelly's and the Pelham. The division of labor on the song is moot; Leslie's later Tin Pan Alley standing was primarily as a lyricist. It is probable that Berlin again supplied the routine music to fit the lyric, and that he and Leslie collaborated on the sometimes spicy words. As he would tell interviewer Michael Freedland some years later, "As much as anything, we did it to see if we could get away with it."

Berlin and Leslie collaborated on a couple more songs that year, then went their separate ways. Leslie would later team with several other songwriters, among them Harry Warren (for "Rose of the Rio Grande" and "By the River Sainte Marie"), James V. Monaco (for the Jolson hit "Dirty Hands, Dirty Face"), Walter Donaldson, and Joseph Burke (for "On Treasure Island," "In a Little Gypsy Tea Room," and "Moon over Miami"). His greatest success would be "For Me and My Gal," written with E. Ray Goetz and George Meyer in 1917.

The sales of "Sadie Salome" impressed Snyder and Waterson, who offered Berlin a job as staff lyricist at a salary of twenty-five dollars a week, plus royalties on any songs of his that the company published. He quit waiting on tables and singing at Kelly's and rounded out his year, 1909, with a spurt of remarkable energy, producing more than a dozen songs, many with his boss Ted Snyder, but others solo. One of these latter would make him one of the best-known songwriters in town.

Among the most interesting, and most successful, of the songs he wrote without a collaborator was "That Mesmerizing Mendelssohn Tune," not only because of the un–Tin Pan Alleyish second word in the title but also because of the tune's musical quotation from Mendelssohn's *Spring Song* for piano. As Berlin later told Michael Freedland, "I had always loved Mendelssohn and his 'Spring Song' and simply wanted to work it into a rag tune." According to Freedland, it sold half a million copies.

Another song from 1909, inspired by an extemporaneous quip, kept Izzy's name—now officially Irving Berlin—in the *Evening Journal* for weeks. It all began one evening at John the Barber's on Forty-fifth Street, where he met George Whiting, a café and vaudeville entertainer and sometime song-writer. One (or the other; the stories vary, with Woollcott making it Whiting) suggested that since both were free for the rest of the evening, they go to the theater, with Whiting adding, "My wife's gone to the country."

"Hooray!" Berlin shot back. He then stopped in his tracks and said something like, "I think we have a song here." The theater forgotten, the two men hurried to the Snyder office on Thirty-eighth Street and went to the piano. Snyder was there and lent a hand with the music. By early morning, "My Wife's Gone to the Country, Hurrah! Hurrah!" was finished; soon after, the authors went next door to Maxim's, a restaurant that catered to the theater and sporting crowd. Wishing to try out their new creation on an audience, they asked the manager to quiet the customers and announce the performance of a new song.

Whiting took the place of the house pianist, and Berlin, standing on a chair, sang:

> My wife's gone to the country—
> Hurray—Hurray!
> She thinks it best—I need the rest—
> That's why she went away;
> She took the children with her—
> Hurray—Hurray!
> I'm with you till the cows come home—
> My wife's gone away.

In the verse preceding this chorus, the song's protagonist, one Brown, has just encountered a "charming female" on the beach at Coney Island, whom he thinks a "peach." (The spelling of the exclamation used in the chorus varies, with the official Berlin catalog giving it as *Hurrah*. The excerpt reproduced here was one of a hundred additional verses and choruses that Berlin prepared for publication in the *Evening Journal* after the song's wildfire popularity led to the sale of three hundred thousand copies.)

Irving Berlin was now definitely a name. His collaborator Whiting's career as a songwriter, in contrast, did not bloom: his one other hit was "My Blue Heaven," written with Walter Donaldson in 1927.

Tin Pan Alley folklore has Whiting's wife divorcing him because of the flagrantly misogynistic lyric of "My Wife's Gone to the Country," and a jilted Whiting trying to atone with the pro-family lyric of "My Blue Heaven." The tale seems dubious, however, considering the time gap between the songs, from 1909 to 1927. While Whiting may have contributed the phrase that gave Berlin the initial idea, it was Berlin himself who provided the *Journal* with the hundred supplementary variants. Did these represent his own perspectives on women and marriage? He was then a twenty-one-year-old bachelor, a man about town, patronizing John the Barber, the better restaurants, theaters. Early photographs show a natty dresser, small and slender, in well-cut suits, high collars, and quiet neckties.

When Berlin, Whiting, and Snyder tossed off this comic song, women's right to vote equally with men was still years away. It was a time when the reality of James Thurber's later coinage the "battle of the sexes" was taken for granted. Men roamed and women "homed"; the phrases "my better half" and "ball and chain" were often heard. Berlin's lyric simply reflected the attitude of half the nation; after all, *someone* bought all those copies—or rather, three hundred thousand someones.

As for Berlin himself, though he was no misogamist, nor misogynist, his dedication to work curtailed his social life to a great degree. He mixed largely with people in the music-publishing business, and the women he knew were mostly theater and vaudeville performers who came by the Snyder offices looking for songs. They were fun, ambitious (like him), and, by the very nature of their personalities and occupation, poor marriage prospects.

Woollcott, in *The Story of Irving Berlin,* glancingly intimates that Berlin had by this time moved back to Cherry Street, to the "crowded home downtown to which he *had long since returned* [italics mine, this being the book's first and only allusion to his return], a contrite son and a puzzling but respected worker." Such a move seems unlikely, as Berlin was now earning enough to continue living as he had done since the Bowery, only at better addresses. He would have disrupted the overpopulated flat on Cherry: his mother, sisters, and brother kept regular working hours (such as they were in 1909), and his own schedule was erratic. He would work on a song, when inspired or driven, through the night; there may even have been a cot for him in the office. And when he wasn't groping for a song, he was making the rounds of cafés, bars, and vaudeville houses to see how Ted Snyder Co. was doing.

The amazing popularity of "My Wife's Gone to the Country" convinced Berlin and Snyder that they, and it, were destined for greater things. At that time, the elite songwriters wrote for the musical theater, among them Victor Herbert and George M. Cohan, whose from-the-heart songs Berlin much admired, calling them "my inspiration, my model."

With some difficulty, Snyder and Berlin got an appointment to audition their song before the mighty Shuberts, who had dominated the musical theater since 1900. They saw J.J. (né Jacob Szemanski), the youngest of the three brothers who had emigrated from Lithuania and founded a great theatrical empire, with a chain of theaters in the United States (sixty-three in New York alone) and London. Their power rendered J.J. and his older brother Lee (the other brother, Samuel, died in a train wreck in 1905) the most formidable producers in the country. They reigned over their dominion with a mixture of arrogance, ruthlessness, and great business acumen. They were pursued if not loved; there were periods when they would not even speak to each other, though they inhabited the same offices.

On the day of Berlin and Snyder's audience with him, J.J. was preoccupied with dictating to a stenographer while Berlin sang and Snyder accompanied. Such rude, if characteristic, disregard unnerved Berlin, and he gave up after the first chorus; he and Snyder left Shubert's office, not to return until the following year.

It wasn't as though they had never placed a song in a show before; it was just that the Shuberts were the biggest among the "managers," as they were termed at the time, and securing their backing would have been a coup. Early in 1909 Berlin and Snyder had succeeded in interpolating "She Was a Dear Little Girl" into *The Boys and Betty,* but that was as far as their success went. The major portion of the score was the work of Silvio Hein, a prolific and mildly acclaimed composer of the day; his lyricist and librettist was George V. Hobart. The "Betty" of the show's title was Marie Cahill, who, as star, incorporated some of her favorite songs into its short run.

Such interpolation of others' songs into a show scored principally by a different writer or writers was a common practice that would continue into the 1930s, especially in revues, which always used teams of writers. In turn-of-the-century musicals, the star often chose to work in songs that displayed his or her talents, with publishers sometimes making deals with producers. Some big stars went even further: Al Jolson, for example, whose star was in the ascendent along with that of his fellow East Sider Berlin, not only interpolated songs but also shared credit for their authorship (his likeness usually graced the sheet-music cover), thus ensuring himself a cut of the royalties from both the sheet music and any recordings of the work made by him or other vocalists.

The following year, Berlin and Snyder would get "Oh, How That German Could Love" into *The Girl and the Wizard* (score mostly by Julian Edwards, Robert B. Smith, and Edward Madden). Additional interpolations came from such beginning composers as Louis Hirsch and Jerome Kern (who placed no less than three songs). Whether Kern and Berlin met during the making of this not very successful show is unknown; they would in time become very close, lifelong friends. (Incidentally, seven years later, another great, George Gershwin, would initiate his own theatrical writing career by placing interpolations.)

The star of *The Girl and the Wizard* was the German dialect comedian Sam Bernard (the "Girl" was Kitty Gordon), a bit of casting that rationalized the inclusion of "Oh, How That German Could Love." The song also has some slight further significance in that sometime in January 1910, Berlin himself recorded it, in dialect, for the Columbia Phonograph Company. The resulting acoustic recording (he sang directly into a horn, backed by what sounds like a distant orchestra; there were no electrically powered microphones in 1910) is dim and distorted. Although Columbia licensed the performance (on a one-sided disk) to other labels, Berlin was not eager to return anytime soon to a recording studio. (His trepidation was fortified fifteen years later, when he recorded a new song, "Always," for the Victor Talking Machine Company; it was never released. It would take a major war to induce Irving Berlin into the studio again.)

Recording his single song from the score of *The Girl and the Wizard* was only half the prize, however: the show itself was a Shubert production, which meant Berlin had succeeded in getting his foot firmly wedged in that pinching door. An even better portal opened later that year, when two of his and Snyder's songs were interpolated into Florenz Ziegfeld's *Follies of 1910,* the fourth in this series of revues celebrated for their stars and opulence.

That year, Fanny Brice made her Follies debut after a career in vaudeville and burlesque. Ziegfeld had discovered her on the burlesque circuit singing "Sadie Salome, Go Home" in a Yiddish accent, one of her specialties (another was heart-wrenching ballads such as "My Man" and "Second Hand Rose"). Then eighteen, she spelled her first name "Fannie." Also making his debut in the show was the brilliant black comedian Bert Williams, appearing in blackface. With or without makeup, his was the only black face in the cast, representing a major breakthrough in the American theater.

As was his practice, Ziegfeld employed several songwriters for the production, though most of the songs were assigned to Gus Edwards and Harry B. Smith. Brice introduced Berlin's "Goodbye, Becky Cohen," no doubt in dialect. The other Berlin song, with music by George Botsford, was "The Dance of the Grizzly Bear" (published as "Grizzly Bear"). Botsford was best known as a conductor, though he would produce enough original songs to become a charter member of the American Society of Composers, Authors and Publishers when it was formed in 1914.

The Follies opened in June; on July 18, 1910, the Shuberts presented *Up and Down Broadway,* with a score primarily by Jean Schwartz and William

Jerome (their hit from the production was the long-lasting "Chinatown, My Chinatown"). Ethnicity continued to fascinate both Broadway and Tin Pan Alley: among the songs by Schwartz and Jerome were "Everybody Is Bagpipe Crazy" and "I'm the Ghost of Kelly." Berlin and Snyder contributed "Sweet Italian Love"; their other interpolation, salvaged from the unsuccessful *The Jolly Bachelors* of the previous January, was "Oh, That Beautiful Rag." Tin Pan Alley was also rediscovering ragtime.

Up and Down Broadway had but a wisp of a plot, something about Apollo and other gods descending from Olympus to improve Broadway's productions. The star was the comic Eddie Foy; also in the cast were Ernest Hare and Emma Carus, the latter a Berlin-born vaudeville entertainer known for her powerful vocal powers and advertised as the "Female Baritone." While not cast in stellar roles, Berlin and Snyder nonetheless appeared onstage at the Casino Theater, singing their songs at seventy-two matinee and evening performances—a bit of moonlighting that curtailed their writing until autumn.

WANDERING MINSTREL

SOON AFTER his and Snyder's vaudeville stint at the Casino ended, in October 1910, Berlin, with Henry Waterson, left for London. On this voyage he traveled not in steerage but as a catered-to passenger on the British luxury liner *Lusitania.* That he was assigned to accompany Waterson on a business trip, to check up on how Snyder and company's songs were doing by visiting the offices of their British distributor, was an indication that Snyder and Waterson now considered him more than just a lyric writer. Creativity was momentarily abandoned for finance.

By November he was back in New York, working on several interpolations; simultaneously, he was planning a piano piece. The latter, initially a reject, would make history. In April 1911, he wrote "I Beg Your Pardon, Dear Old Broadway" (words and music) for Ethel Levey, former wife of George M. Cohan and costar in four of his musicals. Popular in vaudeville and in England's music halls and revues, Levey was a tall, slender singer and dancer. On one of her London tours she recorded Berlin's "Sweet Italian Love"; four years later, she would appear in a Berlin musical and record several songs from it.

Her 1911 show, entitled *Gaby* and subtitled "Folies Bergère Revue," was produced by Henry B. Harris and Jesse L. Lasky, who had decided to bring a touch of Paris to Forty-sixth Street, duplicating, as Berlin recalled, "the Folies Bergère or Des Ambassadeurs. People drank, smoked, had dinner—and there was a show going on."

The partners had not stinted. The *New York Dramatic News* described the decor after renovations of the former 46th Street Theatre were completed:

> It is finished in pink, gray, and turquoise blue, with just enough brown and gold to give character to the lighter shades. The orchestra floor is given over to terraces of tables for diners, and another row of tables circles the front of the balcony. The rear of the balcony and the entire gallery is [*sic*] devoted to usual theater seats. It would be difficult to mention a restaurant where the gastronomic artistry surpasses that at the Folies Bergère.

The diners and smokers, if so inclined, could enjoy a triple bill comprising *Hell,* a profane burlesque in one act, book and lyrics by Rennold Wolf; *Temptation,* a ballet in one act by Alfredo Curtis, with music by Edmond Diet; and *Gaby,* a satirical revuette in three scenes, book and lyrics by Harry B. Smith and Robert Smith. Four Berlin songs were selected for the revue; one was a musical advertisement for the dinner theater itself, "Down to the Folies Bergère," while another was written especially for Levey, alluding to her long absence from the New York stage ("I Beg Your Pardon, Dear Old Broadway"). She was the Gaby of the revuette, a satirical take on the French star Gaby Deslys, who had yet to appear in the United States. The highest-paid French entertainer of her day, Deslys was a singer as well as a dancer, famed for her "Gaby Glide." The Shuberts would import her later in the year to appear opposite Al Jolson.

For her impersonation of Deslys, whom she played as a Spanish, not French, dancer, Ethel Levey sang and danced to "Spanish Love," with words by Berlin and Vincent Bryan and music by Snyder. Berlin also brought one more song, only recently completed—and all his own—which he sang for Lasky and his sister. "[Lasky] didn't like it," he would recall fifty years later with a pleased grin. Although Lasky was not thrilled with the tune, it was in fact once (literally) performed in a tryout of the show—as an instrumental, if that is the word: Ethel Levey's costar, the portly comic Otis Harlan, came on, center stage front, and whistled it. Apparently the Folies audience agreed with the producer's assessment, as "Alexander" was eliminated by the next night.

The Folies Bergère was an utter failure despite *Variety*'s commendation— "a burly show of the highest type"—and shut down after five months (to be reincarnated as the Fulton Theatre). The producers lost a hundred thousand 1911 dollars on the venture. Both Harris and Lasky subsequently faded from the Broadway scene, though the former's wife, Mrs. Henry B. Harris, as she was billed, would achieve a fleeting notoriety when, in 1927, she barred

Walter Winchell from the Hudson Theatre as punishment for writing a bad review of one of her plays. Lasky, wisely and to his profit, would flee to Hollywood, to begin a long and successful career with the production of the historic *The Squaw Man.*

Berlin took Lasky's rejection gracefully, still convinced that he might have a potential hit on his hands. Fifty years later he would recall the history of that song, and some of the relevant people, events, and details of his life at the Ted Snyder Company.

One of the better changes made in the staff came with the hiring of Max Winslow away from von Tilzer to promote the company's publications. When selling his friend Berlin's songs, Winslow plugged even harder. The two, recognizing their compatibility and shared dedication to popular song, eventually became roommates in a small apartment in Union Square; their work hours coincided, and there were no arguments about comings and goings.

Most nights, Berlin and Winslow made the plugging rounds together. "We'd go out plugging till around one or two," he remembered, "then I'd go to Maxim's, next to the office, after which I'd work till three or four." The Snyder Company was housed in a brownstone; on the top floor, a room had been set aside for him so he could compose without the distractions of the workday office, where songs were demonstrated for singers and dancers looking for new material.

Whenever he wished, he could let himself in with a key, climb the stairs, and sit at his special piano, a Weser Brothers model that he had acquired, secondhand, for a hundred dollars. It was a peculiar instrument. On the right-hand side, at the treble end of the keyboard, was a small wheel, not unlike a miniature version of that used to steer an automobile. By turning it, Berlin could shift the keyboard and, still using only the F-sharp black keys, play the melody in other keys. This type of piano was widely used by unschooled pianists, called "fakers," in Tin Pan Alley, vaudeville, and cabaret. Perhaps cued by the wheel, Berlin referred to this contraption as his Buick. A later Buick was equipped with a less obtrusive shift, a crank under the keyboard.

One night in about mid-March 1911, he worked on several song ideas. "In those days I used to start on a song—if I couldn't finish it, I'd go to something else," he explained. "It happened at a time when they were dancing to rhythm." A craze for dancing had begun to sweep America the year before, and the public was demanding songs it could dance to. Up to that time, most songs had been designed primarily for singing, not for dancing. The waltz was still popular, but the younger generation craved peppier numbers, such as the *alla breve* "fox trot," in which the four quarter notes were played as two beats to the measure. In time, this approach would inspire such dances as the Bunny Hug, the Turkey Trot, the Kangaroo Dip, and other, similar fauna. In 1912, when the dance team of Vernon and Irene Castle returned to America with their refined ballroom dancing, they would bring with them the Castle Walk, the Maxixe, and the Toddle. Under their influence, public dancing in the country would reach a high-water mark.

Sitting at his Weser that night, Berlin sensed that "they" wanted a lively rhythm number. This intuitive understanding of popular taste, this sixth sense, was a unique gift, one that his colleagues envied, even resented. The next day, Berlin dictated the song he called "Alexander's Ragtime Band" to Alfred Doyle, the copyist, who was paid fifty cents a page for his work; this tune earned him the sum of four dollars. The copyright date was March 18, 1911.

When Berlin demonstrated "Alexander's Ragtime Band" for the Ted Snyder Co., he ran into some resistance. For one thing, it was longer than the standard thirty-two bars. And even Winslow pointed out that it was too rangy—"an octave and four." True, as a kind of slow march, it would serve well as an accompaniment to the Bunny Hug or the Turkey Trot, but it had another innovative feature as well: in the final, published version the verse is in the key of C, and the chorus in F.

Despite the in-house objections, Berlin prevailed, and "Alexander" was published as a song in September and then as an instrumental—a march two-step—in October. The arranger was William Schultz, who had written out "Dorando" two years before. "He did all the marches in those days," Berlin recalled.

The publication of "Alexander" was predestined even before September—in fact, even before its one-night tryout in the Folies Bergère. (The standing joke for years was that Jesse Lasky was the man who turned down "Alexander's Ragtime Band.") The song's odyssey actually began in April, before Lasky opened his cabaret-theater.

It started with Emma Carus, a German-born star of American vaudeville. Then thirty-two, she was about to embark on a tour of the circuit and stopped by the Snyder office seeking new songs for her act; among her selections was "Alexander's Ragtime Band." On April 19, 1911 (a week before the Folies debuted), the *Chicago News* noted her arrival at the American Music Hall: "Emma Carus is there," the report said, "splendidly dressed and fitted out with a fine repertoire of songs ranging from ballads to ragtime." Although "Alexander" was not specifically mentioned in the *News* review, it is certain that Emma Carus did present it for the first time in public in Chicago. It was so well received there that she made it a part of her repertoire; it was a hit in Detroit as well, and then she swung around and returned to New Brighton, New York, to sing it to an appreciative audience that included a reviewer from the New York *Sun*. Published on May 25, the review enthused:

> It is in her songs that Mrs. Carus is most impressive, and she has five new ones that are worthy of the headliner. "Alexander" has all the swing and metrical precision of "Kelly," which Mrs. Carus brought to this country from England three years ago.
>
> In a few days "Alexander" will be whistled on the streets and played in the cafés. It is the most meritorious addition to the list of popular songs introduced this season. The vivacious comedienne soon had the audience singing the chorus with her, and those who did not sing whistled.

Three evenings later, the songwriter himself introduced the song to New York proper, at a *Friars' Frolic* at the New Amsterdam. The 1911 Frolic was produced as a benefit to raise money for a new "monastery" on Forty-eighth Street.

A social club originally formed in 1904 by press agents, the Friars had soon attracted a membership consisting mostly of vaudeville and burlesque performers denied admittance to the elite Lambs or Players clubs, whose members came from the higher echelons of the legitimate theater. The club applied monastic titles to its officers—Abbot for the president, Dean for the vice president—and called its clubhouses monasteries (one of these was renowned as a place from which a piano was once stolen in broad daylight).

The Abbot in 1911 was Berlin's friend and idol George M. Cohan, who asked the young songwriter to contribute an act and some songs to the revue. Berlin brought a sheaf of songs and demonstrated them for Cohan, who stopped him midway through, exclaiming, "Irvy, that's the song you'll do!" It was the rejected, peripatetic "Alexander."

The Frolic of 1911 consisted of a minstrel show (part 1) and an olio, or miscellany (part 2). The interlocutors for the minstrel portion were comic monologist Fred Niblo (husband of Cohan's sister Josephine and later an eminent director of silent films, including the Rudolph Valentino hit *Blood and Sand* and the classic epic *Ben Hur*) and character actor Emmett Corrigan, who would later star in a couple of Cohan's shows.

Among the "end men" were Cohan and his father, Jerry; the choristers included Ernest R. Ball (author of "Will You Love Me in December As You

Did in May?," "Mother Machree," "When Irish Eyes Are Smiling," "In the Shade of the Old Apple Tree," and "Good Night, Ladies") and Irving Berlin. To round out the the minstrel show, Julian Eltinge, then a sensation in vaudeville as a female impersonator, glided onstage (his Salome was especially popular) to sing Cohan's own "The Pullman Porters' Ball."

Made up of various sketches, the olio opened with a travesty of a Jesse Lasky creation, "Piano Phiends," performed by "The Piano Bugs," who counted among their number composers Ball, Jean Schwartz, Berlin's collaborator George Botsford, and ragtime specialist Les Copeland. Cohan came on with vaudeville comedian William Collier (later a costar in his *Hello, Broadway!*), for "Two Hot Potatoes," a Cohan sketch. Celebrated veterans Weber and Fields then regaled the audience with their "Billiard Room" scene.

In the minstrel-show segment of the Frolic, each of the songwriters presented his wares. Berlin introduced "Alexander's Ragtime Band" with the assistance of Harry Williams. The two men worked up quite an act, punctuated by an impressive flourish on their exit: "We did a double," Berlin told an interviewer. "We sang, did a little dance—and went off with a cartwheel."

The players received an appreciative and generous acclamation from the audience, a goodly percentage of which was made up of their peers and colleagues. But it was the Berlin-Williams acrobatics that stayed with the spectators, not the song itself, in an evening filled with song after song followed by songless intervals. "Alexander's Ragtime Band" "went over" well enough, but there was no particular ado made over it. In far-away-from-Broadway Staten Island, Emma Carus was more successfully promoting the song with the aid of her audience of vocalists and whistlers. She also spread the word among vaudeville luminaries, who, by popular demand, appropriated Carus's number for their own acts. Among these were the popular Eddie Cantor, the rapidly rising Al Jolson, and lesser lights.

Berlin remained with the *Friars' Frolic* for the brief tour that followed, during which the demand for "Alexander" was further stimulated. Requests for professional copies of the song prompted its publication in September, by which time *Variety* would call it the "musical sensation of the decade." Performances and recordings proliferated, and once the sheet music was made available—at ten cents a copy—two hundred thousand copies were sold "overnight." *Variety* soon reported that other publishers were complaining that the song-loving public bought nothing but "Alexander's Ragtime Band," leaving them out in the cold. By November, *Variety* noted that sales had risen to more than a million.

In 1911, it was not only music shops that sold sheet music, but also "five-and-dimes" such as Kresge's and Woolworth's. Some of these even hired resident pianists to demonstrate the latest publications while perched on a small platform in the back of the store. In larger cities, five-and-dimes were regularly toured by song pluggers, a practice that would continue into the thirties.

The sales of "Alexander's Ragtime Band" were phenomenal, and phenomena inevitably generate myths. To begin with, the tune is not a rag in the traditional sense; it does not, for example, adhere to the form of the authentic rags composed by Scott Joplin around the end of the nineteenth century. Classic rags, a fusion of African-American and European musical styles, were created into the teens by such composers as James Scott, Eubie Blake, and Joseph Lamb (who was white). Ragtime's popularity would ebb with the advent of the Jazz Age in the twenties.

Berlin himself maintained that "Alexander" was not a rag but rather a "song about ragtime." Nor was it his first attempt in this line: in 1909 he and Snyder had interpolated "Stop That Rag (Keep On Playing, Honey)" in *The Jolly Bachelors* (in which Emma Carus appeared). A year later Berlin had also written "Alexander and His Clarinet" with Snyder, and, alone, "Dat Draggy Rag." Other rags, by other writers, were also published in this period, among them "That Italian Rag," "Monkey Rag," "That Oceana Roll," and "Gaby Glide," written for the American debut of Gaby Deslys in *Vera Violetta* by Louis A. Hirsch, with words by Deslys's husband, Harry Pilcer.

In short, Tin Pan Alley had discovered ragtime. "I didn't originate it," Berlin said. "Maybe I crystallized it and brought it to people's attention. 'Ragtime' was an inner-circle term [the word was defined differently in Tin Pan Alley than it was in Harlem]. 'Alexander' brought it to the public's attention." Berlin maintained that ragtime was "on the beat" and jazz "off the beat."

The song, and what many thought was ragtime, did not go unnoticed beyond the "inner circle." From another Berlin (Germany), a Dr. Ludwig Gruener contributed his own diagnosis: "Ragtime is not music, it is a disease. . . . Hysteria is the form of insanity that an abnormal love of ragtime seems to produce." Warming up to his thesis, the man of science continued, with scientific imprecision, "It is as much a mental disease as acute mania— it has the same symptoms. If there is nothing to check this form, it produces idiocy." He rounded out his observations with statistics: 90 percent of the inmates at the insane asylums he had visited on a recent trip to America, he claimed, were "abnormally fond of ragtime." Gruener's assessment was published in an American newspaper in October 1911, before "Alexander's Ragtime Band" conquered Europe all the way to czarist Russia.

In December, a report from Philadelphia contradicted the good doctor's hypothesis. The article's headline read:

RAGTIME MELODY PREVENTS PANIC AT FIRE IN FILM SHOW

The fire had broken out during the showing of a film, as a pianist accompanied the visuals with the doleful "Hearts and Flowers." At the cry of "Fire!" the patrons stampeded en masse for the exits—whereupon the cool-headed pianist broke into the strains of "Alexander's Ragtime Band." The scramble stopped, order was restored, and, as the people filed out, "all the boys whistled and the women hummed."

Unpersuaded by this incident, Alexander Blume, an American newspaper writer, mounted his own attack on the entire realm of American popular music. He feared for his country, he said: "What a shiftless, thoughtless and blatantly immoral people we must be if we are judged by our 'popular songs.' . . . What has come over us that decent women can sit in the theater and applaud studied indecency?" (Alas, he did not supply examples to illustrate his point.)

"Popular music is like drink," he argued, in that "it goes to the head [and] unlike drink, in that it goes to the feet. Did you ever notice the diabolical grace with which the popular song so readily lends itself to that sinuous body dance[?]"

Popular song, he declared, laughed openly at the institution of marriage. (No examples here, either, but he may have been considering the likes of "My Wife's Gone to the Country" or Jean Havez and Harry von Tilzer's "I'll Lend You Everything I've Got except My Wife [and I'll Make You a Present of Her].") He blamed the entire shameful state of American popular song on the "disciples of Irving Berlin & Co."

Berlin and company, for their part, could not have been more elated, as sales figures soared. "Alexander" was tinkled out on parlor pianos and belted out in cabarets and vaudeville theaters. In the latter, performers competed to use the song; the rule was that whoever got to the bandleader first got to do the number. Not only vocalists but acrobats, jugglers, and comedians seized on "Alexander" to serve as their "play-off," or exit, music, a surefire stimulus to applause.

Berlin himself experienced that satisfying sound more than a few times. Five days after "Alexander's Ragtime Band" was published, he was booked into Hammerstein's Victoria, in the heart of the theater district on Forty-second Street, where Broadway and Seventh Avenue converge. Originally built by opera aficionado Oscar Hammerstein, grandfather of the lyricist, the theater was managed, while the first Oscar was preoccupied with opera and with feuding with the Metropolitan, by William "Willie" Hammerstein, father of the second Oscar.

The Victoria was notorious for showcasing "freak" acts, a policy inaugurated by the wily Willie that made it probably the most successful vaudeville theater in New York. For a minimal salary, Hammerstein would sign such unlikely talents as famous boxers, wrestlers, and even bicyclists. His most freakish offerings included such luminaries as the Cherry sisters, billed as "America's Worst Act" (which claim they reportedly lived up to), and two attractive young women named Lillian Graham and Ethel Conrad, who between them had managed to shoot socialite W. E. D. Stokes in the leg. In tribute to this achievement, they were billed as "The Shooting Stars."

In the wake of the sensational popularity of "Alexander," Berlin was hired by Hammerstein for a week (at a thousand dollars) and billed, with characteristic Hammersteinian flair, as "The Composer of a Hundred Hits" (though at the time he had published only about half that number of songs, all told). Sime Silverman, of *Variety,* covered the opening of Berlin's stint on September 11, 1911, and reported:

> Next to last [considered the ideal spot on any vaudeville program] appeared Irving Berlin, who sang two of his newest songs, together with a neat medley of his own "hits," woven into a story. When you can do that you can write songs, and to see this slim little kid on the stage with a pianist [Clifford Hess] going through a list that sounded like all the song hits in the world [was] something to think about.
>
> Mr. Berlin looks so nice on the platform all the girls in the house fall for him immediately. He did make some hit. They were still applauding after Rayno's Bull Dogs came on to close the performance, but Irving wouldn't return.

According to Woollcott, that first performance was attended by a Chinatown contingent ("200 of the old gang") led by Chuck Connors; the group was "vociferous but refined." As he was about to enter the Victoria that evening, Berlin was startled to see a couple of his old cronies out front. One confessed that they had been waiting around for hours hoping "to pinch that swell picture of you in the lobby"—a life-size photograph of the songwriter that Hammerstein was using to advertise the Berlin week.

"Alexander's Ragtime Band" decidedly made his name, and to make that official, in November he petitioned legally to take the name Irving Berlin. Further recognition came in December with the formation of Waterson, Berlin & Snyder, a new company in which he was a full partner. Waterson and Snyder were no fools: Irving Berlin's songs had made the company.

Berlin's next major step began comically but would end tragically. On the same day he made his debut at the Victoria, a musical entitled *The Fascinating Widow,* with a score by Karl Hoschna (music) and lyrics by Otto Hauerbach (later Harbach), opened at the Liberty Theatre. Starring female impersonator Julian Eltinge, the show featured one interpolation by Irving Berlin, "Don't Take Your Beau to the Seashore," with lyrics by E. Ray Goetz.

Then about twenty-six, Goetz had left Buffalo for Broadway and begun collaborating on songs with composer A. Baldwin Sloane the year before. In 1911, in addition to their *Fascinating Widow* tune, he and Berlin also interpolated a number into a Sloane musical, *The Never Homes.* That song, "There's a Girl in Havana," had what would seem in retrospect an ominous title. Ted Snyder collaborated on it, as he did on another song by Berlin and Goetz, "Sombrero Land," for a Winter Garden show. Although these few songs exhaust the Berlin-Goetz catalog, the two men became close friends. Goetz would go on to another brief collaboration, with George Gershwin, and then turn to producing. Some of his productions would star his wife, Irene Bordoni (among them *The French Doll* and *Paris,* with songs by Cole Porter).

The final Berlin-Goetz collaboration was a parody of Berlin's own still mass-selling song: "Alexander's Bag-Pipe Band," written with the aid of Sloane, was introduced in *Hokey-Pokey,* which premiered at the Broadway early in February 1912. That same month, Irving Berlin married Goetz's petite twenty-year-old sister Dorothy.

The story of their meeting is both curious and suspect. Dorothy had followed her brother to New York in hopes of breaking into show business; that she and Berlin might have met during the period when he and Goetz were collaborating seems very likely, even inevitable. But according to Eric Bennett, writing in the *Sunday Chronicle* (London) years later, they instead met in Berlin's office during a farcical battle over one of his songs.

According to Bennett, Berlin told him that an attractive girl came to the office one day looking for songs for her act (it is worth noting here that no record has surfaced of Dorothy Goetz's appearing on any stage). Berlin's/Bennett's account continued:

She leaned across the desk to plead for [the song she wanted]. But she had hardly begun to speak when another Broadway adorable swept into the room.

As soon as [the latter] heard what the first girl was asking, she rushed across to the desk, pulling her away [and] shouting, "No! I want it."

Dorothy was a woman of spirit. She swung around a haymaking left and slapped the newcomer across the face. The two closed, swapping punches like a couple of prize-ring veterans, and I [Berlin] was powerless to separate them. They were scratching, tearing hair and shouting in lovely voices that they wanted to sing my song. Well, I had dreamed of people fighting for the right to sing my stuff, but this was the first time I saw that dream come true.

Berlin claimed he gave the other lovely the song, then asked Dorothy for a date.

A likely-enough-sounding tale, and maybe even true—but its self-serving tone is unlike Berlin, and its denouement seems too neat. The next year, when he was in London, Berlin was no longer speaking to interviewers. The story thus may or may not be apocryphal.

However Dorothy and Berlin met, they were married in Buffalo, in the presence of her (non-Jewish) family. Taking a cue from the song written for *The Never Homes*, the newlyweds left soon after for a honeymoon in Cuba. When they returned, they moved into a fine apartment building, the Chatsworth, on Seventy-second Street and Riverside Drive. They planned to redecorate the place and make it their home. (Berlin, at the time of the wedding, had been living in Harlem, on West 112th Street; once the royalties and profits had begun accruing at the Ted Snyder Co., he and Winslow had been able to afford separate quarters. In 1912, the section of Harlem in which Berlin lived had a large Jewish population, second in size only to that of the Lower East Side, and much more affluent. The then-ten-year-old Richard Rodgers lived in the same area, but nearer to Mount Morris Park; his father, Dr. William Rodgers, had his practice there.)

Before the Berlins were fully settled in at the Chatsworth, however, Dorothy came down with a cold and fever, and her concerned husband summoned some of New York's most prominent physicians to her bedside. "The doctors and the decorators were jostling each other in the hallway of this shiny new home," Woollcott wrote in his quasi-biography of Berlin, "while the anxious bridegroom was locked up in the front room trying ludicrously to fulfill his contracts for jaunty songs long over-due."

During the period of Dorothy Berlin's worsening illness, several Berlin songs, some written with her brother, were in fact interpolated into shows, including the ingenious "Opera Burlesque," based on the Sextette from Donizetti's *Lucia di Lammermoor.* In April Berlin played a return engagement at Hammerstein's Victoria, where he made a hit with a song written the year before, "Everybody's Doin' It Now."

In June Dorothy's condition deteriorated, requiring virtual round-the-clock medical attention. There was no medication to cure her illness; antibiotics did not exist in 1912. She died on July 17, at the age of twenty. The cause of death is usually given as typhoid fever, which she presumably contracted in Havana on her honeymoon, typhoid having been epidemic there at the time. In Cuba, even in the finer hotels, one could get the disease from contaminated food or drink, or from casual contact with a carrier. The mystery is, how did Irving Berlin avoid being infected?

While typhoid develops slowly, with initial symptoms resembling those of a bad cold—fever, coughing, fatigue—Dorothy's diagnosis in June was pneumonia, with similar symptoms. Either one would, on its own, have been dangerous enough; the combination of the two was, in this case, fatal. Typhoid fever was most lethal when it struck the elderly, generally running a milder course in children. At twenty, Dorothy might well have survived had there been no complications. The death certificate filled out by her doctor noted the cause of death as typhoid fever and pneumonia.

There is one other troubling question about Dorothy Berlin's illness. Initial symptoms normally appear within two weeks of a typhus infection, but Dorothy died about five months *after* her stay in Cuba. This suggests that her complaint may have been misdiagnosed at first—though considering the nature of the treatment (minimal) and medication (none) available at the time, even a proper diagnosis would probably have made scant difference. Two days after her death, Dorothy Goetz Berlin was interred in the family plot in Buffalo. Afterward, Berlin and Ray Goetz returned to New York, the former in virtual shock and despondent, the latter determined to assist his friend and brother-in-law through the grim and dismal period of mourning that lay ahead.

Berlin was not interested in writing. His mind reeling in a fog of confused indignation—it all seemed a cosmic injustice—he agreed to leave town, to go to Europe, at the suggestion of a concerned and distressed Goetz.

"A week after it was all over," Woollcott reported, "the understanding Goetz picked his new brother up bodily and carried him all over Europe in an effort to pull him together." He does not say where or for how long they went, but concludes, "When, after a long absence, [Berlin] was seen on

IRVING BERLIN

Broadway, everyone said he was himself again. But the folks at the office knew better."

Woollcott added that when the songwriter at last returned to his Buick, his output was mediocre at best: "He tried to turn out jolly things about grizzly bears, bunny hugs and all the fearful menageries of the dance floor of the day. But the tunes were all limp and sorry."

Giving up on the dance crazes, Berlin took what was for him an unusual musical turn by composing a ballad, a waltz, an undisguisedly personal song from the heart. Titled "When I Lost You," it was hardly the typical Irving Berlin parody, comic song, or celebration of the latest ragtime theme—nothing to do with a jockey man, mockingbird, or soldier (all subjects of songs he published that year).

Instead, "When I Lost You" was an honest, almost sentimental, biographical expression of anguish. Publication, when he began writing it, was probably far from his intent. It has been intimated that this song constituted a commercial exploitation of Dorothy's death, but that is nonsense. Berlin wrote it because he felt it; it is guileless, lucid, and memorable, its sentiments simple, even obvious, but timeless. After a brief (and lovely) introductory verse, the words are:

> I lost the sunshine and roses,
> I lost the heavens of blue,
> I lost the beautiful rainbow,
> I lost the morning dew.
> I lost the angel who gave me
> Summer the whole winter through.
> I lost the gladness that turned into sadness
> When I lost you.

When his partners heard the song, they voted for publication, even though ragtime was then still the main inspiration for Tin Pan Alley, and the waltz not especially salable. Vindicating their decision, "When I Lost You" swept through the field; by the beginning of 1913 there were millions of copies in print. (As for Berlin's "exploitation," it is unlikely that every purchaser across the country would have been aware of the story behind the song's composition.) An ideal vehicle for a tenor who could conjure a sob in his throat, it was taken up widely in vaudeville and cabaret; piano rolls brought it into the homes of unskilled pianists. Recordings soon followed. The popularity of "When I Lost You" was second only to that of "Alexander's Ragtime Band."

Back at his Buick, Berlin rounded out this tragic year with two more hits, the spirited rhythm number "When the Midnight Choo-Choo Leaves for Alabam' " and "At the Devil's Ball," whose composition extended into January 1913.

Curiously, there are three versions of this last song. The first of these dated from November 1912; not pleased with it, Berlin reworked it twice to produce the variant that was a hit in the early months of 1913. Although he would place only three interpolations in the coming year, his creative slump was clearly over. December 1912 saw the opening, in London, of an important show with music mostly by Louis Hirsch and lyrics by Arthur George. Entitled *Hullo, Ragtime!,* it starred Ethel Levey and featured some songs from the Waterson, Berlin & Snyder catalog, most notably "Alexander's Ragtime Band." (Levey's success in this show and in one that followed would keep her employed in Britain for a decade.)

Ragtime mania now swept across sedate England, impelling the management of the Hippodrome, which housed *Hullo, Ragtime!,* to invite the composer of the catchy new song to appear in their theater. He agreed (for a salary of £20,000) and late in June 1913 sailed for London with his musical secretary, pianist Cliff Hess.

His impending arrival was preceded by a vigorous promotional campaign in the press, where he was dubbed the "Rag-time King" and a "Song-Writing Genius." On reaching London, he took a cab to the Savoy, only to find that "the kid selling papers, who opened the door, was whistling 'Alexander.' " It was a good sign, almost as auspicious as the window displays in the music stores: life-size posters of him surrounded by sheet music.

The Hippodrome advertised him as the "Composer of a Hundred Hits," who would "entertain and render for the first time his latest melodic efforts." This was followed by a list of no less than twenty song titles. To fulfill the promise of unheard works, Berlin prepared a new number to open the act, appropriately entitled "That International Rag." The Hippodrome program listed him as part of *Hullo, Ragtime!,* under the billing "Irving Berlin in selections from his repertoire"; like the show itself, he was a hit.

Besides putting Berlin's musical ideas on paper, Hess also served as his accompanist. The Ohioan, born in Cincinnati, had begun his professional life as a pianist on Mississippi riverboats. After five years with Berlin, he would strike out on his own as a publisher and in the recording industry, later paying tribute to his old boss with "When Alexander Takes His Ragtime Band to France" (written with Alfred Bryan and the indefatigable Edgar Leslie).

Berlin impressed the British press; one writer found it "almost impossible to believe that this boy—he looks nineteen—" could have written "Alexander's Ragtime Band" (the "boy" had in fact turned twenty-five that May). Although "That International Rag" was a success in London as well as in the United States, its author would later dismiss it, calling it "dated in the sense that it is about the effect of ragtime on people."

Evanescent it might be, but it was still going strong when he and Hess returned to New York late in July. He soon completed another surprisingly popular hit, "Snookey Ookums," lampooning young lovers' baby talk (no doubt some of the success of "At the Devil's Ball" could be attributed to the similar treatment it accorded mothers-in-law), and gave a nod to a growing industry in "I Was Aviating Around" (with Vincent Bryan). "Jake! Jake! The Yiddisher Ball Player" was decidedly *not* a hit. His collaborator on it was Blanche Merrill, who wrote special material for Fanny Brice and Willie Howard, which accounts for the song's ethnicity.

Nineteen-thirteen ended without further excitement. Generally, Berlin's days and nights were a kaleidoscope of sameness, each different, yet routine: the round of cabarets and shows, the late-night and early-morning work, rest, then back to the round again. This formulaic pattern would undergo some slight modification in 1914, though, to accommodate his duties as a charter member of the American Society of Composers, Authors and Publishers (ASCAP); he would serve on its board of directors for four years. The stimulus for the society's founding was a visit to New York in 1910 by the Italian composer Giacomo Puccini, who came to America to attend the world premiere of his *Girl of the Golden West.* He was escorted around town by George Maxwell, representing his publisher in the United States. Puccini was delighted to hear his melodies performed in restaurants and hotel dining rooms, but he was most displeased to learn that in the United States, unlike Europe, such public presentations generated no additional royalties or income for the work's composer.

Maxwell discussed the matter with a successful young composer named Raymond Hubbell (best known for the song "Poor Butterfly," and for writing no less than four different scores for the Ziegfeld Follies). A couple of years later, the two men brought their concept of a performing-rights society to attorney Nathan Burkan, who counted among his clients Victor Herbert, then the towering giant of American musical theater. Herbert was dubious at first, but after two days of persuasion, Maxwell convinced him.

In October 1913 plans were made to hold an organizing meeting at Herbert's favorite restaurant, Luchow's. On the appointed night, however, it was pouring rain, and of the thirty-six top songwriters invited to the meeting, only nine turned up, among them Herbert. Whether because of the rain or because he, like Herbert before him, had doubts, Berlin was one of the absentees.

Undaunted, the nine present formed their society to protect the rights, and income, of all songwriters, whether they attended the meeting or not. When the next meeting was called, for February 13, 1914, at the Hotel Claridge, more than a hundred prospective members appeared, and ASCAP was formally launched. Irving Berlin would be one of its most prodigious members.

The battle was hardly won with the founding of the society; it was merely the call to arms. The real opening shot was not fired until April 1915, when Victor Herbert, the most prestigious member and vice president of ASCAP, initiated a lawsuit against Shanley's, one of New York's most elegant restaurants. Hearing the resident orchestra render one of his songs, Herbert reasoned that if people listened to his "Sweethearts" while dining, then the management owed him compensation for the use of his music; alternatively, as the copyright owner of a dramatic work (specifically, the operetta from which "Sweethearts" was derived), he retained the exclusive right to its public performance.

This argument did not go over well in court, as it had not in a different case the year before, when John Philip Sousa brought suit against the Vanderbilt Hotel. Then, in the Circuit Court of Appeals, the judge had ruled that people came to the Vanderbilt's dining room to eat, not to listen to music; now, in May 1915, Judge Learned Hand likewise decided against Herbert, explaining that music was performed in Shanley's for entertainment, not for profit. Herbert appealed the decision and in January 1916 lost again, but a year later, on January 22, 1917, the two previous decisions were swept aside in the United States Supreme Court by Justice Oliver Wendell Holmes. Victor Herbert and all the members of ASCAP were entitled to payment for the use of their compositions in restaurants, hotels, cabarets, vaudeville theaters, film houses, and dance halls—anywhere, in short, that music was performed (including, in time, on radio and television). A system of licensing was devised, with payment to be made to ASCAP for equitable distribution of royalties among its members. By the midtwenties, it was a million-dollar organization. Songwriters as successful as Jerome Kern, the Gershwins, Cole Porter, DeSylva, Brown and Henderson, George M. Cohan, Walter Donaldson, and others became affluent thanks to Victor Herbert and the original handful who made it to Luchow's that rainy night in 1913.

Irving Berlin, as a member of the society's board of directors, observed the fall and rise of Herbert's litigation with apprehension and then, finally, elation in the knowledge that his own future was secure. He became a member of ASCAP's elite, drawing a substantial annual income over and above his royalties from sheet music and recording sales.

At the time of Herbert's second failed effort, Berlin was reaping rewards from a new type of venture for him, his first fully scored Broadway musical. Before the December 1914 opening of *Watch Your Step,* which starred the dancing Castles, he had made a drastic and wise business move, leaving Waterson, Berlin & Snyder to form Irving Berlin, Inc. Accompanied by the faithful and astute Max Winslow, he set up offices on Broadway, uptown, near Times Square. Waterson and Snyder got to keep the "Berlin" in the company's name, but they lost their major money-maker. Irving Berlin was thus, as of November 1914, in full control of his works, and would be in perpetuity, or until those works slipped into public domain according to copyright law. On the surface, he seemed in charge, businesslike, assured, but in fact, he later admitted, "I was scared to death because I didn't know if I could continue to write hits."

Vernon and Irene Castle were at the height of their popularity in 1914, having recently returned from Paris, where they had scored a major success as a husband-and-wife dance team in 1912. The British-born Vernon had made his Broadway debut in *About Town* (1906) as an eccentric dancer and stooge for comedian Lew Fields; Irene had appeared on Broadway for the first time as a replacement dancer in Fields's *The Summer Widowers* (1910), which also featured Vernon Castle. The next year, 1911, both were cast in yet another Fields production, *The Hen-Pecks.* Unhappy with their less-than-stellar roles in the New York theater, they left for Paris, where they established themselves as the Castles and inspired a mania for ballroom dancing.

When they came back to the United States, they brought with them the Maxixe, the tango, and most notably their own Castle Walk—not to mention the polka. Their timing was perfect: dance halls were thriving in 1914, with the fancier ones being called dansants. Not only were women doing the Castle Walk, they were also trying to dress like the glamorous Irene, and they loved her "modern" coiffure. Men, for their part, wished they could be as slim, and as smooth, as her husband.

Veteran producer Charles Dillingham conceived the idea of celebrating the dance with its most celebrated practitioners, and of complementing their talents by hiring the man who seemed to be writing all the popular dances of the day to score the show. Dillingham was an old hand at producing musicals, beginning with 1903's unsuccessful *The Office Boy* and *Babette*. The latter was significant largely because its score was by Victor Herbert (who did much better that same year with *Babes in Toyland*); it was the first of nine Herbert musicals to be produced by Dillingham, among them *Mlle. Modiste* and *The Red Mill*. Jerome Kern, too, would later write scores for him.

Dillingham succeeded in signing the Castles to appear in *Watch Your Step,* advertised as the "Syncopated Musical Show Made in America," with "Plot, if any, by Harry B. Smith," according to the program credit. He then ensured the score's syncopation by hiring Irving Berlin to write the songs and dances. Now twenty-six, and basking in worldwide success, Berlin unhesitatingly agreed to provide a full score (though on a couple of songs he collaborated with Snyder and Goetz, and used one interpolation by De Witt C. Coolman, "The High Stepper's March," an instrumental).

Somehow, during the period when he was moving into his Broadway offices, he managed to write close to thirty songs for the show, plus an instrumental "Polka." *Watch Your Step* opened at the Globe on December 8, 1914, following a tryout in Syracuse in late November. Berlin dutifully touched all musical bases with such inventions as "I'm a Dancing Teacher Now" (a Vernon Castle number satirizing the proliferation of dancing schools in the country), "Show Us How to Do the Fox Trot," "The Syncopated Walk," "Ann Eliza's Tango Tea," and even a "Ragtime Opera Medley." Then, too, there was "What Is Love?," a waltz.

The current popularity of dancing was acknowledged by Berlin in the lyric to "The Syncopated Walk," with its line ". . . ever since the dancing craze/ Ev'rybody has a syncopated walk." His most ingenious song was "Play a Simple Melody" (really a pair of songs), in which the show's ingenue begins by pleading for the title's simple melody, then repeats the theme against a contrapuntal rag performed by a jazzy character named Algy. While not the standout hit of *Watch Your Step*, "Play a Simple Melody" would become a standard in the early fifties when it was recorded by Bing Crosby and his son Gary.

The show, which was in fact primarily a revue, was replete with peculiarities. Vernon Castle, for example, was cast as "Joseph Lilyburn," the male lead, while Irene was billed as "Mrs. Vernon Castle." At one point in the performance, Castle stepped out of character to introduce his wife, and the two then proceeded to go into their dance. As the *Times* reviewer observed, "Mr. Castle has a name of some sort attached to the character that he is supposed to play [Joseph], but [Frank] Tinney keeps calling him Vern." Tinney was a popular comedian-singer who had begun in vaudeville and was famed for his ad-libs. However, Tinney's addressing Castle by his given, rather than stage, name was neither an ad-lib nor in the script.

The most coherent synopsis of the plot may be found in the *Catalog of the American Musical,* by Tommy Krasker and Robert Kimball:

> Old Jabez Pennyfeather dies and bequeaths his fortune to any man or woman in his family who has never been in love. Two relatives appear: a very proper and bashful Englishman [Castle] and an innocent young maiden, "Ernesta Hardacre" [played by Sallie Fisher], who is spurred on by her greedy father. . . . Pennyfeather's money-grubbing lawyers and married relatives plot to disqualify the pair by luring them into amorous entanglements. Eventually, Joseph and Ernesta fall in love with each other, but don't admit it until after they receive the inheritance.

Perhaps the most concise appraisal, however, was that of the reviewer from the *Press,* who agreed with the playbill's self-assessment of Harry Smith's contribution: "The plot lasted through the first act, but never appeared again in recognizable shape."

Evidently the paying audience did not much mind the lack of a plot: *Watch Your Step* ran for 175 performances in New York before embarking on a successful tour. In May of the following year it opened in London, where it enjoyed an even longer run. During its American tour, Castle left the show to enlist in Britain's Royal Flying Corps; after serving in France (where he would shoot down two German planes), he would be transferred back across the Atlantic as a flying instructor, first in Canada and then later in the United States, after the country was drawn into what was then called the Great War. He would be killed early in 1918 in a plane crash while on a training flight.

The wide range—the variety—of the songs Berlin fashioned for *Watch Your Step* is striking. The show's numerous settings provided some of the inspiration: a Palais de Fox-Trot, the Metropolitan Opera, a Fifth Avenue cabaret, and a Pullman sleeping car (in which a couple must settle for an upper berth for two, only to keep everyone else in the car awake with their song "Move Over"). An opera setting in the second act, part of a long production number, brought out an irate Verdi to protest the ragging of operatic arias. The other sets, meanwhile, were ideal for songs and dances, with titles that read like chapters of a travelogue—"Come to the Land of the Argentine" (to rhyme with "queen"), "Lock Me in Your Harem and Throw Away the

Key" (set in Cairo), and "When It's Night Time in Dixie Land"—juxtaposed with the more homely "Settle Down in a One-Horse Town" and "Homeward Bound."

There were, of course, the requisite love songs (ballads), as well as one hate song. The waltz "What Is Love?" has a strikingly un-Berlinian word in its second verse—"Love, love, out of the darkness I call to thee . . ."—and asks

> *What is love?*
> *Is it gladness?*
> *Or a form of sadness?*
> *Or a sign of madness?*

More imagination is evident in the lyric of "When I Discovered You" (written with E. Ray Goetz). In the first verse "he" sings of all that men have discovered; in the second, "she" counters with:

> *History proves since the World first began,*
> *Ev'rything great was not discovered by man,*
> *Girls can discover what men never can,*
> *I'm a discoverer too,*
> *Though I'll never be*
> *Known to history*
> *This much is true.*

Chorus:

> *Columbus discovered America,*
> *Hudson discovered New York,*
> *Benjamin Franklin discovered the spark,*
> *That Edison discovered would light up the dark,*
> *Marconi discovered the wireless telegraph across the ocean blue,*
> *But the greatest discovery was*
> *When you discovered me and I discovered you.*

"I Hate You" is a typical expression of the young leads who will end up together by the end of the evening; it was an idea that Berlin would return to, even employing some of the same imagery, a quarter of a century later. The two relatives, the Englishman Lilyburn and the girl, Ernesta, are trading barbs. He begins:

> *You're not the girl I'd want to be my wife.*

and she replies:

> *I'd never marry you.*

They go on from there, alternating lines:

> *You don't mean a thing in my young life.*
> *I never wanted you.*
> *I hate your dress because you wear it.*
> *I hate the place where you reside.*
> *Don't ever fret, you will never share it.*
> *Rest assured I'll never walk inside.*

Chorus (which she begins; then they alternate until both sing the last two lines together):

> *I hate the very ground you walk upon.*
> *I hate your great big eyes of blue.*
> *I hate the very phone you talk upon.*
> *I don't give a rap for you.*
> *I hope you never do.*
> *I hate the color of your curly hair.*
> *I hate the clothes you wear all through.*
> *Then besides I must hate someone,*
> *And it might as well be you.*

The first-night audience, and the critics, loved *Watch Your Step.* For Berlin it was a major accomplishment. Just as he had once proved to Waterson that he could write a tune ("Dorando"), he now proved to Dillingham that he could write a full musical-comedy score. Dillingham, for his part, was both impressed and pleased. A year later, in the same theater, he would stage *Stop! Look! Listen!,* score by Irving Berlin.

3

UP AND DOWN
BROADWAY

AS IMPORTANT as it was to Berlin that he had fulfilled Dillingham's expectations, even more important was the fact that he had proved himself *to* himself. And not only had he written a complete show score, but the *Watch Your Step* songs revealed a new sophistication, a self-assurance, an ability to work under the pressure involved in assembling a musical, with all the dropped numbers, new songs, and cast changes such a production inevitably entailed.

A common feature of many of Berlin's earliest songs is that they tell a story, frequently in dialect (ideal for vaudeville) and always about people. They are not objective declarations of love or some other emotion; names are named—Sadie and Moses of "Sadie Salome, Go Home," for example. Another Sadie, in "Yiddle on Your Fiddle," implores Yiddle to play some ragtime. Benjamin Manner and Lucy Brown are the protagonists in "Try It on Your Piano," and Bill tells Liza, "I Just Came Back to Say Goodbye," though sadly.

Typical of this genre is one of the few songs published in 1915 that were not from a show, the droll (and some might say anti-Semitic) "Cohen Owes Me Ninety-seven Dollars." Like most "ethnic" songs that Berlin, and others, wrote in the pre–First World War period, it provoked no protests, bans, or demonstrations over its content. As Benjamin Sears and Bradford Connor point out in their annotations for a 1996 recorded collection of early Berlin songs, *Keep On Smiling,*

Berlin's ethnic songs always have a good-natured quality to them that is not necessarily found in songs of this type by other writers. . . . He invites the listener to join the character in seeing how ridiculous stereotypes can be. Even though in modern terms these songs might be thought to be "politically incorrect," Berlin treats these topics in a manner that is surprisingly lacking in offensiveness. Products of the period, such songs were basically dropped from Berlin's writing by 1920.

Over the years, Berlin wrote songs with Irish, Italian, and black "stereotyping," in addition to Jewish. In the case of "Cohen," Belle Baker, a prominent vaudeville star noted for her comic characterizations, needed a new song, and Berlin complied. The plot of the song is introduced in the first verse, in which Old Man Rosenthal, fatally ill, calls his son to his side and tells him:

> *Cohen owes me ninety-seven dollars*
> *And it's up to you to see that Cohen pays*
> *I sold a lot of goods to Rosenstein on an I.O.U. for ninety days*
> *Levi brothers don't get any credit*
> *They owe me for a hundred yards of lace*
> *If you promise me, my son,*
> *You'll collect from every one*
> *I can die with a smile upon my face.*

In the second verse Belle Baker could inform her audience that "Old Man Rosenthal is better now"—he is both "healthy and very wealthy." Apparently his dutiful son has succeeded in collecting all the outstanding bills. In the second chorus Rosenthal himself explains his miraculous recovery:

> *What could my son do with all that money*
> *If I should leave it all and say goodbye?*
> *It's all right to pass away,*
> *But when people start to pay,*
> *That's no time for a businessman to die.*

Belle Baker's star shone brightest in the early-twentieth-century equivalent of the later Borscht Belt, in the Catskill Mountains of upstate New York. Her fans were delighted with the new number, and it became a popular hit, as did another Berlin song that followed, a touching ballad that was, ironically, the profitable end result of a hoax. The author's serious intent is obvious in the superscription above the title in the published song: "Respectfully dedicated to the memory of Charles Lounsbury [sic], whose legacy suggested this song."

Who was this Charles Lounsbery? He was, it turns out, the putative author of a remarkable last will and testament first published in a trade periodical for bankers and subsequently collected in an anthology entitled *Heart Throbs.* Brought to Berlin's attention by one of his Broadway friends, the wag Wilson Mizner, and an editor named Robert H. Davis, the will was a sad and moving piece of writing, and it touched the songwriter. Charles Lounsbery, so the story went, was an attorney who had spent his final days in an insane asylum and died destitute. Penniless when he prepared his will, he left only simple bequests to two special groups, children and lovers. In part, Lounsbery's testament read:

> ITEM—I leave to children, exclusively, but only for the life of that childhood, all and every, the dandelions of the fields and the daisies thereof, with the right to play among them freely, according to the custom of children, warning them at the same time against thistles. . . .
>
> And I leave to children the long, long days to be merry in, in a thousand ways, and the Night and the Moon and the train of the Milky Way to wonder at, but subject, nevertheless, to the right hereinafter given to lovers. . . .
>
> ITEM—To lovers I devise their imaginary world, with whatever they may need, as the stars of the sky, the red, red roses by the wall, the snow of the hawthorn, the sweet strains of music, or aught else they may desire to figure to each other the lastingness and beauty of their love. . . .

Seeing in this document the potential for a poignant song, Berlin selected as *his* recipients the elderly. The first verse of "When I Leave the World Behind" introduces a millionaire with a "load on his mind" who leaves to "ev'ry wrinkled face" a fireplace, for dreaming of the golden days, adding, "I'll leave them each a song/ To sing the whole day long,/ As toward the end they plod./ To ev'ry broken heart/ With sorrow torn apart,/ I'll leave the love of God." He concludes:

I'll leave the sunshine to the flowers,
I'll leave the springtime to the trees;
And to the old folks I'll leave mem'ries
Of a baby upon their knees.
I'll leave night-time to the dreamers,
I'll leave the songbirds to the blind:
I'll leave the moon above
To those in love,
When I leave the world behind.

The song was debuted early in May 1915, at the Palace, by Fritzi Scheff, a Viennese opera star turned vaudevillian who had scored a great success in Victor Herbert's *Mlle. Modiste* a few years before. That started it; before long, the ballad was appropriated by the still-rising Al Jolson and the established Belle Baker. Once again Berlin had succeeded in touching the public nerve and heart.

(There was a sequel to the moving story and the song's success: years later, Berlin would learn that Charles Lounsbery had never really existed, and that he and his will had instead been invented by a man, possibly an attorney, named Willston Fish. Furthermore, it seems highly likely—though it is not known for certain—that jokester Wilson Mizner was aware of the deception when he brought the will to Berlin's attention. Mizner, who had known the songwriter from about 1910, was a noted con man and wit, once remarking of his young friend, apropos of the limited vocabulary displayed in his lyrics, "Berlin is a man of few words." The original straight man for another of his most-repeated quips was a hotel clerk. Not informed when he took it that his room faced onto an Elevated track, Mizner called the clerk and asked, "When does this room get to Chicago?" In the midfifties, George S. Kaufman, S. N. Behrman, and Berlin considered writing a musical about the Mizners—Wilson's brother was the noted architect Addison—but the project never took off.)

As "When I Leave the World Behind" spread through the vaudeville circuits and the five-and-dimes, and while it was being recorded by a master of sentimental songs, Harry Burr, Berlin was occupied with the composition of a new song.

His friend George M. Cohan paid him affectionate tribute at a Friars banquet at which Berlin was the guest of honor. Cohan's toast, or "roast," in language typical of its time and context, introduced "Irvy" as a Jew boy [who] named himself after an English actor [i.e., Henry Irving] and a German city [Berlin]. Irvy writes a great song. He writes a song with a good lyric, a lyric that rhymes, good music, music you don't have to dress up to listen to, but it is good music.

He is a wonderful little fellow, wonderful in lots of ways. He has become famous and wealthy, without wearing a lot of jewelry and falling for funny clothes. He is uptown, but he is there with the old downtown hardshell. And with all his success, you will find his watch and his handkerchief in his pockets where they belong.

The honored guest was expected to counter with his own after-dinner speech, and the nervous Berlin rose—Woollcott described him as being panicky—to reply "in his own language":

> *Friar Abbot, Brother Friars,*
> *Ladies, Guests*
> *And Music-Buyers.*
> *What am I gonna do?*
> *What am I gonna do?*
> *What can a songwriter say?*
> *What can a songwriter do?*
> *I wish I could make an appropriate speech,*
> *But speech-making simply is out of my reach.*
> *So what can a songwriter do?*

Then he sang:

> *What can a songwriter say?*
> *A fiddler can speak with his fiddle,*
> *A singer can speak with his voice,*
> *An actor can speak*
> *With his tongue in his cheek,*
> *But a songwriter has no choice,*
> *Whatever his rights and wrongs*
> *He only can speak with his songs.*

He then made good on this promise by entertaining the Friars with a selection of his works.

Later he would reveal his feelings about songwriting, its rewards and uncertainties, in another lyric, ostensibly tracing the trajectory of a song but also, and patently, autobiographical:

> *Born just to live for a short space of time,*
> *Often without any reason or rhyme,*
> *Hated by highbrows who call it a crime;*
>   *Loved by the masses who buy it;*
> *Made by the fellows who stay up at night,*
> *Sweating and fretting while getting it right—*
> *Publisher pleading with all of his might*
>   *With some performer to try it;*
> *Heard by the critic without any heart—*
> *One of those fellows who pick it apart,*
> *Cares for the finish, but don't like the start—*
>   *Makes many worthless suggestions;*
> *Sold to the public—that is, if they buy—*
> *Sometimes they do, and the royalty's high—*
> *Most times the statement brings tears to your eye—*
>   *Take it without any questions:*
> *Popular song, you will never be missed,*
> *Once your composer has ceased to exist,*
> *While Chopin and Verdi, Beethoven and Liszt*
>   *Live on with each generation.*
> *Still, though you die after having your sway,*
> *To be forgotten the very next day,*
> *A rose lives and dies in the very same way—*
>   *Let that be your consolation.*

For all his imposing success, Berlin was, as Cohan said, a man whose watch and handkerchief remained in their rightful places. When it came to analyzing what he did, the craft he practiced, he was surprisingly unsentimental: there were few aspects that excited nostalgia or curiosity in him. He was interviewed on the topic for newspapers and magazines and occasionally asked to write for some of them, but in these pieces he waxed even less romantic about popular song, speaking out about the "cutthroat competition," payoffs, and other factors that commonly drove publishers into bankruptcy. One of his outlets was the *Greenbook Magazine,* in which, in April 1916, he asserted in an article written "in collaboration with Justus Dickinson" that we depend largely on tricks, we writers of song. There's no such thing as a new melody. There has been a standing offer in Vienna, holding a large prize, to anyone who can write eight bars of original music. The offer has been up for more than twenty-five years. Thousands of compositions have been submitted, but all of them have been traced back to some other melody.

Our work is to connect the old phrases in a new way, so that they will sound like a new tune. Did you know that the public, when it hears a new song, anticipates the next passage? Well, they who do *not* give them *something they are expecting* are those who are successful.

In short, originality was the key, but not too *much* originality. The ideas here are Berlin's, but the actual writing is Dickinson's.

Berlin put things even more candidly when he said, "Usually, writing songs is a matter of having to pay bills and sitting down to make the money to pay them with."

Although themselves not big money-makers, two of Berlin's 1915 songs nonetheless found him concerned with larger topics than Cohen's ninety-seven dollars. "The Voice of Belgium" memorialized the plight of a neutral country invaded by the German army on the eruption of the Great War in Europe; it was probably inspired by propaganda about the atrocities allegedly committed there. In May, after Germany proclaimed a policy of total submarine warfare, the British liner *Lusitania*—on which Berlin himself had sailed less than five years before—was sunk, with a heavy loss of American life (128 dead). In response, Berlin wrote a paean to America's greatness, "While the Band Played an American Rag." President Woodrow Wilson condemned the Germans' strike but stuck by his policy of keeping the country out of the European war; former President Theodore Roosevelt, for his part, called the sinking an "act of piracy."

Although notes demanding reparations were ignored by the German high command, the kaiser himself decreed in June that passenger liners were safe; at the close of the month, however, the liner *Armenia* was sunk and twenty Americans were lost. In July the German reply to Wilson's communication was the same: the submarine war would continue. Wilson's third warning against "unfriendly acts" was issued on July 20. Five days later, two American merchant ships went down off the Irish coast. On August 10, General Leonard Wood opened a military training camp for volunteers in Plattsburg, New York.

While it would in time impinge on the life of Irving Berlin, this inexorable succession of distant events was forgotten for now in a frantic rush of work.

Early in September 1915, announcements appeared in the press that Charles Dillingham had a new show in preparation. *Blow Your Horn* was to star Gaby Deslys, now a popular American favorite, particularly after her success with Al Jolson, two years before, in *The Honeymoon Express*. Also in the cast were cabaret entertainer Harry Fox, ex-Follies beauty Justine Johnstone, and Marion Sunshine; among the then-lesser-known featured players were Blossom Seeley and Marion Davies. Irving Berlin would write the music.

Dillingham intended to produce a kind of sequel to *Watch Your Step,* once again with a Berlin score, an approximation of a book by Harry B. Smith, and a dance team—this time Deslys and her husband, Harry Pilcer. Putting all other aspects of his life on hold, Berlin again applied himself to the composition of a generous score, in genres ranging from his virtual trademark, ragtime, to the hula (some of the action was to take place in Honolulu). Gaby Deslys was cast as a chorus girl eager to fill the role abandoned by the show-within-the-show's star (Justine Johnstone), who has run off with a millionaire. The producer will, of course, have nothing to do with a mere girl from the chorus, hoping instead to replace the defector with a more exotic type of performer. Persuaded by the show's press agent—no doubt himself smitten with Gaby (also her character's name in *Blow Your Horn*)—that just such a star can be found in Hawaii, the hoodwinked producer leaves for Honolulu, where he has been preceded by the now-exotic chorus girl. Gaby gets the part and becomes a star. Such was the plot, which, if a bit thin here and there, did not disappear entirely, this time around, at the end of act 1.

Sometime during Berlin's most intense period of work, between the September announcement and the start of rehearsals in mid-November, the show's title was changed to *Stop! Look! Listen!* After a Philadelphia tryout beginning on December 1, 1915, it premiered at the Globe in New York on Christmas Night.

The original title number was retained for the first act, sung immediately after the opening ("These Are the Costumes"), with the new title song inserted early in the second; four other numbers were eliminated. The song that garnered the greatest, and long-lived, attention was "I Love a Piano," performed by a piano sextet. Berlin returned to counterpoint and patriotism with "When I Get Back to the U.S.A.," in which a homesick "cranky Yankee" yearns for the land of "peace and freedom," emphasized in the second chorus by the Berlin tune's being sung against the anthem "America." (The following year, when *Stop! Look! Listen!* was presented in London, under the title *Follow the Crowd,* Berlin would revise this song into "England Every Time for Me," fittingly using the same countermelody, but now with a different lyric—"God Save the King," the British national anthem.)

Librettist Smith cued in one of Berlin's songs by having the onstage producer, Coyne (played by Harland Dixon, a comic dancer teamed with James Doyle), say:

> *I have to find some new way to undress the chorus—costumes make the show. Leave me my ponies and my clothes horses, and musical comedy will still go on!*

Berlin's solution was melodically expressed in "Take Off a Little Bit." A "pony," in the jargon of the trade, was a dancer, while a "clotheshorse" was a tall, statuesque member of the chorus whose sole function was to stand around ornamenting the stage like a piece of scenery. If it was not the showbusiness anthem of a later time, "Take Off a Little Bit" nonetheless encapsulated the theme of Ziegfeld's Follies and of its rival productions, such as George White's Scandals and Earl Carroll's Vanities. *Stop! Look! Listen!* did well, though not as well as its predecessor; it would have better luck in its British form.

Although the next year, 1916, would not be as productive as most in Berlin's seemingly formidable hit factory, two events—one professional, the other personal—would make it memorable.

During this period he oversaw the publication of several songs from *Stop! Look! Listen!* and contributed "The Friars' Parade" to that year's fund-raising Frolic, in which he appeared with his brother Friars George M. Cohan, William Collier, and Frank Tinney. The very next evening, *Step This Way* opened, with songs by Bert Grant, lyrics by Berlin's former brother-in-law E. Ray Goetz, and two Berlin interpolations, one of them the comic "I've Got a Sweet Tooth Bothering Me" (Johnnie visits a dentist, but his real problem is his heart, and his sweetheart).

In November a possibly ground-breaking and certainly unique revue, *The Century Girl,* opened at the Century Theatre. Formerly the New Theatre, the Century was a colossal white elephant situated in the wrong place—that is, too far from Times Square (it is now the Century Apartments, at 25 Central Park West). The show was remarkable in that it was jointly produced by longtime rivals Charles Dillingham and Florenz Ziegfeld, Jr. And further, its score was divided in two, with one half to be written by the impressive

Victor Herbert and the other by Irving Berlin. The laboriously assembled show—money was the least of objects—was also singular for being the only successful musical ever staged at the vast Century.

Sometime between the Friars' Frolic in May and November's *Century Girl,* Irving Berlin suffered his own sweet-tooth miss. The instigator was his old Bowery friend Joseph M. Schenck, who had graduated from amusement parks and carnivals into the burgeoning movie business. Schenck, along with Florenz Ziegfeld, Samuel Goldwyn, George M. Cohan, and Sam Harris, belonged to the Sixty Club, which held biweekly parties in the ballroom of the Ritz Hotel. There, in the words of author Anita Loos, "a galaxy of crystal chandeliers shone down on the pick of Broadway beauties."

Among those Schenck encountered at one such party was Norma Talmadge, who, while not precisely a Broadway beauty, had nevertheless recently enjoyed a (none-too-successful) fling in silent pictures. (She would return to greater glory in the twenties, starring as a regal heroine until movies found a voice and her Brooklyn-tinctured articulation ended her career.) Despite the fact that she had come with another man, a smitten Schenck proceeded to ask her for a date (though he himself, at the time, according to Loos, was keeping as his mistress one Peggy Hopkins Joyce, an actress and future Earl Carroll beauty who had a talent for multiple marriages, and whose upkeep must have cost Schenck dearly).

Two months later, Joseph M. Schenck married Norma Talmadge; he was then twenty-nine, and she twenty-three (he was to be the first of her three husbands). Their union had the blessing of Margaret (Peg) Talmadge, the ultimate stage mother, who was confident that Joe could rekindle her daughter's movie career.

Peg Talmadge had not cared much for Hollywood, where she had taken Norma along with her younger daughters, Natalie and Constance, better known as Dutch (so dubbed by her mother because as a child she had been a chubby little blonde). All three daughters appeared in silents. Natalie, the most hopeless on screen, eventually married comedian Buster Keaton; Norma made several now-forgotten films in the three or four years of their West Coast sojourn. It was Constance, then about seventeen, who made the most indelible impression, in D. W. Griffith's awesome spectacle *Intolerance,* released in 1916. In the film's first sequence, set in ancient Babylon, Constance steals the scene as a gamine charioteer chewing on a bunch of scallions.

Constance was a born comedian, while her older sister was more dramatic; their very different qualities would enable them both to have good years in silent Hollywood, with never a hint of sibling rivalry. But Joe Schenck, in 1916, was concerned only with the film career of his new wife, and soon began shooting a picture for her in a vast warehouse on East Forty-eighth Street. What he had not realized was that in marrying Norma, he was also acquiring Dutch and the redoubtable Peg.

According to one anecdote, Irving Berlin came into this circle some while before the wedding, when Schenck asked him to sound out Norma about her feelings for him. One wonders about the truth of this; Anita Loos does not mention the incident in her talky biography of the Talmadges. She does make quite a point, however, of noting Berlin's infatuation with Constance, his admiration for her vivacity, her wit, and her beauty. But the irrepressible, flirtatious Dutch would not take him—or anyone else, it seemed—seriously. She did not, thanks to her mother's supervision, have "affairs," but she did have an affinity for "sugar daddies": all four of her husbands were wealthy. Hers was a pragmatic sweet tooth.

Irving Berlin was certainly rich enough—with an annual income of $100,000—but for some reason nothing came of his courtship, and he gave up. When her daughter married a young Greek tobacco broker, Peg was said to have remarked, characteristically, "I just can't understand Dutch. It isn't a question of choosing between little Irving and some gorgeous Greek god. But why pick a guy who looks like a Greek waiter?" Constance's explanation was that her husband was "different." Berlin's own reaction was perhaps best summed up when he was asked to suggest a title for a film written by Anita Loos and starring Constance: he voted for *A Virtuous Vamp* (released in 1919, the film would be one of Schenck's earliest successes).

In the summer of 1916, Berlin was busy writing his half of the score for *The Century Girl,* and was almost as agitated about it as he had been by his unrequited feelings for Constance Talmadge. Victor Herbert was more than twice his age (fifty-seven to Berlin's twenty-eight) and a recognized musical giant; a composer, songwriter, cellist, and conductor, he even did his own orchestrations. Berlin, the untutored, was embarrassed by the disparity in their musical learning. In Herbert's presence he felt, as he would tell Herbert's biographer, Edward N. Waters, "like a man who could talk, but could neither read [nor] write."

At the piano, however, Herbert, for all his study, was hardly more adept than Berlin. Listening to him play one of his songs for the show, Berlin would feel a little puzzled, but then later, when Herbert came in with his orchestration of the same piece and conducted the orchestra, it would seem to Berlin as if the music "were falling from heaven."

During rehearsals, Berlin and Herbert lunched together at the Lambs Club, where Berlin one day broached the subject of his ignorance of the technical side of music. Should he study? he asked.

Herbert replied that while formal instruction would not harm the younger man's natural talents, he had exhibited the "proper musical instinct for successful writing, and the discipline of formal training seemed unnecessary." Some of Berlin's friends had likewise advised him not to study, fearing it might interfere with his instinctive genius for song. (Gershwin would later receive the same gratuitous counsel from friends unaware of the scope of his early formal music instruction.) As it turned out, Berlin did not follow their advice: he actually began piano lessons, practiced for a couple of days, and then stopped. The time it would take him to learn to read music could, he reasoned, be more profitably spent dictating songs to Cliff Hess.

The writing of the score for *The Century Girl* was divided evenly, with Berlin assigned to compose the ragtime/Tin Pan Alley lighter songs and Herbert the operetta-like melodies and orchestral music in the form of ballets. That the formulation of the revue was intended to exploit the diverse talents of the two men was made obvious in the first act. In a skit entitled "The Music Lesson," both composers, impersonated by actors, appeared onstage, and Herbert's popular "Kiss Me Again" was performed as Berlin's "You've Got Me Doing It," a ragtime-ish number, was sung in counterpoint. This was their one collaborative effort in the score.

The show had no plot (though by design, this time); it was just a series of sketches and numbers. In recognition of the parlous times (*The Century Girl* opened the night before that year's presidential election, and patriotism was in order), songs and dances celebrating the American Way were included. The long evening belonged to the star in the person of the comely blonde Hazel Dawn, who had scored her first major success playing the violin in *The Pink Lady* (1911, music by Ivan Caryll, lyrics by C. H. S. McClellen) and gone on to play the lead in Herbert's unsuccessful *The Debutante* of 1914. Her Berlin song, sung with Irving Fisher, was "Alice in Wonderland," performed against a stunning set based on the original John Tenniel illustrations from the Lewis Carroll book, created by Ziegfeld's brilliant designer Joseph Urban.

Coming more than four hours after the first strains of the overture, conducted by Herbert, the finale was Berlin's "On the Train of a Wedding Gown." (Another Berlin number, "It Takes an Irishman to Make Love," with words by Elsie Janis, who sang it in the show, may have been a subtle tribute to cocomposer Herbert.)

Herbert's most-praised efforts were "The Stone Age," also entitled "Ballet Loose," an allusion to the Ballet Russe, and the march "When Uncle Sam Is Ruler of the Sea," a study in patriotism for this worrying time when clouds of war hovered over the Atlantic. Another Herbert flag-waver was

"Uncle Sam's Children," whose dances, conceived by Ned Wayburn, raised the spirits of the audience at the end of act 1 (little did they realize they still had some three additional hours of gargantuan entertainment ahead of them).

Alexander Woollcott, then the drama critic for the *Times,* like the rest of the audience loved the show but believed it could be improved with a great deal of lopping off. He pronounced it both "spectacle and vaudeville, glorified beyond anything we have had in the music hall world and multiplied by ten."

It was the spectacle—the famed Ziegfeld-Urban staircases, the frilly, abbreviated costumes, the magnificent sets—that most captivated the audience. As for the vaudeville, the Ziegfeld-Dillingham wallets had opened wide. The cast, besides Hazel Dawn and Elsie Janis, included headliner Marie Dressler, comedians Sam Bernard and Leon Errol, and the comedy team of Van and Schenck (the latter, though also named Joe, not related to Berlin's friend), as well as Harry Kelly, Frank Tinney, and a pre-Hollywood Lilyan Tashman. These elements kept *The Century Girl* housed in the Century for an unprecedented (and never to be repeated) two hundred performances.

Not one of the songs by Berlin or Herbert achieved any real popularity, lost as they were in opulence and in the aftermath of the reelection of Wilson to the presidency. The vote was so close that the final result was not announced until November 11, five days after the election. On November 8, the *Times* and other newspapers proclaimed Charles Evans Hughes the victor; three days later, with California's electoral votes in, Wilson won, 272–259. His slogan was the concise "He Kept Us out of War"—and this he did, temporarily, but time was running out.

On February 26, 1917, Wilson asked both houses of Congress to provide him with the means of maintaining an "armed neutrality" to contend with the Germans' unrestricted submarine warfare; as he spoke, the Cunard liner *Lanconia* was sunk, counting among its twenty-five passengers lost two Americans. Over the next month, more than a hundred nonbelligerent ships went down, including the American *Housatonic.* In March the Imperial German Government announced that it would sink every vessel that approached Great Britain, Ireland, or ports in the Mediterranean. Wilson found that to be "reckless" and a waging of "war against all nations."

On April 6, 1917, the United States declared war on Germany. That same day, George M. Cohan responded with his own declaration, "Over There," which was subsequently taken up by vaudeville star Nora Bayes and thousands of others. In May, President Wilson signed into law the Selective

Draft Act, a bill requiring all American men between the ages of twenty-one and thirty to register for possible service in the armed forces.

Irving Berlin was then twenty-nine, but he was not legally an American. *His* patriotic songs were "Let's All Be Americans Now," written with Edgar Leslie and George Meyer, and "For Your Country and My Country," a "jazz one-step" recorded on a Duo-Art piano roll by Rudy Erlebach and a young Tin Pan Alley "piano pounder" named George Gershwin. In November they cut another Berlin roll, "Mr. Jazz Himself," billed as "Irving Berlin's latest effort. The jazziest of all jazz." A new sound was coming into American music, and once again, Berlin's uncanny ear was attuned to it.

Berlin, along with Jerome Kern, was Gershwin's Tin Pan Alley hero. Unhappy pounding a piano in the Alley, and hoping to escape, he applied for a job as Berlin's musical secretary. Their brief meeting was not fruitful; when asked about it later, Berlin could not even recall it. Gershwin informed him that he also wished to write songs; Berlin requested that he play a few, and Gershwin obliged. After hearing them, Berlin told him that working as an amanuensis was not for him, not with his talent as a pianist as well as a song-writer.

Even though Berlin failed to hire him, and did not offer to publish anything he had written, he seemed so kind and interested that Gershwin left his office in a state of elation. He and Irving Berlin would meet again.

Berlin closed out the year with a handful of songs written for *The Cohan Revue of 1918* (which debuted on the last night of 1917); one of these, "Polly Pretty Polly," had words by Cohan himself.

Berlin's next interpolations were slipped into a score by Louis A. Hirsch, Rennold Wolf, and Gene Buck. This edition of the Follies, which premiered on June 18, 1918, marked the Follies debut of Marilyn Miller; also in the cast were Eddie Cantor and W. C. Fields. Berlin's contributions were "I'm Gonna Pin My Medal on the Girl I Left Behind" and "The Blue Devils of France." The latter was attributed to *Private* Irving Berlin.

THIS IS THE ARMY, MR. B

T HE UNFORESEEN BESTOWAL of the rank of private on Irving Berlin came to pass in the normal course of events. On February 16, 1918, he became a legal citizen of the United States of America (qualification number 1); on May 11, he turned thirty (within a year, according to the Selective Draft Act, he would no longer be subject to the draft; the board therefore moved quickly to implement qualification number 2). By June he had been transformed into Pvt. Irving Berlin, 77th Infantry Division, stationed at Camp Upton, in Yaphank, New York.

His future biographer Alexander Woollcott had preceded him into the military and would spend the remainder of the war far from the trenches, writing for *Stars and Stripes* in Paris. Himself a military misfit, Woollcott later recounted Berlin's metamorphosis from Mister to Private: "The board's bland acceptance of him had come as a disagreeable surprise. For all his own doctors had insisted that no army would take him as a gift. Indeed, for years he had writhed with a nervous indigestion which led him from doctor to doctor and made him the profitable plaything of each new specialist arriving in New York."

Berlin's life changed abruptly and drastically. He was plucked from the luxuries of the Chatsworth and transported to the center of nowhere, forced to sleep in a long, narrow barracks shared with numerous strangers. When word got out, across the nation several newspapers ran the inevitable headline: "U.S. Takes Berlin!"

Living conditions in the army were, at least, better than those he had known on Cherry Street and the Bowery. But all that was far behind him by now: in 1918, he was *the* Irving Berlin, a celebrated songwriter with a valet, a cook, his own regimen, and his own hours. The army's day began at reveille—5:00 A.M., Berlin's wonted bedtime.

As a private, Berlin would undergo the same discomforts, indignities, and training as any other draftee. Fame and affluence meant nothing in Upton. According to Woollcott, Berlin arrived at the post in a chauffeured limousine, after a drive of about sixty miles from Manhattan east through Long Island farm country. There Pvt. Berlin was issued an ill-fitting khaki uniform (his tailor would remedy that on his first weekend pass), wraparound leggings, a campaign hat (similar to those worn by Boy Scouts), cumbersome shoes, and a steel helmet. In addition, he received two olive-drab blankets and a gun with a bayonet. This last did not make much sense to Pvt. Berlin.

Nor did "lights out" at ten o'clock and then reveille at five. "I hated it," he said crisply. "I hated it so much that I used to lie awake nights thinking about how much I hated it." He was not alone.

After a day of close-order drills, lectures (from "Personal Hygiene and Care of the Feet" to French lessons), chow lines, and maybe a stint on Kitchen Police (K.P.) duty, he expressed his contempt for the routine in a song:

> *I sleep with ninety-seven men*
> *Inside a wooden hut.*
> *I love them all,*
> *They all love me,*
> > *It's very lovely*
> > BUT
> *Oh, how I hate to get up in the morning,*
> *Oh, how I'd rather stay in bed,*
> *But the hardest blow of all*
> *Is to hear the bugle call:*
> > *You've gotta get up,*
> > *You've gotta get up,*
> > *You've gotta get up this morning.*
> *Someday I'm going to murder the bugler,*
> *Someday they're going to find him dead,*
> > *I'll amputate his reveille*
> > *And step upon it heavily,*
> > *And spend the rest of my life in bed.*

The second time around, he added a final couplet to the end of the chorus:

> *And then I'll get the other pup,*
> *The guy who gets the bugler up,*
> *And spend the rest of my life in bed.*

The song spread through his barracks and then around the rest of the camp, raising his status in the eyes of his fellow draftees. This was subversive stuff, considering the tenor of the patriotic Tin Pan Alley outpouring typified by Cohan's jingoistic "Over There" and other offerings such as "Good-bye, Broadway, Hello, France!," "We'll Knock the Heligo into Heligo out of Heligoland!," and "We're Going to Hang the Kaiser under the Linden Tree." Like Berlin, and unlike many civilians, most American draftees were neither bloodthirsty nor eager for battle, and also like him, they hated their buglers. Cooks weren't too popular, either.

Soon after his arrival at Camp Upton, Berlin read an item in *Variety* about a show entitled *Biff! Bang!*, which had been staged at the Century Theatre for a limited run of sixteen performances. The fact that the U.S. Navy had sponsored the show gave Berlin an idea: Why not the U.S. Army?

What happened next is a bit unclear. According to some versions of the story, the camp commander, Major General J. Franklin Bell, summoned Pvt. Berlin to his office at headquarters to sound him out about something. Now that Camp Upton was filling up with draftees and volunteers with families, he said, it might be a gracious gesture to provide those who visited with a service club where they could have lunch or dinner and meet with their soldiers. Such a facility could be built if they could raise the money—thirty-five thousand dollars, he thought, would suffice—with, say, a musical show. Could Berlin produce such a show?

Possibly the general had already heard about *Biff! Bang!*, even if he was not a regular reader of *Variety*. Or perhaps Berlin actually brought the paper to him and suggested putting on a camp musical to boost morale. Songwriter and pianist Harry Ruby intimated to interviewer Max Wilk that Berlin conceived the idea primarily to avoid the call of the bugler. It's a good anecdote, but one recalled half a century later; a summons by General Bell seems the more likely motivator. Ruby, a civilian, was to work on the show as Berlin's musical secretary.

Yet another explanation—that some sort of service-branch rivalry was at work—seems the least credible of all: Berlin was hardly so enamored with army life that he would want to show up the navy. The promise of a comfortable service club was undoubtedly the real lure for the show that Berlin agreed to do.

Quite suddenly, Pvt. Berlin was promoted to sergeant, and indeed, he was thenceforth not compelled to murder the bugler. General Bell excused him from all regular routines and assigned him a staff ranging in rank from lieutenant to major, comprising three hundred actors, singers, dancers, musicians, and technicians—a complete theater company. Once production was under way, army public relations broadcast the news that Sergeant Irving Berlin was assembling an all-soldier show, to be entitled *Yip! Yip! Yaphank.* Word soon spread, and during the writing of the show, Anita Loos recalled visiting Camp Upton with Constance and Norma Talmadge, the vanguard of Broadway and Tin Pan Alley callers. Camp Upton was now on the map.

Berlin worked in Yaphank as he had in Manhattan, but now he was also literally the producer, conceiving every sketch. With his own room in the barracks, he was virtually on leave. By July the production was far enough along to be staged for a Broadway contingent that was brought to the camp in a special train. Among the luminaries in the audience were Al Jolson, Eddie Cantor, Fanny Brice, Will Rogers, and a real female dancing chorus (all "girls" in *Yaphank* were, of course, men). The professionals pronounced the show good and proclaimed it time to transfer it from Upton to Manhattan.

(The publicity also had another, more peculiar aftermath. One day Berlin was again summoned to headquarters and into the office of General Bell, where, to his surprise, he saw three women seated. Bell asked him to sit and explained, "Berlin, these women are here representing some society [Berlin, in recalling the incident, did not remember which society it was]. Since we are at war with Germany, they feel you ought to change your name." The "wonderful General Bell" [in Berlin's words] then added, "I advise you not to, you've had Berlin for a long time." The disgruntled women left and were not heard from again.)

Advertised as "A Military Musical 'Mess' Cooked Up by the Boys at Camp Upton," *Yip! Yip! Yaphank* was scheduled to premiere at the Century on the evening of August 19, 1918. The show's company, all three hundred of them save one (it is more than likely that Sgt. Berlin bivouacked at the Chatsworth, on West Seventy-second) were stationed at the 71st Regiment Armory on Park Avenue at Thirty-fourth Street. For each performance, plus matinees, they would march up Park, then west on Forty-second Street, and then up Eighth Avenue, which at Columbus Circle becomes Central Park West. The Century Theatre was situated between Sixty-second and Sixty-third Streets.

The nineteenth was a Monday. *Yip! Yip! Yaphank* was booked for a week-long run of seven evenings and a matinee, but Tuesday's reviews, and the audience response at the premiere, changed that.

Berlin had devised a revue of foolproof theatrical fare, familiar yet original, all accomplished with the talent at hand, some professional, some not. Given the number of amateurs involved, the audience did not expect much, and they got a great deal more than they anticipated.

The first act began with a minstrel show in which the song "Sterling Silver Moon" was featured. A black-faced Mandy followed. "She" was portrayed by vaudevillian Dan Healy, one of the show's experienced professionals. After the war Healy would appear in a couple of musicals, one by Rodgers and Hart and the other by Berlin (*Ziegfeld Follies of 1927*), before turning to directing in the thirties at Harlem's Cotton Club. Also associated with the show was dancer-choreographer Sammy Lee, who would be dance director for several Gershwin musicals, among them *Lady, Be Good!* and *Oh, Kay!;* he would be most celebrated for his work in the Kern-Hammerstein classic *Show Boat.*

The minstrel show was followed by a vaudeville segment showcasing jugglers, acrobats, and such. Then Berlin brought on the "girls." The *New York Times* critic reported that the

> chorus of *Yip Yip Yaphank* [is] guaranteed to be one long laugh whether one regards the third from the left, the fourth from the right, or the ensemble in general. Whoever picked its members was nothing less than inspired. And that, of course, was Berlin, who even found Benny Leonard, World Lightweight Champion, in uniform somewhere and brought him into the show to give a boxing demonstration. . . .
>
> The show does not depend on such merit. It is at its best when the music is playing, for Berlin is first and foremost a song writer.

Clearly the evening's star, Berlin carefully husbanded his time onstage. In the first act he appeared as a private, with pail and mop, to plaintively, and with penetrating satire, sing:

> *Poor little me,*
> *I'm on K.P.*
> *I scrub the mess hall*
> *On my bended knee.*
> *Against my wishes*

> I wash the dishes
> To make
> this
> wide
> world
> Safe for democracy.

Although the sentiment expressed was shared by many in uniform, the use of the Wilsonian punch line was a little risky; Woodrow Wilson was, after all, Sergeant Berlin's Commander in Chief, and by extension the backer of *Yip! Yip! Yaphank* (which was "Produced by Uncle Sam," according to the program).

The premiere audience comprised not only military personnel (General Bell sat in a box) but also colleagues of Berlin's and members of society who regularly attended benefits, who "whistled, shouted and cheered every number, and joined in the choruses after the first encore. The enthusiasm of the boys on the stage and the stimulus of the songs swept everyone irresistibly into the spirit of the evening." This reaction was reported in the October issue of *Theatre Magazine*.

Act 1 closed with a jazz finale ("Send a Lot of Jazz Bands over There"). After the intermission, the curtain rose on "A Company Street at Upton," and Berlin came out again to air his antimilitary views in "Oh! How I Hate to Get Up in the Morning." A Follies parody ensued, with a Pvt. Kuy Kendall appearing as Ann Pennington, she of the "flashing legs and dimpled knees"—a description that Pvt. Kendall's gams, to the mirthful delight of the audience, failed to live up to. Another private, Loher, took on the persona of comedian Joe Frisco, while still others presented impersonations of various Ziegfeld luminaries, including W. C. Fields, Lillian Lorraine, and Marilyn Miller. The finale, in a more serious vein, was "We're on Our Way to France."

The reviews, all of them, were unqualified raves, and tickets were sold at a premium, often in blocks (and for sizable donations). The massive Century auditorium overflowed, as did the box office. The run was extended from the original eight performances scheduled to thirty-two, and the expected intake of $35,000 was more than doubled, to $83,000.

After the first-night applause and cheering quieted, General Bell rose and made a gracious speech, closing with, "I have heard that Berlin is among the foremost songwriters of the world, and now I believe it. . . . Berlin is as good a soldier as he is a songwriter, and as popular in Camp Upton as he is on Broadway."

The truth of the latter assertion was demonstrated after Berlin chose not to make a curtain speech, as Bell had requested: members of the cast lifted him onto their shoulders as the audience again burst into cheers and wild applause.

He did not stick around for the traditional opening-night celebration but instead drove his mother, who had been in the audience that night, to the home he had bought for her five years before in the Bronx, on Beck Street. The house, complete with maid, was the second proof of his success in the form of a gift to Leah Baline. The first, early on in his rise, was a rocking chair that was probably the only piece of furniture she took with her when she left Cherry Street for the Bronx. She was comfortable there; her section of the borough was home to a large Jewish population, likewise up from the Lower East Side. No longer crowded with her family into a few rooms in a tenement, Leah Baline now resided in a house all her own. Contemporary accounts indicate that she lived alone: except for Irving, all her children were married by now, and had their own homes.

In September, *Yip! Yip! Yaphank* had its final performance, having been squeezed out of the theater to make way for a new show as the new season began. For that last night, Berlin conceived a memorable finale. As the cast, in full uniform, with rifles and other military regalia, sang "We're on Our Way to France," Sgt. Berlin led them not into the wings but offstage, down the aisle, and out of the theater. The audience, in midcheer, was stunned: clearly, the men were literally demonstrating the lyric of the song. According to reports, there were gasps, muffled outcries, sobs—the soldiers were, it seemed, bound for a troopship, the trenches, possibly death.

Not likely: the beloved sergeant, for one, never even left the country. The service club, planned beneficiary of the box office, was never constructed, for there was no longer any need for it.

By April 1917, at the time of the American declaration of war, the fighting nations, Allies as well as Central Powers, were close to exhaustion: the heavy loss of life, the destruction of cities and towns, and the interruption of industry and agriculture had nearly done them in. That all was wasted seemed obvious to everyone except the military leadership on both sides.

The first American troops, led by General John J. Pershing, debarked in France in late June of that year. (Colonel Charles E. Stanton graced Pershing with immortality when, standing before a tomb, he said, "Lafayette, we are here," which comment was later misattributed to his commanding officer.) In October, after three months of training, the first Americans took position in a quiet sector of the Western Front, where the first American soldiers to die fell in November 1917.

The arrival of young and eager, if inexperienced, American troops raised British and French morale; soon enough, the folks at home were reading about the heroic exploits of their boys on the Somme, at Château-Thierry, and at Belleau Wood. By July 4, 1918, a million American soldiers were on French soil, and the tide was turning. On August 8, around the same time the *Yip! Yip! Yaphank* troops were preparing to move from Camp Upton to the 71st Regiment Armory, sixteen thousand German troops surrendered. There were rumors of peace negotiations. In the second week of September, as the show ended its run, American troops were straightening out the Saint-Mihiel salient; soon after, the Allies would smash through the deadly Hindenburg line. By October the German government would be broadcasting pleas for "peace with honor." On November 11, 1918, the Great War would end with the signing of an armistice.

By early September it was already evident that there was no need to send additional American troops to France. When the *Yip! Yip! Yaphank* company marched out the door of the Century Theatre, it was to return to Camp Upton to be disbanded, a prospect that all, especially Sergeant Berlin, looked forward to with eager anticipation.

Of Irving Berlin's wartime songs, only "Sterling Silver Moon" and "Oh! How I Hate to Get Up in the Morning" (advertised as "Irving Berlin's Bugle Song") would achieve standard status. He discarded another effort, "God Bless America," because he felt its sentiment did not fit well with the lighthearted, irreverent tone of *Yaphank.* He would come back to it in the next war.

Two other sentimental songs did remain in the show, however, one of them excessively saccharine. This was "I Can Always Find a Little Sunshine in the Y.M.C.A.," in which a soldier reassures his "Darling Mother" of his well-being and promises to write her every night from the safety of the YMCA. This would amuse Berlin's hutmates: once off duty and in town, they generally found a number of activities to divert themselves with, of which writing letters to Mom was rarely one. Still, mother songs were popular, and if the lyric is a bit sticky for Berlin, the song's sentiment is sincere enough.

"Dream On, Little Soldier Boy" is another matter altogether, not only because Berlin himself did not write the words (they were contributed by fellow Friar and ASCAP charter member Jean Havez) but because of its lovely melody. The lyric is typical, true to the moment when Tin Pan Alley was flooding the country with mawkish numbers about homesick soldiers longing for the farm, or daughters, usually, not to mention wives and mothers, pining for the return of their daddies, husbands, or sons.

The apposite lyric, good though it is, quickly came to seem dated. That the song did not become popular probably discouraged Berlin from writing new words for it, much as he would recycle "Sterling Silver Moon" as "Mandy" for the 1919 Follies, along with the prescient "Bevo," which deprecates the qualities of nonalcoholic beer (the only kind dispensed on military bases). The latter presaged most Americans' reaction to the impending Volstead Act, the resultant Prohibition, and all they portended for the nation during the Jazz Age.

Other war-inspired Berlin songs were primarily amusing; none was conceived as a big production number. In one, a proud Irish father, after watching his son parade by, informs the listeners that he noticed "They Were All out of Step but Jim." A serious declaration by a soldier was the inspiration behind the simple and touching "I'm Gonna Pin My Medal on the Girl I Left Behind," an original idea at a time when popular taste favored racier songs such as "Oui, Oui, Marie," "Mad'moiselle from Armentieres" (also known as "Hinky, Dinky, Parlez-vous"), and, in 1919, "How Ya Gonna Keep 'Em Down on the Farm (after They've Seen Paree)?" This last, incidentally, was published by Waterson, Berlin & Snyder.

Berlin's take on the wartime coal shortage was a ragtime number entitled "The Devil Has Bought Up All the Coal," which concludes that there will be "a hot time in Hades when the Kaiser gets there." His final swipe at military life, once again echoing the dream of many a doughboy, was 1919's "I've Got My Captain Working for Me Now."

As it turned out, however, that was just his penultimate word on his military career. In 1982, a plaque would be erected on the grounds of the Brookhaven National Laboratory to commemorate what had once been the site of Camp Upton; the dedication ceremonies also celebrated Berlin's ninety-fourth birthday. In acknowledging the receipt of a photograph of the plaque, Berlin said, in a letter to town councilman Donald W. Zimmer, "I can't tell you how much this means to me. Camp Upton was a very important part of my life and having this plaque placed on the grounds of Brookhaven touches me deeply."

By early 1919, the sergeant was Mr. Berlin again and could be reunited with his friend George M. Cohan, whose soon-to-be long-running *The Royal Vagabond* (an "Opéra Comique") was slated to open at the Cohan and Harris Theatre on February 17. Did Irvy have a song for the show? He did; its title was "That Revolutionary Rag."

5

THE MUSIC BOXES

ONCE OUT OF UNIFORM, Berlin hurried back to the Buick and his publishing business. While he was at Camp Upton, the publication and distribution of his songs had been managed by Waterson, Berlin & Snyder (the names on the ends still clinging to the name in the middle), not his own Irving Berlin, Inc.

Royalties from his *Yip! Yip! Yaphank* songs, and from the few others completed in the months before he was drafted, gave him a financial cushion on which he could rest while contemplating his final and permanent break with Waterson and Snyder. Concurrently, he sensed something in the flow of events. In Europe, the "Big Four" (America's Wilson, Great Britain's David Lloyd George, France's Georges Clemençeau, and Italy's Vittorio Orlando) met at the palace of Versailles, near Paris, to wrangle over a peace treaty. The vindictive document they ultimately produced effectively guaranteed that an even greater world war would be waged sometime in the future.

But there were even more immediate, and equally ominous, developments elsewhere abroad. At Camp Upton, Sgt. Berlin had read of a "Bolshevik Revolution" in the land of his birth; soon after, a revolutionary named Vladimir Lenin had proclaimed the formation of the Third International (Karl Marx had formed the First), hoping to spark proletarian revolutions all over the world. Czar Nicholas II and his family had already been slaughtered;

there were bloody eruptions in Hungary and Germany, and unrest in the United States, all fueled by Lenin's Comintern.

Berlin regularly told interviewers that current events supplied him with ideas to set to music. The news from overseas now inspired him to write "That Revolutionary Rag." With Irving Berlin, Inc., in temporary limbo, he took the song to Max Dreyfus, head of the T. B. Harms music publishing company. Harms, thanks to the acumen of Dreyfus, was one of the most successful publishing houses in New York, known for the quality of its publications, especially in the field of musical theater (Rudolf Friml and Jerome Kern were both published by Dreyfus, as would be Richard Rodgers and Cole Porter in the future). Dreyfus himself was one of the few publishers in town who could actually read music.

When Dreyfus said he liked "That Revolutionary Rag" and offered to publish it, Berlin informed him that he would need to have it taken down. Dreyfus called for someone named George to meet with Berlin and write out the song.

A slim, dark young man was sitting at a piano in one of the cubicles when Berlin entered. He started: he knew Irving Berlin. Berlin himself did not recognize Gershwin until he introduced himself and said he had come to Berlin's offices two years before looking for a job. Still only twenty, Gershwin had been on the Harms staff as a composer for a year and was, at the time of this visit, at work on a musical, *La, La, Lucille.*

Gershwin, with his customary grace and much respect, notated the song as Berlin sang it, after which they together worked it over a bit (in fact, Gershwin arranged it). It came off well, and Berlin often joked about the collaboration, saying, "[The song] was so good I didn't recognize it."

The first verse alludes to the current Russian upheaval, while the second, citing historical precedents, sings of "Little Mary [*sic*] Antoinette," who "was a lovely queen you bet." The lyric begins:

Verse:

> *Where the Russian breezes blow*
> *There's a piece of calico*
> *Ev'ry thread dyed in red*
> *You can see it on a pole*
> *Or in Trotsky's buttonhole*
> *Long-haired Russian foxes*
> *Wave it from old soapboxes.*

Chorus:

> *That Revolutionary Rag*
> *'Twas made across the sea*
> *By a tricky, slicky Bolsheviki*
> *Run with your little moneybag*
> *Or else they'll steal it away—wheel it away,*
> *As they go raving, madly waving*
> *That Revolutionary Rag.*
> *It's not a melody*
> *It's a crimson flag:*
> *All the Royalties across the seas*
> *Shake in their BVD's*
> *When they see that Revolutionary Rag.*

The tune is less inventive than the lyric, which may or may not explain why the song was not one of Dreyfus's best-sellers. One particularly clever touch consists in Berlin's construction, with the word *That,* in the first line of the chorus, being held for a full four beats, followed by *Revolutionary,* which syncopates (the touch of ragtime) through a bar in sixteenth notes and dotted eighths. The final *Rag* balances *That* with a bar to itself, a form of stop-go-stop device. It is one of the last examples of Berlin's ragtime style; the references to jazz and the blues in "Mr. Jazz Himself," of two years earlier, show that he was aware of a change taking place in American popular music in 1917, the year the Original Dixieland Jazz Band made its New York debut at Reisenwebber's Restaurant.* While jazz had been around, and recorded, since the late nineteenth century, the five white musicians from New Orleans introduced this free, improvisational style of performance to New Yorkers at just the right moment—the dawn of what would come to be known as the Jazz Age.

No sooner had Berlin left the Harms office with his Gershwin manuscript than George M. Cohan took "That Revolutionary Rag" and found a place for it in his parody of operetta, the "Cohanized Opéra Comique" production *The Royal Vagabond.* Berlin's "Bolsheviki" essay fitted neatly into the story line, which centered on a prince in disguise who falls in love with

---

*A historical footnote: The repertoire of the "Jass Band," as they were originally called when they began their recording career in 1917, was made up of such titles as "Livery Stable Blues," "Dixie Jass Band One-Step," "Barnyard Blues," and "Tiger Rag." The same band would record Berlin's "I've Got My Captain Working for Me Now" during a London appearance in 1920.

a commoner (an innkeeper's daughter). The peasants in the country are simmering with revolution, and the disguised prince ends up becoming the head of a movement bent on removing him(self) from the throne. The convoluted plot (which Cohan borrowed from others) was deftly handled, and the tongue-in-cheek, slangy dialogue spoken by a character based on Cohan himself delighted audiences. The show was an instant hit, and "That Revolutionary Rag" was heard in no less than 208 performances. Cohan's joky style can be glimpsed in a song written "by" his impersonator (Cohan himself was not in the show), Professor "Hoppy" Hopkins (aka "Horrible Harold"), for his lady love:

> *He sipped the nectar from her lips*
> *As 'neath the moon she sat,*
> *And wondered if ever a man before*
> *Had drunk from a mug like that.*

With his Bolshevik song out of the way, Berlin turned to his publishing business. By mid-June he had phased out the old Irving Berlin, Inc., and set up a new firm under the same name, giving his good friend Max Winslow the title of Professional Manager and hiring one Saul Bornstein as business manager (not a wise choice, as he would later learn). Replacing Hess as musical secretary was a well-rounded musician—a composer, conductor, pianist, and arranger—named Arthur Johnston. Then twenty-one, Johnston was to work with Berlin, not only as a transcriber but also as an arranger and conductor, for the next decade. On his own, in Hollywood, he would later become the most successful of all Berlin's former secretaries. Irving Berlin, Inc., was ready for business.

Two days before the new firm was established, on June 16, the thirteenth annual Ziegfeld Follies opened, reuniting Berlin with the master showman for the first in a series of musicals. The 1919 edition of the Follies is widely regarded by musical-theater historians as the best of all Ziegfeld productions (at least until *Show Boat*). As his major contribution, Irving Berlin wrote what would be the theme song for this and all subsequent revues glorifying the American girl, "A Pretty Girl Is like a Melody." As was his practice, Ziegfeld hired several writers to produce the score, leaving the final choice to his chief writer and assistant, Gene Buck, who as a charter member of ASCAP knew all the writers in town.

The project commenced in April 1919, while Ziegfeld was on his annual vacation in Palm Beach, Florida, and proceeded in his customary style, which involved the communication of ideas to Buck via telegrams, many running to several pages. Amazingly, according to show historian Stanley Green, that year's Follies was thrown together in the three weeks before its weeklong Atlantic City tryout. Lavish to a fault, it ran to four and a half hours, forcing the elimination of three Berlin songs: "Bevo," formerly of Camp Upton, "Look Out for the Bolsheviki Man" (a natural sequel to "That Revolutionary Rag"), and "Beautiful Faces Need Beautiful Clothes," which he would interpolate in *Broadway Brevities* the following year, which featured several songs by George Gershwin.

Despite these cuts, Irving Berlin remained the chief songwriter for the 1919 Follies. Gene Buck had mustered, besides Berlin, nineteen other songwriters (most of them teams), including himself. Only Berlin (with the exception of a comic song for Bert Williams, "You Cannot Make Your Shimmy Shake on Tea," written with a lyric by Rennold Wolf) and Herbert worked alone. Herbert composed the score for a "Circus Ballet" for Marilyn Miller and a corps de ballet. Miller herself was but one member of an enormous cast of performers, chorus girls, and dancers. Among the numerous other stars featured were Eddie Cantor, Bert Williams, Van and Schenck, Delyle Alda, Jessie Reed (whom Ziegfeld had enticed away from the Shuberts), the brother-sister dancing team of Johnny and Ray Dooley, the Fairbanks Twins, and the tenor John Steel, in his Follies debut. Hailed as a young John McCormack, Steel would induce Berlin to write the show's most enduring song. The cast greatly outnumbered the large contingent of songwriters: a panoramic photograph of a preproduction meeting on the stage of the New Amsterdam Theatre shows no less than eighty assembled and listening to sketch writer Buck and director Ned Rayburn. And these were only the "girls"—none of the male cast or the principals was present for the photograph.

The premiere of the *Ziegfeld Follies of 1919* on that same stage, on June 16, was as much a social event as it was a theatrical one. "Among the elegantly attired throng," Stanley Green reported, "could be observed such sturdy social pillars as the Reginald Vanderbilts, the Morgan Belmonts, the John Wanamakers, the Frederick Lewisohns, the Lewis Gouverneur Morrises, the Angier Biddle Dukes, and the Condé Nasts."

The curtain was scheduled to rise at 8:10, but "as befitted the social nature of the evening," Green continued,

> the start of the *Follies* was signaled not so much by the posted time schedule as it was by the arrival of the hostess, Ziegfeld's radiant wife, Billie Burke, who floated down the aisle, waved and blew kisses, and eased into her seat at exactly 8:27. That, as everyone was

aware, was the cue for the houselights to dim, the hubbub to subside, and music director Frank Darling to strike up the overture.

Only slightly streamlined (opening night still lasted for a bit over three hours), the revue that had been whipped up in three weeks swept all before it. The *Evening Sun* cleverly summed up the achievement in the head above its review: "Ziegfeld Outziegfelds Ziegfeld."

The two acts were divided into "episodes" rather than scenes, the first of them being "The Follies Salad" (author[s] unknown), in which Eddie Dowling sang to a parade of showgirls dressed as Salt and Pepper, Lettuce, Spice, Oil, Sugar, Paprika, and—for reasons unknown—Bert Williams as Chicken. The next episode glorified its female headliners in a sensual Ben Ali Haggin tableau entitled "Hail to the Thirteenth Folly." It featured former Shubert beauty Jessie Reed and a dozen other loosely draped young women in statuesque poses (Haggin's Ziegfeld trademark). Subsequent episodes highlighted the assorted principals in songs, dances, and their particular vaudeville specialties—as, for example, Eddie Cantor, in blackface, and black Bert Williams, also in blackface, doing comic skits and numbers. In episode 10, Cantor brought on the first Berlin song, the mildly suggestive (especially when delivered with a leer and rolling eyes) "You'd Be Surprised," soon to range through the vaudeville circuit.

The first-act finale employed the entire company. After a quartet harmonized its way through a few standard minstrel-show songs, the stage opened up to reveal the rest of the cast dressed in pink, silver, and white costumes, as the orchestra played Berlin's "I'd Rather See a Minstrel Show." Cantor and Williams appeared as "End Men" in this episode. In the classic minstrel show, the company sat in chairs across the stage. The Interlocutor (not in blackface) sat in the center and the End Men at either end of the line. Their part in the show was to needle the pompous Interlocutor. When this happened the other members of the company rattled their tambourines. Marilyn Miller, in whiteface, impersonated George Primrose, of the Primrose and Dockstader's Minstrels, with a soft-shoe dance. But the showstopper was Van and Schenck's rendition of Berlin's "Mandy," with tambourines banged out to a buck-and-wing by Mandy (Ray Dooley) and her "Follies Pickaninnies."

The second act belonged mostly to Berlin. The first episode, set in a harem, opened to the tune of "Harem Life" and closed with a study in frustration, "I'm the Guy Who Guards the Harem." As the set was being changed for Miller's (and Herbert's) "Circus Ballet," Bert Williams came out (the curtain was down, or "In One," in stage jargon) to sing a couple of numbers in his characteristic style, wearing an ill-fitting suit, with top hat and oversize shoes. His delivery on such topics as money, matrimony, and Prohibition (now less than a month away) was studied, rueful, and skillfully timed.

After the ballet came the evening's major climax. Tenor John Steel, who had serious ambitions, had managed to convince Ziegfeld (no one *told* Ziegfeld what to do) that his big moment in act 2 should afford him the opportunity to break into classical song. Berlin was given the assignment of finding a way to do this by somehow writing a song into which melodies by Dvorak, Schumann, Mendelssohn, Massenet, and Schubert might be woven. His solution was "A Pretty Girl Is like a Melody," intoned by Steel while members of the chorus came forward to represent the classical songs— "Spring Song," "Humoresque," "Trumerei," and so on—against a beautiful urban backdrop. The episode closed with another Haggin tableau underscoring the Berlin lyric, depicting Lady Godiva on her horse, accompanied by handmaidens, heralds, guards, and the "Follies Kiddies."

Two episodes later (after a skit with Cantor in an osteopath's office), Bert Williams returned to lament once more the coming of Prohibition, against a backdrop showing the New York skyline draped in black crepe. After an ensemble rendition of Berlin's "Prohibition," Williams went into "You Cannot Make Your Shimmy Shake on Tea." Delyle Alda then sang "The Near Future," and Miller did "Syncopated Cocktail."

The finale was all-Berlin, beginning with John Steel's serenade of Jessie Reed, "My Tambourine Girl," and concluding with another tableau—this one utilizing an Urban Victory Arch in a tribute to the young women who had served in France with the Salvation Army—set to "We Made the Doughnuts over There."

Despite the hour (past eleven), the opening-night audience, as Green wrote in his monograph on the show, "not wanting to leave so festive an occasion, cheered the company through countless encores."

The cheering continued in the next day's press, but Ziegfeld's favorite assessment would come from a more unusual source. The English playwright-poet John Drinkwater, in New York to oversee the production later in the year of his verse-play *Abraham Lincoln,* was induced to write of his reaction. His response read, in part,

> The composite mind that produced the "Ziegfeld Follies" show is a
> master dramatist with a superb gift. Mr. Ziegfolly, if I may name
> him so, has a vivid and personal zest of grace and wit and fooling. . . .
> I am inspirited by the genuinely organic pattern that informs the

work of Mr. Ziegfolly. He makes holiday with a fine air, and brings
truth to his gesture, and I beg leave to lift my hat to him.

Drinkwater's words were accordingly preserved in later printings of the
Follies program—never mind that he had somehow overlooked the contributions of sketch writers Buck, Wolf, and others, designers Urban and Haggin,
the cast, and twenty songwriters. All of the show's elements, of course, functioned together to make it the hit it was. After the opening, it was trimmed
a bit more to make the evening more endurable: a serious/burlesque dance
episode set in Chinatown, "Perfume of Opium," was eliminated in the first
week. Even Ziegfeld knew when too much was more than enough.

The *Follies of 1919* ran for a considerable 171 performances, longer than
any of the twelve preceding versions. In mid-August, when Actors Equity
called a strike to protest the nefarious practices of managers and producers,
Eddie Cantor, the Dooleys, Bert Williams, and Van and Schenck, though in
comfortable spots and well paid, chose to side with the performers, and the
show shut down for three weeks, as did shows in eleven other New York theaters. It would be some time before Cantor would appear in another Ziegfeld
musical. George M. Cohan, who wore the hats of both actor and producer,
aligned himself with management, a choice that lost him many friends and
curtailed his career for a while.

Berlin and Ziegfeld remained on good terms, a rare thing for the producer, who in general was not highly regarded by songwriters. After the
actors' strike was settled, the Follies resumed its run, and Ziegfeld proceeded
with the other shows he regularly presented on the New Amsterdam's roof.
Berlin's ("I'll See You in) Cuba" was sung in the *Midnight Frolic* later in the
year, and the following March, "Metropolitan Ladies" went into *Ziegfeld Follies of 1920.* The bulk of the "roof" scores were by Dave Stamper (music) and
Gene Buck (lyrics). The songs that were best remembered from these presentations were written by songwriters other than Berlin, among them "Rose of
Washington Square" (James F. Hanley and Ballard Macdonald) and "My
Man" (Maurice Yvain and Channing Pollock), as interpreted by Fanny Brice.

Berlin turned out a few more songs and then, in the spring of 1920, took
some time off to get a little sun in Palm Beach, Florida. One day shortly after
his return, according to Woollcott, he was awakened around noon by a call
from Sam H. Harris, then respected as the former producer-partner of George
M. Cohan. Berlin had first met Harris with Cohan, around the time he wrote
"Marie from Sunny Italy," back in the Pelham Café days; Harris, he remembered, had called him Little Izzy then. Later, after Berlin had written several

ragtime songs and the first four bars of "Alexander's Ragtime Band," they met again: Harris admired Berlin's gift and suggested that the young writer (Harris was sixteen years his senior) look him up someday; maybe they could do a production together. They ran into each other a third time during the *Yaphank* run, and Harris once again expressed an interest in working with him, but as Berlin explained, "I was in uniform; it was easy to get in but not out."

After he did get out, the two met at the Friars Club, where Berlin, brimming over with the success of his Follies songs, blurted, "If you ever want to build a theater just for musical comedy, I've got a great name for it: the Music Box." Harris approved of the name, but they went on to talk of other things.

In his partnership with Cohan, Harris had always handled the money and produced; Cohan had created the plays and staged them. The association began in 1904 with *Little Johnny Jones,* on which Harris was the sole producer, and continued with *The Talk of New York* (1907), the first of fourteen Cohan shows they would coproduce, up to and including *The Royal Vagabond* in 1919. The estrangement that followed that last production was due in large part to the Actors Equity strike: Harris, despite his presidency of the Producing Managers Association, was sympathetic toward the Equity membership, sensing that as the theater expanded, an actors' union would be an inevitable result. Cohan adamantly disagreed, and their partnership, to the incredulity of Broadway, was dissolved. Cohan then disappeared from the scene after announcing his (temporary) retirement from the stage.

Harris went on to produce *Honey Girl* at the Cohan and Harris Theatre, with a score by Albert von Tilzer and Neville Fleeson. Debuting in May 1920, the show lasted barely a month. (Von Tilzer and Fleeson did better with another collaboration that year, the song "I'll Be with You in Apple Blossom Time.")

It was around this time that Harris called Berlin and woke him up with a question: "Irving, remember that Music Box idea of yours?"

Not really, after a couple of years, and given the time of day; Berlin could reply only with an equivocal "Will I ever forget it?" (Fifty years later, Berlin would recall the conversation as having taken place in Harris's office; Woollcott, for all his historical/anecdotal embroidery, was writing closer to the event, making the phone call the more likely scenario. Otherwise, the two accounts agree in all but minor details.)

Harris went on, jogging Berlin's memory back to their exchange at the Friars Club. He had just acquired a hundred feet of property on West Forty-fifth Street, he said, across from the Astor Hotel. He concluded, "You can have your Music Box whenever you want it. You're my partner."

This was a stunner. Berlin knew that Harris was a gambler: he had come to show business from the Lower East Side, via a laundry business that had enabled him to build a stable of racehorses, which in turn had positioned him to manage boxer Terry McGovern. Getting McGovern into the cast of *The Bowery after Dark* had led him first to Cohan and now to Berlin.

The money involved was a considerable sum for 1920—the estimate was $947,000 to pay off the property and build the theater. Berlin, though financially well off, did not have his half of the total. He therefore went to see Joseph Schenck, now well settled in the film industry with United Artists, whose theater chain he had established.

Not quite certain how to begin, Berlin tried a promise of profit: "Joe, I want to let you in on something."

Schenck just listened.

He took a different tack. "Joe, I'm in trouble."

"Who's the girl?" Schenck (himself a known womanizer) inquired.

"Not a girl, a theater."

"Why do you want me?"

"You're my partner," Berlin replied. It had worked for Harris, and now it worked for him: Schenck put up half of his half. (Berlin later bought it back, and he and Harris became the sole owners of the Music Box.)

Two or three brownstones on West Forty-fifth Street were razed to accommodate the new theater. While the building, designed by architect C. Howard Crane, was going up, Berlin busied himself in an effort to keep ahead of the expenses, contributing songs to another composite (involving fifteen songwriters this time) score for Ziegfeld's *Follies of 1920.* One of these numbers pretended to social significance, but with a Berlin twist: "The Leg of Nations." John Steel was given two fine Berlin melodies, "Tell Me, Little Gypsy" and the pluralistic (thus Ziegfollyish) "The Girls of My Dreams." With Harry Ruby and his new collaborator Bert Kalmar, Berlin fashioned a special number for Fanny Brice, "I'm a Vamp from East Broadway" (published as "The Syncopated Vamp").

Meanwhile, skeptical Broadwayites watched the costly erection of Berlin and Harris's small, handsome, and expensive theater. "Rival managers," Woollcott would write, "standing in knots on nearby street corners, could be seen figuring happily on the backs of envelopes and announcing: 'If they sell out every seat [there were to be a mere 1,010] for the next five years, they'll lose money.' " (The Shubert seated 1,400, the Winter Garden 1,570.)

Berlin would remember, too, producer John Golden's dismal judgment: "The boys think they are building a monument, but they're building a tombstone." Comedian Sam Bernard, who would appear in the new theater's first production, observed, "It stinks from class." (It had so much class, in fact, that no one noticed until just before the scheduled opening, in September 1921, that architect Crane had neglected to put in a box office. Hurriedly, a small one was stuffed into the lobby: a bad omen.)

As soon as he finished the songs for the Follies, Berlin was free to concentrate on his Music Box score. No "composite score," this—it would be all, and only, Berlin. The Music Box had the unique distinction of being built as the outlet for the work of a single composer. Harris wanted to name it "Irving Berlin's Music Box," but Berlin objected: "Too much Berlin," he said. Besides, he had originally suggested that it house musicals, not just *Berlin* musicals. (As it turned out, during its first four years, the theater presented only Berlin Music Box Revues.)

By September, the Music Box was ready. Schenck, recently returned from Hollywood, stopped by during a dress rehearsal to visit with an obviously nervous Berlin. As the two men spoke, an elevator designed to lift the chorus from beneath the stage jammed, trapping sixteen extremely vocal members of the chorus halfway up.

"What's that?" Schenck asked.

"Oh," Berlin told him, affecting sangfroid, "that's just one of our little effects."

Laughing, Schenck patted his friend on the back and said, "Never mind, Irving, after all, it's no more than you or I would lose in a good stud game and never think of again." But Berlin *was* thinking of it: with the expenses of the production added to the cost of the real estate and their Music Box, he and Harris would be in debt for over a million dollars before one ticket was sold at the makeshift box office.

To use a cliché, no expense was spared. The Music Box, beautifully detailed inside and out, truly earned its description as a "jewel": Moss Hart, who would later have several plays staged there, called it "everybody's dream of a theater." Unlike Ziegfeld's Follies, however, which were also expensively mounted, the first Music Box Revue did not feature a glittering array of big-name stars. The best-known performer was William ("Willie") Collier, whose career as a comedian-character actor went back as far as 1890, when he had appeared, in his early twenties, as an "actor" in the show *The City Directory*. Successful in vaudeville as well as in the theater, Collier was one of George M. Cohan's best friends and had starred in Cohan's *Hello, Broadway!* in 1914. He contributed considerably to the first Music Box Revue, as comedian, sketch writer, and codirector with Hassard Short.

Lesser lights included Emma Haig and the three close-harmonizing Brox Sisters, who scored a hit with their rendition of the intricate, syncopated

"Everybody Step." (The Broxes would be featured in other, subsequent Revues and in the 1927 Follies; they would make a number of recordings, some with Berlin's musical secretary Arthur Johnston as accompanist.) Comedian Sam Bernard was also in the cast.

The show's most enduring song was assigned to two comparative new-comers, Wilda Bennett and Paul Frawley. It had been circulating in New York for some time (Woollcott says "months") before the show opened, ever since the night Berlin went to Schenck's favorite Sixty Club and just happened to have his music with him. It is unlikely that he had an orchestration yet, so the song was probably played by the pianist. The bandleader promised to play it only the one night, but the members of the Sixty Club demanded more, and after a few renditions, the rest of the orchestra may have joined in, to further demands for encores. By the time the show premiered, the song was already quite popular in Manhattan. "Say It with Music" was to become the Music Box theme song.

On opening night, September 22, 1921, the apprehensive Berlin and Harris, in tuxedos, sought refuge in a suite in the Astor, to pick at an early dinner and, from time to time, look down at Forty-fifth Street, where a sign across the way blazed MUSIC BOX and the marquee proclaimed brightly, "Irving Berlin's Music Box Revue." Soon, fascinated, they were watching the early arrivals, coming in cabs and limousines and on foot in small groups. More surprising were the crowds lining the sidewalks blocking the entrance of the theater until police cleared a path; they had come to see the people who came to see the show, celebrities such as Douglas Fairbanks and Mary Pickford (Mr. and Mrs. Fairbanks), Metropolitan Opera soprano Geraldine Farrar, and socialite Mrs. Lydig Hoyt. It was a comforting sight.

Since Irving Berlin was advertised as one of the cast, it was time for him to descend and cross the street. The partners shook hands, and Harris said, "Go to it, Irving."

"Go to it, Sam."

Harris had alerted the public to this appearance in a teasing press release:

The young man who has puckered the lips of a nation into a whistling position, stimulated the hurdy-gurdy industry and increased the dividends of the gramophone and pianola companies is going on the stage. . . .

Sam H. Harris announces that Mr. Berlin will be a member of the company opening in *The Music Box Revue.* "Mr. Berlin's present working day averages about twelve hours. And I felt that time was hanging heavily on his hands. Accordingly, I offered him a job. I believe that everyone should work. Besides, he is a fine young fellow and I want to see him get ahead. When I expressed my feelings, he took the job."

Berlin's slot in the revue was the coveted last-to-closing number (that is, the one before the finale). He appeared with eight members of the chorus, the "Eight Notes" (referring to the octave on a piano), who "asked me how you write a song," Berlin would tell Mel Gussow fifty years later. "I kidded myself. It was a tough spot, right next to closing. I was a bit of a ham.

"Sam and I were in a room in the Hotel Astor [after the curtain went down on the finale]. Very frightened men. We spent more than we should have on the theater."

One critic agreed. "The Music Box," he wrote,

opened last night before a palpitant audience and proved to be a trea-sure chest out of which the conjurers pulled all manner of gay tunes and brilliant trappings and funny clowns and nimble dancers. Its bewildering contents confirmed the dark suspicion that Sam H. Har-ris and Irving Berlin have gone quite mad. They have builded them a playhouse in West Forty-fifth Street that is a thing of beauty itself, then crowded its stage with such a sumptuous and bespangled revue as cannot possibly earn them anything more substantial than the heart-warming satisfaction of having produced it all.

This was the opinion of *Times* critic Alexander Woollcott. Ignoring, or forgetting, the other "gay tunes" mentioned in the above paragraph, he pro-ceeded to opine magisterially that there was only one song in the entire show—"Say It with Music" (apparently he had missed "Everybody Step" and a couple of others). He then predicted that "by February you will have heard [the song] so often that you will gladly shoot at sunrise any one who so much as hums it in your hearing."

Four years later, when Woollcott published his biography of Berlin, he would compensate for such arch flippancy by declaring the Music Box Revue of 1921 a great hit (*Variety*'s Jack Lait, for his part, had gone so far as to christen it "America's greatest show") as well as a financial triumph. Meticulous down to the last cent, he tabulated production costs from costumes ($66,783.09) to scenery ($28,214.09) and even steamship fares for missions abroad ($2,170.00), and followed up with an accounting of weekly running expenses ($19,065.86) broken down into their component parts, including sundries (whatever they may have been, $128.97).

High though the overhead might be, Woollcott exulted, "the average weekly gross receipts of the first revue during the forty-one weeks of the New York run were $27,788.57, so the goose hung high and an even greater profit was shown nearly every week that the revue toured the country. Wherefore the wiseacres on the curb stopped laughing"—among them, no doubt, the man from the *Times* himself.

It is unlikely that Berlin himself toured with the revue, as that would have kept him from preparing for the next production; as it was, having to be present at the Music Box for all 440 performances—until June 1922—would have interfered with his writing.

Woollcott, in his biography, reported that one June afternoon, a neighbor asked Berlin how his new show was going.

"I don't know yet," Berlin is supposed to have replied. "We've got Clark and McCullough and Grace Moore, but I don't know anything beyond that." While the gist of this remark may be accurate enough—revues were always built around the talent—Woollcott got one detail wrong: Grace Moore would not make her Music Box debut until the third (1923) edition of the Revue. The second edition was to star tall, long-legged comedian Charlotte Greenwood (who would sing and dance "I'm Looking for a Daddy Long Legs") alongside (Bobby) Clark and (Paul) McCullough, a vaudeville comedy team appearing in their second Broadway show.

Inevitably, the Music Box Revue would be compared with the Ziegfeld Follies. While the first in the Music Box series was as expensively, if more modestly, mounted, it was more tasteful than a typical Ziegfeld extravaganza—and more tuneful, given Ziegfeld's penchant for uneven composite scores. (Berlin gave a satiric nod to his rival producer in the 1921 revue's "My Ben Ali Haggin Girl.") The Follies of 1921, despite contributions from Victor Herbert and Rudolph Friml (the latter's with lyrics by Gene Buck), would be musically remembered for the songs interpreted by Fanny Brice, "My Man" and "Second Hand Rose," which she kept alive by making them a part of her act. A greater threat to Ziegfeld than Berlin's Revues were George White's Scandals. White, a young former Ziegfeld dancer, struck out on his own in 1919; by 1921 he had enlisted George Gershwin as his composer. His Scandals put an emphasis on youth and dancing and may have been a bit more vulgar than anything Ziegfeld produced.

Ziegfeld's 1921 Follies had no songs that came near to matching the inventiveness and creativity of Berlin's "Everybody Step," "Say It with Music," or "They Call It Dancing," in which Sam Bernard observed, "A man can squeeze all the shes/ With his arms and knees." The "class" that Bernard had detected before the Music Box opened would pay off.

Some of the Music Box Revue's initial success may be attributed to the novelty of the enterprise, abetted by Harris's press agentry and Berlin's name. As the series progressed, it would become a discouraging matter of diminishing returns. At the beginning, though, it looked like a winner: the first edition not only toured in the United States but also was produced at the Palace in Britain, featuring several from the New York cast, among them the rising Brox Sisters.

In all, there would be four annual Music Box Revues, beginning with the 1921 first edition (440 performances) and going through the second (330), the third (273), and the last, in 1924 (184). Each would have its distinctions. The 1922 production would be memorable for "Crinoline Days," "Lady of the Evening" (sung by Ziegfeld's former fair-haired boy John Steel), and "Pack Up Your Sins and Go to the Devil," which would lead to an interesting lawsuit.

The 1923 revue was to star the operatically ambitious soprano Grace Moore, in from Paris, where she had been studying voice. That June, on a semivacation, Berlin went to France and heard her, then brought her back home with him. In the show she sang "An Orange Grove in California," whose staging included its own (especially pleasing to Berlin) "little effect": as Moore sang, the Music Box was filled with the scent of oranges sprayed into the auditorium. Berlin's "find" also joined John Steel in a song interpolated into the show after the opening, "What'll I Do?" Some of the skits for this Revue were written by George S. Kaufman, among them "If Men Played Cards like Women." Even more important and enduring, however, was Robert Benchley's reading of his own "Treasurer's Report."

The last of the series, which opened in December 1924, would have a cast of Ziegfeldian proportions, with Fanny Brice, Clark and McCullough, Oscar Shaw, and Grace Moore (now on the brink of her Metropolitan debut, as Mimi in *La Bohème*). Moore introduced the pretty "Tell Her in the Springtime" and, with Shaw, the classic "All Alone."

By then, the Music Box partners had realized that the production of costly musicals could eventually cause them serious financial problems. They decided to quit while they were still ahead, and to end the Music Box Revue series at four. The Broadway musical scene was changing; except for Ziegfeld's offerings, lavish musical productions were becoming passé. While the 1924 Scandals did not run as long as the Follies, it had a better score, with its Gershwin hit "Somebody Loves Me"; still, it would be the last year for White's show as well. Gershwin's own *Lady, Be Good!*, a bright, jazzy, unpretentious, up-to-the-minute musical, would introduce new rhythms and bluesy harmonies into the American theater. Significantly, it would open on the same night as the Music Box Revue of 1924.

Berlin agreed with Sam Harris: it was time for a change. They would rent the Music Box to others, for dramatic plays, comedies, and musicals. Berlin had been working with little letup for more than three years, since 1921. The second of those years had been particularly difficult for him. Late in July 1922, Leah Baline had died at the age of seventy-two; his sister Gussie, now married, had helped him arrange for her burial. And then, after the premiere of the 1922 Revue, in October, an obscure songwriter had sued him for plagiarism, claiming that a song he had published in May had been stolen from him and republished by Berlin as "Pack Up Your Sins and Go to the Devil." Clearly the timing, if not the charge itself, was feasible.

When the dispute came to trial, three witnesses testified on Berlin's behalf. Violinist Jascha Heifetz, Broadway star Lenore Ulric (who had enjoyed great success in *Kiki*), and the free-living artist Neysa McMein all swore they had heard him play the song the previous January, at McMein's studio. Case closed.

This distinguished lineup signified, if nothing else, that Irving Berlin was now an accepted member of the exclusive group of artists, writers, musicians, and (more or less) intellectuals who made up the Algonquin Round Table.

A photograph taken in the sand of Miami Beach on what appears to be a virtually sunless day in January 1924 shows, in period swimsuits, Berlin's former brother-in-law Ray Goetz, Neysa McMein, and, next to her, Irving Berlin. Berlin squints, like Goetz, directly into the lens of the camera; now thirty-five, he looks to be only in his midtwenties, his hair tousled and his cheeks hollow, as if the effort of the third Music Box Review had drained him. Filling out the picture are William Emmerich, known in New York for his musical parties, and the most celebrated female member of the Algon-quin Round Table, Dorothy Parker, pensively peering into the sand, hands clasped.

The informal collection of writers, poets, press agents, and show people who gathered regularly at the Hotel Algonquin beginning sometime in 1920 called themselves the Vicious Circle (the Round Table tag would come later). Among the group's charter members were Deems Taylor (music critic for the *World* and an aspiring composer), George S. Kaufman (then drama editor for the *Times*), Robert Benchley (on the staff of the smart, slick Condé Nast pub-lication *Vanity Fair*), Harold Ross (then editor of the *American Legion Weekly,* following his success with *Stars and Stripes;* he would, in time, conceive the *New Yorker*), Heywood Broun (sportswriter for the *Tribune* and later firebrand in the infamous Sacco-Vanzetti case and in labor unions), Alexander Woollcott (who contributed maximally to the viciousness of the Vicious Circle), and, neither least nor last, Robert E. Sherwood (also at *Vanity Fair*).

The original aggregation counted two formidable women in its number. The first was McMein, a very successful commercial artist who specialized in covers for *Woman's Home Companion* and the *Saturday Evening Post,* and presided over one of New York's artiest salons, whose informal sessions were held in her studio; the second was the clever, acerbic, troubled Parker, the circle's preeminent woman member. She, too, worked at *Vanity Fair,* as a drama critic—until Flo Ziegfeld got her fired for questioning the talent of his wife, Billie Burke. In protest, Benchley and Sherwood left along with her; all three would go on to make their mark in writing and drama.

The nominal leader of this wayward, irreverent, often undisciplined gang of noncomformists was the columnist Franklin P. Adams ("FPA" to all), the most established member of the group. As early as 1911, he was a recognized writer for New York dailies; in 1914 he edited a column for the *Tribune,* "The Conning Tower," in which he published works by then-unknown lyricists Ira Gershwin and E. Y. Harburg and by such writers as Sinclair Lewis and Edna St. Vincent Millay, not to mention Dorothy Parker, Alexander Woollcott (who fancied himself the circle's true leader), and George S. Kaufman.

Around the time when the Vicious Circle was formed, FPA was writing a much-read weekly column for the *New York World* called "The Diary of Our Own Samuel Pepys," intended to be a kind of gossip column about the arts in Manhattan but more often merely a stultifying accumulation of trivia, news, and musings. He would become the unelected head of the Algonquin Round Table when the manager of the hotel, Frank Case, set the group up in an out-of-the-way spot equipped with a table of said shape; its members, trading quips and insults, would become as celebrated as some of the Algonquin's other regulars, theater types such as the Barrymores. Berlin was a peripheral but honored member. Shy, self-effacing, he could not bring himself to participate in the self-conscious, though often very witty (if sadistic), badinage of the Round Tablers.

Berlin preferred the unpretentious, often helter-skelter warmth, stimulation, and fun of the studio in which Neysa McMein lived and worked, on West Fifty-seventh Street opposite Carnegie Hall. Everyone was welcome, friends and friends of friends. Afternoons, while Neysa, in a loose smock, turned out her colorful pastel covers (called "pretty-girls") for glossy magazines, artists, writers, and composers would wander in and out; she would greet them and then continue with her work. Various conversations were always resonating through the studio, and there were board games (she loved games, even invented a few), food, and gin, mixed in the bathtub. Her Round Table friends were regulars.

Evenings were often musical but just as informal as the afternoons—and just as clamorous. Attention would be paid, however, when George Gershwin played his "Rhapsody in Blue," and laughs follow when violinist Jascha Heifetz, at the piano, parodied the popular "Japanese Sandman" (retitled "Just a Japanese Sandwich"). Deems Taylor often took time out from his work as a critic to present something of his own.

Even some of the literary Algonquin set sometimes made so bold as to perform in such professional company. FPA, who had first introduced Neysa into the circle, would bring along a piccolo, flute, or harmonica, or maybe all three; Robert Benchley's instrument was the banjo-mandolin, and Dorothy Parker's the triangle (though she was also, like Neysa, a better-than-average pianist).

As Arthur Krock, of the *Times,* would recall in his *Memoirs,* Neysa's

> was the only place where in a single evening one might hear [Robert] Sherwood's gravely ludicrous rendition of "When the Red, Red Robin Comes Bob, Bob, Bobbin' Along"; Heifetz burlesquing the graduation solo of a boy violinist; Father Duffy singing old Irish songs and Ring Lardner spinning such of his fantastic tales as "The Tridget of Greva" with the impassivity of expression found only on the faces of cigar-store Indians.

Neysa McMein, herself quite musical, frequently took her turn at the keyboard to "improvise some raggedy blues in her best nickelodeon manner," according to her biographer, Brian Gallagher. Paul Robeson would sing, and Grace Moore, of the Music Box and the Metropolitan; or Irving Berlin might try out a newly minted future hit, as he did with "Pack Up Your Sins" on that memorable January 1922 evening that would settle the lawsuit that followed the premiere of that year's Music Box Revue.

Neysa McMein was a midwesterner of independent mind whose casual love of people won her the title of the finest salon-keeper in New York (lesser salons, but of greater formality, were run by East Siders on Fifth and Park Avenues, including Mary Hoyt Wiborg, the Condé Nasts, the Sidney Fishes, and the Jules Glaenzers, he of Cartier; Berlin attended these, too, but Neysa's was more to his liking, much more raffish and down-to-earth). Some also called Neysa a tart—"perfectly beautiful . . . tall, Amazonian, as handsome as could be," in the words of one male admirer. But she was no tart; rather, she was a feminist and, in every sense of the word in the twenties, a liberated woman.

One of her more sensational exploits occurred a year and a half or so after she first met Irving Berlin, when, in May 1923, she secretly married a mining engineer named John Baragwanath. The day after they wed, "Handsome Jack," as he was dismissively nicknamed by the Vicious Circle, left for northeastern Quebec on a mining expedition, while Neysa sailed for Europe on a previously booked trip. On the deck of the *Olympia* she encountered Alexander Woollcott, who was aware of her booking but not of her hasty marriage. He inexplicably proposed and was duly rejected, taking it with rare good grace but nonetheless thereafter attaching himself to her. In Paris they ran into Jascha Heifetz, dramatist Marc Connelly, and Art Samuels, editor of *Harper's Bazaar,* all three members of her salon. They joined the Woollcott-McMein party, as did Ferdinand Touhey of the Paris office of the *World.* It was to Touhey that Neysa eventually disclosed the secret marriage, a piece of news that preceded her and her entourage—and, to his dismay, Handsome Jack—to New York. The original plan had been to announce the marriage when both returned, in June.

Gossip soon spread: Neysa McMein had spent her honeymoon with seven—some said ten—men, not one of them her new husband. A chief topic of conversation, speculation, and racy humor around the Round Table, the situation was summed up in the circle's favorite paper, the *World,* in a headline by editor Herbert Bayard Swope: "A New Groom Sleeps Clean."

The marriage would last, and produce a child, but it was what would come to be called an open-ended relationship. Both had affairs with others, yet they remained close.

Irving Berlin was a friend, sitting on the sand of Miami Beach with Neysa and Dorothy Parker (also a friend). He was frequently seen in their company, and often saw his name mentioned in columns with those of these blatantly promiscuous women. Something almost Victorian in him discouraged him from having "affairs," however; if he did have any, they were never detected by those who would have made the news public with relish. Circle members particularly loved tormenting other members over such matters.

As for Neysa's secret vows, Alexander Woollcott, one of the circle's most sadistic tormentors, waspishly accepted the marriage, forgave her, and even, albeit with reservations, acknowledged the existence of Jack Baragwanath.

While Berlin relaxed in Florida, the *New York Tribune,* in its issue of January 4, 1924, printed a brief announcement concerning a concert being planned by Paul Whiteman, leader of the most popular dance band of the moment. Whiteman had conceived "An Experiment in Modern Music" as an attempt to define American music; the concert was booked into Aeolian Hall (Carnegie Hall was taken) for the afternoon of February 12. Various judges were named to provide the hoped-for definition (though in the end, none was ever agreed on). The article closed with a summary of some of the expected highlights: "George Gershwin is at work on a jazz concerto, Irving Berlin is writing a syncopated tone poem and Victor Herbert is working on an American suite."

As it turned out, Gershwin did not compose a jazz concerto; rather, he produced the sensation of the concert, "Rhapsody in Blue." Victor Herbert's "American Suite" consisted of four "serenades": "Spanish," "Chinese," "Cuban," and "Oriental." But Berlin went further than either of the others in contradicting the Whiteman press release. Not only did he write no tone poem, he wrote nothing new at all; instead, Ferde Grofé, Whiteman's pianist-arranger (who also orchestrated Gershwin's rhapsody, there being too little time for Gershwin to do it himself, as he was engaged in preparing a new musical for Broadway), concocted a "Semisymphonic Arrangement of Popular Melodies" comprising "Alexander's Ragtime Band," "A Pretty Girl Is like a Melody," and "Orange Blossoms in California."

Unquestionably, it was the youthful Gershwin who stole the (often boring) show, and Berlin was impressed with "the kid"; as he put it, "George is the only songwriter who became a composer." Throughout Gershwin's tragically truncated career, Berlin would be an unabashed fan, proud of the other's accomplishments in every idiom he tried. Gershwin, for his part, would reciprocate the admiration for a lifetime.

After Whiteman's "Experiment" (which the bandleader subsequently took on a cross-country tour), Berlin's time was occupied by ASCAP business. On April 16 he was among a delegation that went to Washington to protest a bill that would excuse radio broadcasters from having to compensate songwriters for the use of their works on the air.

Victor Herbert led the group, which was made up of Berlin, John Philip Sousa, Raymond Hubbell, and Gene Buck. Their first day there, they entertained sympathetic congressmen at the National Press Club, Herbert on his cello and Berlin at the piano. The next day, at the hearings, Buck put their case succinctly when he said, "The Radio Corporation of America gets money, doesn't it? If they get money out of my tunes, I want some of it, that's all."

When it was Herbert's turn to speak, he was asked to state his full name for the stenographer; his reply was, "Oh, I thought you had heard of me."

He proceeded to present ASCAP's case against Senator Clarence C. Dill's bill from another angle, using his own "A Kiss in the Dark" as an example. Hearing the song as many as eight or nine times on the radio in one evening—"ad nauseam," he complained—deadened its popularity; not only was he receiving no payment for this overuse, but it also diminished the sales of sheet music.

Although the ASCAP delegation had made its point, it was forced to return to Washington for another hearing on May 7. Herbert spoke for all of the group when he addressed the hearing committee and said,

Authors and composers need the protection of the copyright laws. This is our source of livelihood. In the olden days a man or a woman would enter a theatre or a music house, hear a good piece of music and then purchase it. In this way a demand was created for our product. Today these compositions are delivered daily to the homes. They are rendered in an inartistic manner and the public soon tires of them. . . .

What is to become of musical art if the present state of affairs continues? There can be no initiative in the field if the reward is to be denied the men and women who devote their lives to musical culture. If you do not protect us it will be a sad thing for the musical art of the United States. I want to say that I was not driven here by publishers. I came here to fight for our cause, which is a good one.

Herbert's appeal worked: the bill did not pass, a victory for songwriters and for ASCAP itself, which would reap a bountiful harvest from the growing radio industry (and, years later, from television).

Irving Berlin was happy with what had been accomplished by his and his peers' efforts, but he was even happier when, that May, he fell in love.

FACING THE MUSIC

"I AM IN LOVE with Irving Berlin," Ellin Mackay, in confidence, told Nellie Livingston, of the Goodhue Livingstons, residents of Southampton and Manhattan. The Livingstons were old friends of Ellin's father, the stern proprietor of Harbor Hill, Roslyn, and the town house on East Seventy-fifth Street, Manhattan. It was summer—August, in fact—when the affluent fled New York's swelter for the breezes of Long Island's Gold Coast on the North Shore.

Nellie was properly stunned. She knew who Irving Berlin was, but she also knew that Clarence Mackay, a strict, if not devout, Catholic, was a truly devoted anti-Semite.

How on earth had the twenty-one-year-old New York society belle even come to meet the thirty-six-year-old Russian immigrant?

Quite by chance, it turned out.

Late in May 1924, another friend of the Mackays', Frances (Mrs. Allen G.) Wellman, who also commuted between New York and Long Island, had asked the popular, pretty, and outspoken Ellin to a dinner party. When a last-minute cancellation upset the balance of men to women, Mrs. Wellman called her friend Irving Berlin and invited him to the party as well. He was, as was often the case when he was not working, free that night, so he donned his dinner jacket and went off to the Wellmans'. It was there that he first saw the tallish, blond, and beautiful young woman who was introduced to him as

Ellin Mackay. He had no inkling of her position in life, or of her relationship to Clarence Mackay; it is doubtful, in fact, that Berlin even knew who Clarence was. He would soon learn.

Ellin spoke a kind of finishing-school, North Shore English (though she had never actually "finished," having dropped out of Barnard because of its reverse snobbery). At one point during the dinner, Ellin turned to Berlin and said, "Mr. Berlin, I do so like your song 'What Shall I Do?'"

Berlin's eyebrows rose a little, and he told her it was really "What'll I Do?" She was slightly taken aback, but he gallantly put her at ease by confiding, "With grammar, I can always use a little help." (Ellin Mackay was not the only one to mishear the title: when recordings of the song were released in Britain, a number of queries were dispatched to the publisher asking what a "whattle" was.)

The dinner progressed beautifully. "A spark was struck," their daughter Mary Ellin Barrett would write in her exquisite, and honest, memoir.

> She was a great heiress, a spoiled stuck-up darling; he was a world-famous composer, with the pride of a self-made man. Both had life-saving senses of humor, and their humors matched—fast, playful, sometimes a little rough on others.
>
> The rest of the conversation [that first night] is lost, but it continued briskly, no doubt, interrupted by an occasional lighting by him of [her] Turkish cigarette, fitted into a long quill holder, the badge of a young sophisticate.

The party over, the obviously interested songwriter asked the heiress to accompany him to a less elegant spot downtown, Jimmy Kelly's on Sullivan Street in Greenwich Village. (Kelly had moved up from the Union Square venue where Berlin had sung more than a decade before; he would later noise it around that it was at his club that Irving Berlin first encountered Ellin Mackay.)

Thus began one of the most arduous, publicized, and embattled romances of the Jazz Age. The up-to-then-elusive Berlin, seemingly destined to be an eternal bachelor, was taken with Miss Mackay. They took to meeting at smart parties, after which he would offer to give her a lift home in his luxurious chauffeur-driven automobile. They dined and danced at the Astor Roof, and sampled the rides and other amusements at Coney Island in the company of Cole Porter (a good friend of Ellin's second cousin Alice Duer Miller, novelist and member of the Round Table) and, ominously, Frances Wellman.

Word of the relationship was spreading around town, but it had not reached distant Harbor Hill—not yet, at least. Berlin and Ellin found they could avoid the attentions of the tabloid press by seeing each other at his midtown home.

Some two and a half years earlier, in 1921, with the success of the first Music Box Revue behind him, Berlin had abandoned his Chatsworth apartment and bought the building at number 29 West Forty-sixth, then a residential street of brownstones and small businesses. He kept the two top floors for himself, let the ground floor to a grocer, and rented the remaining three floors to assorted tenants. Ironically, his new residence uncannily resembled one of his first New York homes, at 330 Cherry Street, even to the first-floor grocery.

There were differences, of course, not the least of them being that he now had his own staff: a superintendent to make sure everything ran smoothly; a driver, the tall, capable Jack MacKenzie (a tank operator in the Great War); and a cook-butler named Ivan, who would prepare late-night suppers for Ellin and Berlin as they danced to a phonograph playing on the roof. Berlin also frequently whipped up his own culinary chef d'oeuvre—scrambled eggs seasoned with sautéed onions and tomatoes—no doubt to the amusement of his guest, who had never cooked in her life (there were servants to do that at Harbor Hill) and never would.

Another improvement over Cherry Street was the elevator that took him, his guest, and their friends to his duplex. The living room up there was expensively decorated, with bookcase-lined walls (influenced by his friend Jerome Kern, he had begun collecting rare first editions) and a fireplace, near which stood a Steinway grand piano, *sans* crank. A wrought iron chandelier hung overhead, and leaded-glass windows gave onto the street above a spacious window seat.

In this splendid room, Berlin played Ellin the songs he was writing for the fourth and final Music Box Revue, as well as the earlier "Say It with Music" and "Lady of the Evening," the even older "Alexander's Ragtime Band" and "I Love a Piano"—and, undoubtedly, "What'll I Do?"

It was an idyllic interlude, but it did not last. That August, while Ellin was telling Nellie Livingston of her feelings for Berlin, Clarence Mackay was hearing from a guilt-laden Frances Wellman the story of what had resulted from her dinner party in May. Infuriated, Mackay lashed out at the contrite Frances: How could she have been so stupid as to introduce his young daughter (his "angel child") to an older man, and even worse, a Jew? Besides, Ellin was already engaged (if only casually, at least in her opinion) to a diplomat who spent much of his time in Washington. This long-distance, lukewarm romance came to an end when Ellin simply called it off; her only concern, according to her daughter, was whether to return the watch given to her by her part-time suitor. When she discussed this with Berlin, he simply advised her to do whatever she wished. That ended the discussion and the "romance" with the diplomat.

Although Mackay was then in the midst of arrangements for a ball he was hosting in honor of the future King of England (Edward, the dashing Prince of Wales), he at once sprang into vindictive action, hiring detectives to shadow the interloper and making plans to whisk his daughter away from New York as soon as the ball was over. The detectives had little to do except follow Berlin every day from West Forty-sixth Street to his offices on Broadway; at the time, he was busy writing songs for the Music Box.

Mackay then confronted his daughter, stating firmly that she must stop seeing "that man" (he had developed an aversion to the name Irving Berlin) and adding, "You must give me your solemn word."

Her blue eyes flashed, holding his with a strong, defiant gaze. "No, I won't promise," she replied. Mackay realized he had a battle on his hands.

As the story broke, one newspaper printed "A Mackay-Berlin Parallel," pointing out similarities in two brief biographical sketches. There was something rather odd, however, about the chronology provided for the fifty-year-old Mackay, which read: "reached New York as immigrant 1840" (Berlin: 1892 [sic]); "sold papers on Park Row and Bowery" (Berlin: ditto); "worked as shipyard laborer" (Berlin: waiter and boy of all work, singing waiter in Nigger Mike Salter's saloon); "tended bar in Louisville, Ky." (Berlin: moved to Jimmy Kelly's as waiter); "went west as miner and laborer . . . struck silver and riches" (Berlin: became songwriter and found wealth).

As it happened, these anomalous "parallels" were between the lives of the songwriter and Ellin's *grandfather,* not her *father,* dedicated foe of Irving Berlin.

John William Mackay, Irish immigrant, was the founder of a financial empire that had its beginnings in Nevada and a fortune made from the Comstock Lode. He parlayed this into several Eastern businesses, notably the Postal Telegraph and International Telephone and Telegraph companies; he died a billionaire.

John Mackay's fortune maintained the Stanford White–designed, fifty-room mansion at Harbor Hill, where Ellin was born on March 22, 1903. It bought the town house in Manhattan and paid for his son's European education (during which, some suggested, he majored in snobbism). Clarence, who had spent the first two decades of his life in France and England, used some of his inheritance to accumulate a collection of armor and fine paintings, but he also saw to it that Ellin and her siblings—an older sister, Katherine, and younger brother, John William—had a good Catholic upbringing. What Clarence lacked was a good business sense, a failing that would, in time, shatter his world and the life he had come to take for granted.

For Mackay, Ellin's foolish insurrection was more than just a little family problem: the thought of another scandal terrified him. Eleven years before, the papers had been full of the disintegration of his own marriage to Ellin's mother, Katherine Duer.

A few years before that, Clarence Mackay had found out that he had throat cancer. His hunting companion, Dr. Joseph Blake, a convivial New York specialist, operated and was credited with saving his life. During Mackay's recuperation, Dr. Blake made house calls to look in on his patient; he was also attentive to the beautiful Mrs. Mackay. An affair ensued, leading to the breakup of both parties' marriages. Katherine, a Protestant, walked out on Clarence and their children (Ellin was then ten years old) and married Blake once his divorce was final. Clarence, a strict Catholic, did not recognize either the divorce or Katherine's remarriage, and did not himself remarry (though at the time of the Berlin flareup, he was keeping a mistress, opera singer Anna Case).

The deeply wounded Mackay had forbidden his children to have anything to do with their disgraced mother. Ellin defied him on that ukase as well: Katherine Duer Blake would later become one of her few North Shore allies in her newfound self-assertion. Ellin wrote to and saw her mother whenever she wished, but she refused to meet, or speak to, her stepfather, Dr. Blake.

Clarence Mackay's ball for the Prince of Wales was an event of lavish proportions, with the mansion ablaze with lights and filled with gowned women and formally dressed men. Paul Whiteman and his orchestra were hired to provide the music. The servants were instructed to bar Irving Berlin from entering, should he have the cheek to attempt to crash the party; little did Mackay realize that his adversary would find a subtler way in, as Whiteman's band book contained a generous selection of Berlin songs. While Ellin and the prince danced to "What'll I Do?," she told him about her crisis. People stared, for they made a striking couple, especially when the prince laughed at some remark of hers.

Now enlisted as a coconspirator, Edward engaged Mackay in conversation during supper, distracting him so that Ellin could slip away to call her Irving. Later he would remember the encounter as "refreshing": Ellin Mackay was the only young woman he met in America who talked to him about another man, not about himself.

After the party, Mackay resumed his campaign. He proposed a plan: father and daughter would leave for London a few days later, at the end of September, with his mother ("Granny" to Ellin), Ellin's companion Mary Finnerty (who doubled as chaperone), and her French maid, Hermine Tripet. From England they would travel to France and then to Spain and Italy, Egypt and Algiers. Mackay would leave the others in Paris, but Ellin would be away for six months. On her return, her father promised, they would discuss her infatuation, if she still thought she was in love by then.

For now, she *was* in love. She wrote to Berlin frequently from abroad, and he replied, not as frequently, telling her that he was doing nothing but grinding out music. He did admit to being "really . . . delighted with a good deal of my stuff, [but] then again as I told you so many times, the thrill of the Music Box has gone and now it has become a job that I love most when it's finished."

She often cabled him, deftly using Western Union, the family companies' competitor. Berlin's secret cable address was "eyebee." By post and by wire, Ellin kept "my young man" informed of her travels and about the people she met, including opera star Mary Garden, the pope (in Rome), and art expert Bernard Berenson, who had helped Clarence Mackay assemble a valuable collection of paintings.

In Rome, too, she encountered Ray Goetz and the Cole Porters, with whom she celebrated the far-off opening of the final Music Box Revue on the first day of December 1924. How could she forget Irving Berlin? There seemed to be reminders of him everywhere she went. In January she returned to Paris, where Joseph Schenck brought her a message from Berlin: he wanted to come to Europe in February to talk things over with her. Ellin responded that she thought it best to complete, as she had promised her father, the six-month separation; she would be back in March.

She liked the burly movie magnate, and he liked her back. She was touched when he told her that he believed she and his old Bowery friend should marry.

Not long before, out of the blue, she had acquired another coconspirator. During her travels, Ellin wrote from time to time to her mother (though not as faithfully as she did to her "young man"); in December, while she was in Rome, she got a letter back, in which Katherine Blake informed her daughter that she had heard from "various people" of her "admiration for Irving Berlin."

In reply, Ellin confirmed the rumor and advised her mother that if she wanted to know about Berlin's genuine charm and "real niceness," she should speak with her cousin Alice Duer Miller, who knew him well from the Round Table and Neysa McMein's open houses. Ellin then wrote immediately to Berlin to prepare him, saying that she hoped he would meet her mother and adding, "I think you might get on amazingly well." He would, and they did.

Mrs. Blake now wrote again, referring to her daughter's "probation" and promising that when it was ended, and Ellin returned to "tell me you are going to marry Berlin because you love him more than anything else in the world, I shall say, my darling, it's your life & your choice & may your marriage bring you all that's best in love." She did have some reservations, she confessed, about the couple's religious differences (unlike her former husband, she ignored the age gap), and wondered how she, and the rest of Ellin's family, would get on with Berlin's parents, who she heard were Orthodox Jews (she did not realize that both were now dead). She also recalled the serious disagreements she had once had over religion with Ellin's father. Having made this point, however, Katherine renewed her vow to stand by her daughter should she choose to marry Irving Berlin. She concluded her letter on a cheerful note, announcing that she had taken a box at the Music Box to see the fourth annual Revue early in January 1925.

Alice Miller arranged for a meeting between Berlin and Katherine while Ellin was in Cairo. He called on Mrs. Blake, probably at her home in Tarrytown, and quite formally asked for her daughter's hand in marriage—a unique proposal by proxy. She gave her blessing, of course. When Ellin learned this, she wired Berlin, then in Palm Beach, to make their engagement official. Their long ordeal was about to begin: the moment her ship, the *Olympic,* docked in New York, Miss Mackay was engulfed by the press.

She gave as well as she got, denying all rumors of her engagement to Irving Berlin. Tossing a bouquet to a waiting Clarence, she said marriage would force her "to surrender my companionship of my father, and I can't bear to think of parting with Dad."

When one reporter asked if she would consider marrying a man without money, she retorted, "Are you proposing?" and drove off.

Frustrated, the reporters now descended on Berlin. "Engaged?" he replied to their questions. "I'm engaged to Sam Harris" (he was then beginning work on a new musical that Harris was to produce).

But the papers, and the tabloids especially, would not be put off their pursuit of gossip and romance. The *Daily Mirror* went so far as to publish, complete with dialogue, an account of a meeting between Irving Berlin and

Clarence Mackay, culminating in a heated exchange—a meeting that never actually occurred.

Berlin was unhappy and uncomfortable about this fiction; Mackay, for his part, was furious. Through his attorneys, he issued a statement:

> My attention has been drawn to an article this day published in a morning paper. It contained so many false statements that to treat any of them in detail would serve no useful purpose. There are, therein, three statements of very grave import, not merely to me but to others and perhaps even to a substantial part of the community and these I wish to meet with a denial of the strongest character.
>
> 1) His Holiness the Pope has never sanctioned and has never been asked to sanction a marriage between a daughter of mine and the person referred to;
> 2) I have not sought nor held an interview with that gentleman, nor have I ever seen him;
> 3) I know of no engagement between my daughter and him.

It was true that they had not met, but he *had* had others look into the life of the "person referred to" (whose name was still anathema to him). To this end, he had retained the services of the famous/infamous attorney Max Steuer, himself the son of immigrants and formerly of the Lower East Side, as well as being a brilliant graduate of the Columbia Law School. Steuer was highly regarded for his skill at successfully defending clients who were patently guilty, through his clever use of trickery and volatile cross-examination. Among his most notorious clients were fight promoter and fixer Tex Rickert; former member of the corrupt Harding administration and ex–Attorney General Harry Daugherty; and Chicago gangster Johnny Torrio, who left his bootlegging empire to his protégé Al Capone on retiring, a free man, to Italy.

Clarence Mackay had no objection to Jews who could give him what he wanted, and Steuer came through with the goods. Mackay summoned Irving Berlin's lawyer, Dennis O'Brien, to a meeting at which he presented him with what Steuer's detectives had dug up: Berlin was a drug addict, suffered from a venereal disease, and had mobster relatives (a convincing story since Steuer knew and had defended so many mobsters himself).

Not one of these allegations was accurate, O'Brien informed Mackay. The drug-addiction rumor could be traced back to Berlin's early life in Chinatown, where, in fact, he had not even so much as drunk spirits. He was not ill as described, and his brother and sisters were all married and gainfully employed. A disappointed Mackay took the news quite well, considering, though not without making some further protestations as to the hopelessness of the match. He even apologized, but he would not concede.

Unwillingly, Ellin herself was to provide Clarence with another stratagem after she had her tonsils removed in May. During her convalescence at home, she was able to talk on the phone with Berlin thanks to the complicity of Mary Finnerty, who did not tell her father about the incoming calls.

Anxious to see her fiancé, Ellin soon insisted on leaving Harbor Hill for New York, where Berlin took her for a drive during which she talked incessantly. To his horror, blood began to dribble from her mouth; the exertion had brought on hemorrhaging, requiring a return to bedrest.

When she next communicated with him, it was by wire, after her father's meeting with O'Brien. She and Clarence had a talk that evening; Ellin assured Berlin that there was nothing to worry about, but she said their wedding must be postponed until the fall, for "I go west in July for the summer." She promised to get in touch with him later and implored him not to call.

So it was that for two months, beginning in July, Ellin Mackay traversed parts of western Canada and then traveled southward from Vancouver to California. The separation almost brought about the break that Mackay was hoping for. While Ellin, far away, was feeling that the "whole thing seemed hopeless," Berlin was hard at work on a musical he was scoring for the Marx Brothers. The angst he experienced in the making of this show—the time it consumed, the changes required during its tryout tour, and the concentration demanded of him—may account for the apparent paucity of communications, in contrast to the flow that had brightened Ellin's European sojourn the previous winter. This much shorter separation, without either letters or calls, made her think that perhaps their engagement was truly doomed.

Berlin had got himself into his current predicament innocently enough. The previous year, the Marx Brothers (now down to four out of their initial five) had made the transition from vaudeville to Broadway in a nondescript "musical comedy revue," the practically scoreless—and plotless—I'll Say She Is. Onstage, the Marxes virtually rewrote the script, by librettist-lyricist Will B. Johnstone (the music was by his brother Thomas), during every performance. On a given night, a typical Groucho line might go, "You are charged with murder, and if you are convicted, you will be charged with electricity." The show became an instant hit, and the brothers acquired a cult following.

Even as their show continued its successful run, the brothers fielded offers from several producers, including the Shuberts and Ziegfeld. Although they specialized primarily in revues, the Marxes agreed among themselves that they wanted to remain on Broadway. The only major producer who did *not* approach them was Sam H. Harris.

Harpo Marx, like Berlin, was a member of the Algonquin Round Table. A much more active participant than Berlin, he cornered the songwriter during one of his rare appearances there and asked him to talk to Harris about their doing a show together. Berlin kept his promise, but Harris was skeptical; he had heard about the Marxes and their peculiar brand of mayhem, which was hilarious for the audience but not for the producer or the writers. When Berlin persisted, Harris finally gave in and suggested that he invite the Marxes up to run through some of their routines. "The comics hurried over," Scott Meredith would report in his biography of George S. Kaufman, "and soon turned the Harris office into a madhouse, leaving Harris and his associates weak with laughter."

The producer continued to harbor doubts, however, and dismissed them with an "I'll let you know." He felt the decision required more thought. The Marxes were doing *I'll Say She Is* in Syracuse when they heard from Harris, who offered to produce their second show. His next call was to Kaufman, another Round Tabler, whom he asked, "How would you like to write a show for the Marx Brothers?"

Kaufman was familiar with their act and came to the point instantly: "I'd as soon write a show for the Barbary apes." He was aware of what they had done, and kept doing daily, to the script of *I'll Say She Is,* but he granted that the revue's success could be attributed to the Marx madness. At the moment when Harris called him, Kaufman was just completing his own *The Butter and Egg Man,* which was booked to open in September (and destined to be a hit). He had no need of the Marxian frenzy.

Harris told him of his own misgivings and how he had at last made up his mind, saying, "I wanted to be sure myself that I was willing to rent a room in a lunatic asylum." He had undertaken to produce the show for artistic as well as commercial reasons, and he believed Kaufman should do the same.

"How do you write for Harpo?" the writer countered. "All you can say is 'Harpo enters,' and then he's on his own." Kaufman then went through the others, one by one: the good-looking vocalist, Zeppo (real name Herbert), needed straight lines; Chico (Leonard) had to have Italian dialect; and Groucho (Julius)—well, Groucho was Groucho. It was easier to write for Harpo (Adolph).

But in time Harris did manage to talk Kaufman into writing a play for the Marx Brothers—"all seventeen of them," as he phrased it. Now it was Berlin's turn: he had got his partner into the project in the first place, so Harris felt it only fitting that he should score it. He was not busy; he had finished the final Music Box Revue and was spending most of his time mooning over the wandering Ellin. About all he had accomplished since the Revue opened was a single song, written on Christmas Day 1924 and obviously (though he denied it) inspired by her absence: "Remember."

Harris reminded Berlin how warmly he himself had commended the Marxes, and what a great opportunity and honor he had claimed it would be for Harris to produce a show starring the town's hottest new comedy team. Wouldn't writing songs for such a show be just as big a chance for the composer? Berlin conceded the point and began working with Kaufman and his uncredited assistant, Morrie Ryskind. (After writing *The Butter and Egg Man* by himself, Kaufman—who had earlier teamed up with both Marc Connelly and Edna Ferber—felt the need of a collaborator on the Marx Brothers project; Franklin P. Adams introduced him to Ryskind, whose work had appeared in his column.)

Berlin faced a number of obstacles in composing songs for this show. Of the Marxes, only Zeppo sang in a light, passable tenor, while Chico entertained with tricky, often one-fingered pianistics and Harpo played the harp. Whereas Zeppo might be relied upon to sing a song from a Berlin score, Chico and Harpo would interpolate anything that suited their unpredictable fancies.

And then there was Kaufman. The songwriters he worked with suspected that he believed their songs intruded into his book, and that he resented seeing the plot suspended for the sake of a sentimental ballad or "pointless" dance. "Funny thing about Kaufman," Ira Gershwin once mused. "It's very funny, considering he did so many musicals—he hated music, you know."

Kaufman would contradict Gershwin on that score in "Music to My Ears," an article written for the August 1938 issue of *Stage* magazine. "Mind you," he began, "I like music. If the Society of Ascaps or whatever it is wants to take a small ad in the *Times* and quote me, that's fine with me. 'Music is all right'—George S. Kaufman." But in the same piece he went on to admit that he often had to hear a song several times before he "got" it (an honest admission that many a fellow critic could make), and that there were some things he would never get, such as the "unbelievable invention known as swing[, which] is strictly for mental defectives." He concluded by invoking four of the composers he had worked with up to that time: Arthur Schwartz, Richard Rodgers, George Gershwin, and Irving Berlin.

Writing in the *New Yorker* a couple of decades later, Kaufman was to recall one song he liked straightaway—or more or less so. It happened in Atlantic City, where

> Irving Berlin and I went . . . together to work on a musical show for the Marx Brothers. . . . We had adjoining rooms in the hotel, and along about the second week Irving woke me up at five o'clock one morning to sing me a song he had just finished. Now, Irving has a pure but hardly strong voice, and since I am not very strong myself at five o'clock in the morning, I could not catch a word of it. Moving to the edge of the bed, he sat down and sang it again, and again I failed to get it. Just when it looked as though he would have to get into my bed before I could hear it, he managed, on the third try, to put it across.

In short, on his actual first hearing of it, Kaufman liked the song, and "as the dawn broke we leaned out of the window and sang it to the Atlantic ocean—its first performance in any hotel. It was destined to be sung millions of times after that"—though not in their Marx Brothers show, *The Cocoanuts*. True to his penchant for cynicism in the presence of sentiment, Kaufman could not resist a display of his famous wit, being

> presumptuous enough then to question Irving's first line, "I'll be loving you, always." "Always," I pointed out, was a long time for romance. There were almost daily stories to that effect in the newspapers—stories about middle-aged husbands who had bricked their wives up in a cellar wall and left for Toledo with the maid.
>
> I suggested, therefore, that the opening line be just a little more in accord with reality—something like "I'll be loving you Thursday."

As it turned out, Kaufman had outwitted himself, unaware as he was of the songwriter's sensitivity: if Berlin felt the intended recipient did not care for a song, he would file it away and write another. (This would occur again some years later, but in that case the culprits involved would succeed in arguing the song back into the score.) Fated one day to become Ellin's song, "Always" was indeed, as Kaufman noted, sung by millions.

From Atlantic City, Berlin and Kaufman, with a finished score and libretto pristine and untouched by Marxian editing, moved back to Manhattan for auditions, casting, and rehearsals before setting out again for Boston, the first stop of the tryout tour. By then it was September, and Ellin Mackay had returned from her travels, during which she had decided to end her engagement to Berlin. Accustomed to disappointment, he took the news with his customary equanimity. Despite the break, they continued to see one another, though he was preoccupied with the shambles of *The Cocoanuts.* Ellin's mother, for her part, sensed that her daughter was "still in love with [Berlin] and very unhappy."

No more so than Berlin himself, who was nonetheless forced to head north with the *Cocoanuts* company. While he suffered in Boston, Ellin Mackay initiated a literary career. It began when her cousin Alice Duer Miller, a member of the board of the struggling *New Yorker,* encouraged her to write an article expressing some of her opinions on life on the North Shore and society in general. Her first piece, entitled "Why We Go to Cabarets—a Post-Debutante Explains," shocked some of her friends and her father by its frank admission that she frequented such places. Her young friends knew all about it, of course, but not those she called the Elders, who "criticize many things about us, but usually . . . attribute [to us] sins too gaudy to be true." In part, she suggested, this was because the Elders believed the picture painted by the Flaming Youth novels of F. Scott Fitzgerald and Gertrude Atherton. "*Cabaret,*" she surmised,

> has its place in the elderly mind beside *Bohemia* and *Bolshevik,* and other vague words that have a sinister significance and no precise definition.
>
> It is not because fashionable young ladies are picturesquely depraved that they go to cabarets. They go to find privacy. . . . We have privacy in a cabaret. What does it matter if an unsavory Irish politician [this detail cannot have pleased Clarence Mackay] is carrying on a dull and noisy flirtation with the little blonde at the table behind us? We don't have to listen; we are with people we find amusing.

Not only did the article cause flurries of displeasure along Park Avenue and throughout the Hamptons, it even inspired outraged editorials in the press (over which *New Yorker* editor Harold Ross was exultant). Ellin's comparison of cabarets, where a debutante could dance with whomever she pleased, to society parties, at which the same girl was expected to dance with anyone who asked—from a stag line comprising a collection of "extremely unalluring specimens" culled from the Upper West Side or Brooklyn—drew the ire of one editor, who predicted that Clarence Mackay's Postal Telegraph Company would lose some of its Brooklyn customers as a result.

All the to-do boosted the *New Yorker*'s circulation, and Ross soon demanded a sequel. In "The Declining Function," published in the issue dated December 12, 1925, the author asserted that as a liberated woman, she would seek her pleasures and joys where she wished. To her father, one sentence must have seemed particularly ominous: "Modern girls are conscious of their identity and they marry whom they choose, satisfied to satisfy themselves." Three days after the magazine appeared on the stands, *The Cocoanuts* opened at the Lyric Theatre; Berlin's guest that night was the controversial rebel Ellin Mackay.

Even as the *New Yorker* had circulated his beloved's initial apostasy, Berlin had been enduring his own anguish up in Boston. The first-night performance ran forty minutes too long, owing to bits of business and ad-libs gratuitously tacked on to the Kaufman-Ryskind book. Every one of the critics, and some of the audience, left before the final curtain. Berlin, Kaufman, Ryskind, director Oscar Eagle, dance director Sammy Lee, and a concerned Sam Harris worked through the night cutting text, a specialty dance or two, and songs.

The Marxes rehearsed the edited version the next day, but when they performed it that night, *The Cocoanuts* was even longer than it had been the night before. The group assembled again for more cutting, with Berlin's suggesting that if they kept on at this rate, they would eventually "have a musical without music." The overtime continued until a union official threatened to take the stagehands off the job if they were not out of the theater by eleven o'clock.

Kaufman and Berlin conferred with Harris, and all three agreed to confront the Marxes together. They went to their dressing room and waited. Finally deciding to tackle "the boys" by himself, an agitated Harris told the others to await him in the corridor. The brothers at last arrived; the door closed behind them. Moments later, it opened again and Harris's clothing flew out, followed by a nude producer.

Summoning up as much dignity as he could, Harris said to Kaufman and Berlin, as he turned a corner, "I guess you'd better handle it." Writer and songwriter managed to remain fully clothed while pointing out the show's problems, but it didn't do them much good: the Marxes persisted in their antics in the Philadelphia tryout. On December 8, 1925, *The Cocoanuts* had its New York premiere at the Lyric; it was a triumph.

Something inexplicable had happened between Boston and New York. The show was still protracted—the first night on Broadway played until near midnight—but this time no one fled. The critics did light out a bit early to file their raves for the morning papers, but the laughing audience stayed in their seats through the last notes of the finale, after which they cheered wildly. (Not least among the road improvements was simple excision: if a line or a gag, whether Kaufman-Ryskind's or the Marxes', got no laugh, it was out.)

In time, the production took shape despite the unpredictability of the Marxes, whose spontaneous bits made the performances longer, to the delight of their audiences. One night, during one of Groucho's scenes (probably with his long-suffering, unperturbable matron, Margaret Dumont), Harpo persuaded a chorus girl to run across the stage as he pursued her, leering and honking his horn. Proving he could be as composed as the stately Dumont, Groucho waited a beat, looked at his watch, and said, "The nine-twenty's right on time." This gag went over so well it was kept in the show.

Groucho was the most shameless of the libretto-tinkerers. Another night, he broke off in midscene, moved to stage front, peered apprehensively into the auditorium, and inquired, "Is there a doctor in the house?"

A man in the front row rose and said, "*I'm* a doctor."

"How do you like the show so far, Doc?" Groucho asked.

Yet another time, spotting the President seated in a box, he stopped the show to call to him, "Isn't it a little past your bedtime, Cal?" (Coolidge was known for his starchy, abstemious Vermont ways.)

With such irreverent, but funny, improvisation taking place pretty much nightly, *The Cocoanuts* soon assumed cult status. Writer Heywood Broun saw it twenty-one times during its long (377-performance) run; golfer Bobby Jones admitted to (a mere) twelve. The Marxes continued to run riot, in spite of the tightening and admonitions; Berlin and Kaufman-Ryskind were simply overwhelmed (and, to a great degree, overlooked in the reviews). It is unlikely that anyone in the audience had any idea of which lines were whose, though the writers' general plot remained. Groucho was the slippery owner of a run-down hotel named The Cocoanuts—in Cocoanut Beach, Florida— who moonlights as a real estate developer. (The musical's theme was inspired by the Florida land boom of the day, a bubble that would burst in 1926, when lots purchased by speculators, advertised as being "outside of Miami Beach," turned out to be *seventy miles* outside, or even worse, after that year's hurricanes, under water. Kaufman and Ryskind's cynical take thus proved prophetic.)

A subplot had to do with a jewel robbery, with suspicion falling (wrongly) on a young architect-to-be (John Barker) working in a menial job at the hotel. He loves Polly Potter, daughter of the stolen jewelry's rich owner (Dumont), who has another man in mind for her. The mother's candidate is actually a fortune hunter, and in on the jewel heist. All is solved, of course, by the final curtain's "A Little Bungalow" reprise.

The Cocoanuts was a sellout in its Broadway run, inspiring Harris to announce a "New Summer Edition" of the show, slated to debut in June 1926, with "new twists and dialogue" and four new Berlin songs. Among the promised twists was the addition of the soon-to-be-famous "Why a Duck?" routine featuring Groucho and Chico. The critical reception given the revised version would be as ecstatic as the one the previous December. The *Times* would voice the consensus opinion: "Thus refurbished *The Cocoanuts* maintains its prestige among the best musical shows of the season. For Harpo Marx has not improved his manners in the least, nor has the garrulous Groucho lost his instinct for trade at any price, upon any terms that offer— honorable, dishonorable, or blatantly fraudulent." Even as a "best," the show in one respect lived up to Berlin's earlier fear: it remained a musical comedy without music, at least as far as the critics were concerned.

Musical historians and researchers tend to dismiss Berlin's *Cocoanuts* songs as minor efforts. It is true that they were not widely taken up by popular singers, in part because many of them were too "integrated" (before that term became trendy)—"The Bellhops," for example, which began the first act, or "Florida by the Sea," likewise too plot-related (though a good tune nonetheless). But "The Monkey Doodle-Doo," a syncopated dance number whose lyrics advise, "If you're too old to dance, get yourself a monkey gland" (another fraudulent fad of the time), is neatly done, and the lilting ballad "A Little Bungalow" is prime Berlin, as is the lovely, sinuous "Tango Melody."*

In his "Diary of Our Own Samuel Pepys" for December 8, 1925, Franklin P. Adams noted, "All day at my scrivening, and in the evening with my wife to see 'The Cocoanuts,' which had more things I laughed at than anything I can remember at all, in especial the anticks and comick sayings of Julius [i.e., Groucho] Marx. So to H[erbert Bayard] Swope's, and met there Miss Ellin Mackay, the essayist, a fair girl to see and sweetly spoken." There is no mention made of Irving Berlin, who escorted her to the party. The couple continued to meet; his Christmas gift to her that year was a gold cigarette case, for all sophisticated young women (she was now twenty-two) who frequented cabarets smoked—with holders, of course.

---

*The score was sufficiently appreciated to convince the Victor Light Opera Company to record a medley of *Cocoanuts* songs in early March 1926. Among the company were such important vocalists as incipient opera star Richard Crooks and the popular Franklyn Baur, future member of the Ipana Troubadours and a featured performer in an upcoming Ziegfeld Follies.

They danced in the New Year at the Mayfair House on Park Avenue, where he told her he would be leaving for Europe that Sunday, the third. This cast a pall over the beginning of 1926.

On Saturday, January 2, FPA's "Pepys" reported engaging in a game of

cards, and things went ill with me past one in the morning, and then I. Berlin came in, and played with us [Henry Miller, actor and husband of Alice Duer, and George S. Kaufman] till near four, and I won back all I had lost and a trifle besides, owing to Irving's ineptitude and ill-luck. Then he did leave, and we fell to speculating as to whether he would be the Lochinvar to wed the fair Ellin, and I said nay, and offered to wager a great sum that he would not marry at all, but nobody would bet with me.

The "inept," abstracted "Lochinvar" definitely had something on his mind. Before dropping in on the poker game, he had had dinner at the Morgan Harrimans' on Park Avenue. His hostess was the writer Margaret Case Harriman, daughter of the owner-manager of the Algonquin; significantly, the other guests were actress-mimic-songwriter Elsie Janis and her mother. Berlin had known the "Sweetheart of the A.E.F.," who sang for the Yanks in France during the war, since 1916, when they collaborated on "It Takes an Irishman to Make Love"; three years later, they had created "I Never Knew," for which she wrote the lyric. Elsie had also collaborated with Jerome Kern on some of his early songs, and was a fellow charter member of ASCAP. Her own most popular number was "Love, Your Magic Spell Is Everywhere," written with Edmund Goulding. She and Berlin had, over the years, become good friends (she was about a year younger than he), and to the delight of Mrs. Janis, he frequently spent weekends at the family's estate, swimming in the summer and ice-skating in the wintertime.

Mrs. Janis had, in fact, "always been not too secretly in favor of a marriage between Elsie and Irving, who were devoted friends although not matrimonially inclined," Margaret Harriman would later recall, adding that

throughout dinner [Mrs. Janis] kept pointedly remarking on the virtues of married life. "Just look at Margaret and Morgan!"

After dinner Elsie and Mrs. Janis had to hurry down to the Palace Theatre where Elsie was playing, and after a while Irving left too, saying he had a date. The date the little rascal had was to get married to Ellin Mackay.

He missed his boat on Sunday.

On Monday, January 4, 1926, after a telephone call from Mr. Berlin to Miss Mackay, the hurried acquisition of a ring, and the bride-to-be's arrival at West Forty-sixth Street, the wedding party boarded a subway (Ellin's first time), bound for City Hall downtown. The extremely nervous groom was accompanied by his faithful friend and partner Max Winslow, Winslow's wife, Tillie, and—luckily—the Berlin office manager, Ben Bloom.

Winslow later told a reporter from the *World* a little more of the story. "I got a call from Irv at my home at nine o'clock in the morning. Then I knew something was up. He always sleeps until noon or later. 'Come on down,' he told me, 'I want your help in something. And bring Tillie.'"

"I guess he's getting married today, calling this early," was Mrs. Winslow's response.

"When we got down [to Berlin's house]," Winslow continued, "about eleven o'clock, Miss Mackay was there. They told us they were going to get married. They had arranged it over the telephone. Miss Mackay had come down at once. That was the way they always said they'd do it. 'We'll do it on the spur of the minute, when we do marry,' they used to say."

Suddenly worried, Berlin turned to Winslow and said, "There's liable to be a lot of details, better get Bennie. He can put it through for us fast."

"At the Municipal Building Bennie Bloom saw to the details," the reporter filled in.

They required one minute. He caught [Deputy City Clerk J.J.] McCormick, bound for lunch on the fly.

"Irv Berlin's getting married," he said. "Do it fast."

"One minute's all I need," said McCormick. "Who's your friend?"

"Berlin," was the answer.

For a second, the clerk thought *Winslow* was the groom-to-be.

Word soon spread that a famous couple was getting married. When someone recognized Berlin, newsmen covering City Hall and the courts left their beats to investigate the more intriguing event occurring downstairs. It *was* Irving Berlin, and wasn't that the famous, rich "postdebutante"? She was wearing a none-too-stylish dress (when Berlin called, she was just on her way out to have her hair done). Ellin, too, began to feel the pressure.

When they applied for their license, the bridegroom discovered that he had brought no money with him. Bennie Bloom came up with the requisite two dollars. Immediately, this neutral marriage ground excited curiosity:

how could a Catholic marry a Jew without the ritual of conversion and then a proper wedding in a church or a synagogue? And of even greater significance, what did Clarence Mackay have to say about it? The answer was nothing, for he was completely unaware of the proceeding, at least while it was taking place.

After the ceremony, the ever-helpful Bloom provided the newlyweds with cab fare back to Forty-sixth Street, where they made the necessary calls to inform their respective families. Berlin asked his youngest sister, Chasse (or Gussie), to tell their brother Ben and other surviving sisters, Sarah and Rebecca. Then it was Ellin's turn. With trepidation, she rang the Mackay town house on East Seventy-fifth Street. According to her daughter Mary Ellin, the phone was picked up by her faithful ally Mary Finnerty, who, upon hearing the news of the wedding, promptly fainted. A valet came on next, wanting to know what had made "Finny" swoon; when told, he offered to phone Mr. Mackay at his office. Ellin followed up with calls to her grandmother and her mother, neither of whom fainted. Both were happy to learn of the marriage.

Clarence Mackay, predictably, was not. He was even more unhappy when he read the front pages of the next day's papers. The *Times* trumpeted, "Ellin Mackay Wed to Irving Berlin; Surprises Father." Elsewhere it was reported that the newlyweds had sped away, ignoring the bride's Rich Father, whose first postnuptial act was to draw up a new will and cut out his daughter completely.

Speeding away had not, unfortunately, been a feasible option for the besieged "elopers." All through the cold, wet, dark afternoon of their wedding day, they were confined to Berlin's—now their—apartment, with a ringing telephone and reporters waiting outside in the street. Berlin had booked them passage to Europe on the *Leviathan,* scheduled to leave on Saturday, but Saturday was still five days off; in the interim, they needed to get away and hide out alone somewhere. They planned to take a train from Grand Central Station to Atlantic City, reasoning that because it was the off-season, the resort would be sparsely populated. And it was, except for the press horde that followed them there.

Even their friend FPA covered their movements in his quaint column: on Monday he wrote, "Great news this day that I. Berlin hath married Ellin Mackay, and Lord! how glad I am of it, and how happy none did accept my wager that it would not happen." The following day, January 5, he rightly expressed a doubt, "to office betimes, and read all the tayles in the publick prints of Irving and Ellin, and how they have gone to Atlantic City, a poor place, methought, to hide away from the pressmen."

Apparently there was no privacy to be had. They were staying at the Ritz Hotel, having arrived late the night before after missing their train and being driven down by Jack MacKenzie. They had barely settled into their suite when reporters converged on the place, in the lobby at first, and then in the tenth-floor hallway. On the sixth of January the Berlins granted an interview, in which they denied that the marriage had been sudden: "We have known each other for years," Ellin told the reporter from the *Times*. She did admit, "I got married in my oldest dress. I didn't have time to dress because we were married two hours after we decided to go through with it." Of the greatest concern to Ellin was her father's cold silence; a telegram inviting him to come to Atlantic City to see them had so far gone unanswered.

The next day FPA's column noted that he was "reading these tayles of how C. Mackay is wood-wroth that his daughter hath wedded I. Berlin." Some of the less responsible papers had gone so far as to print "statements" that neither the Berlins nor Mackay had actually made. Berlin, uncharacteristically angry over the fictions (though not over the stories in the *Times*, which, though in pursuit like the rest of the pack, was both honest and fair in its reportage), sent a notice to the ruthless tabloids:

> We desire to avoid publicity but we have been misquoted so much that we wish to make this statement in order to set to rest the fabrications that have been published in certain newspapers.
>
> We have never said one word for publication except that we are very happy. That statement we repeat and beyond that we have nothing to say.

Four days after the wedding, Mackay's office would only revisit his original reaction, appending a terse sentence at the end: "The marriage came as a complete surprise to me and was done without my knowledge and approval. Beyond that I have nothing to say. Statements published since were false."

Early on the afternoon of January 6, the Berlins had left their hotel in Atlantic City and squeezed through the crowd of reporters and photographers to catch a train back to Manhattan. All the way to the station they were relentlessly hounded by the "gentlemen of the press," who got an anxious and distraught Ellin to confess that she had not yet heard from her father. The couple gave their pursuers the slip by getting off the train at Newark, where MacKenzie was waiting with the limousine. The *Leviathan* was booked to leave in three days; unfortunately, the *World* had published the name of the ship in its interview with Max Winslow.

On January 8, Alexander Woollcott threw the Berlins a farewell party at his apartment at the far end of West Forty-seventh Street, practically adjacent to the pier where the *Leviathan* was docked. Early the next morning, Saturday the ninth, they managed to sneak out of Woollcott's building unseen and board the liner, which left the dock that afternoon. By Monday the eleventh, Irving and Ellin Mackay Berlin were well out to sea; they had been married for exactly a week. "Some honeymoon," the publicity-battered bride had laconically observed during that helter-skelter seven-day period. The highlight of this trying time was Berlin's presentation of "Always" to Ellin as a special wedding gift; it was *her* song, music, words—especially the words— plus copyright and royalties.

Their suite aboard the *Leviathan* assured them of a week of peace and relative quiet; to provide further comforts, Ivan, Berlin's valet-cook, accompanied them, as did Ellin's "diminutive, ferociously loyal French maid, Hermine Tripet," in Mary Ellin Barrett's phrase. There were occasional interruptions when the steward brought them radiograms from well-wishers (not including Clarence Mackay); Berlin's sister Gussie sent a message and a basket of fruit. In his column, FPA reported that on their one-week anniversary, he received "a wireless cable from Irving and Ellin, saying they were having a wonderful time."

All too soon, their ship docked in Southampton, and with Ivan and Hermine attending to the luggage, the couple entrained for London. Upon arriving at Waterloo Station, they were shocked to see a huge crowd gathered on the platform; suddenly a men's chorus burst into song. Berlin recognized the tune as the "Drinking Song" from Sigmund Romberg's *The Student Prince in Heidelberg,* which had opened in London the day before their marriage and in New York two years before.

They soon learned that the chorus of the show had in fact come to the station to welcome producer J. J. Shubert, in the belief that he would be on their train from Southampton (he had, it eventuated, other plans); mistaking Irving Berlin for their man, they gave him what the *Daily Express* would call an "astonishing reception."

Before entering a waiting car, Ellin informed a reporter that they had had a lovely trip, were happy, and had as yet had no word from her father. They registered at the Carlton, whose management assigned them a uniformed guard to screen all visitors, keeping a particular watch for reporters disguised as waiters or representing themselves as colleagues or friends. They were back on the honeymoon merry-go-round.

One evening they emerged from their suite and braved the flashing of cameras to see Berlin's old friend Sophie Tucker, then at the end of a long run at the Kit Kat Club, the London nightspot of the moment. When she spotted the songwriter in the audience, Tucker coaxed him onstage to accompany her in his "Remember." And so the world's most public marriage spun on, amid cables, letters, flowers by the bushel, and reporters and photographers giving constant chase.

Although a standard, non-Buick piano was at hand, Berlin had no time for songwriting, despite his promise to Harris of some new songs for the summer edition of *The Cocoanuts,* scheduled for early June. Still, he did accomplish a little business, meeting with English librettist Frederick Lonsdale to discuss an elaborate revue to be staged at the Theatre Royal later in the year.

At the end of January, the couple moved on to Paris. Berlin did no further work here; now it was his wife who was the celebrity. The February issue of *Vogue* carried an article by her about that new dance craze the Charleston— new, that is, to society's young flappers. She praised the dancers in Broadway shows: "Anyone who has studied the Charleston, who has undergone the strenuous process of 'stretching and limbering' before being permitted to learn a single step, will never be able to watch with placid, matter-of-fact acceptance the skilful dancing of the chorus in the musical shows." She confided that the westbound streets of New York were "clogged with smart motors bearing ladies to the Broadway dance emporiums. Some go anonymously in taxis. There are ladies who plan to say nothing of their studies until they can startle the world with their proficiency."

And it *was* startling, this energetic, eccentric dance of Flaming Youth, though it had, in point of fact, been around for some time before being discovered by the North Shore and Park Avenue. "The Charleston" was the title of a song written for a 1923 musical, *Runnin' Wild,* with words by Cecil Mack and music by James P. "Jimmy" Johnson. By 1925, when the popularity of the dance had spread, George Gershwin used its characteristic syncopated rhythm in the opening of his Concerto in F; that same year, Ellin's husband had published "They're Blaming the Charleston." Inspired, no doubt, by Mrs. Berlin's article, one of the songs he would write for the summer *Cocoanuts* was to be entitled "Everyone in the World Is Doing the Charleston."

Paris proved to be reasonably quiet, but the weather did not encourage sightseeing. Returning to London only to find the weather there even rawer, they packed and shipped off again to the gentler winds of the Portuguese island of Madeira. Their interlude in the peaceful city of Funchal would be the most relaxed segment of their European travels. Berlin wrote to his sister to tell her he was "happier than I have ever been in my life. Ellin is wonderful and we are having a fine time together." In a burst of creativity he wrote a waltz, "At Peace with the World," describing their idyllic weeks at Funchal. It was all so serene, so enchanting, that when the time came for them to return to London, Ellin wept.

Soon afterward, Arthur Johnston joined their party to notate "At Peace with the World," four new *Cocoanuts* songs, and "How Many Times?," an immediate hit that the ubiquitous Brox Sisters would record in July 1926, while the Berlins were still abroad.

While her husband was working with Johnston, Ellin began to experience what turned out to be morning sickness. Eager to celebrate, the joyful father-to-be dashed out to Cartier (they were now, briefly, back in Paris) to buy her a beautiful jeweled bracelet. Somehow word got out (though Ellin informed only her mother and grandmother, and Berlin himself was tight-lipped), and a reporter from the *New York Tribune* called their suite at the Crillon to check: he had heard she was expecting a baby in June. (The implication was obvious—an explanation, perhaps, for their hasty marriage and subsequent long absence from the United States.)

The newsman managed to get only a couple of "no comments" from Ellin, along with a threat to sue him and his paper if they dared print the scurrilous rumor. He backed down.

By June, Ellin Berlin was four months pregnant and having a rough time of it. Although they hated the thought of contending with the American press, the Berlins wanted their child to be born in America. When, in August, the collaboration with Lonsdale fell through (the librettist could not come up with a book), there was no further reason for them to remain in London. They chose a roundabout route home, taking a train to Glasgow, Scotland, and there boarding the *Montnairn,* on whose passenger list they were registered as "Mr. and Mrs. J. Johnston."

The ship arrived in Quebec on August 21; Ellin was, at six months along, both patently pregnant and pale. They had been away for almost eight months. The "Johnston" ruse had not worked; they were met by reporters, some of whom had come all the way from New York. The daughter Ellin was then carrying would one day write in her memoirs of this homecoming:

> My mother . . . threw a fit, screaming and swearing, remembering
> nothing afterward [about] what she had said—and just as well, my
> father would tell her, it was pretty bad. Much later, a poised Ellin
> Berlin would meet one of those reporters. He recalled his side of
> things, how he had told the group assembled, "If we don't let that

woman alone, she'll lose her baby." He had covered waterfront saloons and longshoremen's strikes, said this newsman to my mother, but never in his life had he heard such language as issued forth from the pretty mouth of Mrs. Berlin. "Put it there, Mackay," said he, an Irishman himself.

Ellin Mackay Berlin was a spirited woman who had at her disposal a number of well-chosen words. Her husband put it more succinctly: "We beg for privacy."

MacKenzie waited for them in Berlin's car while they proceeded through Canadian customs with the aid of Ivan and Hermine, fussing all the while over her Ellin. They drove south more than four hundred miles, crossing the St. Lawrence River into New York. Their destination was the village of Alexandria Bay, some 250 miles from Manhattan, where the Winslows had an out-of-the-way summer cottage; the nearest town of any size was Watertown, about forty miles distant. Max and Tillie greeted them, and the next few days were spent quietly, Ellen resting and relaxing with Tillie, and the men getting in some fishing and a little golf.

Like locusts, the press soon descended upon them, particularly when they went into Watertown, which offered better communications facilities. MacKenzie was able to keep the newsmen away from the cottage, and he ran interference on the trips into town. The frenzied following of reporters and cameramen deeply impressed the townspeople, and even the *Watertown Times* joined the rush to print stories about the celebrated visitors. Deemed especially printable was an item about the Berlins' wiring flowers to the funeral of Rudolph Valentino in New York. The local paper also published their departure date.

After four almost revitalizing days with the Winslows, the Berlins boarded the New York train while MacKenzie drove back with some of their luggage. Arriving on the evening of August 29, they were swept once again into the news maelstrom. They escaped in a cab to the apartment at West Forty-sixth Street, ignoring the same questions as before, the same rumors and rumors of rumors—the most recent of these concerning Berlin's alleged intention to convert to Catholicism now that he was about to become a father. In what faith would the child be raised?

On September 1, 1926, a terse release from Berlin was published in several papers: "The report that Mrs. Berlin and I are to go through another ceremony is untrue. I shall deny no more of these false statements."

Nor was it an easy time for Ellin; hers was not a comfortable pregnancy, and she spent a good deal of time resting in bed. The duplex, while they were away, had been completely redecorated, transformed from a bachelor apartment into the home of Ellin and Irving Berlin, complete with a nursery and all the trappings.

While nervously awaiting the baby's arrival, Berlin turned to the Buick and worked on a song until the day came, late in November. On the twenty-fifth, Franklin P. Adams's "Pepys" reported going up to York House, a private hospital,

> to see my wife [who had had a son five days before], but met I. Berlin there, and he told me Ellin was to have a child soon, so I stopped with him till a nurse came by and told him he had a daughter, and he was greatly overjoyed, and in a few minutes I saw little Mary Ellin, as sweet a little girl as ever I saw. Lord! there have been so many babies born in this nursing home since last Friday.

November 25, 1926, was a Thursday, Thanksgiving Day; Mary Ellin's family would later joke that her birth, early in the afternoon, interrupted the doctor's dinner. It was a difficult delivery, and Ellin had to remain at York House until early December. Needless to say, her homecoming was fully covered by the tabloids; the *Daily Mirror* even published a photograph of Mary Ellin on its front page—only it wasn't really Mary Ellin.

Back at home, all went well with mother and babe, and Berlin completed his latest song and placed it in his files. On Christmas Day, with the apartment a mass of flowers—Berlin invariably sent his wife red roses on special occasions—and Mary Ellin precisely a month old, he took out his song and wrote on it:

For Mary Ellin, Christmas 1926

> *Blue days all of them gone*
> *Nothing but blue skies from now on.*

"Blue Skies," Mary Ellin's song, was destined to be one of Irving Berlin's most enduring creations. Aside from the four summer *Cocoanuts* additions, it was the only song of his to be sung in a Broadway musical that year (1926). Show-business legends have grown up around that interpolation.

The story began a few days before Christmas in Washington, D.C., where a much-troubled Ziegfeld production entitled *Betsy* was floundering. Its major stars were comedian Al Shean and Berlin's friend Belle Baker. Due to wrap up in Washington on Christmas Day, it was a most trying tryout, according to composer Richard Rodgers, who had written the score with Lorenz Hart. The production was one big skirmish, the reception was poor, and all concerned were in panicked contention. Librettists Irving Caesar and David Freedman fought with each other, Rodgers and Hart fought with them and with Ziegfeld, and Ziegfeld himself "went charging around the theatre, screaming like a wounded water buffalo," in the opinion of Rodgers. From Washington, Rodgers wrote to his wife, "I don't like it at all. The book, if you can call it that, is terrible, and the score has been such a source of extreme annoyance that I am anxious only to have done with it."

He would get his wish soon enough. On opening night in New York, three days after Christmas, Belle Baker, with chorus, sang "Blue Skies" at the beginning of act 2. Rodgers and Hart had not written that song; Rodgers had never even heard it before, and Ziegfeld had told him nothing about any interpolation. "Not only did the interpolated number get the biggest hand of the evening at the premiere," Rodgers later recalled, "but Ziegfeld also had arranged to have a spotlight pick out Berlin, seated in the front row, who rose and took a bow."

In this version of the story, Berlin seems to have been merely an innocent cat's-paw in a typical Ziegfeldian maneuver. Rodgers himself believed that the producer, hoping to salvage his messy show with something he thought could be a hit, had asked the songwriter to give him a number for *Betsy*. This is an unlikely scenario, however, for Ziegfeld was no judge of a song; he generally left that task to Gene Buck, who likewise never warned Rodgers and Hart about the interpolation. However it played out, there is no doubting that Ziegfeld personally authorized the insulting treatment of the show's words-and-music men.

Another, more plausible (if somewhat embroidered) explanation of what happened that night is part of Belle Baker's family tradition. According to this version, Baker called Berlin the night before *Betsy* was to open and complained that she was unhappy with her songs (though she had in fact been assigned one of Rodgers and Hart's best but little-known numbers, "This Funny World"). Would he write something for her to put into the show? Berlin informed her that at the moment he did have a song "in his trunk," and he had even thought of it as a good number for her, but it was not finished. Her son Herbert Baker, then six years old, would later recall that Berlin had only the first eight bars of "Blue Skies" and that he came over to the Abrahams' apartment (Baker was married at the time to Maurice Abrahams, with whom Berlin had written "Queenie, My Own" and "The Pullman Porters on Parade") to let them hear it.

The Abrahams, according to Belle's son (who could not sleep because of the noise), practically forced Berlin to expand the eight bars he had brought with him: "He couldn't get the middle [i.e., the release] eight," the then-six-year-old noted. (In fact, the complete song had been registered with the Copyright Office the week before this songwriting marathon allegedly occurred.) In any event, by seven o'clock on the morning of December 28, "Blue Skies" was ready and styled for Belle Baker to spring on an unsuspecting Rodgers and Hart.

The unfortunate irony in all this was that an Irving Berlin song was to be the hit of a Rodgers and Hart musical. *Betsy* ran for barely a month, and "Rodgers and Hart and Florenz Ziegfeld . . . ended 1926 with the biggest flop of their respective careers," Rodgers wrote. The former pair could take some solace in the fact that their *Peggy-Ann,* which opened the night before *Betsy,* would run for more than three hundred performances. Still, in Rodgers's opinion—and he had reason to know—"Ziegfeld was not a nice man." Baker, of course, would claim that the hit song had been written especially for her.

On January 4, 1927, the Berlins celebrated their first wedding anniversary in the company of Mary Ellin, now almost six weeks old. It had been a trying but exciting, beautiful time, and with "Blue Skies," Berlin had proved that he could still turn out a hit, always a cherished ambition.

If Mary Ellin's birth, the holidays, and the couple's anniversary went unremarked by a stony Clarence Mackay, other members of Mackay's set took a more aggressive approach. Their smug hostility was beautifully skewered in a wire-service article entitled "A Hideous Handicap," which appeared in a number of papers in smaller markets across the country (in her memoir, Mary Ellin Barrett cites the *St. Paul Herald,* the *Elmira Advertiser,* and the *Bridgeport {Conn.} Times,* but the piece obviously originated in some large syndicate in New York). In part, it read:

The name of Ellin Mackay[,] who before she married Irving Berlin, America's foremost songwriter, was herself America's foremost heiress, has been stricken from the chaste sheets of New York's Social Register.

Strangely enough, the latest edition of the Register made its annual debut on almost the very day that the Berlins' latest edition in the person of a blue-eyed seven-pound daughter was born.

The infant therefore faces life with a hideous handicap of neither its mother nor its own small self being given a paragraph, a sentence, even a period or comma in that arbiter of human destinies, the Social Register.

Perhaps the fact that Dad Irving is one of the best-known men in America, that his face looks down from the sheet music on millions of pianos, that his lilting tunes give joy to millions of people the world over, may compensate a bit. Perhaps, too, the fact that the names [in] the impeccably correct Social Register are put there for reasons of pedigree rather than of achievement may compensate the young lady, too.

Deciding to ignore such petty slights, Berlin took his little family to Palm Beach, Florida, whose gentle weather, sun, and tranquillity would, he believed, be good for Ellin, despite her abhorrence of Palm Beach and its social snobbery. Her predictions proved correct: her North Shore friends, even her relatives, snubbed them. Berlin shrugged it off; true, they were barred from the Everglades Club (which had a no-Jews policy), but the only clublike organizations that had ever meant anything to him anyway were ASCAP, the Friars, and the Lambs. He was reunited with two friends from the early days in Tin Pan Alley, Wilson Mizner and his brother Addison. Ellin, for her part, could claim one Gold Coast friend who had not deserted her, Nellie Livingston, Mary Ellin's godmother.

Anita Loos was there, too, and was spotted in a local dance hall with Ellin, doing the new dance craze, the Black Bottom, which had supplanted the Charleston. Berlin worked on a new song, the minor-keyed "Russian Lullaby"; he had also begun thinking about his next show for Ziegfeld, due to open in the summer.

When they returned to New York in the spring, Berlin's concern for Ellin took them, before the summer heat set in, to the bucolic Hudson River village of Dobbs Ferry, in Westchester County, an easy commute from Manhattan by automobile or train. In a quiet residential section (which description fitted most of the town), he rented a fine old stone house complete with a big lawn that stretched to a wooded area. The most modern feature of the place was a swimming pool. It was a graceful, green, birdsong-drenched environment in which one would hardly expect to find the likes of Irving Berlin.

By early summer he had been transformed by work into an absentee husband and father, which in time would nettle Ellin. After working all week on the songs for what was to become the *Ziegfeld Follies of 1927,* he would manage to drive up to Dobbs Ferry only on weekends. Ellin found herself resenting the isolation, with no friends nearby and only a weekend husband. She chafed to return to Manhattan.

The 1927 edition has been accorded a special significance in the history of the Follies, as the only production in which all the songs were the work of a single songwriter (not precisely true, but close enough). Of the dozen or so songs that Berlin wrote for this revue, which was among Ziegfeld's most lavish efforts, only one, "Shaking the Blues Away," would become a standard. It was introduced by a fashion designer turned vaudeville singer from Chicago, Ruth Etting, in her Broadway debut (she was to record her song and another from the show, "It All Belongs to Me," two weeks after the premiere).

The major problem with the show was that Ziegfeld, going against his usual practice, featured Eddie Cantor as his star and only Big Name; the lesser lights were comedians Harry McNaughton and Dan Healy and, besides Etting, vocalists Franklyn Baur, Claire Luce (who had appeared in the last Music Box Revue), and the dependable Brox Sisters, among others. For "Jungle Jingle," Luce made her entrance seated on an ostrich, backed by an elaborate Urban curtain splashed with tropical flora and fauna, including monstrous cobras and flamingos.

Ziegfeld laid out a total of $289,000 for this production (his most expensive to date), and while a good deal of that was spent on designer Urban's sets and costumes, the star money, and much of the burden of the show, belonged to Cantor. He did his standard blackface number, impersonated Mayor James Walker ("Jimmy" was the title of the song), and interpolated a hit by Walter Donaldson and George Whiting, "My Blue Heaven." The song was extraordinarily popular by the summer of 1927; if Berlin objected to its incursion, there is no record of it. Besides singing a couple of other songs, Cantor also appeared in several skits. When he began to complain of exhaustion, the show was forced to close after an investment-losing run of 167 performances.

Ziegfeld hauled Cantor into an Equity hearing and won his case, but the show remained closed. It was the producer's penultimate Follies, and his last for four years: in 1931, his final production would be staged with the usual squads of songwriters and stars, including a rising Ruth Etting. Ziegfeld would die the next year, aged sixty-five, bankrupt. It seems that of all the songwriters he employed, Berlin was the only one he treated respectfully (he was, in turn, the only producer the Gershwins ever sued). Despite its inauspicious beginning with *Betsy,* 1927 would end triumphantly for him when *Show Boat* premiered at the Ziegfeld Theatre in December.

The *Ziegfeld Follies of 1927* was no high point for Berlin, either, though he was pleased when some of the cast made a two-sided Victor recording of favorite numbers from the show: the Broxes sang "It's Up to the Band" and "Ooh! Maybe It's You" and were joined by Franklyn Baur for "It All Belongs to Me." Fairchild and Rainger, the show's duo-piano team (an idea borrowed from Gershwin), performed "Ticklin' the Ivories."

The critics pronounced the Follies "immense for the eye and ear," but they generally ignored what Berlin had created for the latter organ in favor of Ziegfeld et al.'s confections for the former. The *Tribune*'s Percy Hammond found the "First Minstrel's verse and music as naive as in the past" but predicted wide popularity for "It All Belongs to Me," "Shaking the Blues Away," and "Ooh! Maybe It's You." Burns Mantle of the *News* agreed and ventured that Berlin's "sense of melody [is] as perfect as any can be."

Such compliments seemed small consolation in light of the success that year of other musicals by other songwriters, notably *Good News!* (by DeSylva, Brown, and Henderson, 551 performances); *A Connecticut Yankee* (Rodgers and Hart, 418); *Funny Face* (the Gershwins, 244); and finally, in December, the big winner, Ziegfeld's *Show Boat* (Jerome Kern and Oscar Hammerstein II, 572). It was not Berlin's year, a reality that made him uneasy and restless.

Soon after the premiere of *Show Boat,* Berlin, having heard the siren song of Hollywood, left for the West Coast. It was not purely a business move, however: Ellin's doctor believed that her anemia and weight loss mitigated against her spending the winter in New York. Still, new things always excited Berlin; when Al Jolson's *The Jazz Singer* opened at the Warner Theatre in October, it was a revelation for him to hear "Blue Skies" sung on the screen. He sensed that the recently developed sound picture could be a wonderful vehicle for song.

The Berlins, in January 1928, celebrated their second wedding anniversary in a house they had rented adjacent to the just-opened Desert Inn, in Palm Springs, about a hundred miles east of Los Angeles. The dry desert air would be good for Ellin; Mary Ellin had a nanny, Hermine kept the household in order, and Jack MacKenzie eventually arrived in the family's new Rolls-Royce.

Irving Berlin was about to be initiated into the workings of a strange new industry. He would not have an easy time of it.

CROSS-COUNTRY
TRAUMA

T*HE JAZZ SINGER* was neither the first sound film nor precisely a musical, but a "feature" with songs. A year prior to its release, in the summer of 1926, the Warner brothers—Harry, Albert, and Jack—had introduced a newly developed (and still-evolving) device called the Vitaphone at the Metropolitan Opera House. The Vitaphone film (created "By Arrangement with Western Electric and Bell Telephone Laboratories") starred John Barrymore; *Don Juan* was in fact a silent, but it had recorded background music performed by the New York Philharmonic.

The Vitaphone was a primitive system that synchronized film using a disc and was limited in time by the amount of sound, whether speech or music, on the disc. This was good for short subjects and cartoons but hardly ideal for full-length features.

In fact, the ideal system already existed: Lee De Forest had introduced his Phonofilm in 1923. This method photoelectrically photographed the sound waves simultaneously with the visual action. The sound and picture were thus synchronized perfectly. In time this system would supplant the Vitaphone after Warner Brothers released their first all-talkie *Lights of New York* in 1928. When De Forest had initially introduced his Phonofilm it was dismissed as being inferior to sound from a disc. But by 1927 it had been improved by sound engineer Theodore W. Case, working with the Warners' rival William Fox, to produce the first Movietone newsreels, among them the Washington, D.C., reception of Atlantic flier Charles Lindbergh.

In 1928 the Warners lost their exclusive rights to sound and the race was on.

The first words spoken from the screen were imbued with the midwestern inflections of Will H. Hays, president of the Motion Picture Producers and Distributors Association of America and head of the Hays Office, formed to keep Hollywood "clean." In his introduction, Hays prognosticated an exciting new era for pictures and music.

To underscore the possibilities for the latter, several brief musical sequences had been shown before the full-length *Don Juan*. Among the musical celebrities performing were violinist Efrem Zimbalist and pianist Harold Bauer, who played a movement from Beethoven's Kreutzer Sonata, and Metropolitan Opera notables Marion Talley, Giovanni Martinelli, and Anna Case (mistress of Clarence Mackay).

Industrial panic ensued. A later presentation in Los Angeles proclaimed the experiment a major success, and *Variety* devoted its front page to the event. Below the banner headline VITAPHONE THRILLS L.A., articles were headed "Remarkable First Night Crowd Acclaims Vitaphone" and "New Era in Pictures, Says Hays of the Vitaphone." Naysaying Hollywood executives predicted that sound films were merely a flash in the pan; the fad would not last, and converting equipment and facilities to produce and show such novelties threatened to bankrupt the industry. The Warners were skirting ruin by investing in Vitaphone (and, moreover, borrowing to do it). But when short sound films began appearing here and there and proved to be good for the box office, the writing on the studio wall became obvious.

With their coffers jingling nicely (other studios converting to sound were now forced to license the Vitaphone technology from them), the Warners tried to persuade Al Jolson to star in *The Jazz Singer,* a silent with dubbed-in songs. (George Jessel, star of the stage version, had already turned them down.) Not yet completely solvent, the studio heads offered Jolson stock in the company in lieu of a salary, but he insisted on being paid in cash (a profound mistake in the long run).

Besides "Blue Skies," Jolson was programmed to sing a couple of traditional Jewish songs, including "Kol Nidre," and a few of his own trademark numbers. In a scene set in a cabaret, having done "Dirty Hands, Dirty Face" and preparing to launch into "Toot, Toot, Tootsie, Goodbye," the singer exclaimed to the applauding audience of extras, "Wait a minute! Wait a minute! You ain't heard nothin' yet. . . ." This spontaneous bit of dialogue was recorded on the soundtrack, and director Alan Crosland decided to keep it in and add a little more. Thus was the "talkie" born.

When the Berlins arrived in Los Angeles soon after New Year's, 1928, the studios, particularly Warner rivals Fox, First National, and Paramount, were in a frenzy of converting to sound and scrambling to raise the millions the changeover would require. Though a mediocre film at best, *The Jazz Singer* was a raging success in New York, as well as in Boston, Philadelphia, Chicago, and other large cities. Competing studios were forced to abandon any lingering hopes of fighting the "Warner Vitaphone peril," junk their silent technology, and resign themselves to paying royalties to the Warners for the rental of sound equipment. They could only pray that their long-term contracts with their silent stars would not prove to be a liability (many would, as a number of those actors' voices or accents would not record well). Contract directors, with no experience in filming music or dialogue, presented yet another opportunity for disaster.

As Hays had predicted, music became an important factor in movies with the advent of sound. But the studio heads and technicians had a lot to learn, as did Irving Berlin. If Tin Pan Alley had been a murky jungle, Hollywood, he would discover, was a glittering desert of quicksand.

He was not venturing solo into the unknown, however. Joseph Schenck was associated with a distribution company, United Artists (UA), formed in 1919 by reigning luminaries Mary Pickford, Douglas Fairbanks, Charlie Chaplin, and director D. W. Griffith. Schenck had joined the firm in 1924 as its head, bringing with him Rudolph Valentino, Buster Keaton, and Samuel Goldwyn.

The United Artists Corporation had an office but no studio. UA financed other companies' films as well as its own, and saw to the distribution of what it advertised as high-quality motion pictures. Its stars were among the most celebrated in the world, Griffith was the leading director of the day, and Schenck and Goldwyn were both shrewd showmen and businessmen. But there was not one musician among them.

When not basking in the sun in Palm Springs, Berlin dictated an occasional song to Arthur Johnston or drove in to Hollywood to meet with Schenck and company. During this period Berlin, Schenck, and Goldwyn also indulged in an inveterate, and often very costly, passion for poker.

As Hollywood retrenched for sound, the studios experienced anxiety and much bafflement over the technical aspects of shooting sound pictures with music; one difficulty was that the cameras had to be installed in soundproof booths because they made so much noise when running. With technicians, directors, and actors all floundering in their attempts to adapt to new ways, no new film musicals were produced in the immediate wake of *The Jazz*

Singer, though Jolson himself would repeat his earlier triumph in 1928's *The Singing Fool,* another part-talkie with a few songs that was to gross millions in the United States and Canada. (Berlin wrote "My Little Feller" for the film, but Jolson, by then given to imperious star turns, insisted on changes, and Berlin, as was his wont, withdrew the song.)

Until February 1929, the bulk of Hollywood's musical fare amounted to little more than the odd number or two or a theme song to promote a film. A classic example was "Ramona," from the movie of the same name, with words by L. Wolfe Gilbert and music by Mabel Wayne. Sheet music and recordings sold in the millions, and the picture profited accordingly.

Berlin's first Hollywood songs were, in a sense, also historic "firsts"—for Vilma Banky's first talkie, *The Awakening,* he wrote the waltz "Marie," and for Mary Pickford's sound debut, in *Coquette,* he penned the title song, another waltz. But these were no more than conventional theme songs. When *The Cocoanuts* was made into a film in 1929, it was conceived as a Marx Brothers vehicle with incidental songs, including a new one, "When My Dreams Come True." If some of the original score got lost in translation, the music was nonetheless all Berlin, and consisted of more than the single song featured in most movies. As a filmed stage show, it comes off as a rather shoddy production, of little more than minor interest, but the chorus dances are rather fascinating to watch.

By spring Ellin was feeling better, but also isolated. The Berlins moved closer to Hollywood, into a house in Santa Monica, where Ellin and Frances Goldwyn (wife of Berlin's poker adversary Samuel Goldwyn) became close friends, and Mary Ellin and young Sammy Goldwyn played together often.

While he waited for something to happen career-wise, Berlin got to know character actor–comedian James Gleason, also recently arrived in Hollywood. A lifelong show-business veteran, Gleason was an established playwright who had seen two of his plays successfully produced in 1925: *Is Zat So?* and *The Fall Guy* (the latter written with the multitalented George Abbott). Berlin and Gleason soon began sketching out a musical with a minstrel-show background, *Mister Bones,* for Al Jolson.

Around this time, Ellin discovered that she was pregnant; her physician, worried about her fragile health, suggested an abortion, but she refused.

Concerned about his wife, now two months along, Berlin in May moved his family back east to Port Washington, New York, so Ellin could be closer to her regular doctor—and within an easy drive of Clarence Mackay's mansion, though she had not heard from her father in more than two years. When she felt well enough, they attended musical-literary parties at the home of

Margaret and Herbert Bayard Swope. (Then executive editor of the *New York World*, Herbert was also a Pulitzer Prize winner and an enthusiastic poker player.) The Swopes' pseudo-salon attracted writers and show people who had settled in the more glamorous neighborhoods of Long Island, including Woollcott, the Kaufmans, and Harpo Marx.

Although he was not getting a great deal of work done during this period, Berlin did manage to write a couple of songs for *Mister Bones,* as well as some others, among them the poignant "How about Me?" He was going through what he called a dry spell, though in August he could write Ellin, then summering at the more comfortable Loon Lake in the Adirondacks, in upstate New York, that he was still working on the Gleason musical and had even had an idea for a short, operalike piece for Paul Robeson. Not long before, Otto Kahn, a fellow Russian immigrant made good, a Gold Coast resident, and a member of the board of the Metropolitan Opera, had approached several well-known songwriters and suggested that the Met might be willing to produce an American opera based on jazz themes and popular song. One of his targets was George Gershwin, who, though interested, wanted to defer his decision for a few years; Berlin, in the end, never got any further with his idea.

In September Ellin, now six months pregnant, was called back to Harbor Hill to see her grandmother, who had suffered a severe heart attack. Louise Mackay died on September 4, 1928. At the funeral services in Roslyn, Ellin sat in the front pew with her sister, Katherine, her brother, John William, and her father. Clarence was cordial but distant; Berlin did not attend.

Father and daughter had an incipient reconciliation after the funeral, when Mackay presented Ellin and her sister with some of their granny's possessions—jewels, furs, books, even handkerchiefs. Ellin closed one of her letters of thanks to her father with the words "I want so much to see you soon."

She *would* see him—and all *too* soon.

With the coming of the cooler months, the Berlins left Port Washington for a house in Sutton Place, where they awaited the birth of their second child, due around the end of November. After a strenuous and painful labor, Ellin gave birth to Irving Berlin, Jr., on December 1, 1928. Elated at having a son and relieved that mother and child had survived the ordeal, Berlin arrived at the hospital one day with a sapphire ring for his wife. If all went well, they should be at home in time for Christmas.

When Ellin was strong enough, Berlin happily took her and his son back to the Sutton Place house. All turned tragic, however, early Christmas morning, when the nurse found the baby dead in his crib. The cause was probably what is now known as sudden infant death syndrome, or "crib death," which kills children under a year old in their sleep, through a sudden cessation of breathing (possibly resulting from some defect in the central nervous system).

Mary Ellin, now two, could not understand the comings and goings at their house that Christmas Day. Her godmother Nellie (now Mrs. Frederick Cromwell) came over to help her distressed parents, and it was she who answered the bell to admit an ashen Clarence Mackay. Saying "Ellin is waiting for you, Mr. Mackay," she nodded her head in the direction of the stairs. On that grim, fateful Tuesday, Irving Berlin met his father-in-law for the first time, almost two years after the disputed marriage.

Some months later, in mourning and emotionally exhausted, her frailty still pronounced, Ellin allowed Berlin to take her down to Miami for a little sun and quiet, leaving Mary Ellin in the care of her "bossy" nurse. In Miami they encountered Ellin's brother, Willie, and his new bride, Gwen Rose. The Berlins had missed their February wedding, feeling unable to deal with celebration and laughter so soon after the death of their son. But now, in Miami, they found the newlyweds great fun. Willie, like his father no businessman, was a sportsman, a nightclubber, even a bandleader with his own little group; Clarence had spared him tenure in the Postal Telegraph Company by selling out in 1928, the year his son turned twenty-one.

As Gwen Mackay would recall this time years later for Mary Ellin Barrett's memoir,

> Irving was delightful; comfortable, so relaxed, and so attractive. That black hair, those bright eyes. He whipped us off on a boat for the day, but I also think they lived on a boat. We had a perfectly lovely time.
>
> Ellin was sweet and very quiet. I had the feeling she didn't want to see anyone much; and she didn't talk about the baby, not one word. You [Mary Ellin] were not there. I'd remember if you had been, because as a little thing you never stopped talking.

In March, after their return to New York, Berlin left for California again to write some songs for another historic film "first," King Vidor's *Hallelujah!* for Metro-Goldwyn-Mayer. "For several years I had nurtured a secret hope," Vidor would confess in his autobiography:

> I wanted to make a film about Negroes, using only Negroes in the cast. The sincerity and fervor of their religious expression intrigued me, as did the honest simplicity of their sexual drives. . . .

The answer from the studio executives to my pleading had always been a positive no. Now, with sound pictures, I had a new argument. . . . I made a list of scenes suitable for an all-Negro sound film—river baptisms, prayer-meetings, accompanied by spirituals, Negro preaching, banjo playing, dancing, the blues.

In other words, every stereotype in the book, and then some.

Vidor's next step was a meeting with Nicholas Schenck, brother of Joe and chairman of the board of Loew's, Inc., which controlled the monies that went into the films produced by Metro-Goldwyn-Mayer. The answer was still no: while there was a modest market for all-black films, a big production such as the one Vidor had in mind would not do well in the general market and would not be shown at all in the whites-only film houses of the South.

Vidor, whose silent war film *The Big Parade* had done very well for Metro two years before (grossing fifteen million dollars for the studio and putting it on its financial feet), now made an offer: he would match his considerable director's fee with Metro's backing to make the film.

Schenck, like his brother, was a gambler. "If that's how you feel about it, I'd let you make a picture about whores," he purportedly told Vidor.

The Texas-born director had grown up knowing the blacks who worked in his father's sawmill towns, and recalled, with nostalgia, his sister's being rocked to sleep each night "to one of the best repertoires of Negro spirituals in the South." While indigenous music was appropriate to, and used in, the film itself, Schenck felt Irving Berlin should contribute some popular songs for promotional purposes. Berlin's name, along with Vidor's, would also add some cachet to the production; the featured actors would not be well known in Hollywood, even if they lived there.

As his leading man, Vidor selected Daniel Haynes, who had been understudy to Jules Bledsoe, "Joe" in the Broadway production of *Show Boat*. Perky sixteen-year-old Nina Mae McKinney was plucked from the chorus of *Blackbirds of 1928* to portray the scheming temptress Chick; the rest of the cast was utterly unknown. Although Vidor had not counted on having to insert new songs into the film's score, Haynes sang Berlin's dignified, hopeful "Waiting at the End of the Road," and McKinney sang and danced (energetically) his "Swanee Shuffle." The former song was originally written for *Mister Bones,* but that musical had since been (temporarily) abandoned: around the same time *Hallelujah!* was being shot, James Gleason was appearing in a film he had written, *Oh Yeah.*

For all its clichés and stereotypes, *Hallelujah!* was a sincerely made film, often beautiful in its handling of light, shadow, and sound. The sequences featuring the Berlin songs were filmed at the studio, but the outdoor scenes—the spirituals, the prayer meetings, the singing in the cotton fields—were shot on location, near Memphis, with the sound added later in the studio. Synchronization was a difficult, and daunting, job. Vidor said he once "saw a cutter literally go berserk at his inability to get the job done properly. . . . [He] fell on the floor sobbing helplessly. I unwound him from the tangled maze [of film] and drove him home to the care of his wife. He remained in bed a week before he could again undertake the task of editing the film."

His must have been a total recovery, for some of the most favorable comments made about the film after its release in August 1929 were those praising its fusion of sight and sound. Because Vidor moved his camera around for the location scenes, the film often has a kind of impressionistic softness, a very different feeling than that generated by the static camera work that vitiated Hollywood's earliest musicals. *Hallelujah!* is in this sense a true "movie," its photography extraordinary for the composition of the frames and its range of shadings. Regrettably, Schenck had been right in the first place: while the film did well in larger cities—in New York it premiered in Times Square and Harlem simultaneously—it flopped in smaller markets and in the South. For Berlin, it was a more suitable assignment than mere theme-song writing, though it wasn't really a musical. But Hollywood wasn't finished with him yet.

He, however, had had enough of Hollywood—for now, at least. After *Hallelujah!* opened, in August, he and Ellin dropped off Mary Ellin with her aunt Katherine O'Brien in Southampton and took a break from everything, especially work, to do some traveling in Europe. Their itinerary included London, Paris, Italy (with a stopover to sun on the beautiful beaches of the Lido de Venezia), and Germany (with stays in Munich, Baden-Baden, and the Black Forest). It was a time of rest, sea and mountain air, and trees. Ellin's health improved, and Berlin shed the tension accumulated during his frustrating Hollywood sojourn—so completely, in fact, that he was ready to try it again.

He returned to America before his wife and arranged to rent a house in Hollywood that belonged to Joseph Schenck. The Goldwyns lived nearby, so Mary Ellin, almost three, was able to renew her friendship with Sammy Goldwyn, and Ellin hers with his mother, Frances. Berlin, for his part, took up pokering again with Schenck and Goldwyn.

Although Hollywood remained musically barren, Berlin was involved in two productions simultaneously. The project originally entitled *Mister Bones* would become *Mammy,* another star vehicle for Al Jolson (the story is credited to Irving Berlin, adapted by L. G. Rigby). *Photoplay,* the unabashed fan magazine, would describe the film as a "minstrel piece" in which Jolson "rises above his story to make an entertaining movie, singing good Irving Berlin songs . . . tunes that leave the theater with you." Berlin himself did not agree with the latter assessment, judging the Jolson staple "To My Mammy" one of his worst efforts ever, though he would later lift a couple of phrases from the release for another hit. "How Deep Is the Ocean?" would be the title and theme of one of his major songs, an answer to the question asked in the lyric's first line: "How much do I love you?"

The other Berlin-scored film starred Broadway nightclub and revue personality Harry Richman. Entitled *Puttin' On the Ritz* (after two alternate suggestions, *Playboy* and *Broadway Vagabond,* were rejected), it also featured Joan Bennett and James Gleason, Berlin's quasi-collaborator, who played Richman's partner in a vaudeville team. *Photoplay*'s appraisal was to the point: "There is some good Irving Berlin music, particularly 'Alice in Wonderland.' Harry shows little in looks or acting, but you'll like his warbling." Richman had learned well from his model, Al Jolson, and managed to interpolate a couple of his own songs into the score, one being the popular "There's Danger in Your Eyes, Cherie." But *Photoplay*'s reviewer was correct about his screen presence; Richman's Hollywood career would be brief. He did better on records and in clubs, including his own Club Richman and later the Desert Inn in Las Vegas and New York's Latin Quarter.

The shooting of the "Alice in Wonderland" sequence (the song was first written for the 1924 Music Box Revue) was particularly memorable for Mary Ellin, not yet three, who accompanied her parents to the United Artists studio to observe the confusion that was filmmaking. The same week that "Alice in Wonderland" was shot, Irving Berlin, along with countless others across the nation, lost a fortune. The disaster was succinctly—if a bit flippantly—summed up in a headline on the front page of *Variety* for October 30, 1929: WALL STREET LAYS AN EGG.

Berlin, unlike many other Americans, was still employed after the crash, but his investments and the bulk of his savings were wiped out. With Max Winslow managing the business back in Manhattan, the Berlins remained in Hollywood. They celebrated Christmas with a tree and presents for Mary Ellin, who was too young to realize it was also the first anniversary of her brother's death. The family was still in the Schenck house on Hollywood

Boulevard for Mary Ellin's Easter party, attended by Sammy Goldwyn and two little girls, all dressed in their Easter best and carrying baskets and candy eggs. Berlin supervised, with the help of Hermine, as Ellin was in New York taking care of her mother.

Now divorced for the second time, Katherine Blake was seriously ill. Some years before, she had suffered from a type of eye cancer, but by removing the eye (she would live the rest of her life with a glass prosthesis), her doctors believed they had entirely excised the malignancy. Meanwhile, her doctor husband was consistent, if not considerate: during his wife's recuperation, he took up with her nurse. On learning of the affair, Katherine sued for divorce and won. Dr. Blake, gentleman that he was, then married the nurse.

Around the time of the crash, the cancer recurred, now in her liver, where it proved to be inoperable and fatal. Katherine Duer Mackay Blake, not yet fifty-one, died on April 21, 1930. Berlin and Mary Ellin stayed in Hollywood, where Ellin joined them for a couple of weeks in July as she prepared to take Mary Ellin back east. When they left, Berlin remained behind to write the songs for a film he had conceived.

The idea had come to him shortly after the stock-market crash, a calamity he dismissed with the observation "I'm lucky, I have a rich wife." (She was now in better financial shape than her father, for he, too, had been broken by the depression, which forced him to live more frugally, move out of the big house into a smaller one on the estate, and sell his art collection. The legend that Mackay's songwriter son-in-law bailed him out is untrue; Berlin was having his own money problems.)

Although he would have preferred to return to Manhattan with his wife and daughter, Berlin thought he owed it to Joseph Schenck to finish what he had begun in Hollywood. Through Schenck, he had been signed to work on a United Artists film starring Douglas Fairbanks, initially entitled *Love in a Cottage* but finally released as *Reaching for the Moon.* (The title change came about because of a Berlin song of the same name, a brooding, minor-key waltz that he felt was his best effort in that form since "What'll I Do?") Also to be featured in the film was a rising young singer, one of the Rhythm Boys from Paul Whiteman's band: Bing Crosby.

The movie's protagonist (Fairbanks), a workaholic stockbroker who goes broke when Wall Street collapses, is obsessed with a beautiful woman aviator (a blond Bebe Daniels) who seems nothing less than a blend of Charles Lindbergh and Amelia Earhart. (Earhart herself had flown the Atlantic—as a passenger—in June 1928, and since that flight had regularly written and given talks about women in aviation.) The film's plot twists around Fairbanks's pursuit of the aviatrix, despite her engagement to another man and his own penchant for overwork; in the end, of course, the hero's monetary acumen regains him his fortune.

Photoplay, in its prerelease publicity, credited Irving Berlin with the script, but the final result would turn out to be yet another nonmusical, and undoubtedly the worst production he was involved in during his early Hollywood forays. Not that he had been expecting all that much; in June, *Photoplay* published his formula for the structure of a film musical, which was as follows: "In my opinion," he said, "no picture except an operetta should have more than four songs, but these four should be sung often. Even a musical comedy should have no more than four, or at the most, five songs, of which two are almost certain to become hits."

In August he wrote Ellin to say that the screenplay wasn't working and the original director had been replaced by Edmund Goulding, "a genius." He felt that the two of them were blessedly in tune. The British-born director-writer had a reputation for knowing how to get the best out of the big women stars of the thirties; before taking on *Reaching for the Moon,* he had directed Greta Garbo in *Love* (whose theme song was "The Melody of Love" by Walter Donaldson and Howard Dietz) and, in 1929, Gloria Swanson in *The Trespasser* ("Love, Your Magic Spell Is Everywhere," music and words by Elsie Janis and Goulding, who also wrote the screenplay).

Given Goulding's previous credits, it would seem only logical that Berlin should believe they were speaking the same language—but in due course, they would not be speaking at all.

As the filming of *Reaching for the Moon* progressed, Berlin's admiration only increased. He informed Winslow, in New York, that Goulding was "doing a great job on the story" and that the musical numbers were "well placed." But Goulding had some ideas of his own about the film. When it was released, late in December 1930, the titles read: "Joseph Schenck Presents *Reaching for the Moon*/ Based on a story with music by Irving Berlin/ Written and directed by Edmund Goulding/ Additional dialogue by Elsie Janis." Unfortunately, in the interim between Berlin's letter to Winslow and the release of the film, the actual songs—all except one, that is—had somehow disappeared.

It seems that in midproduction, Goulding decided that the film should be not a musical but a straight comedy. Since Fairbanks could not sing, the inclusion of songs would necessarily shift the emphasis away from him. While Daniels was a trained vocalist, she was also, like Fairbanks, a skilled comic, and thus could survive the film's transformation. (Among her lines, probably written by Janis, were some words of advice to her fellow women fliers: "Keep your tanks clean, your landing gear on the ground, and don't go into tailspins.") As for the athletic Fairbanks, he spent much of his time on screen dashing about, jumping over railings to get from one deck of a ship to another, and, while intoxicated, climbing walls (this last may have been the scene that Charlie Chaplin purportedly directed when he came by the set one day to watch Goulding at work).

All that would be left of the Berlin score by the time the film opened was the title song, played instrumentally, under the credits and in the background. Later in the film Crosby, as a shipboard crooner, also sings "When the Folks High Up Do the Mean Low-down" with Daniels. Several months of concentrated work on Berlin's part thus went down the drain. In October, after an incendiary argument with Goulding, the songwriter walked off the set, never to return. Arthur Johnston remained, and kept his boss informed, but the situation was hopeless. Tired, angry, embittered, and depressed, Berlin again fled Hollywood. (Johnston would stay on to launch his own Hollywood career, which was to have a happier beginning than Berlin's.)

To recover from the whole dreadful experience, Berlin spent a month in a spa in French Lick, Indiana. By Christmas of 1930, he and his family were settled in the Warwick Hotel on West Fifty-fourth Street and Sixth Avenue in Manhattan, close to his office on Broadway at Forty-ninth; he also retained the building on Forty-sixth Street, but only as a landlord. The Warwick was described in its advertising literature as having been

> designed for discriminating people accustomed to superior living, who wish to live close to business and prefer apartment house life to the cares and responsibilities of keeping up a home. Warwick suites have large closets, completely equipped pantry, automatic refrigeration, and the rooms themselves are spacious, light and ideal in their appointments.

Completed in 1926, it was one of New York's finest buildings; the Berlins would spend all of 1931 there.

Berlin's Hollywood experience had shaken him, and to some degree he blamed himself for his failure to accomplish anything of significance there. But in fact, the men who ran the studios had misused, and underemployed, not only Irving Berlin but also the Gershwins and Rodgers and Hart, all during the same brief period. Western technicians, for their part, were seeking out knowledge, learning a new trade, searching for skilled directors who understood song and dance and how to film them.

The trend had first emerged—if not very impressively—with the release of *The Broadway Melody* early in 1929. A "backstage" movie, it was fully scored, had musical sequences that made sense, and spun out an actual plot. It spawned a series of similar films that would reach a peak four years later in *42nd Street.* Some of the most knowledgeable directors of these early film musicals were imported from Europe: Ernst Lubitsch came from Germany to direct the fine *Love Parade* (1929), and Rouben Mamoulian from Russia for *Love Me Tonight* (1932). Late in 1933, a new era in film musicals would be ushered in by *Flying Down to Rio,* featuring Fred Astaire and Ginger Rogers in secondary roles.

Hollywood was at last ready for Irving Berlin, but for the moment, he was happily at work elsewhere.

8

COMEBACK

THE BERLINS celebrated Irving's return to New York by attending a New Year's Eve party at the Swopes' home in Port Jefferson. Berlin accompanied Franklin P. Adams in a dozen of his own songs, "to the delight of a majority of listeners," Adams reported. In his column for January 8, 1931, FPA related that "Mary Ellin Berlin and her mother came [to our house], and she played all afternoon with my boys and all three enjoyed it mighty much, but Mary Ellin kept calling me Mr. Timothy, whereupon my boys told her that I was not Timothy, but Papa, so she called me Mr. Papa, and a very sweet girl she was."

Her father, feeling fit and eager to work, met with Sam Harris, ready to try anything except another musical film. While he was on the Hollywood shuttle, Broadway had changed, primarily because of the financial wreckage wrought by the Great Depression. Although a number of musicals had been produced during those years, they were fewer and less lavish than before. Despite the innovations introduced by George and Ira Gershwin, Rodgers and Hart, and Cole Porter in the twenties, operettas were still doing well: in 1928, before the crash, Romberg and Hammerstein's *The New Moon* ran for more than five hundred performances. More Berlinesque (that is, more lighthearted, tune-filled) musical comedies were now being written by DeSylva, Brown, and Henderson. For three years running (1928–30), this team scored the musicals that came closest to matching *The New Moon*'s record: *Hold Everything, Follow Thru,* and *Flying High.* All were quite topical—concerned with prizefighting, golf, and flying, respectively—and designed for younger audiences than those that typically favored operetta. But that the traditional melody-filled musical could still attract theatergoers was proved by the success of Jerome Kern's *The Cat and the Fiddle*. Whatever the latest musical fashion, Berlin realized—be it ragtime, jazz, or swing—operetta, like the waltz, would always have a place.

Yet another kind of show achieved increasing popularity during the depression. More refined than vaudeville, and more intelligently written, revues were simpler, less lavish, and therefore less expensive to produce than extravaganzas such as Ziegfeld's Follies, a form that would (essentially) die with the crash, as would its creator not long after.

The revues of the late twenties and the thirties were freewheeling compendia of satirical (often political) sketches, specialty dances, and songs, the joint work of several hands and minds. One of the first hit revues was *The Little Show,* with a brilliant cast—Clifton Webb, Fred Allen, and Libby Holman—and songs mostly by the new songwriting team of Arthur Schwartz and Howard Dietz, whose big hit was "I Guess I'll Have to Change My Plan." An interpolated song entitled "Can't We Be Friends?," written by Kay Swift and her husband, Paul James (né James P. Warburg), also went over well. *The Little Show* ran at the Music Box for more than three hundred performances.

In 1930, the Warburgs followed up that success with their own revue, *Fine and Dandy,* with its popular title song, the distinguished "Can This Be Love?," and the comic "Let's Go Eat Worms in the Garden." Schwartz and Dietz returned with *Three's a Crowd* the same year, and the next year crafted one of their greatest scores for *The Band Wagon,* the last musical to star Fred Astaire and his sister Adele. Also in 1931, the Gershwins scored a political satire that was produced by Sam H. Harris at the Music Box. *Of Thee I Sing* was a quasi-sequel to the brothers' 1930 antiwar musical, *Strike Up the Band;* the later show had a book by George S. Kaufman and Morrie Ryskind, while the earlier book was written by Kaufman and revised by Ryskind.

As Berlin pondered his future, Broadway, though constricted by the impact of the depression, cheaper-ticketed movies, and free radio, was nonetheless flourishing musically with satire, politics, and what were called smart songs, combining literate lyrics with beautifully formed melodies over inventive harmonies. Harris felt that for his return to Broadway after an absence of almost five years, Berlin might find an ideal creative partner in a bright young writer named Moss Hart, a stagestruck playwright who had earlier collaborated with Kaufman on the hit *Once in a Lifetime*. Hart was then twenty-six, sixteen years Berlin's junior. Once introduced, the two men talked about the approach they might take. Hart suggested a revue, in the vein of *Fine and Dandy* or *Three's a Crowd,* but Berlin was doubtful: his last such effort, the 1927 Follies, had not been successful, and times had changed. He wanted to write songs for a book show.

Berlin readily admitted that the idea of attempting a new Broadway show frightened him to death. He would tell Percy N. Stone of the *Herald Tribune* that he and Hart at one point even considered writing a revue with a connecting story running through it. They finally found their plot in the political scandals that would eventually drive New York's part-time mayor, Jimmy Walker, out of office and into an extended European exile.

As Hart later recounted the story in *Stage* magazine, Berlin suggested that he come to Sands Point, Long Island, for two weeks.

> I stayed for four months and then moved back to New York and lived with him for eight months more [the Berlins were still at the War-wick; the collaborators also did some work in the songwriter's favorite refuge, Atlantic City]. You not only write a show with Irving Berlin, you live it, you breathe it, eat it and were it not for the fact that he allows you to sleep not at all, I should also say sleep it.

A lifelong insomniac, Berlin confided to reporter Stone, soon after their show opened, that during its writing, "I grew nervous and I couldn't sleep. I lost ten pounds trying to make songs. . . . If I could have revived any self-assurance it wouldn't have been so tough, but a song writer is only as good as his last show, and I was constantly afraid." However great his past successes, he always felt his next effort had to be even *more* successful, an attitude that would haunt him throughout his professional life.

According to Hart's timetable, he and Berlin spent a year on their show, which they titled *Face the Music.* Berlin himself attributed the long pull to their rejection of three initial versions and to his own anxiety over whether he could produce the necessary songs: "What if I can't write any more good ones?" he wondered. But in the end he did, though songs, too, went into the discard pile if, when he tried them out on Winslow or other staff members—such as his new musical secretary, Helmy Kresa—anyone expressed doubts. In the midst of the collaborators' final struggles with the show, Ellin Berlin became pregnant again, yet another cause for worry for her already nervous husband.

By January 1932, *Face the Music* was ready for rehearsals at the New Amsterdam. Berlin's own Music Box was unavailable because the Gershwin musical *Of Thee I Sing,* likewise produced by Sam H. Harris, had opened there

Rhynland passenger list, September 14, 1893. Moses Beilin heads the family at number 49; Leah's name, next, is partly obliterated. In the background, steerage passengers gather on deck for air, a scarce commodity in their quarters belowdecks. *Courtesy of the National Archives, Northeastern Region, New York/Library of Congress.*

Hester Street was the Lower East Side's Broadway, the shopping and social center of New York's Russian-Jewish population around the turn of the century. *Library of Congress.*

The Pelham Café on Pell Street, where Izzy Baline worked as a singing waiter, contrived comic lyrics to popular tunes, and wrote his first song. *American Society of Composers, Authors and Publishers (ASCAP).*

I. Berlin's first published song initiated his career and gave him a new name. *ASCAP.*

The original sheet-music cover for Berlin's first enduring hit song, published only four years after "Marie from Sunny Italy." *Irving Berlin Music Co.*

From another world: Clarence Mackay and children (*left to right*) Ellin, John, and Katherine on their Long Island estate in 1911, the same year "Alexander's Ragtime Band" was published. Ellin was then eight years old. *Bryant Library Local History Collection, Roslyn, N.Y.*

Berlin circa 1914, at his desk in the offices of Waterson, Berlin & Snyder on West Thirty-eighth Street. By this time Tin Pan Alley was in the process of moving uptown from Twenty-eighth Street. A shareholder in the new firm, Berlin was also its greatest asset. *Irving Berlin Music Co.*

Barracks interior at the recently constructed Camp Upton on Long Island, where newly drafted soldiers were trained. The camp was isolated, muddy, and crowded—discomforts Berlin had not known since he left the Lower East Side. And as he would soon chronicle in a song, the reveille bugle woke him up every morning at about the hour he would have been slipping into bed back in Manhattan. *Brookhaven National Laboratory, Upton, N.Y.*

Sergeant Irving Berlin flanked by two members of the *Yip! Yip! Yaphank* chorus. Berlin is in costume for his "Kitchen Police" number, "Poor Little Me, I'm on K.P." *Brookhaven National Laboratory, Upton, N.Y.*

Ceremonial opening of the Music Box. Berlin's partner and friend, producer Sam H. Harris, wields the key as Berlin and State Senator (and future Mayor) James J. Walker observe. For Walker's mayoral campaign in 1925, Berlin would write "It's a Walk-in with Walker." *ASCAP.*

Berlin, here surrounded by the chorus, appeared in the first Music Box Revue in 1921. In the back row, at far right, is Miriam Hopkins, who would later leave Broadway for a long and successful career in Hollywood. *ASCAP.*

The Music Box a decade after its opening. The marquee heralds *Of Thee I Sing,* the Gershwins' Pulitzer Prize-winning political operetta, which saved the theater from bankruptcy. *Gershwin Archive.*

Newlyweds Ellin and Irving Berlin dash for the train in Atlantic City with the press in hot pursuit, January 6, 1926. One reporter heard Mrs. Berlin say she was having the "worst honeymoon that ever befell a bride." A few days later they boarded a ship bound for Europe, and the honeymoon sweetened. *Bryant Library Local History Collection, Roslyn, N.Y.*

Hollywood, March 1928: Berlin is greeted at the station by his old friend producer Joseph Schenck and his wife, silent-film star Norma Talmadge. Berlin was about to experience his first stressful stint in Hollywood, while Talmadge's film career would come to an abrupt end with the advent of sound. *Photofest.*

En route to Nassau, 1933: Ira and Leonore Gershwin, George Gershwin, and the Berlins. Berlin had good reason to be happy, with *As Thousands Cheer* a major success; George Gershwin was about to compose *Porgy and Bess. Ira and Leonore Gershwin Trusts.*

Berlin's second Hollywood excursion was happier than his first, beginning with his participation in what many film historians consider the quintessential Astaire-Rogers musical, *Top Hat.* Berlin himself judged it his best work for films. *Photofest.*

Hollywood celebrated the silver jubilee of "Alexander's Ragtime Band" a few weeks early, at the Ambassador Hotel on January 20, 1936. Berlin is shown here accompanying "The Boys" on a piano with a standard keyboard. Joseph Schenck is standing directly behind him; lyricist Ted Koehler peers over Schenck's shoulder, while Jerome Kern, to the right of Schenck, beams down at his friend. Zeppo and Harpo Marx (*front right*) vocalize. *ASCAP.*

Beverly Hills, 1937: Berlin sat for Gershwin's camera portraits in the Gershwin house on North Roxbury Drive. Using a delayed-action shutter, Gershwin joined his subject in some of the shots. These were among the last photographs taken by Gershwin before his untimely death in the summer of 1937. *Ira and Leonore Gershwin Trusts.*

to great acclaim just weeks before, in late December 1931. It, too, had a Jimmy Walker–like character (Wintergreen, who runs for President) and a libretto (by George S. Kaufman and Morrie Ryskind) based on a jaundiced view of the political scene. But where *Of Thee I Sing* set its sights on national politics, *Face the Music* took a bead on its local equivalent: politics New York–style.

In a somewhat unusual move, Harris hired Kaufman to direct the book and Hassard Short the musical portion of *Face the Music*. Short, a Harris favorite, had directed several Music Box Revues, including one in London, plus the more recent *Three's a Crowd* and *The Band Wagon.* This division of labor would create some friction in the beginning, while the show was being prepared for its Philadelphia tryout.

On the day of the musical's first reading, Kaufman listened attentively as the cast members went through their lines, but when Berlin went to the piano to play the full score for the first time, the oblivious "book director" rose and left the theater. Berlin was furious and would not speak to him for weeks. An apology and explanation helped a little: the music was not his job, Kaufman argued; the *book* was. He pleaded his notorious ignorance of music. As he put it to a friend, "I don't know the difference between Handel's Largo and—well, Largo's Handel."

That issue settled (or at least tabled), the show could go on. After its Philadelphia tryout, *Face the Music* opened in New York on February 17, 1932. In a rave review, Robert Garland of the *World-Telegram* listed the targets of Hart's take-no-prisoners book:

> Everything is spoofed, nothing is spared. And by everything, I mean policemen with little tin boxes, Miss Mae West and the clean show crusaders, automatic restaurants and torch songs, the bills at the Palace and the penthouses on Park Avenue, the 18th Amendment and the hotels where missing judges stay, the nouveaux riches and dear old Crinoline Days, Police Commissioner Mulrooney and Judge Seabury . . . the drama critics and the Empire State Building, the Depression and the Messrs. Shubert.*

---

*The missing judge referred to was Joseph Crater, recently appointed to the State Supreme Court by Governor Franklin D. Roosevelt. After dinner out one evening, Crater got into a cab, waved to some friends, and was never seen again (nor was the five thousand dollars in cash he had in his wallet). The other judge, Samuel Seabury, led the investigation that would soon drive Jimmy Walker out of office.

Face the Music's first scene is set in an Automat, where the affluent—because of the depression, which would reach its nadir in 1932—now dine. The chorus fills in the audience:

> *Come along and you will see*
> *Mrs. Astor with a grin*
> *And a dab of ketchup on her chin.*
> *With pearls around her neck*
> *Mrs. Woolworth eats her mutton,*
> *And then she splits the check*
> *With her girlfriend, Mrs. Hutton.*

This leads into the show's first hit song, "Let's Have Another Cup of Coffee," sung by the romantic leads (played by J. Harold Murray and Katherine Carrington).

Enter a producer (Andrew Tombes as Hal Reisman, more Ziegfeld than either Shubert brother), who describes his planned new show, *The Rhinestones of 1932*. Thanks to the depression, he is having trouble raising money. The audience is advised on the state of show business in New York: for a nickel, the Palace is offering a stellar bill featuring Ethel Barrymore, Albert Einstein, and Tony the Talking Horse; the Roxy, for a dime, promises four feature films plus a room with a bath.

Enter Mrs. Martin Van Buren Meshbesher (Mary Boland), expensively furred and glittering with jewels—"On a clear day," she states, "you can see me from Yonkers." More important to producer Reisman is the fact that she is "lousy with money." Her husband, a police sergeant with his tin box of graft money, is being pursued by an investigating committee. Why not hide that loot by investing it in a surefire flop, *The Rhinestones*?

Before act 1 ends, two more hits are sung by the romantic couple: the Latin-inflected "On a Roof in Manhattan" and one of Berlin's most distinctive melodies, "Soft Lights and Sweet Music."

Following the entr'acte, act 2 opens with "Well, of All the Rotten Shows." (*The Rhinestones*—and the audience—have now suffered through its premiere, with its theme song, "My Rhinestone Girl," Berlin's parody of his own "A Pretty Girl Is like a Melody.") The next song was inspired by a *New Yorker* cartoon in which a preadolescent girl says to her mother (who is insisting that she eat her broccoli), "I Say It's Spinach (and the Hell with It)."

The Rhinestones becomes a hit when Reisman takes the advice of his policeman-investors and adds a dash of prurience and ribaldry to the show.

Not only do the backers make some reasonably honest money, they also keep out of the reach of the Seaburyesque committee investigating police corruption. Mrs. Meshbesher makes a spectacular entrance at a hearing, seated atop a papier-mâché (Republican?) elephant, another Ziegfeldian touch. Other songs of note in act 2 are "Dear Old Crinoline Days" (also known as "The Nudist Song," evidently one of the numbers added to make the show-within-a-show a hit; it is not the same song as "Crinoline Days," from the 1922 Music Box Revue) and "Manhattan Madness," which sings of "sensational headlines," peddlers with things to sell, "Noisy cafés and whispering bread-lines,/ Children that scream and yell." The finale, "Investigation," brings Mrs. Meshbesher and the elephant back onstage for a tuneful, happy ending.

The critical reception of *Face the Music* was uniformly positive. The songs as well as the libretto were praised (though there were some gratuitous comparisons between the latter and the book for *Of Thee I Sing,* already well on its way to a long stay at the Music Box). In his review, Robert Garland predicted that *Face the Music* would itself still be "running when Mr. Hoover is again popular" and the "Empire State Building is filled with tenants." (President Herbert Hoover, fated to be swept out of office that November by Franklin Delano Roosevelt, was widely blamed for both the depression's spread and the disastrous occupancy rate of the new Empire State Building. The "world's tallest building," as it was billed, had officially opened in May of the previous year, but many of its eighty-six floors of office space remained untenanted in the spring of 1932.)

Despite the recognition accorded it as one of the best musicals of the period, *Face the Music,* too, would succumb to the depression, as would many other shows that year, including *Through the Years* (after 32 performances), *Marching By* (12), *Blackberries of 1932* (24), and *There You Are* (8). The major survivors were the Gershwins' *Of Thee I Sing* (441) and a handful of others such as Kern and Hammerstein's *Music in the Air* (342), Cole Porter's *Gay Divorce* (248), and the multiauthored *Take a Chance* (243).

The Berlin-Hart show, after a run of 165 performances, was to close in the summer, when audiences dwindled. If not a failure by any means, neither was it a hit show, though several of its songs did become hits, enjoying good sheet-music sales, numerous recordings, and much airplay. Berlin was back in form. The critics' reception encouraged Sam Harris, even if the too-short run didn't, and he almost immediately put Berlin and Hart to work on another musical, to be produced at the Music Box the following year (after *Of Thee I Sing,* which did well for the Berlin-Harris partnership, vacated the theater).

But back in February 1932, when *Face the Music* opened, Berlin was pleased to read Percy Hammond's declaration, in the *Tribune,* that the "score is out of Irving Berlin's top shelf," and Robert Coleman's assertion, in the *Mirror,* that the work was the "best that Mr. Berlin has yet placed on display in a song and dance and guffaw extravaganza." The *Times*'s Brooks Atkinson meanwhile pronounced it "sharp, caustic, beautiful and beguiling." In truth, not only were the ballads themselves beauties, but Berlin's lyrics evinced a wit and bite more often associated with Cole Porter or Lorenz Hart.

Thrilling as such notices were, Berlin had other, even happier matters on his mind. Five days after the premier of *Face the Music,* on February 22, 1932, he took a bundled-up, now five-year-old Mary Ellin out for a ride, promising her a surprise. When they arrived at a large building, the child was beguiled by the elevator, the long hallways, and a room they entered that was filled with flowers. Inside, her mother lay in bed, and in a bassinet nearby was her new sister, Linda, born exactly one month before her mother's twenty-ninth birthday. Ellin had survived another difficult delivery.

When questioned in an interview about the new baby—another girl— Berlin replied, "What could be better than two girls?" In answer to a different query, he said, "Little Mary was very much surprised when she saw her sister. You see, she didn't know a thing about it." (In fact, however, Mary Ellin would later remember having pestered her parents for a sister.) Soon they were all settled at the new home they had moved to just before Christmas, when they left the Warwick Hotel for a triplex penthouse at 130 East End Avenue, overlooking Carl Schurz Park at East Eighty-sixth Street.

It was a magical, roomy, and airy place for little Mary Ellin to grow up in, with a staff of butler, cook, two maids, and Hermine to keep an eye on her, as well as a nurse for Linda. The bedrooms were on the first floor; the spacious living room, on the second, had the Steinway (on which Mary Ellin had begun piano lessons soon after her fifth birthday) and a terrace with a sweeping view of the city and the East River. The top floor boasted an impressive library and Berlin's latest Buick, on which he frequently worked late at night (as always).

Berlin was especially proud of his collection of rare first editions and often compared his acquisitions with those of another avid collector, Jerome Kern. He felt particularly triumphant whenever he happened to beat Kern to a particular prize (such as, on one occasion, a Shakespeare set that Kern coveted).

One day, in a discussion of their rarities, Berlin remarked that he had a first edition of Alexander Woollcott's *The Story of Irving Berlin.*

"Was there ever a second, Irving?" Kern retorted.

Primarily for the sake of Ellin's health, the family spent most of the summer of 1932 in the Adirondack Mountains, at Loon Lake again, about forty miles south of the Canadian border. Jack MacKenzie drove the car or rowed the fishing boats they rented. He also cleaned any fish they caught, which Berlin would then fry up in an old iron pan, skillfully flipping their fare. "And it was delicious," Mary Ellin recalled, "crisp on the outside, sweet and firm inside, so different from the disgusting fish of winter Fridays" (Ellin Berlin had kept up this practice of her Catholic upbringing, with no objection from her husband).

Their days were filled with simple, outdoorsy pleasures: more fishing (her father taught Mary Ellin how), rambling through the woods, boating, and picnicking. For Berlin it was a time of rest; for Ellin, one of recovery. Mary Ellin helped her father pick wild strawberries for her mother, and brought her Loon Lake pillow, stuffed with pine needles, back to the East End Avenue penthouse as a memento for her bed.

During their absence, a concerned Max Winslow, sensing that his friend and boss was feeling low, rummaged in the Berlin files ("the trunk") and found a song he believed would be an ideal vehicle for the most popular crooner of the day, Rudy Vallee. Vallee liked it and broadcast it on his Fleischman's Hour radio program; "Say It Isn't So" became an instant hit. Prompted by this success, Winslow dug into the trunk again for the song that Berlin had fashioned from words buried in the release of the detested Jolson number "To My Mammy"; "How Deep Is the Ocean?" served as both the title and the main theme of the song.

Why Berlin himself had discarded these two efforts, considering their quality (both words and music), is difficult to understand. It may have been his perfectionism, combined with an underlying depression that was made worse by Ellin's own postpartum near-breakdown that spring and summer. *Face the Music*'s closing in July was another cause for gloom, mitigated only by the fact that its songs were heard everywhere (except for "I Say It's Spinach," which could not be aired on the radio because its lyric contained the word *hell*). But that was consolation enough: the popularity of the *Face the Music* songs and the two others that Max Winslow had published literally behind his back brought Berlin home to New York at the end of the summer ready to work. And he returned, too, with an idea for a new show.

This time he agreed with his collaborator: they would do a topical revue. But according to Hart, Berlin did not want it to be a "conventional sort of revue with the usual blackout sketches, songs and dances. So we hit upon the idea of writing a show right off the front pages of the newspapers." Instead of just basing their characters on people in the news, they would have the cast impersonate actual headline-makers, or "column fodder"—some of whom, Berlin believed, were little more than caricatures in real life: many of those who would later be described as the "beautiful people" made the tabloids with public displays amounting to self-parody.

The show took the form of a standard newspaper, with front page, comics, rotogravure (the picture section), and even a lonely-hearts column. With this conception and an outline in mind, Berlin and Hart shipped out the following spring for the clement quiet of Bermuda. The island's sea air and agreeable winds were invigorating to the collaborators but hard on Berlin's Buick, whose strings corroded and whose hammers required a change of felt. They began working on the first act during the summer of 1932 and continued into the winter. During April and May 1933, they completed the first act and sketched out the second. Besides the time out for Buick repair, there was one other interruption, a pleasant one that was supposed to be a "surprise": Ellin Berlin arrived to celebrate her husband's forty-fifth birthday. Bennie Bloom, who saw to such details in the Berlin office, arranged for her passage and, as a precaution, sent a telegram ahead to Bermuda: "She is coming to surprise you on May 11th." This would become a long-standing family joke, with Ellin, in a typical Jazz Age wisecrack, suggesting that Bloom had sent the message to give the boys "time to get the girls out." Bloom, of course, merely knew that Berlin was not fond of surprises.

On their return, the Berlins moved into a house at Montauk, Long Island, near the ocean. Berlin would, after a week of work in town, come out on Fridays and go back in on Mondays. To Ellin's occasional annoyance, on these weekends he was restless, drumming his fingers, chewing gum, smoking, running to the telephone, humming, and fidgeting at the piano. But he also had time to go boating, fishing, and swimming with Mary Ellin (a swimming student of the watchful Jack MacKenzie), and to attend Ellin's sumptuous Saturday-night formal parties. Mary Ellin remembered one especially memorable evening when she was permitted to come downstairs briefly to meet a pianist who was playing jazzy songs; her father introduced him as Mr. Waller (Thomas Wright Waller was better known as Fats). Mary Ellin was fascinated by his inventive style—she was now well into her own piano lessons—and her father told her, "Listen to him, kid, you can learn a thing or two."

Before the end of the summer, the new score was complete, and rehearsals could begin at the New Amsterdam. The show was titled *As Thousands Cheer,* a venerable phrase appropriated from the sports pages. It would star the petite singer-dancer Marilyn Miller; the elegant Clifton Webb (also a singer and dancer); comic Helen Broderick, she of sardonic, deadpan delivery; and blues singer Ethel Waters, recently come downtown from Harlem's Cotton Club. The major dancers were Letitia Ide and José Limón, from the celebrated modern dance troupe of Charles Weidman.

When all agreed the show was ready, the company began its tryout tour in New Haven, went on to Philadelphia, and then opened at the Music Box on September 30, 1933—in the depths of the Great Depression. Although working with Hart again had been a pleasure, easy and full of fun, Berlin had encountered some minor snags along the way. The first act, which they had finished in Bermuda, presented a problem: they wanted to close it with a spectacular scene based on the rotogravure section. A staple feature of newspapers in the earlier part of the century, rotogravure was by now in decline; the sepia tones of the printing process gave it a nostalgic, old-hat feeling.

As the finale of the act, the scene would need an elaborate song-and-dance number; Berlin would have to come up with something appropriate to the setting, New York in the late nineteenth century. As he later told historian Stanley Green,

> I was stuck for a song for the Rotogravure Section. I'd written a couple of old-fashioned-type songs but they were lousy. So I reached back to something I had written in 1917. It went, "Smile and show your dimple, you'll find it very simple. . . ." It was a poor imitation of the cheer-up kind of songs of the day, like "Pack Up Your Troubles in Your Old Kit Bag."
>
> But I always liked the main four-bar theme. So . . . instead of trying to write a new old-fashioned melody I simply used a real old-fashioned melody. Except that now, of course, I made the words apply to an Easter Parade.

The scene opened with the cast standing motionless behind a scrim; then the music began, the scrim vanished, and strollers paraded along Fifth Avenue as Webb and Miller sang "Easter Parade." The entire company then joined in the procession, bringing act 1 to a triumphant close.

The second act opened on a much grimmer note, after a sketch in which a broadcast of the Metropolitan Opera's *Rigoletto* was disturbingly and regularly interrupted by a sponsor's commercials. A headline, enlarged and printed on the curtain, appeared: UNKNOWN NEGRO LYNCHED BY FRENZIED MOB. Curtain up, and a woman was seen in a southern hovel setting the table for her children; she knows her husband won't be home.

Berlin was inspired to write the song that followed after hearing Ethel Waters sing Harold Arlen and Ted Koehler's bluesy lament "Stormy Weather" at the Cotton Club, on his return from Bermuda. Impressed with the singer, and with a specific idea in mind for her, he called Dan Healy (the "Mandy" of *Yip! Yip! Yaphank*), who masterminded the Cotton Club Revues, and offered to buy out Waters's contract. There was none; the mobsters who owned the club preferred not to get caught up in too many legalities (including any prohibitions against the sale of their own brand of beer and other spirits in the club). Evidently either Healy or the Berlin name (no one knows which) had some influence: Ethel Waters was released from her "noncontract" in time for the summer rehearsals of *As Thousands Cheer*. (This was an unusual act of gallantry on the part of the Owney Madden mob, which was jealous of its stars, and packing in audiences with Waters and "Stormy Weather." Cab Calloway had had a rougher time of it when he left the Cotton Club to appear at the rival Plantation Club: early one morning, after closing, a Madden work crew arrived, ripped out the entire interior of the Plantation, and scattered it in the street outside. Calloway and his band subsequently returned to the Cotton Club.)

Waters's emotional rendition of "Stormy Weather" (she had just broken up with her boyfriend, and her career seemed at low ebb) deeply moved Irving Berlin and gave him a notion for a song that could hardly have been more topical. "People told me I was crazy [to do] a dirge like that," he recalled for Stanley Green. "But I was equally convinced that a musical dealing with headline news needed at least one serious piece, and I knew that Ethel Waters had the quality to sing something real dramatic."

The song was "Supper Time," Berlin's bitter commentary on a series of savage lynchings in recent years. The victims were predominantly blacks, taken by mobs from jails or from their homes and killed by hanging, shooting, or beating. Most lynchings took place in the South. In 1930, twenty Negroes—some convicted of crimes, some not—were murdered by mobs; in 1931, the year the infamous Scottsboro Boys trial began in Alabama, the number was twelve, in 1932 six, and in 1933, when most of the work on *As Thousands Cheer* was accomplished, twenty-four. One of the most vicious instances, a double lynching, occurred in Texas, where a mob practiced target shooting on the swaying bodies before cutting them down, splashing them with gasoline, and setting them on fire. Such atrocities were widely reported in the newspapers, with the tabloids' often printing graphic photographs.

Repelled by such inhumanity, Berlin emphatically protested it in the song he wrote for Ethel Waters, who believed that "if one song can tell the whole tragic history of a race, 'Supper Time' was that song."

The show returned to lighter matters in the next scene, a sketch involving an unlikely duo of much-in-the-news personalities, India's Mahatma Gandhi (Clifton Webb), then being held in a British prison (the headline was GANDHI GOES ON HUNGER STRIKE), and American evangelist Aimee Semple

McPherson, who faithfully preached that the road to Heaven was paved with dollars. The point Hart made in the sketch was that both figures were headline grabbers. Gandhi (portrayed by Webb) insists on being photographed fasting in a restaurant; MacPherson (Helen Broderick) arrives to talk him into joining forces with her to sell religion. The couple leaves doing a soft-shoe.

A ballet, "Revolt in Cuba," followed, succeeded in turn by a satirical swipe at Noël Coward's British accent and a skit about a society wedding, in which a young man and woman were seen in bed together and then rushed off to church singing "Our Wedding Day." A couple of headlines later, Ethel Waters returned to parody the attitudes of Josephine Baker, then known as the "Rage of Paris," in "Harlem on My Mind." Despite her newfound wealth, her evenings with members of the French aristocracy, her fame, Baker as imagined by Hart and Berlin still missed Harlem, with a "hi-de-ho."

The scene, too, was quite topical: Baker's residence in France and her unique popularity had altered her demeanor, and her new hauteur alienated many blacks. An anecdote—a true one, for a change—tells of an encounter between her and Lorenz Hart's feisty maid, Mary Campbell. At a dinner party given for her by Hart, Baker imperiously said to Mary, *"Donnez-moi une tasse de café, s'il vous plait."*

Mary Campbell was admired among Hart's friends as a woman who brooked no nonsense from anyone, including her boss. Her reply to Baker was direct: "Honey, talk the way your mouth was born."

This was the Josephine Baker whom Berlin and Waters caricatured in "Harlem on My Mind," a song incidentally written for the singer in Philadelphia, where it was discovered that the show was lacking in what Berlin called the "music department." Waters's other song was the great "Heat Wave."

A strange and difficult complication arose during the tryout tour. Show people are, generally speaking, free of bigotry, but to Berlin's shocked dismay, Miller, Webb, and Broderick all objected to taking curtain-call bows with their black costar, Waters. While he conceded that they had a right to be wrong, Berlin stated simply that in that case, there would be no bowing at all. The three white stars, of course, quickly changed their minds about the whole thing, and the show opened without incident in New York.

The critical consensus was summed up by Brooks Atkinson in the *Times:* "No doubt someone will be able to suggest how *As Thousands Cheer* could be improved but this column can only give its meek approval to every item in the program. As for Mr. Berlin, he has never written better tunes or more sparkling lyrics. In these circumstances there is nothing a reviewer can do but cheer."

The irreverent tone of the show was established straightaway, in the prologue, set in a Park Avenue dining room. A wife is fussing over her Pekinese, and her husband is clearly annoyed; the dog bites him, and then he bites it back. A momentary blackout opens onto the city room of a newspaper, whose editor is so excited that he stops the presses for a special edition. On Columbus Circle newsstands, the paper trumpets the event, and the chorus, before a curtain of columns of type, explains:

> *Not a great big manly he-dog—a little she-dog, a bitch,*
> *Which gives us a headline off the beaten track:*
> *"A Bitch Bit a Man and the Man Bit the Bitch Right Back."*

Percy Hammond, in the *Herald Tribune,* noted that "Mr. Berlin contributes a lot of satin songs. But, perhaps fearful that his efforts might be too mellifluous, he collaborates with Moss Hart, a sarcastic chap with an acid, cruel sense of humor. It is an ideal combination."

Cruel may have been too strong a word for Hart's wit, but there was sarcasm aplenty, unerringly aimed at such public figures as outgoing President Hoover, much-married Woolworth heiress Barbara Hutton (wooed and won by a suitor singing the very mellifluous "How's Chances?"), the Rockefellers, the Prince of Wales and his wedding plans (a prophetic skit), and Douglas Fairbanks, Jr., and his divorce from Joan Crawford (which is forced off the front page by the divorce of his father from Mary Pickford).

Also lampooned were more serious topics such as the war debts, much in the news then because most of the countries that owed the United States money on loans made during the First World War were defaulting. In one scene, a ship sailed out of New York Harbor carrying representatives from Britain, Germany (which owed reparations), Italy, and France, as the Statue of Liberty (played by Helen Broderick) sang, to the tune of "The Star-Spangled Banner,"

> *Let the pound go up,*
> *The franc go up,*
> *The mark go up as well,*
> *Uncle Sam will be in Heaven*
> *When the dollar goes to Hell.*

The *Post*'s John Mason Brown shuddered to think of the fate of all connected with the production had they ventured to win laughs of the kind they won so freely Saturday night while living in the shadow of the Kremlin, in Mussolini's Italy, in Hitler's Germany . . . even in the liberal England of George and Mary[: they would have faced] Siberia, a firing squad, exile, or the darkest dungeon in the Tower. [As *Thousands Cheer's*] satire is as daring as it is convulsing, and proves conclusively in its own gay way that in spite of the many jibes and much evidence to the contrary, America is still the land of the free, at least as far as entertainment is concerned, and that the Music Box continues to be the home of the brave.

Brown's sole objection was to "Supper Time," which he suggested should be dropped from the show. The producer and authors did not follow this advice.

One of Berlin's finest contributions to the score was the sadly wistful "Lonely Heart," a letter-song addressed to an advice-to-the-lovelorn columnist (typified at the time by the real-life Dorothy Dix and Beatrice Fairfax). After the lyric was touchingly sung by Harry Stockwell, it was stylishly interpreted in a dance by Letitia Ide, José Limón, and the ensemble. (It would later be recorded by society dance-band leader Meyer Davis and then by opera star turned Broadway singer Everett Marshall, who did the song as an aria, complete with at least one operatic sob—not quite what Berlin had in mind, we may assume, but an interesting interpretation nonetheless.)

The show's finale represented an ingenious solution to a staging problem. The scene was to have been a Park Avenue–like party at which all the guests/cast members wore roller skates, a bit of business that proved difficult for Marilyn Miller and some of the others. But when the company arrived in Philadelphia for the tryout, it was discovered that the stage was unsuitable—even unsafe—for roller skating. There was no time to prepare another surface for the stage, so Berlin and Hart put their heads together and came up with an alternative ending. Berlin would revise one of their discards and close with a song that had not been heard earlier in the show. This approach was in itself an innovation. The headline before the finale read: SUPREME COURT HANDS DOWN IMPORTANT DECISION.

The decision? That Broadway musicals could no longer end with a reprise of their most popular songs. As the cast members attempted to do the conventional thing, they were silenced by the Supreme Court Justices. Clifton Webb and Marilyn Miller then introduced the newly crafted "Not for All the Rice in China," in which number they were joined by the rest of the cast. The audience's reaction, capped off by several multiracial curtain calls, proclaimed *As Thousands Cheer* a hit, the major success of a dismal depression season.

The Broadway musical year had begun unpropitiously in January with the Gershwins' *Pardon My English* (featuring one of their best scores), which lasted for an ominous forty-six performances; its nadir came in April with Alexander Hill's *Humming Sam,* which closed after its opening night. In that same month, the first American production of Kurt Weill's masterwork *The Threepenny Opera* managed to survive for only an even dozen performances. Of the fourteen musicals produced in 1933, only three were unqualified successes: Jerome Kern's *Roberta* (295 performances); an Earl Carroll production with a composite score, *Murder at the Vanities* (207); and *As Thousands Cheer,* whose four hundred performances ran well into 1934.

At the opening-night party given by the Swopes, Berlin, excited though he was, could relax without the usual waiting-for-the-reviews jitters: the Saturday premiere meant that the notices would not appear until Monday. By Tuesday, *As Thousands Cheer* was playing to standing-room-only audiences.

It was time again to take it easy, tend to the other business, and spend more time with the family. A happy Irving Berlin marked the Christmas holidays by taking Mary Ellin, now seven, to a matinee of the show, which she enjoyed except for all the "boring talk" (i.e., the comic skits that her father and Hart had written, which the adults in the audience seemed to find hilarious).

That Christmas was a truly celebrated one. The day began once the insomniac man of the house arose (Ellin kept their daughters busy until he was ready for the day). Presents—lavish, even extravagant gifts—were opened, and then came the curious gathering of family for an ecumenical Christmas dinner, mingling the Balines and the Mackays around the towering tree in the library. Clarence Mackay arrived with more presents and the girls' new aunt Anna, whom he had married after the death of his first (ex-)wife, Katherine Blake. She was now Anna Case Mackay, retired opera and concert singer. Berlin addressed his father-in-law respectfully as "Mr. Mackay," though Ellin believed he had never really forgiven him for his treatment of them after they were married.

The children's uncle Ben Baline, now a prosperous designer of furs with a shop in New London, Connecticut, came down with his wife, Nettie; Aunt Gussie, married to salesman Edward Rice, brought special gifts, as always— jellies and jams she had canned herself.

The 1933 Christmas season also marked the release of *Flying Down to Rio,* the forerunner of one of the richest cycles in American musical film. It was significant for several reasons, not least of them being that it saved RKO Radio Pictures from bankruptcy (with a little help from the monster hit *King Kong*). Graced with an exceptional score by Vincent Youmans (with lyrics by Edward Eliscu and Gus Kahn), it starred the glamorous Delores Del Rio and Gene Raymond as a dashing aviator-bandleader. But in truth, *Flying Down to Rio* virtually belonged to the two lesser stars billed in fourth and fifth place, Ginger Rogers and Fred Astaire.

Quick to recognize a potential bonanza, RKO quickly followed up with a film starring their new "King and Queen of 'Carioca,' " *The Gay Divorcée* (the Hays Office–approved title for what had been called *Gay Divorce* on Broadway). Because Astaire had made the greater impression in *Flying Down to Rio*, his name was now billed above Rogers's, and the new song-and-dance team of Fred Astaire and Ginger Rogers (in that order) was established. Unfortunately, only one of the original Cole Porter songs from the stage version—"Night and Day"—was retained for the film; new numbers by others were added, with Con Conrad and Herb Magidson's "The Continental" being sold as the stars' big dance number.

Thereafter, the formula would vary only slightly: Astaire and Rogers were the stars, with members of the RKO stock company—Edward Everett Horton, Eric Blore, or Erik Rhodes—standing by to provide laughs, and a wisecracking older woman, usually played by Helen Broderick, to add interest. The producer of seven of the ten Astaire-Rogers films was the young, knowledgeable Pandro S. Berman, who in turn selected the other important members of the production team. The director for five of the pictures was Mark Sandrich; the various musical directors included Nathaniel Shilkret, recruited from the radio and recording studios of New York, and the veteran Viennese conductor-composer Max Steiner, who had scored *King Kong* and would write the music for *The Informer* and *Gone with the Wind*.

In short, in the few years since Irving Berlin had walked off the set of *Reaching for the Moon*, Hollywood had learned how to make musicals. The Astaire-Rogers cycle uniquely exemplified how witty if slight plots, bright dialogue, and likable stars could be combined with dance songs by some of the greatest songwriters of the day.

But there was also another factor at work here, too. Almost from the moment Hollywood first got into the musical-film business, it elbowed its way into the music-publishing business as well. Warner Brothers, for example, as early as 1930, controlled the output of some of Tin Pan Alley's major houses, among them M. Witmark and Sons, DeSylva Brown and Henderson, T. B. Harms (publisher of Gershwin, Kern, Rodgers, and Youmans), and Remick's.

Rather than negotiating for the rights to the publications it wanted, Warner's would simply buy the companies that held those rights. Other studios followed suit, with Metro-Goldwyn-Mayer acquiring Robbins Music, and Paramount, Famous Music.

The handful of independent holdouts included Harry von Tilzer, Edward B. Marks, and, notably, Irving Berlin Music, Inc.

When he saw *Flying Down to Rio* in December 1933, Berlin realized that real strides had been made in the technical aspects of musical filmmaking; when *The Gay Divorcée* was released, in October 1934, he would feel certain that musical creativity on the West Coast had evolved apace. By this time, word had come back east that Astaire and Rogers were making a film of *Roberta,* the relatively successful 1933 Broadway musical scored by his friend Jerome Kern. Kern approved of the project, even to the degree that he agreed to write additional music to words by Dorothy Fields.

The impressive success of *As Thousands Cheer* put Irving Berlin back in the game. In May 1934, his forty-sixth birthday was observed with a *Time* cover. Gulf Oil went even further, sponsoring a five-week series of radio programs on NBC devoted to his work, showcasing no less than a hundred of his songs. The programs hailed—a couple of years late—the twenty-fifth anniversary of Berlin's career as a songwriter, beginning with "My Wife's Gone to the Country" and closing with his most recent hit, "Easter Parade." *Face the Music* and *As Thousands Cheer* dramatically ended his dry spell, though he would never shake the fear of reaching for a tune and not being able to find it. His self-confidence back, he and Hart began working up a new revue, *More Cheers,* only to abandon it after he finished one song, "Moon over Napoli." Hart renewed his collaboration with George S. Kaufman to write *Merrily We Roll Along,* a quasi-comedy told in flashback about a successful but unhappy composer (Stephen Sondheim would set it to music in 1981); they followed up with an even finer play, the depression comedy *You Can't Take It with You.*

By December Berlin was on his way to California: Pandro Berman had asked him to come west to score an Astaire-Rogers musical. He was particularly excited by the prospect of writing for Astaire. Because Berman wanted him to be in California before Christmas, he took Mary Ellin, now a rebellious eight-year-old, to a fine restaurant for an early holiday lunch and then to F.A.O. Schwartz to buy toys. Soon after, alone, he flew to Los Angeles.

There had been a number of changes in his company that year. The peerless Max Winslow had preceded him to Hollywood to head the music department of Columbia Pictures, founded by his brother-in-law Harry Cohn, who had once worked as a song plugger for Berlin. (Cohn was married to Rose, sister of Tillie Winslow.) Winslow's departure created a large vacuum in the company. Replacing Arthur Johnston as musical secretary and professional manager was German-born Helmy Kresa, a colorful all-around musician (as well as a photographer and pilot) who had become a permanent member of Berlin's staff during the production of *As Thousands Cheer,* for which he had also done orchestrations. He had studied composition with American-Hungarian composer Tibor Serly and had written a number of songs, one of the best of which was "It Was a Sad Night in Harlem," published by Berlin. His biggest success would come in 1947 from a tune written before he joined Berlin, in 1931. Entitled "That's My Desire" (with a lyric by Carroll Loveday), it would lead to some friction between employer and employee until Berlin learned more about its publication history. The two at times had a testy relationship, as Kresa was a born wheeler-dealer.

Berlin's own were not the only songs his firm published; its catalog also contained quite a few works by others, the most popular of which, significantly, had been written for films. In 1933 its publications also included two nonfilm songs, "Annie Doesn't Live Here Any More" (by Harold Spina, Joe Young, and Johnny Burke) and Burton Lane and Harold Adamson's "Tony's Wife." Business manager Saul Bornstein argued that the latter needed a new title, but after Lane played and sang it for Berlin, he published it as it was, and made a profit on it.

Among the longer-lasting film songs the company handled were Harold Arlen and Ted Koehler's title song from their first film, "Let's Fall in Love." There were also a couple of novelties, one of which would have been difficult to escape on radios in 1934. With Ben Ryan and Harry Donnelly, Jimmy Durante wrote what would become his signature song, "Inka, Dinka, Doo," for the movie *Palooka;* and Ann Ronell, with help from Walt Disney's composer-in-residence, Frank Churchill, composed the ubiquitous "Who's Afraid of the Big Bad Wolf?" for the cartoon *The Three Little Pigs.*

Radcliffe graduate Ronell was a classically trained musician who had decided to try her hand at popular music after interviewing George Gershwin for her college paper. The composer took her under his wing, got her jobs as a rehearsal pianist, and considered her his protégée. She, too, had had a run-in with Bornstein, when she came to the Berlin office in 1932 with an extraordinary song entitled "Willow Weep for Me." Bornstein had two objections to it: first, it was dedicated to Gershwin, and second, the release introduced a sudden, almost frenetic tempo change before returning to the original, blueslike A section. It was an unusual form for a popular tune, but like Lane the next year, Ronell prevailed once she managed to get to Berlin himself: her song was published as written and dedicated.

When he boarded his plane for California in December 1934, Berlin was confident that he was leaving the office in good hands. Besides the successful movie songs, his own "Heat Wave" and "Easter Parade" were doing well. Bennie Bloom was still with the company, as was composer-pianist Dave Dreyer, whose hit songs "Me and My Shadow" and "There's a Rainbow 'Round My Shoulder" the firm had published. Berlin's personal secretary, the sharp, observant Mynna Granat, could attend to the details her boss found bothersome. (An office romance between Granat and Dreyer would culminate in his divorcing his first wife to marry her.)

Believing his house to be in order, Irving Berlin was elated at returning to Hollywood to do the Astaire picture, whatever it might be.

9

NEW DEAL

EVEN AS RKO was being danced into solvency on the shoes of Fred Astaire and Ginger Rogers, and a cheerful future appeared inevitable, history and faraway events were conspiring to change everything: soon enough, there would be little to sing about. Meanwhile, at home, the depression carried its own load of gloom, making the rest of the world seem distant and insignificant.

Early in 1933, as Berlin and Hart were blocking out the script of *As Thousands Cheer* in preparation for their trip to Bermuda, something happened that was to have an impact on both of their lives—but especially Berlin's. One of the most critical events of the century seemed trivial at the time; it was barely noticed by most Americans. On January 30, 1933, a loud-mouthed politician named Adolf Hitler was appointed German chancellor by a reluctant, befuddled President Paul von Hindenburg. Thirty-two days later, Franklin Delano Roosevelt was inaugurated as President of a depression-afflicted United States. Less than three weeks after that, Hitler, outwitting the aged von Hindenburg, was appointed führer of Germany; the former Austrian corporal was now the German dictator.

Preoccupied with the domestic economy, Roosevelt and his handpicked advisers from academia, known as the brains trust, moved quickly, taking steps that the voters did not always understand (and often hated): they declared a bank holiday, scrapped the gold standard, and proliferated acronyms. The AAA (Agricultural Adjustment Administration), TVA (Tennessee Valley Authority), and NRA (National Recovery Administration) promised, with cooperation from labor and management and with government guidance, to "put people back to work, to let them buy more of the products of the farms and factories and start out [in] business at a living rate again." Roosevelt expressed the hope that through these programs, hundreds of thousands of unemployed Americans would be "back on the payroll by snowfall." In March, he initiated the broadcasting of his "fireside chats," in which he spoke directly to the people about the state of the nation and what he was doing to better it. His patrician voice and delivery served to reassure a stricken populace.

While there was some general economic improvement by the end of the year, 1933 was a disaster for Hollywood, with a drastic fall in attendance that theater owners tried to mitigate with such inducements as free dishes, double features, bank nights, and screeno (a form of gambling, and thus technically a violation of the lottery laws). In that dismal year, *Flying Down to Rio* rescued RKO, and the Vitaphone saved Warner Brothers, along with *42nd Street* and the gritty, socially conscious *I Am a Fugitive from a Chain Gang,* a genre that Warner's excelled in. Good films continued to draw audiences; one of the most successful movies of the year was a British effort, *The Private Life of Henry the Eighth.* Its popularity made the front offices of Hollywood uneasy, preferring as the studio heads did to export rather than import celluloid.

The New Deal's initiatives eventually proved effective; their ripple effect pulled the film industry out of the red and into the black in 1934. (That same year, at Roosevelt's urging, the Twenty-first Amendment repealed the Volstead Act, ending Prohibition and consequently putting a stop to gangland shootings, particularly in Chicago and New York.) Hollywood released several high-quality (and profitable) movies that year, notably *It Happened One Night* and *The Thin Man.* And then there was *The Gay Divorcée.*

A month after the Astaire-Rogers hit was released, in November 1934, negotiations over the Berlin-RKO contract were concluded. Berlin's attorneys had asked for $100,000 for the first of the two Astaire musicals that Berman wanted from their client, but the producer pleaded poverty: RKO was not yet completely out of the financial woods. The compromise agreement gave Berlin $75,000 plus 10 percent of the gross after the film's earnings topped $1,250,000 (a gamble that would pay off).

When he registered at the Beverly Wilshire Hotel in Beverly Hills that December, Berlin had a sheaf of songs with him, one of which would be used in the film. By this time scriptwriter Dwight Taylor had finished a "treatment" that included some suggestions for song spots; a month or so later, the first draft of the screenplay was ready. This in turn was worked on by screenwriter Allan Scott, with input from director Mark Sandrich.

Taylor had written the book for Broadway's *Gay Divorce,* the Cole Porter musical from which the movie *The Gay Divorcée* was derived. Although Taylor was not involved in the latter, a number of parallels have been noted between its screenplay and the new one he was preparing for Irving Berlin.

"Berlin sat in on all our conferences," Sandrich later recalled, "with the result that all the songs grew out of the scene structure itself." During one of these conferences, Sandrich told Berlin that Astaire had a notion of reviving a dance he had done in the 1930 stage flop *Smiles,* to a Vincent Youmans song entitled "Say, Young Man of Manhattan." The choreography called for him to be dressed in formal attire, down to a top hat and cane, and pitted against a dancing chorus, also wearing top hats, and seemingly threatening him. The dance ended with Astaire's mowing down the chorus, wielding his cane like a machine gun. Astaire had evidently liked this dance so much that he wished to repeat it in his next film.

On hearing this curious description (had the finale perhaps been inspired by the Saint Valentine's Day massacre in Chicago?), Berlin responded with an idea for a song about putting on one's top hat, tying a white tie, and brushing off one's tails. The film now had a title: *Top Hat.*

In his December treatment, Taylor had introduced Astaire as a careless, fancy-free dancer "with no yens, no yearnings"—a characterization that led smoothly into the first lines of Berlin's "No Strings" and the dance that, at midnight, disturbs a sleeping Ginger Rogers in her bedroom in the apartment below. From there the plot was to build around a case of mistaken identity (a theme also germane to *The Gay Divorcée*), with Rogers thinking Astaire is the philandering husband of her best friend.

Another scene sketched out in the treatment was to take place at a zoo; Taylor suggested a song entitled "In the Birdhouse at the Zoo," and even went so far as to supply a line or two of the lyric. That would then segue into a scene at a carousel and Berlin's "Wild about You," ending up with Rogers's taking refuge in a convenient bandstand, where Astaire would busy himself by cracking peanuts. (By a lucky chance, there would happen to be a piano on the bandstand.) The entire sequence, including "Wild about You," was ultimately junked, but the rain gave Berlin the idea for another song that *did* remain: "Isn't This a Lovely Day (to Be Caught in the Rain)?"

The number Berlin had brought to California with him was based on "Moon over Napoli," from the abandoned Hart show *More Cheers.* Since most of the action of *Top Hat* takes place in Venice (as interpreted by RKO's masters of Art Deco), it made sense to Berlin to use his Italianate orphan. With assistance from Hal Bourne, whom the studio provided to make piano copies, he transformed the song into the incomparable "Cheek to Cheek." Alec Wilder, in his study *American Popular Song,* classes this tune among Berlin's experimental songs, which he created primarily for the theater, not for Hollywood. What made it work in this instance was Astaire: "He's a real inspiration for a writer," Berlin would later say of the performer. "I'd never have written *Top Hat* without him."

The innovative "Cheek to Cheek" runs to no less than seventy-two measures, in the form A-A-B-B-C-A, a decided departure from popular-song norms and particularly remarkable for a Hollywood musical. Designed as a dance as well as a song, the number has a surprising touch in its extra C section of eight bars ("Dance with me, I want my arms about you . . ."), a kind of climax, now in the minor, rising almost out of Astaire's range to a near falsetto, then slipping back into the sixteen bars of the A section—yet another novelty in that this section ("Heaven, I'm in Heaven . . .") is thus heard three times instead of the conventional two.

Despite the song's structural inventiveness, the melody itself moves flawlessly and seamlessly from beginning to end, with no attention being called to its disregard for the customary practices of popular songwriting. It is, quite simply—or not so simply—a hauntingly beautiful song.

The film's Venetian setting was to inspire the finale, a big dance number featuring Astaire, Rogers, and ensemble, like those that had closed their previous hits. Berlin arrived at one of the production conferences bearing his finale candidate, a song he called "The Piccolino" (literally, a very small flute). Ensemble dance director Hermes Pan objected, pointing out that it was a song about a *song* ("And *hear* them *play* the Piccolino"), not about a *dance.* He wanted something more along the lines of "The Carioca" or "The Continental." Not missing a beat, Berlin suggested an alternative:

> *Come and do the Lido*
> *It's very good for your libido.*

What Pan finally got was a song parodying the preceding films' big dances, though "The Piccolino" itself was no less extravagant a production. Borrowing from Busby Berkeley, Pan utilized overhead patterned shots to film the many dancers. After Rogers sings a song about a Brooklyn "Latin" who writes popular tunes for Venetians, she and Astaire dance, first together and then with the rest of the company on the casino's spacious dance floor. The couple's canonical misunderstanding is at last cleared up (she learns he is not her friend's wayward husband), and with Astaire in top hat, they exit with a dancing flourish.

The film finished shooting early in the summer of 1935. Berlin had by then left the Beverly Wilshire and rented a house in Santa Monica, where he was joined by Ellin and their daughters. *Top Hat* was ready for its California previews in July and scheduled to open at Radio City Music Hall late in August. Audience polling at the previews led to the elimination of about ten minutes' worth of film, but the overall reception was favorable, and Berlin could look forward to the picture's release confident in his achievement.

This otherwise happy time, however, was punctuated by sad news from Brooklyn. Berlin's sister Sarah, the eldest of the Beilin children who had immigrated to America, died, according to newspaper accounts, at the age of fifty-three after plunging from the roof of her apartment building in the Brownsville section. She had been the most distant of the siblings, often morose, quiet, and unhappy. She had married badly: Abraham Henkin, also from Russia, had proved to be a poor provider without ambition. Nor was Brownsville in the depression an especially cheerful environment. Until improvements began, in the twenties, it had been a replica of the Lower East Side of Sarah's earliest years in America, filled with tenements, sweatshops, and pushcarts; a decade later, it was not much better. In 1935, the neighborhood remained a jumble of old tenements, two-family homes, and apartment buildings. The Henkins could not afford the better housing; though Berlin sent his sister a weekly allowance, her husband, unfortunately, did not add to that income.

In any event, it was probably depression and poor health, rather than poverty, that drove Sarah to take her own life. The more considerate newspapers reported that she might have fallen, or suffered an attack of vertigo; others asserted that she had leapt to her death. (Her family, for its part, was certain that she had committed suicide.) Common to all accounts was the fact that she was the sister of the famous songwriter Irving Berlin.

Berlin immediately boarded an airplane for New York (in 1935 even a nonstop flight took about eighteen hours) and arrived in time for her Sunday burial. He was greeted by his brother Ben, their surviving sisters, other members of the immediate family—and the curious press. Berlin and Ben Baline were accompanied by their pretty niece Mildred Kahn, daughter of their sister Ruth.

When the grimly sad service was over, Berlin returned to Santa Monica, to his own family and his next Astaire-Rogers musical. The critical and public reception of *Top Hat* and its songs encouraged RKO to exercise its option and hire him to score a second film for its star dance team. (In *Top Hat*'s first week, Radio City Music Hall's box office took in $134,800; after three, the figure would rise to $350,000. This gladdened many an RKO heart. The film had cost $620,000 to make and would ultimately gross $3 million, earning Berlin twice the fee he had asked for when his contract discussions began.)

Even more gratifying than the high praise accorded the songs by reviewers, however, was the recognition brought by their being broadcast nationally on a radio program that had premiered that July. "Your Hit Parade" was an hourlong show, with guests, that aired on Saturday nights. During the course of each program, the week's fifteen top popular tunes, "determined by a nationwide survey," were performed in no particular order (later the top three would be saved for the final minutes of the broadcast). "Your Hit Parade" soon became a much-relied-on indicator of a song's popularity, as proved by sheet-music and record sales, performances by bands, and number of radio plays. How the weekly selections were arrived at remains unclear, but in the thirties and into the forties the roster was of major importance to both music publishers and filmmakers.

During the "Hit Parade" broadcast of September 28, 1935, *Top Hat* made history: all five of its songs were played, with "Cheek to Cheek" in first place. The week before, the same song had been in third, with "Top Hat" in eleventh, "Isn't This a Lovely Day?" in thirteenth, and "No Strings" at number fourteen. For the next month, "Cheek to Cheek" stayed in first place, as some of the other songs moved around from spot to spot. "Cheek to Cheek" was on "Your Hit Parade" for no less than twelve weeks in all—a most salutary success for Berlin and RKO, not to mention Irving Berlin, Inc. As his friend Joe Schenck pointed out, as much as publishers had traditionally distrusted radio—which they knew could kill a song in weeks and curtail record sales, as Victor Herbert et al. had testified to Congress in 1924—this was one instance in which they might actually profit from it, since musical films were readily plugged and promoted by the medium, and often even publicized into top box-office rank.

The shock of his sister's death began to ease with the heady success of Berlin's first major film score and the beginning of hard work on the next. He labored in the Santa Monica house, sharing a piano with Mary Ellin. When not at the keyboard, he swam in the Pacific with her and Jack MacKenzie and enjoyed his usual late breakfasts in the hot sun. His wife insisted the sun was backward in California, where it set; in the East, she maintained, it rose as it should.) Despite her jibes about life on the Coast, Ellin made a new friend in the patrician Phyllis Astaire, wife of Fred, who had himself become close to Berlin. Another regular in their circle was Mrs. Irving Thalberg, married to the very young but powerful producer at Metro-Goldwyn-Mayer (he would die suddenly the next year, at thirty-seven); she was better known as the film star Norma Shearer. The Thalbergs lived next door to the Berlins, with old friends the Goldwyns just a few houses away.

The Goldwyns had settled in Santa Monica in February 1935, with the *Hollywood Reporter*'s recording the event of their housewarming,

> an elegant tea party honoring the Cole Porters. Among the guests were the Fred Astaires, the Irving Berlins, Mary Pickford and Connie Bennett with Gilbert Roland. The same crowd was also at a party the Berlins gave the next night for the Porters and Moss Hart. In the wee hours of the morning, the guests of honor, who hadn't been to bed, departed on an around-the-world cruise [which would result in their Broadway musical *Jubilee*].

The Berlins' house on Ocean Front, like virtually all others in the area, came equipped with a guest house and swimming pool (though the ocean was only a short walk away). Among their houseguests during this period were composer Harold Arlen and his wife-to-be, model (and bit player in several musicals of the day) Anya Taranda. Other good musical friends were Jerome Kern and Max Winslow and, a little later, the Gershwins. Joseph Schenck—"Uncle Joe" to Mary Ellin and Linda—was also a frequent visitor.

The same team that had created *Top Hat* was reassembled for the next Astaire-Rogers film: Berlin, Pandro Berman, Mark Sandrich, and Hermes Pan (as Astaire's assistant this time). Dwight Taylor and Allan Scott were again credited with the screenplay. For their plot, Taylor turned to a 1922 play based on a novel, both entitled *Shore Leave*. In 1927 it had been reworked as a major Broadway musical, *Hit the Deck,* with music by Vincent Youmans; RKO bought the rights and made it into a film, with some of the score intact, in 1930. Since the "property" was RKO's, Taylor was free to use the story.

In contrast to his three previous movies, this one would not have Astaire dressed perpetually in fancy clothes—in fact, he wears them just once in *Follow the Fleet,* in which he plays a gum-chewing sailor who used to be a dancer. Ginger Rogers was cast as a performer (but not a dancer) in a dime-a-dance hall, a hangout for sailors on shore leave in San Francisco.

Rogers and Astaire were not the picture's only love interest; the nominal romantic leads were Randolph Scott and Harriet Hilliard (recently married to bandleader Ozzie Nelson). Initially the studio had wanted Irene Dunne for the latter part, hoping to repeat *Roberta*'s successful pairing of her with Scott, but she was too busy starring in the film version of *Show Boat.* Hilliard's and Scott's characters, Connie Martin and Bilge Smith, were drawn from the original novel (and play, musical, and film), while Rogers's and Astaire's were newly conceived by Dwight Taylor and Allan Scott. Interestingly absent are the familiar secondary comic characters of the RKO stock company, not to mention the customary big ensemble dance numbers.

Another break with tradition concerned the time frame. *Follow the Fleet* was set in the present, whereas the three previous Astaire-Rogers musicals had been fixed in some never-never-land of the past—the twenties before the crash, when everyone always dressed formally and no one ever seemed to work. There are no spacious ballrooms in the film, just a battleship deck, a dance floor in the Paradise Club, and the deck of a smaller ship, the *Connie Martin* (refurbished by the lovesick Connie for Bilge to captain as her husband, a proposition that causes him to flee; theirs is a troubled romance).

The script explains Astaire's unfashionable gob's attire: when his onetime dancing partner (Rogers) refuses to marry him, he simply joins the navy. Their wisecracking banter gives the plodding plot its sparkle—that and the Berlin songs and, of course, the dancing. (Although the film was not scheduled to begin shooting until early November, Astaire, the consummate professional, started rehearsing the dances in September with Hermes Pan and pianist Hal Bourne, who had already worked with Berlin in setting down the music.)

Never one to waste a good effort, Berlin brought out a song intended for Ginger Rogers in *Top Hat* but not actually used in that film. "Get Thee behind Me, Satan" was given to Harriet Hilliard as a kind of soliloquy, an inner questioning of her emotions as she waits for Scott, whom she plans to invite back to her place.

This latter made for an interesting plot point, especially in light of the vehemence with which the Hays Office and the Legion of Decency were then decrying the morality of the products of sinful Hollywood. A line adroitly delivered by a smart-tongued Lucille Ball slipped by both.

Hilliard was cast as Rogers's dowdy music-teacher sister, who wears glasses not because she needs them but because she wants to impress her students; her clothes do nothing for her, nor does her matronly hairdo. When Bilge first sees her at the Paradise Club, he is not in the least attracted. But thinking she should have more fun, her sister makes her discard her glasses (a sure disguiser of beauty in the films of the period), change her hair, and dress more glamorously. Bilge, of course, won't know what hit him.

The makeover job is assigned to Kitty (played by Ball), who studies her subject skeptically and then pronounces, "Clothes make the man." (Evidently the wordplay was too subtle to sound the censors' alarms.)

The now-knockout Connie, having resolved to seduce Bilge, tries to silence her own doubts in Berlin's brooding ballad. Marked "slowly," it is in the key of C and has no verse, but all songwriting canons end there. "Get Thee behind Me" is a complex, extended song of thirty-six measures. In the A section, the initial sixteen bars are followed by a variant form of the same section as the melody rises, then descends. The B section of six measures leads into yet another variant of the A section, which concludes almost abruptly after the lines "Get thee behind me [pause]/ Stay where you are, it's too late."

It is a hauntingly beautiful song, amazingly adventurous for its time and place. Although Hilliard is appealing in the role, her voice isn't quite up to the task. Her other solo, sung to an audience at a party, is the more conventional yet despondent "But Where Are You?" This and "Get Thee behind Me" are the only songs in the film that are related to the plot; all others are performances, save for the sea chantey "We Saw the Sea" (in which Berlin manages to rhyme "Black Sea" with "taxi," and the singing sailors admit that though they are never seasick, they *are* awfully sick of the sea).

The most ambitious dance sequence—with Astaire in tails and Rogers in a ravishing gown—takes place on the deck of the *Connie Martin,* as part of a benefit staged to pay for the ship's newly fabricated seaworthiness. The dance finale of the film, it is set to one of the finest songs ever written by any composer: "Let's Face the Music and Dance."

Originally created for Irene Dunne when she was to appear as Connie, it was clearly *not* a song for her replacement, Harriet Hilliard. (Dunne, a trained soprano, had had her share of success in Broadway musicals; as the star of the 1929 touring company of *Show Boat,* she had won a Hollywood contract on the strength of her presence and voice. After a tentative start, she had gone on to sing in *Roberta,* the fine film *Show Boat,* and other movie musicals.) Fascinating (if fruitless) though it is to contemplate what Dunne might have done with "Let's Face the Music," assigning it to Astaire was one of the wiser decisions made by Berman and Sandrich—and Berlin, too, was pleased. He and Astaire worked well together, and he listened respectfully to the dancer's opinions and suggestions.

Ultimately, however, as a songwriter, Berlin kept his own counsel. As Pandro Berman later recalled for Mary Ellin Barrett's memoir,

Irving Berlin was the toughest trader I've ever met in the film business, the hardest-headed businessman I've ever known, [but once negotiations were concluded,] there wasn't anything I needed to do. . . . [We] talked over the script. You could tell him this or that was needed. But you couldn't tell him how to do things. You wouldn't. My job was over when I engaged him. . . . He was a brilliant fellow.

"Let's Face the Music" is Berlin at his best—a ballad at once "majestic and somber," according to John Mueller, "the kind of throaty, melancholy melody the cello seems to have been invented to play . . . and Astaire sings it with appropriate ardor and insistence." In the film, the song is sung in the show-within-a-show on the deck of the *Connie Martin,* by one near-suicide to another, so the melancholy tone is fitting. Unlike the big dance finales of the previous films, this number features only Rogers and Astaire. A sort of self-contained, miniature drama, it begins with Astaire's gambling away all his money and being shunned by his former socialite friends; he strolls out onto a deserted terrace (the most opulent set in the film—Art Deco, of course), with city lights in the background. Snubbed again by his "friends" (there is no dialogue; the richly orchestrated music alone sets the brooding indigo mood), he takes a pistol from a pocket and puts it to his head, only to turn and spot Rogers on the terrace railing, apparently about to plunge into the river below. He stops her and, in pantomime, reveals his own suicidal predicament: he shows her his empty wallet, smiles, and tosses it into the river, then produces his gun, which she attempts to snatch from him; he throws that, too, into the water. With the scene thus set, the song begins.

What follows is the longest musical sequence in the movie, lasting almost eight minutes (by way of contrast, "Get Thee behind Me" runs for little more than a minute and a half; "Let Yourself Go," sung by Rogers and a trio, takes up only a minute and forty-nine seconds). Although composed in a deceptively simple A-B-C-A form, the song has an unconventional structure. The A section is a fourteen-measure statement of the theme in a bluesy C minor, slipping in the eighth bar into an unexpected E natural, then brightening into C major. The sixteen-measure B section commences with a restatement of the first four bars before introducing a variant ("Before they ask us to pay the bill"). The release (C section) is once again brighter in feeling—eight bars of hope ("Soon we'll be without the moon . . .")—but then the final part logically returns to the morose mood, this time for eighteen measures, with four of these serving as a concluding tag, repeating the title with an added "dance."

The composition thus adds up to an unorthodox fifty-six measures. Berlin was not following any rules of popular songwriting here, only meeting the needs of the screenplay, as determined through his talks with Berman, Sandrich, and Astaire. The pantomime and dance sequences were conceived jointly by Astaire and Hermes Pan; the music was arranged by Max Steiner and orchestrated by Maurice de Packh.

The gown worn by Ginger Rogers in this scene seems to have a life of its own. Designed by Bernard Newman, it is svelte, glovelike in fit, a bit see-through whenever Rogers dances in front of a light. Even the rather peculiar, extraneous fur piece about the shoulders cannot detract from the seductiveness of the remarkably slinky dress. The sleeves, full and wide, hang heavily from Rogers's wrists, and the hem whirls poetically in graceful patterns as she and Astaire dance. These effects were achieved by a bit of costume "magic": lead weights were sewn into both sleeves and hem. Astaire estimated that the sleeves weighed "a few pounds each," and he would have known: during a spin, he was clocked by one of them in the eye and on the jaw, after which he continued to dance despite being "somewhat maimed." Ironically, though another twenty takes would be filmed, the one selected for the final cut was the first, in which Astaire was walloped.

Follow the Fleet would premiere at New York's Radio City Music Hall on February 20, 1936, to a mixed reception from the critics, who all loved Astaire's dancing but largely overlooked the contributions of an exquisite Rogers and some first-rate songs. Inevitably, comparisons would be made to *Top Hat,* both pro and con. The negative reviews would have little impact on the box office, however: the film was a hit, second only to *Top Hat* as the most profitable in the Astaire-Rogers series.

Berlin's songs would suffer a curious fate. Not one was to be nominated for an Academy Award, though three would figure on "Your Hit Parade" from March through May. "Let Yourself Go" would start in fifteenth place on March 7 and close the *Fleet* song run in fourteenth on May 23, managing to reach second place in the course of its eleven airings. "I'm Putting All My Eggs in One Basket" and "Let's Face the Music and Dance" would be performed nine and eight times, respectively.

Berlin, and Hollywood, would keep an eye on these ups and downs. Successful as the songs were, for Berlin they were not quite successful enough. Ever the gentleman, though, he did not mind at all when Jerome Kern and Dorothy Fields took that year's Oscar for their lovely ballad "The Way You Look Tonight," from another Astaire-Rogers film, *Swing Time.* The song made the "Hit Parade" fourteen times and was in the top notch for seven of those. *Swing Time*'s August 1936 release signifies that America's most popular dance team must have had to begin work on that film almost the moment they completed *Follow the Fleet.* In March, RKO announced that they would do yet another picture, entitled *Never Gonna Dance.* (Eventually it was filmed as *Swing Time* with music by Jerome Kern.) After that, Astaire and Rogers would go on to do a film scored by the Gershwins before being reunited with Berlin.

During the break between wrapping *Follow the Fleet* and beginning his next project—this one for Joe Schenck at Twentieth Century-Fox—Berlin took his family back to New York, where Mary Ellin was enrolled at the Brearley School. Ellin was not feeling well, so Berlin celebrated his older daughter's ninth birthday himself, taking her and twenty of her classmates first to the Rodgers and Hart musical *Jumbo,* starring Jimmy Durante (whose antics were greeted by a shrieking assemblage from Brearley) as an elephant among other circus elephants, and then to see Paul Whiteman and his orchestra at the Hippodrome.

Ellin's "illness" was, in fact, another pregnancy. In December, now three months along, she was well enough to attend the annual Christmas party at Brearley. Sensing it would do his wife good to have a bit of a respite from the often boisterous Mary Ellin, Berlin on Christmas Night boarded a train for Miami and from there flew to Nassau with his elder daughter and Gabrielle Amuat, the governess whom the Berlin girls addressed as "Mademoiselle." Linda, then three, remained at home in Manhattan with her mother and a nanny.

For ten days father and daughter fished and sat in the sun. Young Mary Ellin felt quite grown up mingling with British residents and New York friends of Berlin's, among them Hassard Short, who had worked on three Music Box Revues, *Face the Music,* and *As Thousands Cheer.*

Mary Ellin got back to New York in time for the spring 1936 semester at Brearley, and Berlin returned to Hollywood to start work on his new picture for Joe Schenck. On January 20, a Silver Jubilee celebration of the publication of "Alexander's Ragtime Band" was held at the Ambassador Hotel in Los Angeles. More than 150 of Hollywood's most powerful personalities attended the formal dinner, among them studio heads Schenck and Samuel Goldwyn, producers Irving Thalberg and Darryl F. Zanuck (newly installed at Fox by Schenck), and many from the musical world in Hollywood, including Max Winslow, Al Jolson, Al Piantadosi (who had unknowingly inspired Berlin's first published song), Harold Arlen, and Jerome Kern, who served as master of ceremonies. Johnny Green, the bandleader and composer who had recorded the *Top Hat* songs with Fred Astaire, led one of the bands, and several of the other songwriters present serenaded the honoree with his own songs.

Variety, in its coverage of the gala evening, reported that Berlin was visibly surprised to find that one had to pass through swinging doors to enter the dining room, which had been redecorated as a replica of Mike Salter's Pelham Café, complete with sawdusted floor and an upright piano on which a "Feed the Kitty" box was placed. The festivities kicked off with a medley of songs sung by Berlin, accompanied by Piantadosi, beginning with "Alexander's Ragtime Band" and ending with "Cheek to Cheek." Dinner and speeches followed, with Berlin himself briefly thanking all who had come, especially those of his colleagues who had sung his songs.

When the party was over, it was time to get to work again. Screenwriters Gene Markey and William Conselman obviously took some cues from their composer (Markey was credited as producer, but Zanuck clearly had his untutored fingers in the musical pie): the film's title was to be *On the Avenue,* a line from Berlin's earlier hit "Easter Parade." The plot would center on a successful satirical revue of the same title, one of whose sketches lampoons the richest girl in the world, her father, and her dogs. What might have happened, the writers asked, had (for example) Barbara Hutton or the Rockefellers sued all concerned with *As Thousands Cheer* for their treatment in that show?

The resulting film is a backstager with an ingenious twist. It is not, for once, about getting a musical on the stage; rather, the story is about how the heiress (portrayed by the nonsinging Madeleine Carroll, a beautiful British blonde who might easily have doubled for Ellin Mackay) schemes to get a hit musical *off* the stage, or at least get the offending sketch dropped. The show-within-the-film's writer, and star, was played by Dick Powell, who had moved to Fox from Warner Brothers (with Zanuck) and in the process graduated from his usual juvenile singing roles, mostly opposite Ruby Keeler. Alice Faye, a rising singing star at Fox, portrayed a revue cast member in love with Powell, who himself of course falls in love with the vindictive rich girl (and, of course again, vice versa).

Because all of the musical numbers except one were to be presented as part of the interior revue, there was no need for them to be integrated. The exception was "You're Laughing at Me," which is pertinent to the plot: Powell sings it to Carroll when they stop to park during a drive (the car radio, fortuitously, supplies the music). The song dated back to the late twenties, though it was never published then—some sources say because Berlin considered it "so bad." He did preserve it, however, and it is, in fact, a fine number.

A throwaway verse adroitly sets up the theme of the song in conversation, when Gary (Powell) tells Mimi (Carroll) that though she listens to his declarations, she never gives him any inkling of her own feelings; she always has her tongue in cheek.

Although the song is in standard thirty-two-bar form, its structure ranks it among Berlin's most innovative creations. The A section takes up only eight measures, followed by the B section in an ambiguous key, also eight bars long (the A section is not repeated, as per usual practice). The final A section slides into another key and, over sixteen measures, works through a variation on the original statement, ending with a repetition of "You're laughing at me" a third higher.

Berlin did not deliberately set out to write a "different" song, a rangy song with a compass of thirteen steps, or key shifts. But since he often conceived words and music simultaneously, he could build the melody of the chorus on the words that would become the song's title. From there he readily moved on to the next comment, "I can't be sentimental for you're laughing at me . . . ," adding an unexpected tag (and key change) with "I know." It is as logical as it is surprising.

Similarly exceptional and inventive (in its use of chromatics in the chorus, that is; there is no verse) is "I've Got My Love to Keep Me Warm." During the film's production, Berlin was irritated to learn that Zanuck was planning to drop the number. Zanuck was no Pandro Berman: as the producer in charge, he intended to control every aspect of *On the Avenue.* Berlin sent him a memo in which he acknowledged that Zanuck knew a good story when he read one, but asserted that his own judgment of songs was, he thought, "pretty good." The song stayed in and vindicated Berlin's persistence by making the "Hit Parade" in March of the next year, a month after *On the Avenue's* release.

Alice Faye was assigned the song that would become the picture's biggest hit, "This Year's Kisses." In the standard key of C and in common four-four time, it is a frugal composition (less the verse) of a mere twenty-eight bars: A section (twelve), B section (eight), and repeated A section (a concentrated eight measures). On "Your Hit Parade" for a total of eight weeks, it topped the list three times.

Working with Zanuck (luckily with Joe Schenck pulling strings in the background) was not as relaxed or as pleasant as turning out a musical for RKO; nor were Fox's efforts as sparkling and witty as the other studio's Astaire-Rogers productions. *On the Avenue's* musical numbers were well done, but the show-within-a-show's sets lacked the RKO Art Deco sweep: with most of its musical sequences shot on a stage, the Fox film was necessarily more realistic.

Berlin was, if not precisely eager, at least ready to start on his next Zanuck assignment, but screenplay problems postponed the production. It was to be a grand musical panorama encompassing about a quarter century's worth of popular tunes, all of them by Berlin. The score would comprise twenty songs from the Berlin catalog, beginning with "Alexander's Ragtime Band," as well as a couple more written especially for the film. Because it was to draw so heavily on the songwriter's oeuvre, and because the lead was to stage a First World War army revue, Fox and Zanuck suggested turning the film into a musical biography of Irving Berlin. Berlin would not hear of it, and the idea was abandoned, but when *Alexander's Ragtime Band* was finally released (more than a year was spent on it), popular belief still held that it was Berlin's own story.

While Zanuck was driving his writers to come up with a screenplay, Berlin was occupied with more important concerns: on June 16, 1936, his wife gave birth to their third daughter and last child, Elizabeth Irving. While Ellin recuperated, Janet Tannant was added to the staff, primarily to look after the new baby while Mademoiselle tended Mary Ellin and Linda.

Around this same time, word reached Berlin that George and Ira Gershwin were heading out to California to write songs for Astaire at RKO. Enthusiastically, Berlin wrote them, "There is no setup in Hollywood that can compare with doing an Astaire picture, and I know you will be very happy with it." His letter was dated June 23, 1936; on the twenty-sixth, the Gershwins signed a contract with Pandro Berman that would result in *Shall We Dance?* (with Rogers and Astaire) and *A Damsel in Distress* (Astaire only).

While the script-wrangling over *Alexander*—with various writers coming and going—continued under the vigilant eye of Darryl Zanuck, Berlin, bored with waiting, elected to take his own advice and return to the salubrious "setup" at RKO. After *Follow the Fleet,* Astaire and Rogers appeared together in the Kern- and Gershwin-scored musicals *Swing Time* and *Shall We Dance?,* but there was trouble in this paradise. Rumors spread of the team's breakup, even whispers that they resented one another (which was not true). When Rogers, in 1936, became difficult during contract negotiations, RKO itself fueled the flames of gossip by hinting that she might be replaced by Carole Lombard, Ruby Keeler, or British singer-dancer Jessie Matthews. Actually, both partners were seeking a change: Rogers hoped to appear in dramatic films (and eventually did), and Astaire wanted to dance with someone new (he would get his wish in the person of Joan Fontaine for the Gershwins' last RKO effort, *A Damsel in Distress,* which preceded *Carefree,* the Astaire-Rogers rapprochement with Berlin songs).

RKO also had another, more immediate concern: the bottom line. *Shall We Dance?,* though a success, had not taken off at the box office like the dance duo's earlier pictures; the consensus was that they were all too much alike. While Astaire's *A Damsel in Distress* was being prepared and shot, Rogers appeared, to critical acclaim, in two nonmusicals, the comedy *Having Wonderful Time* (1938) and the excellent comedy-drama *Stage Door* (1937), in which she held her own on the screen opposite Katharine Hepburn.

When the time came for Astaire and Rogers's contracted reunion, Berlin teamed up once again with Berman, Sandrich, and Pan. Scriptwriter Dwight Taylor had since moved on, but Allan Scott remained; his new collaborator was Ernest Pagano, who specialized in comedy dialogue. Their screenplay was based on a story by Dudley Nichols and Hagar Wilde, which was in turn derived from an idea by Marian Ainslee and Guy Endore. There were more plot twists than musical cues this time: Astaire was cast not as a dancer but as a psychiatrist who once had show-business aspirations; Rogers's character is a popular radio vocalist.

Ralph Bellamy plays a stuffy, humorless, longtime friend of Astaire's who is in love with Rogers. She refuses to marry him; a trip to an analyst, he feels, will cure her hesitation. Deadpan comic commentary fell to Broadway-seasoned Luella Gear (appearing in her film debut as Ginger Rogers's youngish aunt), who in one scene turns away a hopeful, rather pompous judge who wants to dance, with a stern "Joe, you know I don't dance at your age."

Carefree constitutes a real departure from the usual Astaire-Rogers formula: there are no mistaken identities, no fallings-out, no reconciliations—just one misunderstanding that is quickly patched up. As Stanley Green has noted, the settings—Astaire's office and the country club where most of the action takes place—"endowed the picture with . . . the trappings of believable affluence rather than the implausible elegance" of the pair's earlier films.

Once the original story had passed through several hands, including Berman's and Sandrich's, the screenplay was given to Berlin to spot the songs. But the abundance of plot left little room for song; the score Berlin turned in in the spring of 1937 contained only five numbers. Not really a musical, *Carefree* was instead a comedic play with music—and even some of that, as it eventuated, was incidental. One song, the memorable "The Night Is Filled with Music," is heard as dance music in the club, and again later as underscoring, but it is never actually sung. Astaire does his first number while practicing his golf swing as, for a few moments, Rogers watches. In an earlier scene, she huffed out of his office after inadvertently listening to a tape recording in which he referred to her as "one of those dizzy, silly, maladjusted females who can't make up her mind"; now, observing him from a bridge above the tee, she disconcerts him with sarcastic laughs and comments, whereupon he demonstrates his golfing and dancing skills to the tune of Berlin's (again unsung) "Since They Turned 'Loch Lomond' into Swing." He accompanies himself on the harmonica, does a traditional Scottish sword dance (using golf clubs), tosses in a few turns, and smacks several balls onto the green without a hitch. The number was Astaire's own idea; in devising an appropriate musical complement, Berlin took his cue from the fact that golf was a Scottish invention.

Producer Berman presented the composer with his next cue. Astaire's psychiatrist character induces his patient Rogers to eat a revolting dinner that will cause her to have vivid dreams, thus giving him something to work with the next day. All in the party are queasy by the time the evening ends, but the menu works: Rogers has her dream. Berman's notion was to film the dream (and only the dream) in color; Berlin's contribution was the song "I Used to Be Color-Blind." But with RKO again sliding toward bankruptcy, economics ruled out Technicolor, and the sequence was shot, like the rest of the picture, in black and white.

The song has a simple, direct melody, with a clever lyric to match. At the beginning (the A section), Astaire states that he was once color-blind but now, having met Rogers (in her dream, that is), has become aware of green grass, a golden moon, and blue skies. In the final four bars he makes it more personal: "The red in your cheeks, the gold in your hair, the blue in your eyes."

The dance that follows, in a dream-world of giant lily pads and tall mushrooms, with a black-and-white rainbow in the background, lapses, after a few moments, into slow motion, and closes with the duo's first full-scale on-camera kiss (Hollywood legend had it that Phyllis Astaire had proscribed her husband's on-screen kissing—untrue, of course).

The dream reveals to Rogers that she is in love with her analyst, but she can't tell him that. When he suggests terminating their sessions, she persuades him to prolong her treatment with a wild story about a recurring nightmare she has been having—"a perfect mass of the most horrible neuroses and inhibitions." To cure her of the latter, Astaire puts her under anesthesia, then leaves the room. At that moment, Bellamy rushes in to wake her: she is due at the radio station. The scene that follows displays Rogers's remarkable comedic talents. Relieved of all her inhibitions, she fluffs Bellamy's tie, annoys people, and mischievously smashes a large plate-glass sheet (after winking at the driver on whose truck it is being transported), using as her projectile a nightstick "borrowed" from a policeman, whom she also manages to kick before the anesthesia wears off. She is finally brought up before the pompous judge, who places her in Astaire's custody and warns her not to run amok again.

At dinner that evening at the club, after beaning the judge with a bread roll, Rogers forces Astaire to dance with her. "The Yam" is the film's requisite big dance number, and the only one to employ other dancers—a "traveling dance" that moves through the club, out to the patio, and back onto the dining room's dance floor. In other Astaire-Rogers musicals, such a number would have ended the film on a grand note, but *Carefree* instead goes on from here.

After "The Yam," Rogers tries to tell Bellamy that she is in love with Astaire, but he thinks she is talking about him and blurts to their party that the two of them are engaged. Rogers and Astaire then dance again (to the "Color Blind" music), and she admits to her love for him. Rattled, he insists that she come to his office the next day.

Another scene of mayhem ensues, after Astaire hypnotizes her and attempts to convince her that she is in love with Bellamy, not him, and that he himself deserves to be shot "like a dog." Taking him at his word, after escaping again, she proceeds to shoot up the country club with a skeet gun in her eagerness to put a bullet in Astaire. A shocked Bellamy turns on his friend, and the judge forbids the doctor to come anywhere near his patient again.

Disregarding the judge's order, Astaire shows up at the Bellamy-Rogers engagement party at the country club that night (by now he has realized that he is in love with her, having discussed the situation with himself by means of a mirror). Still persuaded that she is in love with Bellamy, but evidently no longer homicidal, Rogers treats her former analyst with cold disdain, refusing to dance with him. While fiancé and fiancée take a turn on the floor, Astaire dances with Rogers's aunt, who knows who really loves whom (and vice versa).

The final song, "Change Partners," is an ingenious plot device. As the two couples circle each other on the dance floor, Astaire plants an idea in Rogers's mind through the lyric of this conversational, and verseless, ballad, one of Berlin's stateliest melodies:

Must you dance ev'ry dance with the same fortunate man?

Astaire then suggests, "Won't you change partners and dance with me?" In counterpoint to the brooding tune, the contrasting rhythmic release introduces another proposal: "Ask him to sit this one out, and while you're alone,/ I'll tell the waiter to tell him he's wanted on the telephone." When Rogers complies, Astaire's assistant engages Bellamy in a fake phone call (the fact that they are in adjoining booths, however, enables the duped Bellamy quickly to catch on).

Meanwhile, Rogers has wandered out to the club's pavilion, where Astaire hypnotically induces her to dance to Berlin's indelible melody. Afterward, when they are seated again, she stares blankly into space. Bellamy hur-ries over, followed by the aunt and the judge, who threatens the doctor with imprisonment if he does anything untoward—and especially if he interferes in any way with the Bellamy-Rogers wedding, set for the next day.

On the day of the wedding, with the connivance of Rogers's aunt, Astaire and his assistant sneak onto the grounds of the house where the ceremony is to take place. While skulking in the shrubbery, the assistant has an idea: what Rogers needs to bring her out of her hypnotic state is some sort of a shock, like a sock on the jaw (psychiatric theory be damned). Concurring, Astaire manages to slip into the house and then into the room where Rogers is getting dressed. He makes a fist, preparing to punch her, but can't go through with it. Bellamy, once again bursting in, solves the problem by taking a swing at Astaire, missing, and striking Rogers—who, after a little more business with hypnotism, marches down the aisle with her smiling analyst/groom. The patient/bride is smiling, too, though she has a noticeably black eye.

The film ends there, without the customary big dance finale. For the most part, the critical reception would be favorable, though there would be some quibbling about the less-than-simple plot. The dance team was warmly welcomed back, but *Carefree,* as Stanley Green has remarked, was their most forgotten film, and their least successful financially.

Of Berlin's songs for the score, only "Change Partners" was to achieve any real popularity, airing on the "Hit Parade" nine times, in the number-one spot twice. Ironically, the same week that "Change Partners" was sung on the program for the first time (in third place), two more Berlin tunes, from his *other* 1938 film, were also on the hit roster: "Now It Can Be Told" and the old favorite "Alexander's Ragtime Band." Although the two pictures were scored many months apart, they were released within three months of each other, with *Alexander's Ragtime Band* coming out first. Nominated for an Academy Award, "Change Partners" would ultimately lose out to "Thanks for the Memory" by Ralph Rainger and Leo Robin, sung by Bob Hope and Shirley Ross in *Big Broadcast of 1938.*

Carefree itself would be likewise overshadowed by *Alexander's Ragtime Band,* the major film musical of the year, a lavish ("big-budget"), well-promoted, and bountifully scored (with twenty-two songs, all by Berlin) production. Once the film finally got under way, Zanuck did not stint. The same could not be said for the composer, however: of the twenty-two songs, only two were written specifically for the film.

Back in the summer of 1937, with the *Carefree* songs completed, Berlin, still waiting for a Zanuck-approved screenplay, took some time off. In July there was the shock of George Gershwin's premature death at thirty-eight.

Since the Gershwins' arrival and their move into a fine house in Beverly Hills, the friendship between the songwriters had blossomed. In a letter written to a New York friend late in 1936, Gershwin had noted,

> We have many friends here from the East, so the social life has . . . improved greatly [since his first Hollywood experience, in 1931]. All the writingmen and tunesmiths get together in a way that is practically impossible in the East. I've seen a great deal of Irving Berlin and Jerome Kern at poker parties and dinners and the feeling around is very "gemutlich."

One night in mid-June 1937, the Berlins invited the Gershwins—George, Ira, and Ira's wife, Leonore—and Oscar Levant and his fiancée, actress June Gale to dinner. As they were leaving, Levant and Gale came upon George Gershwin sitting on the curb, his head in his hands, in obvious pain. He had been complaining of severe nauseous headaches over the past few weeks, though medical examinations had revealed nothing. (Some suspected he was faking because he no longer found Hollywood quite so gemütlich; he was unhappy working for Samuel Goldwyn on *The Goldwyn Follies.*)

Less than three weeks later, on July 11, 1937, Gershwin died following surgery for a brain tumor. The stunning news unfurled a pall over Hollywood, especially among his fellow tunesmiths. Berlin was unable to attend the funeral services and interment in New York, but he did get to the impressive memorial concert held in the Hollywood Bowl on September 8. A year later, when Merle Armitage, a designer and impresario who had produced the first revival of *Porgy and Bess,* prepared a volume of essays in honor of Gershwin, Berlin contributed a poem alluding to Paul Whiteman's "Experiment in Modern Music" concert and "Rhapsody in Blue," praising Gershwin's way with a melody and rhythm (". . . just rhythm will soon gather 'corn' ") and grand opera. Its final stanza reads as follows:

> And this morning's *Variety* tells me
> That the last song he wrote is a hit,
> It's on top in the list of best sellers,
> And the air-waves are ringing with it.
> It remains with dozens of others,
> Though the man who composed them is gone;
> For a song-writer's job may be ended,
> But his melodies linger on.

The "last song" referred to was "Love Walked In," from *The Goldwyn Follies*. It comforted Berlin to know that his friend had gone out with a hit, and that the apposite self-quotation embedded in the last line of his poetic tribute was, in this instance, so palpably true.

Before the sudden jolt of Gershwin's death, Berlin had made plans for a family vacation, chartering a yacht for a month's cruise to Alaska in August. He was finished with *Carefree*, and while *Alexander's Ragtime Band* still stewed in the cauldron of rewrites, he felt he had earned a rest. All the Berlins, along with Hermine Tripet, Jack MacKenzie, and special guest Samuel Goldwyn, Jr., boarded the luxurious vessel in Seattle. Young Sammy, Mary Ellin later recalled, was surprised to see his host at the piano in the lounge and to learn that he was working: having observed Berlin with his own father and their friends, he had assumed that all Mary Ellin's father did was play cards.

Their travels took them to Juneau, with a stopover in Sitka and side trips to forests and inland streams and lakes, where Berlin, MacKenzie, Mary Ellin, and Sammy fished. "My father was my father even in Alaska," his daughter has written. "He chewed gum while fishing. He rarely sat still." As usual, he also prepared their catch, flipping the fish in a frying pan or over a campfire.

With August nearly over, they shipped out for Seattle, only to panic at sea when Linda, then five, was stricken with a high fever caused by an unidentified virus. (In 1937 parents, and their children, lived in deadly fear of infantile paralysis, or polio.) Terrified, the Berlins radioed the Coast Guard for a plane but were told it was impossible because of the bad weather. At last they located an Alaskan bush pilot who was willing to pick up the feverish Linda and her apprehensive parents and fly them to a Seattle hospital. Fortunately, no serious illness was found; the fever soon subsided, allowing the "girls" to return to New York, and Berlin and young Sammy to Hollywood.

As early as March of 1937, Berlin had worked on a script with Fox writer Richard Sherman, loosely based on his own rise as a songwriter, beginning with the success of "Alexander's Ragtime Band" and drawing on his catalog of hits for most of its score. Featuring a love triangle among a female singer, a bandleader, and a composer, it was emphatically *not* the Irving Berlin Story; he would not permit his two marriages to be trivialized as part of the plot. His songs were available for use, but not the more important personal incidents of his life.

Zanuck, however, was not happy with Sherman's treatment, nor impressed with the projected musicology, which was to move chronologically through various musical styles as it traced Berlin's professional output. As the rethinking of the script dragged on with wordy memos from the producer, Berlin lost interest and left the plotting to others. The screenplay was worked over, and revised, by staff writers Kathryn Scola and Lamar Trotti, who retained the general outline for a story covering the period from 1911 to 1937, evolving musically from ragtime to jazz to swing.

If there was any biographical parallel to be discovered in the film, it was closer to the life of Paul Whiteman than to that of Berlin. Tyrone Power was cast as Roger Grant, a classically trained violinist (like Whiteman) whose little band begins its rise in a San Francisco dive called Dirty Eddie's (a stand-in for Berlin's Pelham Café). Things get off to a bumpy start when Grant and his band arrive at Eddie's for their first audition, only to discover that the pianist, Charlie (Don Ameche), has left their music behind on a trolley car.

Luckily for them, a singer named Stella (played by Alice Faye), in from New York, happens to have a copy of Irving Berlin's "Alexander's Ragtime Band," which she hopes to use as her own audition number. Her sheet music is swiftly appropriated by Roger and the boys, who have some trouble playing the strange piece until they decide to turn it into ragtime. An incensed Stella first tries to stop them and then, having failed, joins in. They are a smashing success, but there's one hitch: bandleader and singer are from different sides of the social tracks. He, fresh from a recital and in formal dress, while she, with feather boa, looks like a denizen of a Barbary Coast saloon. The manager wants both band and vocalist together, but neither Stella nor Roger will have anything to do with the other. Peacemaker Charlie at length talks them into an armed truce, and Alexander's Ragtime Band is born; accordingly, for the rest of the film, Power's character is addressed as Alex.

The band, now complete with singer, is soon moving from one cabaret to another, each more elegant than the last, presenting songs by Berlin in what amounts to a filmed variety show. An occasional dash of plot reveals that both bandleader and pianist are in love with their vocalist, who is herself smitten with her boss, Alex. Eventually she gets her chance to appear on Broadway without the band, and becomes a Marilyn Miller–like star. Taking this as a betrayal, Alex dismantles his band and joins the army.

An authentic Berlin sequence follows, with an army show and three songs from *Yip! Yip! Yaphank.* Power's character conducts the orchestra, while Jack Haley (also a band member) does "Oh! How I Hate to Get Up in the Morning." At show's end, the entire company marches off to war singing "We're on Our Way to France," as Stella, who has come to the theater to confess her love for Alex, watches misty-eyed.

When Alex comes home from the war, he is surprised to learn that his onetime singer and pianist have married. Although briefly broken up by the news, he reassembles the band and takes on another vocalist, Ethel Merman. The Whiteman thread is picked up again as the band enjoys international acclaim before finally triumphing at Carnegie Hall. While Alex is on tour, the plot twists once more: composer Charlie, though married to Stella for some time already, informs her that she is really in love with Alex, not him, and the two of them agree to divorce.

Years pass—at least a quarter of a century—though as Green points out in his *Encyclopedia of the Musical Film,* "none of the principals ages a day." When Charlie applies for a job with Alexander's now symphonic band, he tells the leader about the divorce and notes that his ex-wife (who, he confides, truly loves Alex) has given up the theater and disappeared into the world of nightclub entertaining.

All are at last reunited on the stage of Carnegie Hall, where Stella belts out a reprise of "Alexander's Ragtime Band," accompanied by what could be the Philharmonic, before a sellout crowd. Happy ending.

In the film's trailer, Fox proclaimed that *Alexander's Ragtime Band* had taken more than two years to make, at a cost of two million dollars (over eighty different sets were used). The film's premiere was advertised the week before its general release, in May 1938, by a studio-sponsored promotional broadcast joining the cities of New York, Chicago, and Hollywood and combining the talents of Walter Winchell, sports announcer Ted Husing, Ethel Merman, Eddie Cantor, Al Jolson (who, as master of ceremonies, proved that he was not above seizing any opportunity to promote his own radio show and sponsor), and others. John Steel, of Follies fame, came on to sing "A Pretty Girl Is like a Melody," and the Brox Sisters (of the Music Box) emerged from retirement to revive their 1921 hit "Everybody Step," sounding in remarkably good voice. Merman did her new number from the film, "My Walking Stick" (the scene as shot has her impersonating the ever-elegant Astaire in top hat and tails).

From California, Alice Faye introduced *her* new song, the memorable "Now It Can Be Told," with its deft dissonances in the harmony, and a melody consisting of repeated eighth notes leading into a half, then a whole, note—an unusual melodic balancing act of contrasting themes. One of Berlin's most inventive creations, it was never to achieve the popularity it deserved. In discussing the song with a writer, Berlin would dismiss it with the terse sentence "It wasn't a hit," but in fact it did rank among the top ten on "Your Hit Parade" for over two months, getting as far as the second spot. In its final weeks it was joined on the list by two other Berlin tunes, "Alexander's Ragtime Band" and "Change Partners." (Dominating the number-one position during that period was the novelty number "A Tiskit, a Taskit," spurred by Ella Fitzgerald's best-selling record.)

Berlin himself appeared on the Fox broadcast to recite-sing his old Friars Club roastee's response, "What Can a Songwriter Say?," and to banter with Jolson and Cantor, with whom he reprised "Mandy." No mention was made of the fact that the broadcast virtually coincided with the composer's fiftieth birthday, on May 11, 1938.

Alexander's Ragtime Band, besides being a hit in itself, was also the first in a whole series of musical films showcasing collections of songs by individual songwriters, organized either biographically (in biopics of Cohan, Porter, Gershwin, et al.) or as anthologies. Berlin himself would eventually claim no less than four more of the latter type. Notably, his name was featured above *Alexander*'s title, as had been the case, too, with *On the Avenue*—a practice that would continue with his next Fox film and most that were to follow later, at other studios. His was a name to reckon with, even in Hollywood.

When *Alexander* had its klieg-lit, star-crowded press preview, much of Hollywood turned up. In the forefront were Mr. and Mrs. Darryl F. Zanuck, trailed by smiling, chattering groups, couples, and singles, including Irene Dunne, Merle Oberon, James Stewart, and the widowed Norma Shearer. Among those who stopped to speak into a microphone was composer Berlin, unaccompanied because Ellin and the girls were back in Manhattan. The film's stars then made their entrances: Tyrone Power with diminutive Janet Gaynor, Alice Faye with rising singing star Tony Martin, and Ethel Merman with Hollywood's current Cisco Kid, Cesar Romero. All were in black tie, with furs and overcoats to shield their twinkling glamour from California's cool night air.

Life soon after published a spread ostensibly generated by the film but in fact concentrating on the life of Irving Berlin; the editors asserted that more emphasis on the latter might have rescued the (rather insipid) former, an opinion widely shared by the critics. The magazine compensated for this negative view by pronouncing *Carefree* its movie of the week on its August release. By then, Berlin had begun work on his next Fox film, again starring Power, now considered a major studio asset.

Early in September, Berlin put aside this new movie to return to New York, where he was scheduled to board a ship bound for England and the London premiere of *Alexander's Ragtime Band*. But first there was a grim family situation to deal with: Clarence Mackay's throat cancer had recurred and required further surgery and hospitalization. Her father's poor health and approaching death upset Ellin Berlin deeply. Although Berlin was his customary supportive self, there was little that anyone could do after Mackay left Roosevelt Hospital and sought refuge in his town house on East Seventy-fifth

Street. Ellin visited faithfully but would not permit the inquisitive Mary Ellin to see her grandfather, even going so far as to reassure her with lies, telling her he was suffering merely from infected tonsils or a throat abscess.

Berlin had no choice: he had to go to London. For one thing, his English music representative was blocking the release of *Alexander* pending Fox's remittance of payment for the British song rights. The problem was eventually straightened out, but not until Berlin personally intervened; the experience left him determined to revoke his arrangement with Chappell and Co., Ltd., and open his own London office. When the BBC approached him with an offer to produce a radio show similar to the one that had heralded the film's American premiere, the contractual wrangling precluded his acceptance. In any event, he was anxious to return to the States.

While Berlin was in London, there was disturbing news from Germany, Italy, and Japan: word came from Tokyo that Japan would back Hitler and Mussolini with arms if war broke out. Near the end of Berlin's stay, Prime Minister Neville Chamberlain flew to Munich with French Premier Edouard Daladier to confer with Hitler and Mussolini on the future of Czechoslovakia's Sudetenland; no Czech representative was permitted to attend the meetings, under threat of war. Czechoslovakia lost its claim, of course, and the gulled Chamberlain returned to London, where he waved a piece of paper and muttered something about "peace in our time." While he was away, gas masks had been distributed in the city.

The defensive preparations, the news from Munich, the talk of war—all were most distressing. Berlin discussed these matters with his friend Alexander Korda, a Hungarian-born new Londoner and successful film producer. This brief English visit would inspire Berlin to write a special, heartening song for Korda, "It's a Lovely Day Tomorrow."

The British critics didn't like *Alexander's Ragtime Band* any more than their American counterparts had. The *Daily Express* voiced the consensus:

> Every cinematic cliché as it comes up is covered up by the ingredients of the producers, who insist on covering it up with one of Mr. Berlin's more memorable numbers. It is nice not to have to worry [about] how bored you are with boy-meets-girl, boy-loses-girl. Every time the yawn comes, so does Mr. Berlin to remind you by his melodies of some great point in show business.

Despite its cool critical reception, however, *Alexander* was a hit with audiences, thanks primarily to the cavalcade of Berlin songs.

It was time, now, for Berlin to contemplate his return to Fox and his final chores there. He had had about enough of the movie business; as he had told a reporter before his departure for London, "I feel slow in Hollywood. The tempo there is slow. So I think it is good once in a while to get back to the theater. I have a feeling that if I don't get back, I'll never see Broadway again."

The new Fox picture proved his point: production was postponed while, as usual, the screenplay was worked over, and over. October in New York can be lovely, but that year Clarence Mackay's illness cast a long shadow over the Berlin household. The news from Europe was worrisome, too: Hitler's army had moved into the Sudetenland. The American people's collective uneasiness was evident in the hysterical reaction accorded the radio broadcast "War of the Worlds," Orson Welles's adaptation of an H. G. Wells story about a Martian invasion. Basing his approach on the radio dispatches then crackling in from Europe, Welles sent listeners nationwide—at least those who missed the "fiction" disclaimer at the top of the show—into a frenzied panic.

Across the ocean the next month, reality was no less horrifying in its own way: young Nazis ran wild in Berlin, smashing the windows of Jewish-owned shops, ransacking and looting homes, and burning the city's largest synagogue. More than ninety died during the infamous *Kristallnacht*.

Ever since his trip to London, Irving Berlin had been thinking of writing a song about peace, not about war. With Hitler on the march and civil war raging in Spain (where Germany and Italy were providing Francisco Franco with not only bombers but also the pilots to fly them); with the news from Asia that despite international denunciations, the Japanese continued to bomb Chinese civilians in Canton; and with newspaper and radio correspondents reporting on all these events, and newsreel cameras catching the atrocities on film, it was a time for patriotism. So long as war remained safely distant, across an ocean or two, Americans felt quite secure, but still they were concerned.

Berlin wanted to express the feelings he and, he hoped, others had about their country. After a couple of false starts, he recalled an almost-forgotten song he had written but not used twenty years before for *Yip! Yip! Yaphank*, "God Bless America." With a little editing and the deletion of a couple of bellicose phrases, he had a new song declaring his love for the country to which he believed he owed everything he had.

He had barely dusted off the old manuscript when he was contacted by Ted Collins, manager of the extremely popular radio and recording personality Kate Smith. (Smith's screen career was slight—only three films in all, including one entitled *Hello, Everybody*, after her greeting at the beginning of every broadcast. The cheerful, Virginia-born "Songbird of the South" was portly and not at all in the Hollywood glamour mode, but she had a great presence on the air.) When Collins explained that he was seeking a patriotic number for Smith to sing in honor of Armistice Day on her weekly radio show, Berlin gave him a copy of "God Bless America"; Smith introduced it on November 11, 1938.

By the summer of 1939, the song was being sung in schools and churches, and sales of sheet music were up for the first time in years. Kate Smith and Bing Crosby both recorded it and enjoyed best-selling records. The notion spread that "God Bless America" should be adopted as the national anthem in place of the less accessible "Star-Spangled Banner," but Berlin himself was adamantly opposed, saying, "There's only one national anthem, which can never be replaced." As a further gesture, he assigned all royalties from the song to the Boy Scouts and Girl Scouts of America; within a decade, this would amount to about $200,000.

The day after Kate Smith's debut performance of "God Bless America," Clarence Mackay died at the age of sixty-four. Family members gathered at his East Seventy-fifth Street mansion three days later to attend the mobbed funeral services at St. Patrick's Cathedral. Mackay's position in the community, and the contretemps a dozen years earlier with his even more famous son-in-law, made his death news. The *Times* published an editorial extolling his accomplishments in business (an exaggeration), his charitable contributions, and his work for the Metropolitan Opera and the New York Philharmonic. Members of the Philharmonic provided the music during the services, while the police kept the crowd outside under control.

Ellin went into mourning for her father, and Berlin, out of respect for her feelings, wore the traditional black armband. Mary Ellin would remember that he still had it on when, later that year, he presented her mother with a Christmas surprise—the deed to a house and fifty-some acres of land near the tiny town of Lewbeach (named for its founder, Lew Beach), in the Catskill Mountains, about ninety miles northwest of Manhattan.

The rustic setting boasted a rambling house with a brook, a modest waterfall, and plenty of evergreens. Nearby, a well-stocked trout stream flashed through a pinewoods. The house, not counting the upstairs attic, contained seven rooms, with three bedrooms on the second floor; in viewing it with his family a few days after Christmas, Berlin pronounced himself excited but conceded that the place needed "a little work" (a typical understatement).

Leaving the renovation of their new country house to others, in early 1939 the Berlins gave up their East End penthouse for good and moved to

Los Angeles, where they settled into a hilltop home. Berlin still had to finish his score for the Tyrone Power film, which was now to costar Sonja Henie, the Norwegian figure skater and Olympic gold medalist turned actress. *Second Fiddle* would be her fifth film since her debut in the 1936 money-maker *One in a Million;* she and Alice Faye had evolved into Fox's most profitable blond stars.

Second Fiddle was written by George Bradshaw, who conceived the notion of constructing a satirical film around the long, heavily publicized, and highly dramatic search for an actress to appear as Scarlett O'Hara in *Gone with the Wind,* David O. Selznick's film version of Margaret Mitchell's best-selling novel. To this basic recipe was added a dash of *Cyrano de Bergerac.* In the film, Henie's character—the 436th candidate to be tested—lands the lead in *Girl of the North,* following a three-year search by the producers. A simple country schoolteacher from Bergen, Minnesota, with no acting ambitions or ability, she wins the part after a friend submits her photo, unbeknownst to her, to the studio.

Power plays a cynical, wily public-relations man whose assignment is to go out to Minnesota, collect the producers' new discovery, and bring her back to Hollywood in a blaze of publicity. To this last end, he concocts a phony romance between her and a novice studio vocalist (portrayed by former bandleader/crooner Rudy Vallee) who needs all the press he can get. The singer is reluctant to participate in the scam because he has a fiancée (vocalist Mary Healy, in her film debut), but Power convinces them both that no harm will come of it. Emulating Cyrano, he offers to spare Vallee the trouble of wooing Henie: he will have flowers delivered daily in Vallee's name, accompanied by poems—even a song—credited to him and dedicated to her.

Naturally, the plan works all too well: Henie falls for presumed suitor Vallee, who in time reciprocates. Power, meanwhile, realizes that he, too, is in love with Henie, and that he meant every word of every poem and of the lyric he sent her (one of Berlin's best ballads, "I Poured My Heart into a Song"). When a furious Healy exposes the plot, an even angrier Henie storms home to Bergen, determined never to set foot in Hollywood again.

Needless to say, *Girl of the North* is a massive hit. Once again, Power is dispatched to Minnesota to retrieve the studio's newest star. On his arrival, he learns that Henie is about to marry a local farmer, evidently for no better reason than to eradicate the memory of her Hollywood sojourn. Finding an ally in Henie's aunt (the wonderfully wry Edna May Oliver), Power attempts to stop the wedding, but they get there too late: Henie has just said "I do." In one of those happy coincidences that occurs only in comedies, it turns out that the justice of the peace who conducted the ceremony has neglected to renew his license; the marriage, therefore, is not legal. After Power confesses to Henie that he, not Vallee, was the author of the poems and writer of the song, all is forgiven. A properly licensed official then performs another marriage—same bride, different groom.

Berlin's task was to squeeze some songs into all this plot. Early in the film, Vallee is seen singing a number in a Hollywood musical, the charming "An Old-Fashioned Tune Always Is New" (a favorite Berlin theme). The verse announces the death of ragtime, jazz, and swing, leading into the chorus about old songs never going out of style. One especially delicious couplet is a kind of inside joke by the songwriter on himself:

> *A simple melody will always linger.*
> *I mean the kind you pick out with one finger.*

Vallee also has another fine ballad, "When Winter Comes," which is sung at a Hollywood poolside but gives way to a dream sequence in which Sonja Henie (as she must) skates. Perhaps the most inventive song in the skimpy score is "The Song of the Metronome," rendered by Henie's young pupils as she conducts. Punctuated by *tick-tock*s and endowed with a beautifully arched, chromatic release, it is the film's musical high point.

Second Fiddle was not well received on its July release. By then the Berlins had abandoned their house-on-a-hill in Los Angeles, and Berlin had given up on Zanuck and Twentieth Century-Fox. Any behind-the-scenes flareups were never discussed, but he was not happy with the picture, and his score betrays that—the dance "Back to Back," for example, is little more than a throwaway number. Plans for a projected sequel to *Alexander's Ragtime Band* were meanwhile discarded.

Back east, the house they had left at Lewbeach in January was a revelation in June. Their decorator, Anne Urquhart, had opened up the two parlors on the first floor into one long living room, with a fireplace and the inevitable bookcases. The dining room and kitchen had been modernized. The main bedrooms remained on the second floor, but the attic space had been converted into three additional bedrooms for Mary Ellin, Linda, and Elizabeth. What had been a barnlike garage was now the servants' quarters, and the former tea house had become a guest house. Some distance from the main house was a little white-painted retreat that would come to be known as "Mamma and Daddy's Cottage."

Berlin loved this place, loved its serenity and its trout stream, and he would keep it for the rest of his life. But he was at heart an inveterate New

Yorker, and at summer's end he moved his family back to Manhattan, to a five-story brownstone on East Seventy-eighth Street, near Lexington Avenue.

Berlin had told Ellin of his Hollywood malaise that spring, when they talked over the possibility of their buying the hilltop Angelo Drive house and joining the landed gentry of California. "There's no Lindy's in Los Angeles," he complained. (On Broadway near Forty-ninth Street, close to his office and to the Brill Building with its several music publishers, Lindy's was a hangout for songwriters and show people. Berlin was particularly fond of the restaurant's strawberry cheesecake.) Its other shortcomings? "No paper at two in the morning. No Broadway. No city."

His wife agreed. Soon after their return to Manhattan that September, Berlin was happily at work on a Broadway musical after a hiatus of more than six years.

The news from Europe grew more ominous. As the Berlins moved into their new brownstone, German armies were smashing their way into Poland; two weeks later, the Russians attacked from the west. Britain and France subsequently declared war on Germany (but not on Soviet Russia). What would eventually metastasize, like a military cancer, into the Second World War had now erupted in deceit, bloody bombings, invasions, and panzer attacks. President Roosevelt proclaimed America's neutrality even as American industry geared up for war: in August the War Department had ordered $85 million worth of military equipment, the bulk of that sum going toward bombers and aircraft engines.

The Great Depression was virtually over, but worse was yet to come. "God Bless America" was truly an anthem for the times—its lyric no longer just a patriotic paean but a fervent hope, a prayer.

10

TWICE IN A
LIFETIME

S UCCESSFUL FILM PRODUCER and even more successful songwriter
B. G. "Buddy" DeSylva had an idea for a musical, a comedy with song
about corrupt politics. It was inspired by the antics, while he lived, of
Louisiana senator and quasi-dictator Huey "The Kingfish" Long, whose presidential ambitions had come to an abrupt end in 1935, when he was shot to
death by a political opponent. For a time, the state was run by Long and his
family as if it had seceded from the United States. It occurred to DeSylva that
the illegal practices of the Long regime would be a fitting subject for a satirical musical; after all, a similar theme had worked profitably in the Gershwins' 1931 show *Of Thee I Sing* (though much less so in *Let 'Em Eat Cake,*
which had followed two years later).

DeSylva was a facile and witty songwriter, particularly as one third of the
partnership of DeSylva, Brown, and Henderson; he had also collaborated
with George Gershwin, Victor Herbert, Jerome Kern, Vincent Youmans, and
others. After splitting with partners Brown and Henderson in Hollywood, he
turned to production, beginning at Twentieth Century-Fox (where he had
several hits starring moppet Shirley Temple), then moving to Universal. In
1941, Paramount would appoint him its executive producer.

On Broadway, his production experience consisted of the Cole Porter–
scored *DuBarry Was a Lady,* which premiered in December 1939. His work
complete on that show (for which he had also cowritten the book, with

Herbert Fields), DeSylva discussed his idea for the Long musical with his attorney, A. L. Berman, who had earlier represented DeSylva, Brown, and Henderson. Berman was a unique and trusted figure in the world of show business, serving as both agent and attorney to a client list that included Ethel Merman (star of *DuBarry*), Harold Arlen, Youmans, and Irving Berlin.

DeSylva turned over his outline to Morrie Ryskind, who by mere coincidence had collaborated with George S. Kaufman on the Gershwins' political operettas. In Hollywood Ryskind had again worked with Kaufman on *A Night at the Opera* and other Marx Brothers movies, among them *The Cocoanuts,* and had been a member of the writing team that scripted the brilliant *My Man Godfrey.* To the left politically (until in his later years he veered far right), he was the ideal choice to take a jaundiced look at a peculiar southern brand of American politics.

In his discussions with DeSylva, Berman quite naturally brought up the name Irving Berlin. Berman knew Berlin had returned to New York from California and had no interest in going back; knew, too, that he was hoping to do a Broadway musical. DeSylva needed no convincing, and Berlin agreed to write the songs for what was to be called *Louisiana Purchase.*

Ryskind's script was about Long's special sort of political knavery, rather than about the man himself; after all, an alleged musical comedy in which the principal protagonist is assassinated might come up a bit short on laughs. Therefore, the plot (taking its cue from DeSylva's story) has an honest Republican senator—honest but bumbling, that is, and moreover feared as a hard-hitting investigator of political corruption—pay a visit to New Orleans to look into the shady dealings of the city's most powerful politician-businessmen. Senator Oliver P. Loganberry (played by Victor Moore) meets his nemesis in slick attorney Jim Taylor (William Gaxton), who is under orders from the machine to use any means necessary to stop the investigation. Since the senator refuses to be bribed, he must be compromised: as a bachelor, so the reasoning goes, he will be susceptible to feminine charm.

The casting was no coincidence: Moore and Gaxton had appeared together before, in *Of Thee I Sing,* the former as the clumsy Vice President Throttlebottom and the latter as the unctuous President Wintergreen.

Of the enticing-female roles, the most important went to ballerina Vera Zorina (fresh from a recent Broadway triumph in *I Married an Angel* and from the likewise recent but not so triumphant film *The Goldwyn Follies*). Her husband, George Balanchine, was hired to choreograph her numbers. The secondary seductress was played by an old trouper, the very French Irene Bordoni. Bordoni had made her Broadway debut in 1912 and ten years later starred in her first major show, *The French Doll,* produced by her then-husband, E. Ray Goetz, Berlin's former brother-in-law. Her song hit from that one was "Do It Again," with music by George Gershwin and lyric by B. G. DeSylva. In 1928 she had introduced Cole Porter's wicked "Let's Do It" in the show *Paris.* Her latest Broadway appearance, for a total of only twenty performances, had been in *Great Lady,* with music by Frederick Loewe in his bleak pre–Alan Jay Lerner phase.

A Berlin discovery, twenty-one-year-old Carol Bruce, would be making her own Broadway debut after several years spent singing with bands and in the road company of the *George White Scandals of 1939.* Her rendering of *Louisiana Purchase's* title song and a spiritualesque number, "The Lord Done Fixed Up My Soul," would turn her into a star—but a star whose light would dim soon after, when she disappeared from the stage and headed west to make a series of mediocre films. (She would return to Broadway in an equally unimpressive variety show, *New Priorities of 1943,* before reigniting her original spark as Julie in a 1946 revival of *Show Boat*—a production that was to have a crucial impact on Irving Berlin's personal and professional lives.)

As had become their custom, the Berlins spent the summer of 1939 at their Catskills estate. Berlin kept his ear to the radio a good deal of the time, listening to the news from Europe, where Hitler's war had begun. Against this distressing backdrop, the songwriter began scoring *Louisiana Purchase,* revealing his mood by interpolating his Korda tune, "It's a Lovely Day Tomorrow," into the show.

Although the score for *Annie Get Your Gun* is widely considered Berlin's finest, that for *Louisiana Purchase* must be ranked a very close second. An exercise in creative versatility, its musical modes range from spiritual to swing (Berlin did not, as many believed, detest the latter in and of itself; he merely disapproved of many swing bands' distortion of his melodies). The title song, in deft tribute to its city of origin, is a kind of declamatory blues. In addition to the Korda number, the score also features two typically fine ballads, one a look backward to a simpler time in Broadway scoring, "You're Lonely and I'm Lonely," and the other an enchanting duet, "Fools Fall in Love." This last particularly captivated Alec Wilder, who pronounced it "simply delicious" and noted with pleasure that "the form of the song is unusual. It is A (6 measures); A' (6 measures); B (8 measures); A' (6 measures); B' (8 measures). At the end of the first B section the music upsets the applecart, bringing envy to my eye and ear." This paragraph begins with "I should be able to put all my feelings aside. . . ."

"Fools Fall in Love" is one of Berlin's most majestic melodies, but it was never a hit. Wilder was not alone in his bafflement over its not becoming a standard.

Berlin was at his most ingenious when he wrote the new verse to "It's a Lovely Day Tomorrow," whose lyric suggests that since the front pages of current newspapers are "bound to make you sad, especially if you're the worrying sort," it may be best to take some "consolation in the weather report." This leads into the dignified, straightforward melody.

More inventiveness and wit are evident in the show's prologue, listed as "Apologia" in the program but entitled "Opening Letter" or "Opening Chorus" in the published vocal selections. An attorney, Sam Liebowitz, has his secretary take a letter, in which he assures the producer of a musical that he can avoid lawsuits by setting his at-times-libelous story in a mythical state named Louisiana.

In a later scene, the straight-laced senator makes a plaintive admission in song. "What Chance Have I with Love?" recalls the disheartening precedents set by such great lovers as Mark Antony, Romeo, and Napoleon. A sample:

> *Look what it did to Samson,*
> *Till he lost his hair he was brave.*
> *If a haircut could weaken Samson,*
> *They could murder me with a shave.*

A comic love/hate number sung by warring lovers Zorina and Gaxton, "Outside of That I Love You," belongs to the genre of the challenge song. (An earlier example would be the Gershwins' "Let's Call the Whole Thing Off," with its "You say *ee*ther and I say *eye*ther.") Even as the singers gamely attempt to top one another in vituperative commentary or contradiction (as in the Gershwin song), their covert affection is betrayed by artful turns of phrase. Berlin's challenge song begins with a very pointed diatribe on the part of the man: "I hate the ground you walk upon/ I hate the phone you talk upon/ I hate 'most ev'rything that you do." After a bit more of this comes the surprising twist:

> *I hate the rouge upon your lips*
> *The polish on your fingertips*
> *I hate your eyes of heavenly blue . . .*

The "heavenly" gives him away, and the inventory concludes with the confession, "Outside of that I love you," an ingenious rewrite of *Watch Your Step*'s "I Hate You."

If the production of *Louisiana Purchase* was punctuated by rehearsal or out-of-town vicissitudes, bickering, frenetic rewrites, or walkouts, there is no record of them. After a New Haven tryout beginning on May 2, 1940, the show opened at the Imperial in New York on May 28. In the interim, three songs were eliminated to tighten the pacing; the never-wasteful Berlin would salvage two of them, "It'll Come to You" and "Wild about You" (a holdover from *Top Hat*).

"It's a Lovely Day Tomorrow" proved all too optimistic that May: the front pages of the newspapers saddened even the most determined weather-checker. On the very day of the show's New Haven premiere, the British were driven out of Norway by the Nazis, and halfway through the tryout, Winston Churchill replaced Chamberlain as prime minister, promising the House of Commons "nothing . . . but blood, toil, tears and sweat." Two days before the opening at the Imperial, the British were forced to pull out of Europe by evacuating Dunkirk, invoking a reminder from the realistic Churchill that "wars are not won by evacuation." Following these reports closely, Berlin realized that if Hitler's armies and *Luftwaffe* defeated Britain, the United States—his beloved America—would be in grim danger.

But if Rome was burning, there was still fiddling to be done: *Louisiana Purchase* opened as scheduled. Abel Green, writing in *Variety,* called it a "svelte" musical and said it contained "many highs," notably "Irving Berlin's set of songs[, which] are already asserting themselves via radio and dance bands." Throughout his review he spotlighted individual performances, especially praising Irene Bordoni's "handling of two of Berlin's best tunes, 'Tomorrow Is a Lovely Day' [*sic*] and 'Latins Know How.' " The first-act high points, Green opined, were Zorina and Gaxton's "Outside of That I Love You" and Zorina and Moore's "You're Lonely and I'm Lonely." Interestingly, whereas *Variety*'s Green thought there was too much plot, the *Times*'s Brooks Atkinson felt there wasn't enough, and accused Ryskind and Berlin of "duck[ing] the satiric implications of their topic"—implying, perhaps, that the book should have been more Kaufman-and-Hartish. He conceded, however, that they had succeeded "in putting together a good-humored and enjoyable show." Which, no doubt, was what they had in mind from the beginning.

Louisiana Purchase was one of the musical hits of the season; its run, of 444 performances, was exceeded only by that of Cole Porter's *Panama Hattie* (another DeSylva production, starring Ethel Merman). Other successful musicals of the season were Vernon Duke and John Latouche's *Cabin in the Sky* and Rodgers and Hart's *Pal Joey,* ground-breaking in its creation of a heel-hero

(Gene Kelly in his first, and last, starring Broadway role). Just around the corner, Kurt Weill and Ira Gershwin's *Lady in the Dark* would open in January 1941.

The popularity of Berlin's songs was inhibited by a dispute that arose, around the time of the show's opening, between ASCAP and a group of broadcasters that objected to its licensing practices. The broadcasters formed their own licensing organization, called Broadcast Music, Inc. (BMI), and banned ASCAP songs from the air. "You're Lonely and I'm Lonely" aired on "Your Hit Parade" twice in July—first in tenth place, then in ninth—and was never played again. Radio listeners tuned to that program and all others began hearing lots of Stephen Foster (in public domain), as well as songs by younger writers who had been rejected by publishers before the ASCAP-BMI feud. A classic case was that of Joan Whitney, Alex Kramer, and Hy Zarat, whose songs, written a year before, now came to dominate the "Hit Parade"; among them were "My Sister and I," "It All Comes Back to Me Now," and "High on a Windy Hill."

The disagreement would not be resolved for a couple of years, during which period no songs by Berlin, Gershwin, Kern, Arlen, Rodgers, Porter, or the like were heard on the air. Vocalists such as Bing Crosby, who had a weekly radio show, soon tired of "I Dream of Jeanie with the Light Brown Hair," as did their listeners.

If the music going out over the airwaves left something to be desired, however, the news dispatches from Europe were cause for grave concern. That summer Adolf Hitler preened in Paris, and the Battle of Britain, as Churchill dubbed it, began, pitting the Royal Air Force (RAF) against the *Luftwaffe*. At the end of October the United States initiated its first-ever peacetime draft, the Selective Service Act, which called for draftees, chosen by lot, to serve for one year in the U.S. Army.

Berlin devoted the early months of 1941 to the composition of patriotic declarations such as "Any Bonds Today?," "Angels of Mercy" (celebrating the Red Cross, with all royalties going to that organization), and "Arms for the Love of America" (promoting Roosevelt's Lend-Lease Act, which enabled the neutral United States to sell or lend Britain war materiel ranging from food to old battleships). He paid tribute to embattled Britain with "A Little Old Church in England" and expressed his own reaction to the rush of events in "When This Crazy World Is Sane Again." Another song, about Hitler, "When That Man Is Dead and Gone," was a rare (for him) excursion into sanguinary wishful thinking.

During this same period he was also involved in misfortune closer to home, when his old friend Joseph Schenck was tried for income-tax evasion.

The ever-loyal Berlin testified on Schenck's behalf, stressing his good character—which, unfortunately, had little to do with the hard facts of his accoun-
tant's creative bookkeeping, or the bribes, payoffs, and other "traditional"
Hollywood practices he took part in. To Berlin's unbelieving dismay, Schenck
was found guilty, fined, and sentenced to prison for a year. Paroled after four
months, he would immediately return to Hollywood and his position as chief
executive at Twentieth Century-Fox; a decade later, he would be presented
with a special Academy Award for his contributions to the film industry.

In the 1940 presidential campaign, both Berlins had been active partici-
pants in the effort to reelect Roosevelt. Ellin, having abandoned her ancestral
Republican views, stumped vigorously; her husband sang at rallies. To both
Berlins, Nazism seemed a growing threat, as did the isolationist, anti-
Roosevelt fulminations of the America First Committee, which opposed all
American aid to Britain. Among the high-profile members of America First
were *Chicago Tribune* publisher Robert McCormick and flying hero Charles A.
Lindbergh. Lindbergh had visited Germany with his wife in the late thirties
and come home believing that the *Luftwaffe* was superior to both the British
RAF and the U.S. Army and Navy air forces; by 1940 he could be heard
regularly on the radio, revealing himself as pro-Nazi and an anti-Semite.
Unimpressed by the couple's fame, Ellin Berlin spoke out vehemently against
Anne Morrow Lindbergh's book *The Wave of the Future,* which predicted an
inevitable Nazi victory.

In the spring of 1941, with FDR successfully reelected for a third term as
President, Berlin turned his energies back to his work, gathering song ideas
for a film that Paramount was to produce and Mark Sandrich to direct. The
project had been conceived, albeit in a different form, some years earlier,
when Berlin and Moss Hart, taking a cue from the popularity of the song
"Easter Parade" in *As Thousands Cheer,* had had the notion of creating an
entire Broadway revue around the theme of American holidays. But like the
sequel *More Cheers,* the holiday revue had never got much further than the
planning stage: Berlin went to Hollywood, and Hart went on to write first
You Can't Take It with You, with George S. Kaufman, and then the Rodgers
and Hart musical (also in collaboration with Kaufman) *I'd Rather Be Right.*

Sometime in 1940, during a chance meeting with Mark Sandrich, who
had left RKO for DeSylva's Paramount (where he was directing and producing Jack Benny musicals), Berlin had outlined the holiday-revue idea, suggesting it might work as a film. Sandrich agreed, and contract negotiations
began. Although these seemed to drag on interminably, Berlin was confident
that all would eventually be resolved; accordingly, in September 1940, he
wrote a holiday song and filed it away for future use.

A year later, in September 1941, with everything at last legally tidy, Berlin took his holiday number and other song ideas to Hollywood. In the seat next to him on the plane was a teenager named Rose Choron, a refugee from the war in Europe who had traveled alone to New York, and now to Los Angeles, while her parents remained behind in Switzerland. Rose was excited, nervous, and not a little airsick, and Berlin could not help but be aware of her discomfort; she was about the same age as his oldest daughter. As Rose squirmed and strained against her seat belt, her seatmate gently took her hand.

"You'll feel better as soon as we land," he assured her. He distracted her by inquiring about her destination, where she had come from, and other such things. When the plane began its descent and was approaching the runway, he asked her name. She told him, then shyly asked his.

"Irving Berlin," replied the smallish man with the jet-black hair.

On the ground, Berlin escorted her from the plane to a group of her waiting relatives, then hurried off with a wish of "Good luck." Her uncle wanted to know who the man was, and Rose repeated his name.

"Do you know who Irving Berlin is?" her astonished uncle demanded. She didn't, but she was soon fully informed by her Hollywood-savvy relations.

Berlin began work almost immediately. In their first preproduction discussion, Sandrich agreed with Berlin's suggestion that Bing Crosby star in the film. Crosby was then Paramount's major money-maker, particularly after the success of the first "road" pictures (*Road to Singapore* and *Road to Zanzibar*), which exploited his radio feud with Bob Hope and the sarong exoticism of Dorothy Lamour.

Crosby had established an on-screen persona as a lighthearted crooner who sailed through life nonchalantly, always ready with a quip. In the "road" films, he and Hope obviously did not take anything about the enterprise very seriously; they ad-libbed constantly and often spoke directly into the camera to address the audience. Their informality and easygoing charm contributed to the wide and continuing popularity of these excursions.

The Berlin-Sandrich conception would cast Crosby as a former song-and-dance man who quits his performing partnership to retire to a farm, then converts the farmhouse into a most exclusive inn open only on holidays—thus the title, *Holiday Inn.* Berlin and Sandrich both felt Fred Astaire should appear as Crosby's ex-partner. Paramount's front office balked, arguing that Astaire would want a lot of money, but when Sandrich threatened to quit the film, the studio gave in. Economizing was accomplished with the hiring, for the female leads, of the relatively unknown Virginia Dale (who played the third ex-member of the Crosby-Astaire act) and the equally unfamiliar—but also unsinging—Marjorie Reynolds, whose vocals were dubbed by Martha Mears.

Berlin's outline was assigned to dramatist Elmer Rice (author of *The Adding Machine* and *Street Scene*) for adaptation, and then to Claude Binyon for the actual screenplay. The plot is the least of the film's appeal, serving merely to move the action, and song, from one holiday to the next (eight holidays in all, including, of course, Easter, with the interpolated "Easter Parade"). The parallel scenario pits the two male ex-partners against each other as rivals for the hearts of the two women, employing tactics that prove the cliché of all's fair in love and war. A curious aspect of the plot is Astaire's role as the ambiguous "friend" who schemes his way into, and tries to ruin, Crosby's romance with Reynolds. In the original screenplay, he does not get the girl (*any* girl); in the final cut, however, he winds up with Dale, his other former partner, who earlier ran off with a millionaire. Crosby and Reynolds have by now reconciled, and all four share in the happy ending, promising to perform together once a year at (it may be presumed) the Holiday Inn.

Despite the none-too-convincing story and the ill-defined characters of both Crosby and Astaire, *Holiday Inn* would be hailed as the "best musical drama of the year" in the *New York Post* and pronounced a "clear occasion for hat-tossing" by *PM,* Manhattan's most self-consciously intellectual tabloid. Even better, the *World-Telegram*'s reviewer would declare that the film was "full of the most tuneful songs any movie score has had in years." If this last was, perhaps, a slight exaggeration, the score nevertheless did contain one of the most popular, most durable songs ever written: "White Christmas" was one of the sheaf Berlin had brought with him when he came to California in September 1941.

Within a month of his arrival, Berlin could inform Dave Dreyer, in his New York office, that the score for *Holiday Inn* was virtually complete, and the preliminary response encouraging. While the film was being shot, he stayed in California, looking in from time to time to check on its progress. Ellin flew out to join him there. He was pleased with his efforts, as were all concerned at Paramount. His work in Hollywood had consumed no more than a month, but it would be almost a year before *Holiday Inn* was at last released, and much was to happen between September 1941 and August 1942.

Possibly because the bulk of *Holiday Inn*'s score was functional, only two of its new holiday songs outlasted the film. One good tune that particularly impressed everyone in charge, "Be Careful, It's My Heart," was obviously well promoted, for it made "Your Hit Parade" in July 1942, the month before the movie opened; it stayed on the hit roster for fully fifteen weeks but never got above second place (by this time the ASCAP-BMI feud had been settled). A pleasant enough ballad, pleasantly crooned by Crosby, it featured a piquant key change in midsong and apposite imagery—for example, "It's not my watch you're holding, it's my heart"—but it may have been just too morose to become a Valentine's standard.

In another, even less well known number, "I'll Capture Your Heart Singing," Berlin sketched the film characters of the leads. This first song presented by the trio (as it happens, on Christmas Eve) has Crosby and Astaire wooing Virginia Dale with their respective specialties—one sings, the other dances. Each also parodies the other's talents. When Crosby sits on and destroys a bouquet Astaire has brought for Dale, Astaire retaliates by stepping on Crosby's box of candy. With cool aplomb, Crosby selects a posy for his lapel and discards the rest of the flowers; Astaire takes a chocolate and then throws the box away. Fed up, Dale walks out on both, and they finish the number alone.

While Berlin himself had no part in creating the choreography (that was done by Astaire, with assistance from Danny Dare of Paramount), his song worked perfectly to set up the quirky, good-humored, but sometimes cruel relationship of the two men, a theme that runs through the film.

"White Christmas" needs no introduction. After *Holiday Inn*'s release, it aired on "Your Hit Parade" on October 17, 1942, in seventh place; "Be Careful, It's My Heart" was then in the second spot. By the following week, "White Christmas" had risen to second, and on October 31, it was at the top, where it remained for ten weeks. Over the next thirteen years, it would make the list every December (excepting only 1953). The success of the song was phenomenal, with the sale of recordings and sheet music rising into the millions (Crosby's recording alone sold twenty-five million copies) and earning it an entry in the *Guinness Book of World Records*.

That October night when "White Christmas" made its debut on the "Hit Parade," it was also preceded, in fourth place, by "I Left My Heart at the Stage Door Canteen," yet another Berlin composition, this one from his newest Broadway hit. Despite the perilous times, and because of them, this show had come together amazingly quickly.

During the production of *Holiday Inn* the previous winter, while Ellin Berlin was visiting her husband in Hollywood, the war that had so concerned them at last hit home: on December 7, 1941, Japanese aircraft took off from carriers in the Pacific to wreak havoc on Pearl Harbor, Hawaii. When the Japanese bombers and fighters finally withdrew that fateful Sunday, the American aircraft on the ground, both army and navy, were little more than smoldering junk. Navy ships anchored in the harbor sank, leaving more than 2,200 people, civilians as well as military, either dead or missing.

This shattering news at once reverberated throughout the world. With the German army now deployed in Russia to engage a former ally (one of Hitler's greatest military mistakes), and the Japanese "running wild" (as the planner of the Pearl Harbor attack, Admiral Yamamoto, phrased it), it was literally a world war, unlike any waged before in history. Suddenly, no place seemed safe. Many Californians feared an invasion by Japanese troops landing from warships lurking off the coast; even some members of the military, who should have known better, got caught up in the hysteria. (Their fears were to prove unfounded, though later in the war, the Japanese would attempt, and fail, to occupy bases in the Aleutians.)

It was during this anxious interval that Berlin, early in 1942, now back in New York, approached the War Department with an idea: why not stage an all-soldier show, which he would be happy to write, to raise money for some worthy cause? In reply, the War Department suggested that he revive *Yip! Yip! Yaphank* to benefit the Army Emergency Relief, which helped needy soldiers and their families in the event of illness or a death in the family.

Berlin, at fifty-three, was ineligible for military service, but in his own way, he enlisted. Not only did the War Department get its show, it also acquired a musical bonanza. For the second time in his life, Irving Berlin went to war.

And he went to work. He decided against a straight *Yaphank* revival, though he would retain the revue format and, as he had done in 1918, make use of the talent to hand. Because he was an unpaid civilian employed by the War Department—and, too, because he was Irving Berlin—he would have little trouble reaching the high command, if necessary, and cutting through any military red tape or paperwork (in triplicate). He had virtually his pick of the army's manpower, a boon since many from the music, theater, and film worlds were serving in one branch or another. By the time he was finished recruiting, he would have his own small army of three hundred.

The revue Berlin called *This Is the Army* closely followed the precedent established by *Yaphank,* opening with a minstrel show that led into a vaudeville segment (with acrobats, jugglers, and a magician), interspersed throughout with musical numbers and dances. Once again, impersonations of celebrities peppered the second act, set in New York's by-then-famous Stage Door Canteen (where soldiers were served by the likes of Helen Hayes, Lynn Fontanne and her actor husband, Alfred Lunt, Vera Zorina, and Gypsy Rose Lee). Private Alan Manson garnered much attention for his portrayal of actress Jane Cowl, and fittingly, comedian Joe Cook was mimicked by Private First Class Joe Cook, Jr.

There were sentimental and romantic songs, patriotic songs, and comic numbers at the mild expense of the military and the enemy (e.g., "Aryans under the Skin," known also as "Jap-German Sextette"). It was Berlin's own brilliant idea, in the next-to-last scene, to appear in his First World War khakis to sing "Oh! How I Hate to Get Up in the Morning," a moment that never failed to bring down the house. The finale that followed had the entire company declaiming the song "This Time," with its vow that it would be "the last time." Also borrowed from the 1918 show were "Mandy" ("Sterling Silver Moon") and "Ladies of the Chorus." Using *Yip! Yip! Yaphank* as a guide, Berlin readily blocked out his new revue; by late April 1942, he was back at old Camp Upton working on songs and recruiting his company, many of whom were theater professionals.

Among the first to be called up was Sergeant Ezra Stone, who was to direct. As an actor, Stone was a veteran of the hit 1938 comedy *What a Life,* in which he had portrayed an adolescent at the voice-change stage, with a gift for mischief and trouble. That success had fostered a popular radio adaptation the following year, in which a frequent bit of business had the mother yelling his character's name—"Henry, Henry Aldrich!"—and Stone answering, "Coming, Mother," in a voice that cracked midway through (this gimmick, or shtick, would be used in Berlin's show as well, immediately identifying young Henry Aldrich in uniform). During the radio run of "The Aldrich Family," Stone had directed a comedy for producer George Abbott, *See My Lawyer,* starring Teddy Hart and Milton Berle. Soon after that show began its own long run, he had been drafted, and in time earned his sergeant's stripes in Special Services, a unit devoted to raising soldiers' morale through entertainment. Stone seemed a natural choice to direct a revue whose songs and skits would present a view of army life as seen by that lowly soldier, the enlisted man.

Selected as musical director was Corporal Milton Rosenstock, a Juilliard graduate who after the war would continue as a theater conductor and composer. For his orchestra, Berlin could draw musical talent from a very large pool; not having to bargain with the Musicians Union allowed him to assemble a full complement of forty-four pieces, a prohibitive number had *This Is the Army* been a standard Broadway production. The backstage staff, meanwhile, ran the gamut from stage manager (Sergeant Alan Anderson, son of playwright Maxwell) and assistant business manager through a troop of carpenters (all of whom received program credit). Important civilians associated with the show, aside from Berlin himself, included his attorney friend A. L. Berman, gratefully acknowledged in the program for his "legal advice on the theater and production matters," and musical aide-de-camp Helmy Kresa, assisting either on site at Camp Upton or over the phone from the Berlin office.

Except for Ezra Stone, there were no "big names" in the show's large cast. Hollywood's elite were serving elsewhere: Clark Gable went into the air corps; Tyrone Power enlisted in the marines; Robert Taylor joined the navy; Ronald Reagan was attached to the air corps but rarely left Hollywood; and James Stewart flew missions as a bomber pilot in Europe. After the war, a handful from *This Is the Army* would remain in show business, among them singer-actor Burl Ives, comic Julie Oshins, and actor Gary Merrill. Best known as one of Bette Davis's husbands, Merrill would leave the company in 1944 to do another show, this one celebrating the air force: Moss Hart's *Winged Victory* (in its filmed version).

By early May, cast and crew were settled at Upton, and the score was complete and ready for rehearsals. When not rehearsing, the men drilled, marched, and stood for inspection like any other soldiers. Meanwhile, army public-relations forces were spreading the word. Expectations rose as the show's carefully selected opening date—July 4, 1942—approached.

News from the war zones continued to be worrisome, especially from the Pacific, where Americans faced the victorious, and often fanatic, Japanese. Three weeks after Pearl Harbor, the Pacific outpost of Wake Island had fallen; a few days earlier, on Christmas Day, 1941, the British had surrendered in Hong Kong. Early in 1942, as the first U.S. troops were landing in Ireland, the Japanese were menacing Manila; in February, they took Singapore, and in March the Philippines, capturing a number of American prisoners.

In April, as Berlin was composing the final songs for his revue, there was a small piece of good news when Colonel James Doolittle, a former racing pilot, led a bombing mission that struck Tokyo, to the surprise and dismay of the Japanese high command. While of little strategic consequence in itself, the Doolittle Raid nonetheless quickened American morale after the fall of Bataan, and caused the Japanese to blunder into both the Battle of Midway, in which American carrier planes inflicted severe damage on Japanese aircraft and ships, and the fruitless invasion of the Aleutians. At the time, neither the Japanese nor the Americans apprehended the significance of Midway: Japan had ceded control of the Pacific and, in effect, lost the war.

Although American troops were not yet active in the European theater, they were already moving into Britain with their materiel, including air corps bombers and fighters. German Field Marshal Rommel's Afrika Korps pushed British forces out of Libya and into Egypt, while great tank battles flared across Russia in what to most Americans seemed vast, bloody, inconclusive conflicts in places with strange names. On July 4, six American bombers would accompany half a dozen British ones in a joint attack on German airdromes in Holland. This display of British-American cooperation would be good for morale, but the mission itself was a failure, though it was not broadcast as such.

Back at Camp Upton, earlier in the summer, Berlin's own morale had suffered. His instincts told him the show did not hold together; it needed tightening. Worse, he and Ezra Stone did not see eye to eye: the sergeant did not care for the minstrel-show routine, and they disagreed on other points as well. The precise cause or causes of their differences cannot be identified, but it has been suggested that Berlin's ego and self-doubts drove him to seek aggressive control of the production, a development that did not go over well with Stone, himself a famed Star of stage and radio. In any event, Berlin was the Boss, and he had access, even as a civilian, to the top brass, from General George Marshall in Washington to Upton's own Colonel H. Clay M. Supplee. Had Berlin been vindictive, he could easily have had Sergeant Stone transferred out of *This Is the Army* and back to his original unit. But he wasn't, and he didn't.

The one vague explanation he offered to his family vis-à-vis Stone was "We had a falling-out." The problems likely began sometime around mid-June, because it was then that one Private Joshua Logan, stationed at Fort Dix, New Jersey, got an interesting call. Logan was lusting for combat, but he had just managed to fail his IQ test ("I ranked low among the idiots," he would later recall). One day, ordered via loudspeaker to go to a phone, he was surprised to hear a "high-pitched, slightly hoarse voice" on the other end of the line say, "Hello, Josh?"

"Who is this?" he demanded, only to be told it was Irving Berlin. When Berlin explained that he was familiar with the private's work and liked it, Logan interrupted, "Thanks, Mr. Berlin, but I'm in the army now, so—"

Berlin stopped him, saying, "That's why I'm calling you." *This Is the Army* was due to open in a couple of weeks, but he felt it wasn't ready: Logan had to come to New York to "get it in shape." His transfer from Dix had already been arranged. That very afternoon, Logan reported at the Broadway Theater, where he first met the "fabled Irving Berlin"—a man he claimed to have worshiped since he was a kid. Berlin informed him that he had nine days in which to doctor the show, which, the newest member of the company privately agreed, was a "badly arranged jumble."

Logan had taken an immediate liking to the nervous—"in a black panic"—Berlin, but he came close to panic himself when his new boss announced to the cast and crew that the private was now in charge ("complete charge," as he put it) of the show. Stone and choreographer Robert Sidney had contributed to the direction thus far, according to Berlin, as had "lots of others," he added cryptically (in the minstrel show, for instance, the dance to "Mandy" was directed by Fred Kelly, brother of Gene).

Since Sidney was responsible primarily for the choreography and movement, it was Stone who suffered the strongest rebuke by the very fact of the newcomer's presence. As a director, Stone lacked Logan's experience. The former Texan had started in the musical theater in 1938, when he directed both Rodgers and Hart's *I Married an Angel* and Kurt Weill and Maxwell Anderson's *Knickerbocker Holiday.* The next year he had directed Ethel Merman and Jimmy Durante in *Stars in Your Eyes,* which was followed by two more Rodgers and Hart musicals, *Higher and Higher* (1940), on whose book he collaborated, and *By Jupiter,* which premiered in June 1942, around the time its director was called up.

Still, experience or no, Logan was uncomfortable about tampering with Stone's and Sidney's routines, and after seeing a run-through of the show, he enthusiastically turned to Berlin and exclaimed over its excellence, only to hear Berlin say, "It's not right. . . . You've got to fix it."

But "how could I fix a show that to my mind was bulletproof perfection?" Logan wondered, writing in his autobiography. At Berlin's urging, however, and after viewing the show several more times, he did manage to identify a "few songs that might be reprised, dialogue that could be snipped a bit. . . . I rearranged the acrobatic scene and put orchestral reprises under it." He also restaged the ballad "I'm Getting Tired So I Can Sleep," to Berlin's delight, making it less stiff and stagy and, sensibly, dimming the lights. When *This Is the Army* premiered, Sergeant Ezra Stone was listed as director, and former Private Joshua Logan, by now a corporal, was credited with "additional direction." Once the show was up and running, Logan resumed his military career—with the air force in Europe.

Variety pronounced *This Is the Army* the "show business sensation of 1942," and its opening on Saturday night, the Fourth of July, was a gala of the grandest sort, something to celebrate in spite of the grim news coming in from most fronts. Fashionably dressed couples crowded into the lobby of the Broadway, mingling with star-spangled military brass and their well-dressed wives. The house was sold out, though as always, there were a few seats available free of charge for enlisted men. Kate Smith was said to have contributed $10,000 for her two opening-night seats, while Berlin himself had reserved two boxes at a thousand dollars apiece (he sat, until the second act, in the fourth row with Ellin, fifteen-year-old Mary Ellin, and Mary Ellin's date for the evening, Timothy Seldes, son of Berlin's friend the writer Gilbert Seldes). Even before the curtain rose, most of the audience knew that the premiere had brought in $45,000 and that Warner Brothers had paid $250,000 for the film rights (as would be reported by John Anderson in his review in the next Monday's *Journal-American*).

The army's public-relations people had done their job well, with the aid of some of Berlin's professional staff. All that was missing was the marquee lights, thanks to the dimout that had darkened Times Square to foil the German U-boats skulking offshore in the Atlantic: the bright lights that once characterized Broadway would have silhouetted all too clearly any ships leaving New York Harbor by night.

But if the Broadway's exterior was dark, inside it was resplendent with light and anticipation. Berlin was his usual fidgety self. When the overture began, the curtain, decorated with rows of steel army helmets, went up on "A Military Minstrel Show," with its opening chorus:

> *You thought that many, many years ago*
> *You saw the last of ev'ry soldier show*
> *But here we are, yes,*
> *Here we are again.*

This led smoothly into the title song, "This Is the Army, Mr. Jones," followed by the appealing "I'm Getting Tired So I Can Sleep" and "I Left My Heart at the Stage Door Canteen." Stone got his opportunity in a skit with Philip Truex and Oshins, who delivered a show-stopping line: when Corporal Truex upbraids him for his unsoldierly conduct, he retorts, "Break me. Go ahead, make me a civilian." (The taunt would become a favorite, oft-repeated slogan among enlisted men, while the mildly derisive attitude of the show as a whole would endear it to soldiers of all ranks.) Stone's reply to this was "The Army's Made a Man out of Me," in which Berlin treated a popular fallacy of the day with a well-deserved touch of satire.

The first act closed with a reprise of "This Is the Army" and another ingenious Berlin tribute, with "How about a Cheer for the Navy?" The air corps got its due in a couple of songs written for, and dedicated to, its commander, General Henry H. Arnold, "American Eagles" and "With My Head in the Clouds." The Stage Door Canteen dream sequence ("A Soldier's Dream") followed as the show built toward the high point of the second act.

Nervously, Berlin left his seat and hurried backstage to his dressing room. When the curtain rose on the seventh scene of act 2, he was onstage, lying in bed. Mary Ellin Barrett recalled every detail in a classic reminiscence:

> And then, there he is at last, sitting up sleepily, swinging his legs over the side of a cot and standing up, alone, stage center. A small, black-haired man in an old doughboy's uniform with a high-necked jacket and puttees. It is the first perfectly still moment since the evening began. He looks down, then up, and out at the audience, mouth open, ready to sing. Then the silence is broken by a roar, as sudden as thunder, and the pounding of applause. Everyone around us is rising, cheering now; and we are on our feet, too, applauding furiously—there is no question of family modesty. The demonstration continues for a full ten minutes as my father stands there looking down, looking up, opening his mouth, closing it again. . . . Finally, he is allowed to begin his song ["Oh! How I Hate to Get Up in the Morning"].

As Logan recalled, *This Is the Army* opened to the biggest roars of applause and laughter I have ever heard. . . . If any show ever took the town, this one did. And why not? It was conceived and written by the astounding theatreman of his time."

The final descent of the curtain, after the company's "This Time," generated more cheering and standing ovations. As some in the audience noticed, even the critics stood to applaud, an unusual response that was vividly underscored in Monday's reviews. The *Times* called it the "best show of a generation," no less. John Chapman approached ecstasy when he reviewed the audience as well as the show: "Of all the sparkling audiences of Broadway's first-night history, this one was the Five-Star Final Tops. For most of the evening, the select had been beating their hands together with unaccustomed violence. But all of this [was] just a warmup." He went on to describe Berlin's reception:

> It was the sort of demonstration that made you want to cry, it was so good. If you had been that little guy, you would have busted right out in tears. . . . His is the only voice I ever heard that is at once squealy and husky. But on that night he would have drawn audiences away had Caruso been singing across the street. The only thing that can stop *This Is the Army* is the end of the war.

(In this last, he was right.)

In the *Herald Tribune,* the town's most perceptive judge of musicals, Richard Watts, Jr., was only marginally more restrained, pronouncing the show

> at once delightful entertainment and a song of American democracy. . . . Because *This Is the Army* does not try to capitalize on patriotism it is one of the most truly patriotic works I have ever encountered. Because it always keeps its sense of humor and never tries to be emotional it is one of the most moving events in theatrical history.

Realizing that he and his little group of three hundred had pulled off a hit (the show was booked into the Broadway for four weeks but would end up running for twelve before going on tour), Berlin was relieved but a bit dazed backstage. His daughter studied his face, which she remembered as showing a "mixture of wonder, satisfaction, and exhaustion. Under his eyes black circles showed through the greasepaint. But his eyes danced."

After the cast party at the Biltmore, Mr. and Mrs. Berlin decided to celebrate further at the Stork Club. A disappointed and slightly grumpy Mary Ellin had to settle for a burger and a malt before Tim Seldes dropped her off at home.

One publication called Berlin the "happiest man on Broadway," but clouds were hovering in his blue skies. Immediately after the show's opening, a period of exciting euphoria rejuvenated him, as he spent sanguine moments, when he was free of his work at the theater or the office, writing letters of thanks to friends and colleagues who shared in his joy (a meticulous practitioner of civilities, he would acknowledge even a birthday card with a note of thanks). What should by rights have been a glorious time, however, was saddened and soured by a series of unpleasant events. The recent death of his friend Max Winslow affected Berlin, but even more difficult was the loss of Ellin's cousin Alice Duer Miller, his most faithful friend from the days of the Algonquin Round Table. He had taken great pride in the major success of her brief narrative poem "The White Cliffs," which was published around the time of the beginning of the Battle of Britain (and, coincidentally, not long before his own composition of "White Christmas") and went through more than twenty printings that fall. The poem's final quatrain was particularly meaningful for him:

> I am an American bred,
> I have seen much to hate here—much to forgive,
> But in a world where England is finished and dead,
> I do not wish to live.

Alice Miller was in the hospital being treated for terminal cancer when *This Is the Army* opened. She wrote to congratulate Berlin on the reviews and to say that she planned to leave the hospital later in July: she was "getting well in order to see the show," she promised. She died in August without fulfilling that wish. Ellin Berlin was especially stricken by the death of this dear friend and relative, a rebellious free-thinker like herself, who had been like a second mother to her.

Soon after the premiere, Berlin also had to contend with what he called office headaches. His partner and business manager, Saul Bornstein, had been in a state ever since the publication of "God Bless America" and Berlin's announcement that he intended to present the royalties to the Scouts—the very idea of giving away all that money! He had tried to talk Berlin out of it, but the songwriter had adamantly refused to back down, and Bornstein had finally ceased his campaign. Inwardly, though, he had continued to seethe. Now here was *This Is the Army,* a major money-maker despite its limited run—and Berlin was signing those profits away, too! Bornstein believed the company was entitled to a cut. Berlin once again prevailed, but he realized he needed an anodyne. He would confront his partner later, at a more appropriate time.

The Shuberts, too, were willing to let this charity stuff go only so far. Having agreed to let the U.S. Army use their theater free of charge, they recognized that they now had a potential gold mine in the Broadway. They figured Berlin should pay them a rental fee for the hall; after all, they had sacrificed three months' income by reserving it for his show. Berlin had to convince them that it was the War Department—or "Uncle Sam," as the program credited the producer—that was booking their theater, not he. (His own Music Box was hosting a quasi-burlesque show, *Star and Garter,* with former stripper Gypsy Rose Lee and comedian Bobby Clark; it had opened two days before *This Is the Army* and would enjoy a run of more than six hundred performances.)

The Shuberts knew when they were beaten: if they were not famed for their philanthropy, any imputation that they were lacking in patriotism could have meant serious trouble at a time when such feeling was running high. Still, they did not take the outcome of their little battle lying down, characterizing their tenacious adversary as a "dirty little rat."

Even worse were the potshots Berlin suffered at the hands of some of his Tin Pan Alley colleagues—or rather, rivals. The real Tin Pan Alley was long gone by 1942, its former denizens having moved uptown and westward, with a concentration of songwriters and publishers working out of the Brill Building, at 1619 Broadway, close to Lindy's and the theater district. Berlin's offices were in the same area, on Seventh Avenue. Although somewhat more civil than they had been on Twenty-eighth Street, the former Alleyites still lived by their jungle mores. They were competitive, aggressive, and envious to a fault. Nothing hurt so much as a competitor's success, and Berlin was having a very visibly successful run—first "God Bless America," then *Louisiana Purchase,* and now *This Is the Army* (*Holiday Inn* and "White Christmas" were yet to come).

The music business, like any other, occupies a small world, and amid the huge popularity of the army show, word soon began circulating around Tin Pan Alley: it was all a scam. Berlin was exploiting the war for his own benefit, effectively mounting a massive publicity campaign that cost him nothing. (To be sure, the nearly ten million dollars that *This Is the Army* would ultimately bring in for the Army Emergency Relief would have paid for an imposing advertising campaign, but Berlin hardly needed such plugging: he was already a celebrated American icon before he wrote the show.)

Some of these charges reached the ears of Cole Porter, a member in good standing of the new Alley. Porter's own (for-profit) army show, *Let's Face It!,* was by now a major success, and had made a star of Danny Kaye. He wrote a characteristically kind letter to Berlin:

> I can't understand all this resentment of my old friend, "The Little Gray Mouse." It seems to me he has every right to go to the limits towards publishing the music of his Army show, as every cent earned will help us win the war. If I had my way, he would have been given the Congressional Medal for years, because even you must admit he is the greatest songwriter of all time and I don't mean Stephen Foster. It's really distressing in these days of so much trouble to know that envy still runs rampant even on that supposed lane, Tin Pan Alley. I am sure you will agree about this? . . .
>
> [signed] *Rat Porter*

Despite all the jealous griping, *This Is the Army* went its own triumphant way, aided by ticket sales and the generous advertising included in its program. One curiosity still catches the eye—a full-page ad for the

Auto-Ordnance Corporation
Bridgeport, Connecticut.
Manufacturers of the
THOMPSON SUBMACHINE GUN
"TOMMY GUN"

Few in that first-night audience can have been in the market for a machine gun, once an indispensable accoutrement of certain elements in Prohibition Chicago and New York; in essence, of course, the ad was a corporate contribution to the Relief fund. Another full page announced the world premiere of the Paramount film *Holiday Inn,* on August 4, to benefit the Navy Relief Fund.

A month to the day after *This Is the Army* began its run, *Holiday Inn* opened in New York, heralded two weeks before by the inclusion on "Your Hit Parade" of "Be Careful, It's My Heart." On August 8, in tenth place, it was joined by the army revue's "I Left My Heart at the Stage Door Canteen" in sixth. That fall, as envy simmered in the Brill Building over this prodigious coupling (a show song and a film song), Berlin was gratified to see "Be Careful" reach number two and "I Left My Heart" number four, with "White Christmas," which had lain dormant for more than two months, in the seventh spot.

Two weeks later, Berlin's holiday tune was the number-one song in the nation, and remained so for ten weeks (significantly, the number-two slot was occupied by the rather more combative "Praise the Lord and Pass the Ammunition"). "White Christmas" would slip off the "Hit Parade" after the turn of the year—to return the next winter and many more thereafter—but it was still solidly number one on the broadcast of December 26, 1942. The entire Berlin family celebrated with a reunion at the Book-Cadillac Hotel in Detroit, where *This Is the Army* was playing on one of its stops in an extensive national tour. Ellin Berlin arranged for a (quite skimpy) tree to be delivered to their suite, and everyone pitched in to decorate it. Mary Ellin was now sixteen, Linda ten, and Elizabeth six.

The phenomenal "White Christmas" was well on its way to becoming one of the most popular secular Christmas songs in musical history, second only to "Silent Night." Its success had begun with the American public and taken off with the American soldier, or GI (short for "Government Issue," a sardonic acknowledgment that men were as expendable as any other military equipment; there were few flag-waving doughboys who found the Second World War to be a Great Adventure). This was the first Christmas that American troops spent away from home—whether stationed in Britain, posted on Guadalcanal in the Pacific, or facing combat in North Africa—and the nostalgic sentiment of "White Christmas" struck a most responsive chord that was truly heard around the world. There was hardly a Post Exchange (PX) coin-operated jukebox anywhere that did not feature Bing Crosby's recording of the song. It was also heard in restaurants, in hotels, in ice cream parlors, and at school dances—in short, everywhere.

Before the army show began touring, Berlin eliminated the original verse of "White Christmas," and with it the reference to a nonwhite California Christmas (not that it mattered much, since most popular bands skipped the verses of songs anyway). With or without its California allusion (in the film, Crosby, stuck in Hollywood, expresses his longing for a Vermont Christmas), the song's motif remained intact and touched many a GI heart.

Sigmund Spaeth, in his history of American popular music, explained the unique appeal of the song. "Like 'God Bless America,' " he wrote, "it was singable and understandable, besides which it avoided all the doctrinal questions of religion that enter into most of the Christmas hymns and carols. Even a heathen or an atheist could agree heartily with the sentiments of 'White Christmas.' " He went on to expand on its history and its fiscal implications:

> No wonder the song sold a million copies in the first four months of its life, bringing back the good old days of Tin Pan Alley for the first time in years. The total sale has since gone up [Spaeth was writing ca. 1948] well beyond three million in sheet-music and five million in records. "White Christmas" has become a "standard" and still sells about 350,000 copies a year.

Berlin's other success was also thriving. On the night of September 26, 1942, when the cast of *This Is the Army* sang "This Time (Is the Last Time)," it was literally true, at least for that venue: the show was closing, after 113 standing-room-only performances, and going on the road. No less appropriate would have been the *Yip! Yip! Yaphank* finale, "We're on Our Way"—not to France but to Washington, D.C., where the curtain went up three days later. President Franklin D. Roosevelt watched the show from a box in the National Theatre; Ellin Berlin sat in the orchestra with her husband, who sneaked out as usual for his second-act number.

The by-now-customary reception from audience and press was capped off by a not-so-customary cast party at the White House, where the President and Mrs. Roosevelt, herself a great fancier of the show, greeted the company. Another evening, the Berlins dined with the Roosevelts and the Hopkinses (Harry Hopkins was Roosevelt's trusted friend and personal assistant before and during the war; his wife, Louise, was a member of the Roosevelts' small circle of nonpolitical friends). For Berlin, it was the high point of the Washington run.

After Washington came Philadelphia, Chicago, St. Louis, and other points west, until on February 1, 1943, the show opened at the War Memorial Opera House in San Francisco. Two weeks later, cast and crew boarded their special train, bound for Los Angeles and a tent city that had been erected especially for them near the Warner Brothers lot. As Berlin and the studio executives and technicians prepared *This Is the Army* for filming, the company returned to soldiering, with reveille, drill, inspections, and passes into town—the town this time being Hollywood, which boasted its own Hollywood Canteen, staffed by film stars.

This routine continued for a month and a half before shooting began. The filmed *This Is the Army* does not replicate the staged revue; for one thing, it has a plot. The Warners, loath to attempt filming a stage show (a genre that had gone out of style by 1930), commissioned a screenplay from veterans Claude Binyon and Casey Robinson. The former had written *Holiday Inn,* and the latter *King's Row,* featuring Ronald Reagan, who was signed to star in *Army* (the future President was by now a lieutenant in the United States Air Force, as the air corps had been redesignated).

The Robinson-Binyon plot took its cue from *Yip! Yip! Yaphank* and the First World War. Mirroring Berlin's own wartime experience, song-and-dance man George Murphy produces an army show comprising several of the original songs from *Yaphank;* also heard are a few bars from "God Bless America," which is rejected. Added were a couple of other Berlin songs of the period, "My Sweetie" and "Goodbye France," with its line "We won the war to end the wars."

One war later, Murphy, no longer a dancer due to a war injury, has a son, played by Reagan, whose turn it now is to put on his own army show. The scriptwriters included a war-shadowed romance between Reagan and Joan Leslie (she wants to get married but he is reluctant, not wanting to leave her a war widow; they of course wed before the final fadeout).

Making this romantic subplot possible (if much less comic than it might otherwise have been) was the incorporation of women into the formerly all-male cast. Besides Leslie, there was Kate Smith to sing the revived "God Bless America," and Frances Langford to do one of the new numbers written for the film, "What Does He Look Like?" Another addition was boxer Joe Louis, by then in the army himself, who takes a turn at the punching bag to introduce the grotesque (in both staging and costuming) "That's What the Well-Dressed Man in Harlem Will Wear." The urban background for this scene is modernistically distorted, with giant caricatures of three men wearing then-stylish (and outlandish) zoot suits, a fad whose popularity had recently spread from Harlem to young America, to much parental consternation. The dancing soldiers in the foreground, "well dressed" (i.e., properly attired) in khaki, merit Sergeant Joe Louis's salute.

Berlin made his only appearance in the movie singing "Oh! How I Hate to Get Up in the Morning," leading into "This Time" and "Dressed Up to Win." The title of this last was changed from the stage version's "Dressed Up to Kill" at the request of Jack Warner, under pressure from local clergy. (The original title, a play on the common expression meaning "alluringly dressed," seems hardly more offensive than the popular "Praise the Lord and Pass the Ammunition," an exhortation allegedly uttered by some unknown army or navy chaplain in the heat of battle. But director/cast member Ezra Stone reportedly objected to the first lyric of "Dressed Up" and may even have been behind the crusade. Seemingly overlooked by all parties was the fact that soldiers are *trained* to kill.)

Shooting was finished by June, and Berlin could return to Manhattan, to the family's new, smaller quarters in Gracie Square. Thus he missed the film's big Hollywood premiere in August but made it to the New York opening on the same date; that would have to be good enough, for by this time he was tired of the army-Paramount grind and ready to prepare for the next phase of the stage show. The film was a financial success, bringing in more than nine million dollars for Army Relief, but it was less rewarding artistically. Aside from some of the musical moments, it has little to recommend it but patriotic fervor.

With the film in the can, the company returned to Camp Upton to await its next billeting: England. It would have been impracticable to retain the full complement of performers, given the travel involved, so Berlin had to carefully prune his cast; among the first to go (or rather, to stay behind) was Staff Sergeant Ezra Stone, that thorn in his side. The *This Is the Army* contingent was halved, with most of the cuts coming from backstage and the orchestra: the stops on the projected overseas tour, which would take the show virtually around the world, would not provide the theatrical conveniences that the troops had grown used to during their national tour and in Hollywood, or even at primitive Camp Upton. All that remained of the crew when Berlin was through was a small group of advisers and technicians who would attend to the details of travel and housing and the shipping of equipment, sets, and so on, the U.S. Army way.

Next Berlin selected the soloists, dancers, and others who would go on tour, among them Alan Manson (as a fetching Jane Cowl in the Stage Door Canteen sequence) and comedian Oshins. Rosenstock would conduct the reduced orchestra, while stage manager Alan Anderson would keep the show running smoothly and his right-hand man, Corporal Benjamin Washer, would carry out a number of tasks ranging from public relations to travel arrangements.

This done, Berlin in mid-October boarded an Air Transport Command plane for London; the rest of the company had shipped out earlier from New York, bound for Liverpool. Arriving first, Berlin settled into Claridge's and began preparing for the show's opening at the Palladium. As soon as he could, he called on Joshua Logan, now an air force officer and recently landed via the *Queen Mary,* and told him about an idea he had for a skit. As Logan remembered it, Julie Oshins would play a private married to a lieutenant in the Women's Army Corps (WACs). He wants to spend the night with his wife, but his mother-in-law, a WAC sergeant, makes it difficult for her daughter to get the required pass. (Some of the specifics in Logan's account seem unlikely—for example, a sergeant would not have had the authority to deny a pass, so perhaps the mother-in-law was a captain—but the point of the skit seems clear enough: it turned on the prohibition against officer–enlisted man fraternization.)

When Berlin found him and asked for his help again, about three weeks before *This Is the Army* was set to open in London, Logan envisioned difficulties: he did not think his commanding officer, Colonel Julian M. Chappell, would release him, since "the invasion of the continent was imminent" (another anomaly in Logan's story; this incident took place in October 1943, and no invasion was scheduled until the late spring of 1944).

When Berlin asked that Logan be assigned to three weeks of detached service with the show, General Eisenhower, who had come to England to command the invasion, approved the request, only to be contravened by Chappell. According to Logan, a furious Berlin then phoned General Arnold in Washington, who seconded Eisenhower's approval; Chappell once again demurred. (All of this makes for a good, show-bizzy kind of anecdote, but it seems most implausible that a mere colonel would have crossed his theater commander and the commander of all the air forces of the United States to keep one soldier in his unit.) What finally made the difference, Logan recalled, was Berlin's telephone call to Colonel Chappell himself:

"Colonel Chappell? This is Irving Berlin." There was a long pause and Berlin called out, "Hello? Hello?"

Finally Chappell said in a strained voice, "Did you say you were Irving Berlin? *The* Irving Berlin?"

"That's right. Now I want Logan for three weeks, and no more beating about the bush."

"Of course not. Anything you say, Mr. Berlin. Irving Berlin, huh? Jesus Christ, *Irving Berlin.*"

Whatever the embellishment, Logan got his transfer, and the skit improvised around Berlin's idea proved to be a "riot." In Logan's appraisal, "The opening night at the Palladium must rank high in London theatrical history."

So it did. The Palladium premiere, on November 10, 1943, was surrounded by a generous display of pomp, with King George, Queen Elizabeth, and their daughters, the princesses Elizabeth and Margaret, attending and going backstage afterward to meet the author. The queen confided to Berlin, "I've never seen anything like it. 'My British Buddy' brought tears to my eyes."

"Thank you, Ma'am," Berlin replied, adding, somewhat incongruously, "I wrote the song in a bathtub."

He had planned to come up with a special song for the London production, something almost reverential about British-American relations, which at the time were somewhat troubled. The Allies were cooperating well enough in Italy and North Africa (they had driven the Afrika Korps out of that continent in May), but back in Britain, where the U.S. Air Force had its base in East Anglia, with more GIs arriving almost daily, resentments surfaced. Dismissively described by their hosts as "overpaid, oversexed, and over here," the brash young Yanks, confident, cocky, and indeed flusher than most British soldiers, filled the pubs (frequently provoking brawls) and attracted all manner of Englishwomen, from prostitutes to lonely wives.

Aware of such tensions, Berlin returned to his London hotel one night during a true blackout (still enforced, though by the fall of 1943 the nighttime bombing of London was over) and soaked in a hot tub. Meanwhile, he pondered the song, and "by the time I was through with the bath, I had it all worked out."

Far from being maudlin, the resultant number is tongue-in-cheek, wryly alluding to American-British soldier rivalry. The verse introduces a GI from the USA who proclaims, "My British buddy/ We're as different as can be/ He thinks he's winning the war/ And I think it's me." He closes on a more serious note, predicting that their cooperation will beat Germany (rhymed with "tea"): "When the job is done/ And the war is won/ We'll be clasping hands across the sea."

"My British Buddy" did all Berlin had hoped it would, and more: only a couple of days after *This Is the Army*'s premiere, the Associated Press could report, "A new American song is sweeping over London and its psychological punch is equal to another big chunk of lend-lease or a fresh troopship of soldiers. . . . Mr. Berlin has presented the rights to the song hit to the British Services Charities Committee, Lady Louis Mountbatten, co-chairman of the committee, announced."* (In the small-world department, Edwina Mount-batten, a good friend of George Gershwin's and habitué of Harlem's Cotton Club in the thirties, was married to Lord Louis Mountbatten, son of the very Prince Louis Battenberg who had heard Berlin sing at the Pelham Café so many years before.)

In wartime, however, nothing was easy: even the song's popularity caused some anxiety when Berlin's London publisher, Louis Dreyfus, of Chappell, could not secure enough paper to publish the sheet music (newspapers, magazines, and writing paper were all in short supply). But Berlin took the problem to Lady Mountbatten, and somehow the song was soon available in music shops all over London.

The musically appealing "My British Buddy" was only the first in a series of songs that Berlin would compose on *This Is the Army*'s global itinerary. "The Fifth Army Is Where My Heart Is" would be written in Italy, as would "There Are No Wings on a Foxhole," a tribute to the Fifteenth Air Force at the base at Bari. Yet another entry in his postcard song series, "I Get Along with the Aussies," would come out of the company's tour in the southwest Pacific, where GI-Australian relations were strained for much the same reasons as in Britain.

Almost two weeks after the London opening, Berlin and some of his soldier-performers went on British radio, where the songwriter introduced "My British Buddy" and "This Is the Army" to all those who had been unable to see the show. Soon after, cast and crew embarked on a tour around the British Isles. When they were in Bristol, Queen Mary (the mother of King George) enjoyed the show and asked for a signed copy of the score. During the breaks between performances, Berlin went off on personal excursions: from Glasgow, he traveled, bringing gifts, to a nearby village to call on Mrs. Tannant, mother of Janet "Tenney" Tannant, nanny to the Berlin "girls"; in Dublin, he visited with the retired Irish tenor John McCormack, whose repertoire encompassed "Mother Machree," "The Rosary," and "Always." He and Berlin had met during the First World War, when he had assumed American citizenship; like Berlin at the time, he had been an indefatigable war-bond salesman. On his retirement, in 1938, he had returned to Ireland. The reunion was warm and nostalgic, but Berlin realized that his friend, then only fifty-nine, was ailing (he would die two years later).

The company returned to London early in February of 1944. General Eisenhower, now in Britain preparing for the cross-Channel invasion of

---

*It should be noted that not only the song's royalties but also the show's were signed over to British relief agencies.

Europe, saw the show and made arrangements for *This Is the Army* to go on another tour, this one closer to the combat areas. Irving Berlin was now truly off to the wars. What is especially striking about this is that he was then a fifty-five-year-old, nondraftable (the cutoff age was thirty-eight) troubadour who could have stayed home instead. In this, his second war, he was often in more danger than most men in uniform.

Berlin sensed a difference between the attitudes of the doughboy and the GI. "In 1918," he recalled,

> the boys in the trenches sang together. But the fellow in a foxhole is not apt to sing to himself. Believe me, he has other things to think about. Dropping bombs are not good accompaniments, even for war songs.
>
> Remember how the doughboys went across during the last war? They marched down the Avenue singing "Over There" or "It's a Long Way to Tipperary." They were anxious to get over there and make the world safe for democracy, and they sang about it.
>
> Today the boys are grimmer.

Expected to mingle with the brass, he was fonder of being with his "boys"; he knew all the generals, American as well as British, from Eisenhower on down, but the GIs were his special charge. He wrote to their families to reassure them, even on behalf of some fellows who were not associated with the show. In the battle areas he and a few of the men made the rounds of field hospitals between performances. In the wards, or outdoors, on a makeshift stage, they would improvise a short entertainment for the wounded and the dying.

These performances were grim for Berlin, who was distressed to see young men, some barely older than his daughter Mary Ellin, in beds or on stretchers. Hardest to face were the amputees. Benjamin Washer noted in his diary that a touched, compassionate Berlin leaned over one soldier who, in a weak voice, asked him to write to his wife. Berlin took down her name and address and promised he would; he kept his word, but by then the young woman was a widow.

On more formal occasions, Berlin dressed in his usual neat suit and tie, but once out of Britain and in Algiers, North Africa, he turned GI himself, adopting the enlisted man's field jacket and garrison cap. Like any member of the military bound for the war zones, he suffered through inoculations, from the jolting antitetanus shot to the ingestion of Atabrine tablets in areas where malaria was a problem (after a few weeks on Atabrine, even the ruddiest soldier would appear to have a case of yellow jaundice). In these areas the water tasted of chlorine; in the tropics, where he would go later, salt pills were a daily requirement. And then there was the army food—for Berlin a far cry from the fare at Lindy's or Claridge's.

After a couple of weeks in Algiers, *This Is the Army* moved on to Naples, Italy. In March 1944 the Germans and the Allies were fighting ferociously over the possession of the Anzio beachhead, between Naples and Rome. Naples had been bombed by the *Luftwaffe,* and its buildings destroyed during the German army's retreat, but miraculously, the San Carlo Opera House was still intact, and the company began its Italian tour there. The audience no longer had to buy tickets; GIs simply came down by truck from the fighting areas, when they could, to attend. The Allies were by now pushing north toward Rome, trying to break through the heavily fortified Gustav line, on which stood the Benedictine abbey on Monte Cassino, a German observation post. Reluctantly, the air force pulverized the centuries-old abbey, and the road to Rome was open.

The Fifth Army entered the Eternal City on June 4, 1944; a week later *This Is the Army* was playing at the Royal Opera House. Throughout April and May the company had entertained the troops of the Fifth and visited hospitals. In Rome, performing in a real theater again, they garnered international goodwill by giving a special performance to benefit Italian war orphans. Berlin won the hearts of the audience, made up mostly of Roman civilians, by taking requests for some of his popular hits and closing with an Italian folk song he had learned as a boy on the Lower East Side.

The war was going well for the Allies. Their first week in Rome was brightened by news of the Allied invasion of France on D day, June 6, and later that month a thousand-bomber attack targeted the city of Berlin. In the Pacific, the U.S. Army, Navy, and Marines were moving closer to the Philippines, and the air force had initiated its deadly bombardment of the Japanese homeland.

From Rome, the *This Is the Army* unit traveled east to the massive complex of air bases on the coast, at Foggia and Bari. From the latter, Berlin wrote his wife that performing "for the Air Corps is thrilling and they can't do enough for us," though he confessed that the heat bothered him a bit. He joked that at least he would have a healthy tan for his homecoming. Soon after, at the end of July, he took a leave of absence from the show (which went on to Egypt and Iran) to return to New York. There were two good reasons for his furlough: he admitted to being quite tired, and there was trouble at Irving Berlin, Inc. It was time for him to deal once and for all with the problem of Saul Bornstein.

Although tanned, Berlin was clearly weary from his travels and distinctly disinclined to discuss his office headaches when he joined his family at Lewbeach. Ellin had been contributing to the war effort in her own way, raising money and working in a hospital. Mary Ellin, now a young lady of seventeen, was spending her summer vacation in nearby Chappaqua, helping out at a home for convalescent needy boys; Linda was twelve, and Elizabeth had just turned eight. How they had grown in the nearly ten months their father was away!

He had been in Algiers on Ellin's forty-first birthday, in March, but he had expressed his affection in letters home. When her first novel, *Land I Have Chosen,* was published, he was proud and especially happy with the favorable review it received in *Time.* Throughout this time she had remained as poised, outwardly calm, and lovely as ever, never revealing to her husband, despite his lighthearted communiqués, how anxious his absence made her. She had also kept this apprehension from their daughters, even when her husband and his troupe moved up the boot of Italy behind the advancing Fifth Army and came within range of German aircraft. Now, with Irving back in their retreat at Lewbeach, she could at last relax.

He, however, could not. He had learned that his trusted partner, Saul Bornstein, who ran the business end of Irving Berlin, Inc., had been surreptitiously cheating him; then, too, there had been the disagreements over the disposition of royalties from "God Bless America" and *This Is the Army,* which Bornstein counted as a big loss to the firm. For Berlin, the implications were chilling: did the copyrights of his songs belong to him or to his company?

Bornstein put up a serious legal battle over this point but wisely backed off when evidence came to light that he had been skimming profits for years. This wrangling went on from the moment of Berlin's arrival in the United States in August until that December, when a curious deal was struck: Berlin would keep his own copyrights and buy out Bornstein's share of the firm for $400,000. Bornstein would then form his own company (to be named Bourne Inc.) and assume the copyrights for all the non-Berlin songs that Irving Berlin, Inc., had published, including such hits as "Moon over Miami" (by Edgar Leslie and Joe Burke), "Love, Your Magic Spell Is Everywhere" (by Edmund Goulding and Elsie Janis), the songs from Disney's *Snow White* and *Pinocchio,* and perennial favorite "Who's Afraid of the Big Bad Wolf?" (by Ann Ronell and Frank Churchill).

So Bornstein did not leave empty-handed; in fact, he did not leave at all—*Berlin* did. He turned over the Seventh Avenue office to his former partner and set up his new Irving Berlin Music Corporation at 1650 Broadway. All this begs the question, With proof in hand that Bornstein had been accumulating an illegal income from their firm, why didn't Berlin sue him or have him prosecuted? The answer seems to be that even though the music business teemed with dishonest manipulators, a scandal of that nature involving Irving Berlin, Inc., would have been too much for Berlin the man. He would not have wanted a public airing of his differences with Saul Bornstein, nor was he vindictive: he was glad simply to be rid of him and done with it. He hired a business manager he trusted, Alfred Chandler, to run the office, and kept Helmy Kresa on as his musical secretary.

With the Bornstein wars over, Berlin was ready to return to the real war. At the close of December 1944, he flew west to rejoin the well-traveled *This Is the Army* company in New Guinea, first stopping over briefly in Hollywood to discuss a musical that Mark Sandrich wanted to do for Paramount after the Pacific tour.

During the period when Berlin was away from the troupe, from July to December, the war in Europe had inched closer to its bloody but inevitable end. On the eastern front, the Russians had pursued the retreating German troops as the Allies began their determined squeeze from the west; by August the Allied forces were in Paris and in southern France. By September, American troops of the First Army had broken into Germany.

In the Pacific theater, meanwhile, General Douglas MacArthur, as promised, had waded ashore in the Philippines in October. His commander in chief, Franklin D. Roosevelt, made history in November by being elected to an unprecedented fourth term as President of the United States; Ellin Berlin's campaign efforts on his behalf earned her an invitation to the White House.

Late December brought a brief detour into gloom. Three days before a white Christmas in New York, German panzers smashed through the Allied lines near Bastogne, Belgium, in a surprise attack that launched the Battle of the Bulge. For Hitler it was a wasteful last gasp, as the Allies spread into Austria and Germany and the Russians raced for Berlin. (By May 1945, the führer would be dead, a suicide, and the German high command unconditionally surrendered.)

By the beginning of 1945, the Pacific war had moved up the northern spine of New Guinea and into the central Pacific and the Philippines. Given their sheer number, countless small dots of islands in the vast expanses of water had to be bypassed as the Allies pushed northward and westward toward Japan; the isolated Japanese troops on those islands would quite literally wither away over the months and years to come.

A Dutch freighter was commandeered to transport the *This Is the Army* company to entertain the men in uniform—army, navy, and air force both American and Australian—in ports held by the Allies. In January 1945 parts of northern New Guinea remained in Japanese hands, but Buna to the south was secure, as was neighboring Oro Bay, whence the company could ship out once the other islands had been cleared of the enemy.

Berlin did not tour to those outlying islands, which would be fought over and won later in the year. New Guinea was bad enough for him, with its hot, swampy, treacherous jungles, some inhabited by Japanese soldiers who had been left behind in the retreat and now refused to surrender. Then, too, Japanese bombers stationed at New Britain, within striking distance, posed a more organized threat.

Other, drearier discomforts included the requisite injections, the Atabrine, the food (not least the unpalatable dehydrated potatoes, the powdered eggs, and other strange inedibles from Australia), and the weather—not to mention the insects. The *This Is the Army* company was not alone in doing its part, in this forbidding war zone, for the boys; Bob Hope and Jack Benny also did Pacific tours. But when Hope came to the area, he brought along glamorous vocalist (and *This Is the Army* film costar) Frances Langford, and Benny entertained with not only his off-key violin but also popular band singer Martha Tilton, plus Hollywood starlet Carol Landis; Berlin's troupe, in contrast, offered only fellow servicemen. (Some, it is true, were *dressed* as women—the Eileen, for example, who stole the heart of the soldier at the Stage Door Canteen—but never too convincingly.) Even without the glamour, however, the show was as popular in the Pacific as it had been in Britain and Italy. It provided a touch of home and, like *Yaphank* before it, a view of army life through enlisted men's eyes. Once the show went on its island-hopping way, Irving Berlin headed back to the States; he had spent three uncomfortable but "thrilling" months in the Pacific. Not yet fifty-seven, he admitted that the experience had aged him. One of the last songs he wrote for *This Is the Army* may have expressed his own feelings no less than those of tens of thousands of others in uniform: "Oh, to Be Home Again."

He left his boys early in April to return to his girls in New York. The cast and crew would go on to Guam, the Philippines, Okinawa, and other dots in the Pacific—Iwo Jima, Kwajalein—over the next six months. They were in Guam on August 6, when the B-29 Superfortress *Enola Gay* took off from nearby Tinian with orders to drop an atomic bomb on the city of Hiroshima, a strike that forced the Japanese to sign an Instrument of Surrender the following month.

Toward the end of October, Berlin flew to Honolulu in an airplane loaned him by Eastern Airlines' Eddie Rickenbacker, to join the company for *This Is the Army*'s final performance, at Haleakala, Maui, on the twenty-second.

Now, he believed, they could all go home.

What had Berlin really accomplished in the three years, more or less, spent touring with *This Is the Army?* Calculated in human terms, the answer must be a great deal, as proved by the enthusiastic reception of so many cheering, laughing audiences, and the praise, the accolades, and, later in October of 1945, the Presidential Medal of Merit (second in prestige only to the military Medal of Honor) he was awarded. But what had he actually produced, aside from the score to *This Is the Army* and a handful of songs written for special places en route? Barely two dozen songs over some forty months, only half or a third of the total he might be expected to write at any other time—peacetime, that is.

Consider the example of Dick Rodgers. During the very period that Berlin devoted to his army show, Rodgers composed the scores to *By Jupiter* with Lorenz Hart and, with Oscar Hammerstein II, the historic *Oklahoma!* and *Carousel*—three full musical scores, and all of them major hits.

Since *This Is the Army* had first left on its overseas tour, no new Berlin songs had made "Your Hit Parade" (though the evergreen "White Christmas," of course, was an annual fixture). Berlin realized he must make up for his time away from the Buick. Despite his own brand of battle fatigue, he must go to work again for the new Irving Berlin Music Company.

OLD-FASHIONED SMASH

B ERLIN APPROACHED his next venture, a film, with little enthusiasm. Its beginnings dated back several months, to the time when, en route to rejoin the *This Is the Army* tour after tending to the Bornstein headache, he had stopped briefly in Beverly Hills to discuss a possible *Holiday Inn* follow-up with Mark Sandrich at Paramount. To be titled *Blue Skies,* it would be another Irving Berlin anthology, with an unobtrusive plot and a handful of new songs.

When he returned from the Pacific in April 1945, home to stay at last, he admitted that he was tired. He was also depressed. In the war zones he had seen destruction, suffering, and death, more so than many servicemen. Now approaching sixty, he had mortality on his mind; over the last few years, a number of those closest to him had died.

In addition to Max Winslow, his champion from the old days on the Bowery, and his beloved cousin-by-marriage Alice Duer Miller, two other good friends had passed away during *This Is the Army*'s first year. His songwriting hero and chief booster, George M. Cohan, died while the show was touring the country, and news of Alexander Woollcott's death came during the San Francisco run. The latter was stricken with a heart attack in the midst of a radio broadcast.

Woollcott's death was not entirely surprising, considering his girth and appetite; what stung Berlin most was that it seemed, also, largely unlamented.

Some of the obituaries emphasized the writer's more unpleasant traits, notably his supposed bitchiness and his slashing tongue. Berlin was one of the few who had never been lacerated by his longtime friend's often cruel wit.

Two years later, in March 1945, as Berlin prepared to leave the Pacific, word reached him that Mark Sandrich, who was to have produced and directed *Blue Skies,* had himself died of a heart attack, at the young age of forty-four. But the show, as usual, must go on: the studio would find a new producer and director.

The general idea for *Blue Skies,* a virtual steal from *Holiday Inn,* had again originated with Berlin. The protagonists were to be yet another song-and-dance team who went their separate ways. As in the earlier film, the dancer remains in show business, but this time the vocalist goes into nightclub ownership; instead of a single inn, he thus has several clubs in which the Berlin songs may be crooned. The singer's peculiar business flair earns him a reputation for instability—as soon as one of his clubs achieves success, he sells it and opens another in another town. This penchant eventually wrecks his marriage.

Bing Crosby was cast as the itinerant club proprietor, but when production began on the film, it was Paul Draper, not Fred Astaire, who was signed to play the dancer. Draper was a curious choice, as he was inexperienced in films and, worse, unknown in Hollywood, having appeared only in revues and nightclubs, often with harmonicist Larry Adler. His solo work as a dance recitalist had acquired him a faithful following in New York; he was an elegant dancer, slim and even a little reminiscent of Astaire, but he was no Fred Astaire.

As originally conceived, *Blue Skies* was to have reunited Crosby, Astaire, Berlin, and Sandrich—money in the bank. Rumor had it that Astaire was offered the part but turned it down. Then came another turn: during an early script reading (before Mark Sandrich's death), it was discovered that Draper, though he danced smoothly, stammered when delivering his lines. Sandrich rather unrealistically believed that as filming progressed, Draper would conquer his nervousness. Crosby disagreed, and since by this time he was Paramount's fair-haired boy—tops at the box office with his several "road" pictures and an Academy Award winner the year before for his priestly role in *Going My Way*—he got His Way.

So it was back to Astaire. He had been making noises about retiring for some time, but when the second call came, he grabbed the opportunity. Astaire biographer and film historian Stanley Green attributes the quick about-face to the dancer's unhappiness over his recent M-G-M film *Yolanda and the Thief* (he was right to be unhappy: when it was released, it was a box-office failure). At that moment, rejoining the team of Crosby, Berlin, and Sandrich must have looked like a good thing.

Nine days into the filming, Sandrich suffered his fatal heart attack. Personally sad as the loss was, it also initiated a sequence of new professional headaches, as Berlin called them: new producer, new director, and general front-office panic. The score was all set and thus no problem; more than two dozen songs from the Berlin catalog were distributed throughout the story, along with four more written especially for the film.

When Berlin arrived in Hollywood with his family that July, he learned that Sol C. Siegel had taken over the production and Stuart Heisler the direction. Paramount had budgeted *Blue Skies* at a generous three million dollars; that was Siegel's department. Heisler, for his part, was a riddle. He had never before, to Berlin's knowledge, directed a musical, though his credits included a well-received mystery starring Alan Ladd, *The Glass Key,* and the recent *Along Came Jones,* with Gary Cooper. No matter: whoever directed this new film, Crosby would be Crosby, and Astaire, Astaire. No headaches there.

Berlin's original idea was first adapted by Allan Scott and then transformed into a screenplay by Arthur Sheekman (who had some experience, most lately in writing Danny Kaye's *Wonder Man*). As before, the story casts the former partners as rivals for the same young woman (Joan Caulfield); the plot twist here is that the "unstable" Crosby wins her twice (marriage-divorce-remarriage), and Astaire ends up as the bachelor friend of the family. If Crosby, as usual, projects insouciant mobility in the film, Astaire comes off as a capricious ladies' man, an unsympathetic but nonetheless likable character. It is he, retired from his dancing career because of a drunken fall, who finally brings the other two together through his radio show.

An anthology along the lines of *Alexander's Ragtime Band, Blue Skies* traverses about a quarter of a century's worth of American history, beginning immediately after the First World War. The songs are placed in chronological order as written, with appropriate period orchestration. The first interpolation is 1919's "A Pretty Girl Is like a Melody," presented in a lavish Ziegfeldian setting (Paramount's advertising boasted that no fewer than forty-seven sets were used in the film), in which Astaire sings and dances with the Ziegfeld girls. Among the chorines is Caulfield, who unwittingly provokes Astaire's unwelcome attentions.

He soon convinces her to accompany him to his old partner's current nightspot, where she falls in love (of course) with the singer-proprietor. As the setting moves on from club to club, the Berlin songs are ingeniously woven into the plot. Thus, at the Hole in the Wall Club, operating during

Prohibition, the chosen number is "(I'll See You in) Cuba," celebrating an accessible seaport where the wine flowed freely. The featured song at the Little Spot is "The Little Things in Life" from 1930; at the Chop Suey, Crosby sings "Not for All the Rice in China," and at the Balalaika, "Russian Lullaby."

One of the score's new songs actually dated back to 1943 and may have been written while Berlin was in New Guinea. Presented by Crosby at the Song Book and entitled "You Keep Coming Back like a Song," it would be the only number from *Blue Skies* to be nominated for an Academy Award after the film's 1946 release. Although it would end up losing the Oscar to Harry Warren and Johnny Mercer's "On the Atchison, Topeka and the Santa Fe," Berlin could take some consolation in the fact that it ran on "Your Hit Parade" for eleven weeks. A typical Berlin ballad, if a bit too much in keeping with the general bland mood of the film, it contained one line that invoked an earlier hit: "A song that keeps saying 'Remember.' " This was obviously meant for Ellin Berlin.

After he completed the other new songs, there was little for Berlin to do except rest, something he had never learned to do well. Instead, he would visit the studio to watch the filming or listen to soundtrack playbacks. No fewer than six arranger-orchestrators plus one vocal arranger were on Paramount's payroll, seeing to a musical background that ranged in style from ragtime through jazz to swing, including a big-band version of "Puttin' On the Ritz" (Astaire's most spectacular dance number) and a percussive, pulsating "Heat Wave," for which the dancer laid down his own eight-to-the-bar, boogie-woogie piano solo.

The two months the Berlins spent in Beverly Hills were pleasant ones, filled with dinners with Joe Schenck, June and Oscar Levant, Anya and Harold Arlen, Phyllis and Fred Astaire (the latter a frequent gin-rummy adversary), and others. Author Somerset Maugham was a special favorite of eighteen-year-old Mary Ellin.

While Berlin and his family socialized and lounged in Beverly Hills, the war came to a definitive if frightful end with the atomic bombing of two Japanese cities; V-J (Victory over Japan) Day was declared on August 15, 1945. It was a time of subdued celebration. The young men who had recently shipped out to the Pacific, among them U.S. Army Lieutenant Samuel Goldwyn, Jr., would return; the slaughter was over at last.

Throughout this period, Berlin kept in touch with the *This Is the Army* company. Even after V-J Day, the show continued to tour, entertaining the troops who were stationed on the various islands waiting to go home. At the end of that historic summer, the Berlins themselves were homeward bound.

Once back at Gracie Square, Berlin was surprised and thrilled to receive an invitation from General George Marshall to come to Washington, where, in the company of Ellin and Robert Sherwood, he would be presented with the Medal of Merit for "the performance of extraordinary service to the United States Army." This memorable occasion marked his first official recognition by the nation he so manifestly loved.

Back in Gracie Square after the ceremony, Ellin Berlin began searching for new quarters for the family. Because they had decided once and for all to make Manhattan their home, with summers at their Catskills spread, they required a real house, not an apartment. Berlin, meanwhile, ignoring his physician's advice that he take a six-month sabbatical, tended to some last details regarding the reorganization of his publishing company. In October he flew to Hawaii for the final performance of *This Is the Army,* an event he could not miss.

Soon after his return, yet another death shocked him.

In mid-September, Oscar Hammerstein II had spent a week in Beverly Hills writing a song, "Nobody Else but Me," for a revival of his and Jerome Kern's classic *Show Boat,* which the two men were planning to coproduce. With the song finished, Hammerstein broached with Kern the subject of another musical that he and his new collaborator, Richard Rodgers, wanted to produce (Rodgers and Hammerstein had already been successful in their first effort as producers, the nonmusical *I Remember Mama,* which opened in 1944 at the Music Box and ran for 714 performances). The musical Hammerstein had in mind for Kern was *Annie Oakley,* conceived by Dorothy Fields (who had written several fine film songs with Kern). Her brother Herbert was her collaborator on the libretto.

Kern had his doubts about returning to the theater after a six-year absence. His last musical had been the failure *Very Warm for May* (out of which had come the incomparable "All the Things You Are," lyric by Hammerstein). Although he was not always well treated in Hollywood, he still preferred it to Broadway; life on the West Coast was sedate, lush, and, from time to time, profitable (even when the films themselves turned out poorly).

But Hammerstein proved to be persistent as well as convincing, and by the time he left, he had secured Kern's promise to come east for *Show Boat*'s casting and rehearsals (the revival was due to open early in January 1946). Once that show was under way, they could begin discussions on *Annie Oakley.*

Kern, with his wife, Eva, arrived in New York on Friday, November 2, and registered at the St. Regis on Fifth Avenue. They spent the weekend with friends. Chorus auditions were scheduled for two in the afternoon on Monday; at noon, having decided to find a gift for his daughter Elizabeth, Kern set out for an antique-furniture shop near the hotel. He never got there, however: as he turned the corner at Fifty-fifth Street, he collapsed.

The stricken composer was taken immediately to a city hospital (i.e., a facility for indigents) on Welfare Island. His only identification was his ASCAP membership card, but that was enough, eventually, to enable Hammerstein to track him down to the ward, where he learned that his colleague had suffered a severe cerebral hemorrhage. On Wednesday, after some slight, though not very hopeful, improvement, Kern was moved to a private room at Doctors Hospital in Manhattan. On Sunday, November 11, he slipped into a coma and died in the early afternoon.

Berlin had been happily looking forward to a reunion with his longtime chum and was stunned to read of his death; Kern was only sixty, three years his senior. Like Hammerstein, Berlin mourned the loss of a good friend and a great composer. And now what?

He would find out a month later, when Oscar Hammerstein called him. Kern's death had upset the *Show Boat* scheduling and thrown plans for *Annie Oakley* into disarray. As it eventuated, *Show Boat* would open on time, and to great acclaim. But Rodgers and Hammerstein were blocked on the *Annie* production, which had substantial backing from Twentieth Century–Fox in anticipation of a film if the show succeeded. A frantic search thus began for Kern's replacement.

News had gotten around town that Irving Berlin was home from the wars (both Pacific and Hollywood), and his was the first name that came to the minds of the anxious producers. But they agreed that Berlin would never accept the job: he was too big. Also, on this show he would not be, as he usually was, in full charge.

Still, Hammerstein reasoned that they had nothing to lose by asking; until they did, they would not know Berlin's answer.

"It's not up my alley," Berlin replied after Hammerstein outlined the plot for him. He did not do folksy musicals like this one, about a sharpshooting heroine from backwoods Ohio who joins a circus.

Nevertheless, the patiently tenacious Hammerstein talked the skeptical Berlin into reading the libretto. This presented another obstacle in the person of Dorothy Fields, who was slated to write the lyrics; as everyone knew, Berlin worked alone. (It turned out that Hammerstein needn't have worried about this: Fields graciously offered to bow out should the producers manage to persuade Berlin to score the show.)

Berlin, most expeditiously, received a "very skinny first act," as he put it, whose primary function was to introduce the protagonists, the performers of Buffalo Bill Cody's Wild West Show and the Oakleys. Annie and her siblings—three younger sisters and a brother—were described in the stage directions as an "unwashed brood of ragamuffins." The plot had the showmen inviting the townspeople to the fairgrounds, where the handsome, vain sharpshooter Frank Butler (to be played by Ray Middleton) challenges all comers to a shooting match.

A shot rings out, ripping a stuffed bird off a woman's hat. Annie (Ethel Merman), in buckskins, a rifle in her hand and a brace of quail over her shoulder, enters, followed by the ragamuffins. She is such a clean shot that a hotel manager offers to pay a premium for two dozen pelletless quails for his kitchen, but it soon becomes clear that the Oakleys cannot count that high (nor can they read).

The first-act sketch may have been thin, but it was enough for Berlin, who called Hammerstein back to tell him, "I can't do hillbilly lyrics."

"Don't be silly, Irving," Hammerstein retorted. "All you have to do is to drop the final *g* from most of the verbs." (Hammerstein's own proficiency at writing dialect songs had earned him a reputation among other writers as a master of a special language dubbed Apostrophe.) This advice amused, but did not convince, Berlin. Rumors have persisted that the major reason for his hesitation was his reluctance to step into the considerable shoes of Jerome Kern, or, alternatively, his petulance at being the producers' second choice. Neither story is true. Kern had been a dear friend—"I loved Kern," he once said—and professionally, though different, they had been equals. As to the other, when Hammerstein first met with Kern, Berlin was not available.

Berlin's quick, searching mind sparked his curiosity. He went to see the producers. If they were so set on doing *Annie Oakley,* why not with a Rodgers and Hammerstein score? They had done extremely well in the Early Americana genre with *Oklahoma!* and *Carousel,* both replete with apostrophied participles. "Why don't you do it?" Berlin inquired.

Taking over where his partner had left off, Rodgers explained. They were planning another musical (the less-than-successful *Allegro*) and the production of a comedy, *Happy Birthday,* starring Helen Hayes. They had their hands full. Rodgers pressed his case, suggesting that Berlin keep the script over the weekend and give it some more thought.

Berlin was dubious; his last book show, *Louisiana Purchase,* had been produced six years before. Since then, while he had been touring with *This Is the Army,* the Broadway musical had undergone a great metamorphosis. The current watchword was *integrated,* an approach he detested. Even before *Oklahoma!,* the pivotal musical of record, there had been such integrated musicals as *Pal Joey* and *Lady in the Dark,* followed by *One Touch of Venus, Bloomer Girl,*

On the Town, Up in Central Park, and, of course, *Carousel.* All had had reasonably literate books and lyrics, with songs that illuminated the plot and dances, even ballets, to further the action. Not one had been a revue, a Berlin specialty.

Rodgers persisted, now joined by Hammerstein, and Berlin yielded a little. It was a Friday; he promised to see what he might accomplish over the weekend. Returning to his office, he drafted Helmy Kresa for a couple of days in Atlantic City. Since it was December, the resort town would be practically deserted; Berlin's late-night/early-morning work at the piano would disturb no one.

On Monday he returned to the Rodgers and Hammerstein office and pleaded, "Give me another week."

Rodgers, approaching the end of his temperamental rope, snapped, "Either you want to do it or you don't! Which is it?"

"I'll do it."

Berlin did not inform them that he had in fact come home from Atlantic City with two good songs—"Ham songwriter that I am," he would later admit. They were "Doin' What Comes Natur'lly" and "They Say It's Wonderful," the first a nod in Hammerstein's direction and the second a sturdy ballad. (In his *Musical Stages,* Rodgers remembers things a little differently, claiming that Berlin "came bounding into the office with a big grin on his face and handed over three songs.") He had requested the extra time because he wanted to be able to demonstrate at least half a dozen songs, rather than a mere two, pleased though he might be with them.

He and Kresa came back a few days later with perhaps seven songs, "all brilliant," in Rodgers's estimation. But Hammerstein had a quibble with a line in "They Say It's Wonderful" that went, "To bill and coo like a dove is wonderful."

"Irving," he asked, "do you really like 'To bill and coo like a dove'?" Berlin saw his point: the line was weak. On the spot, he altered it to "And with the moon up above, it's wonderful," which satisfied everyone, himself included. He respected Hammerstein and later described him as no less than a "genius" and a "great talent. He's never been given the credit he deserves. There's only one lyric writer," Berlin believed, "[who] came close to being a poet and that's Oscar Hammerstein."

With Berlin committed to the project, the delicate subject of a contract arose. Three musical giants were involved, not to mention their batteries of attorneys. In the art of songwriting they might be equals, but in production, Rodgers and Hammerstein were *more* than equal; honest as always,

Hammerstein confessed to Berlin that they had no idea what to offer him for his score.

"How about five percent of the gross?" Berlin suggested.

Relieved, the producers found that arrangement most satisfactory; it spared them the complex negotiations over an advance, royalties during the run of the show, and other details that would have required weeks of legal gymnastics and reams of paper.

Then there was the question of billing, a matter taken very seriously in the theater. Obviously it would be in the established format "Rodgers and Hammerstein/ Present," followed by Ethel Merman's name above the title, with the songwriter, the book's authors, and the director below.

Since Merman's 1930 debut in the Gershwins' *Girl Crazy,* "belting" out "I Got Rhythm," the onetime secretary had appeared in a series of profitable musicals, introducing songs by Brown and Henderson ("Life Is Just a Bowl of Cherries"), DeSylva and Richard Whiting ("Eadie Was a Lady"), and Cole Porter ("You're the Top," "Ridin' High," and "Blow, Gabriel, Blow"). Her ability to project a number, keeping it both musically and lyrically crystal-clear, to the "last row of the second balcony" had made her a star overnight.

In the sixteen years since *Girl Crazy,* Merman had become a dependable and tough trouper, jealous of her position as the Star and mistress of a coarse vocabulary. Cross her in any way, step on her line, or upstage her, and you were out on the street, at liberty, before you could say "Diva." Berlin understood her talent and character. But in his songs for her, he expanded her emotional scope. Later Merman would say, "With all due respect to the Gershwins [she omitted Porter], Irving had given me range, allowing me a kind of vulnerability that was missing" in her usual "tough broad" roles. Irving Berlin, she declared, made a lady of her.

Next came the issue of the credits. Berlin proposed that he, Rodgers and Hammerstein, and Dorothy and Herbert Fields all have their names printed in the advertising, in the playbill, and on the sheet music in the same type size. That solved that.

There was one further detail. Having learned at some point that the Fieldses were to get only 4 percent of the gross, Berlin asked the astonished producers to reduce his portion by half a percent and add the difference to theirs: 4½ percent for the libretto, and the same for the score.

"You know you don't have to do it, Irving," Hammerstein told him. Berlin did know that, but he explained that since his songs had grown out of their script, Dotty and Herbie had in a sense had a hand in writing the score as well. That, too, was agreed upon.

"Generosity such as this," Rodgers concluded, "is an exceedingly rare commodity."

One final decision was made: the musical would be retitled *Annie Get Your Gun.*

The producers were now free to put together the rest of their creative staff, hiring choreographer Helen Tamaris (*Up in Central Park* and *Show Boat*) to do the dances (Agnes de Mille, who had pioneered the form, was busy at the time with Lerner and Loewe's *Brigadoon*), Lucinda Ballard to attend to costume design, and Jo Mielziner to light the show and design the sets.

Berlin was happy over the producers' choice to direct: Joshua Logan. Rodgers and Hammerstein had signed Captain Logan almost the instant he was separated from the service (a day or so before Kern's death), and even before rehearsals began, Logan reworked the book. "The first act was funny," he later wrote, "but there were craterlike gaps in the second. I worked with Dorothy and Herb for days rearranging scenes, writing new ones and, because I insisted on it, giving Annie some character growth before the curtain came down."

Such involvement would seem to be way above and far beyond the typical purview of a director, skilled though Logan undoubtedly was (years later he would be credited with turning a flop show, *Wish You Were Here,* into a hit). The Fieldses were seasoned "professionals" (a term that carried profound implications in the theater), as was Hammerstein, a librettist himself. Logan contributed considerably to *Annie Get Your Gun,* but his fondness for the illuminating if slightly overdeveloped anecdote may have got the better of him here.

Such anecdotes abound about this particular show. One of the most colorful maintains that Berlin returned from his weekend in Atlantic City with the complete score; another has Logan (though Rodgers, in his own book, claimed the distinction for himself) saving "There's No Business like Show Business" from the wastebasket. When Berlin demonstrated the number for the staff, so the tale goes, an unhappy expression on Rodgers's face (Logan said it was on *his*) prompted the composer to discard it.

When the full score was played again, everyone noticed that "Show Business" was missing. Rodgers was distressed and told Berlin that he thought it was one of the best tunes in the show and should be reinstated; director Logan joined in the chorus, insisting on its restoration and yelling (as he recalled it), "That's one of the greatest songs ever written!"

"Nonsense," was Berlin's reaction to these accounts. The song was deliberately written for use during a change of scenery, he said, when the curtain would be lowered ("in one") and the vocalists would sing a song to fill the interval. At the turning point in the first act when Annie has decided to join Buffalo Bill's show, Bill, her rival Frank, and Charlie, the manager of the circus, together sing of the vicissitudes and joys of being in the business; Annie joins in song also. As they render "There's No Business like Show Business," the backstage crew prepares the set for the more intimate duet, "They Say It's Wonderful," that followed.

Berlin considered the position of the song in the plot: it came right after the laugh-provoking "You Can't Get a Man with a Gun," in which Annie realizes that she is in love with Frank but does not know how to show it. The "in-one" song would serve as a transition from the comic to the more serious, though still noncommittal, duet. It should be amusing but not *too* funny, lest it spoil the effect of the previous song; nor should it have any overtone of wistful wondering, like the next.

Berlin recalled discussing the song's function with Hammerstein, who agreed with his notions. He soon came back with "Show Business," which the producer proclaimed good: it was as simple as that. In recollecting the incident, Berlin said, "Oscar never threw his hat in the air about anything. That's why I trusted him."

In not quite three months, Berlin had a complete score. After rehearsals in March, *Annie* was ready for an out-of-town presentation at the Shubert in New Haven on March 28, 1946. The producers' confidence in the show's condition was evidenced by that booking, less than a week before the Boston tryout was due to begin.

There was a big glitch before the New Haven premiere, however—a musical flaw that caused Berlin to become visibly distressed during a rehearsal. As Rodgers remembered it, "We were in New Haven for the tryout, and with opening night just a few days away, we spent one morning listening to the first orchestra rehearsal. I was not satisfied with what I heard, and I was sure Irving wasn't either."

The two left the Shubert to grab some lunch at Keysey's Restaurant across the street. They found a table, and Berlin spoke: "Well, Mr. Rodgers, I'm very unhappy about the orchestrations."

"*Mr.* Rodgers"? Not "Dick"? It was apparent that Irving Berlin was most upset. The orchestrations had been done by one Philip J. Lang, a relative newcomer to the Broadway scene (his one Broadway credit at that moment was Morton Gould's score for *Billion Dollar Baby,* a brassy musical set in the twenties). The orchestra overwhelmed the singers, some of whose words were drowned out by the brass; the comic songs were lost.

Rodgers immediately phoned publisher Max Dreyfus in New York and asked him to send up the dependable, respected Robert Russell Bennett (himself then out of town as well with a new show). Bennett arrived the next morning and, according to Rodgers, reorchestrated the entire score.

Here again, Berlin's memory was different. During that rehearsal, he said, hearing the orchestra obliterate his carefully wrought words, he moved to the back of the theater, took a seat, and brooded. Conductor Jay Blackton, recognizing that they had a problem, stopped the music and found the saddened composer. They talked briefly, with Blackton reassuring Berlin that it could all be fixed.

"Irving," he said, "go out, take a walk, have some coffee. Give us a couple of hours, let me take the bugs out of the orchestrations."

Berlin spent the requisite two hours elsewhere, and when he returned to the Shubert and heard the "debugged" orchestra, he was ecstatic. The songs went over wonderfully, he thought. "I don't know much technically about music," he later claimed, "but I think Lang overorchestrated. Jay, who is an orchestrator besides being a conductor, really took the bugs out." (The playbill credits the orchestrations to Philip J. Lang, Russell Bennett, and Ted Royal.)

Blackton himself offered up yet another variant of the story. In an interview with theater historian and scholar Miles Krueger, he recalled that he had spotted the fault the night before the rehearsal when looking over the score in his hotel room. He said he "sensed with dismay that [the orchestration] lacked the warmth and charm needed to put over Irving Berlin's great songs." That premonition was confirmed in the Shubert the next morning. From that point on, Blackton's account tallies with Rodgers's, detailing the call to Dreyfus and the arrival of Bennett, to the ensuing satisfaction of all concerned.

The disparity among the stories seems to underscore Berlin's reluctance to interfere with those facets of the production that he felt were not his bailiwick, other than to inform "Mr. Rodgers" of his displeasure over Lang's work. It was Rodgers's job as producer to deal with the problem. For his part, Blackton apprehended the signs of uneasiness as Berlin jingled the coins in his pocket, but he emphasized that the composer always kept his distance from all but the songs, and never proffered advice on any aspect of his handling of the orchestra. At the same time, he always seemed eager to hear whatever Rodgers had to say about the score. Like Hammerstein, however, Rodgers was not given to throwing his hat in the air over much, and that tended to exacerbate Berlin's anxiety.

After four New Haven performances, *Annie Get Your Gun,* a musical now in fine fettle, moved to the Shubert in Boston on April 2 for a sold-out run of three weeks. After that the show was slated to settle into the Imperial in New York.

The otherwise trouble-free Boston run was dramatically enlivened during the first matinee, when an unexpected response greeted Annie's first entrance, early in act 1. In the audience that day was Ethel Merman's daughter, known as Li'l Bit, then not quite four years old and accompanied by her father, Robert Levitt. Li'l Bit loved animals, and witnessing her mother shoot a bird—even a decorative frill of the milliner's art—horrified her. Screaming, she pulled her father from his seat, up the aisle, and out of the theater.

Trouble of a more serious nature struck in New York, where the show was to premiere on April 25. On the twenty-fourth, as Mielziner supervised the hanging of the sets, a loud cracking sound echoed through the house. An alert stagehand rushed over to Rodgers and pushed him offstage and into the wings (Berlin was not present for this near calamity). An inspection revealed that a bolt securing a structural beam had popped and a girder had buckled—a threat to the sets as well as the building's roof. The theater was emptied, and its license suspended by the city until repairs could be made. That would take time; opening night was accordingly postponed.

Rodgers and Hammerstein soon confronted Lee Shubert, telling him, according to Rodgers, that

> he had to give us an interim out-of-town booking. At first he blamed the scenery rather than his theatre, but eventually let us play the Shubert Theatre in Philadelphia while the necessary repairs were being made. There was the small matter of another show then playing at the [Philadelphia] Shubert, but Lee managed to have it transferred to Boston [where a show had prematurely expired], and a week later we moved in.
>
> Though we had taken out only a tiny ad in the Philadelphia papers, we were sold out for our entire two-week run before the opening.

Annie Get Your Gun finally premiered at the restored Imperial on May 16, 1946, and remained there until February 12, 1949, for a total of 1,147 audience-packed performances. Its off-Broadway progeny would be just as successful: a road company headlined by Mary Martin began a cross-country tour in Dallas, Texas, on October 3, 1947, and closed in Detroit in May 1949, while the London production, starring Dolores Gray, would enjoy a run of 1,304 performances at the Coliseum. A Paris production, *Annie du Far-West,* was to open in February 1950; in Austria and Germany the show would be known as *Annie Schiess las* and sung in German. The film version, with Betty Hutton (replacing an ailing and troubled Judy Garland) and Howard Keel, would be released in April 1950 to become the box-office hit of the year.

Likewise on Broadway in 1946. In the original, Ethel Merman proved to be a triple talent, not only a prime vocalist but also an actress and comic who could deliver her lines with incisive timing. The darling of the critics (to the neglect of her costar Middleton), she took the year's Donaldson Award for acting; Logan won for his direction, and Irving Berlin got the nod for music and lyrics.

Annie's score is one of Broadway's richest. When Brooks Atkinson later dismissed the songs as "undistinguished" (excepting the exuberant "I Got the Sun in the Morning"), an incensed Josh Logan would point out to him that this one show had also introduced "There's No Business like Show Business," "The Girl That I Marry," "Doin' What Comes Natur'lly," "Moonshine Lullaby," "I Got Lost in His Arms," "I'm an Indian Too," and "My Defenses Are Down"—"all of which," Logan argued, "have become a part of our heritage."

A slight exaggeration, perhaps, but close enough. Curiously missing from Logan's list was the show's major hit, "They Say It's Wonderful," which was broadcast on "Your Hit Parade" only a week after the musical opened and stayed on the roster for no less than six months.

Atkinson was a perceptive theater critic, a Pulitzer winner for his reports from Soviet Russia, and a fine nature writer and biographer, but he had a tin ear. Berlin's reaction was both philosophical and succinct: "Aren't we lucky that the critics only *write about* the music and don't try to *write* it themselves?"

Alec Wilder, a songwriter as well as a composer of charming miniatures, was staggered by the prodigious score and unabashedly called it a "fantastic piece of work." In his study of popular song, Wilder's principal bête noire consists in the use of the repeated note (a practice for which he frequently scolds Gershwin). Interestingly, the *Annie Get Your Gun* song on which he lavishes the most praise and space, "I Got Lost in His Arms," the show's loveliest ballad, is itself built on repeated notes; its melodically hypnotic chorus is a series of the same tone (in other words, the melody is the rhythm). Here Berlin adroitly achieved variety by repeating a single tone eight times in the initial three bars and then, on the final note in that last bar, raising the melody a tone and following the same pattern through to another final note and another step up—and so on until the melody has risen five tones in all above its first. In the four-bar release, where this occurs (on the word *There* in "There you go"), the melody dips down a sixth (on the final "go") before the phrase is repeated.

Although in the key of C and in common 4/4 time, the song has the feel of a waltz, as the rhythmically contrived melody skips along in a pattern of half note, two quarters, half, and two quarters. In this instance Wilder gladly grants Berlin the repeated-note technique, conceding, "It's absolutely marvelous."

Another Wilder favorite is "Moonshine Lullaby," marked "slow blues tempo." In the scene in which it is heard, Annie is singing her sisters and brothers to sleep, a quiet moment. A beautiful, bluesy tune, it nonetheless seems an odd sort of cradle song, for the moonshine originates in a "busy little still"; there are sly references to the children's "lovin' Paw [who] isn't quite within the law" and to a jug of mountain rye. This is Berlin with his tongue in his cheek, writing words that conflict with and play off the music.

"They Say It's Wonderful" is one of the most subtle and inventive songs in the score. Annie has just fallen in love for the first time, having known the emotion only by hearsay before this. She sings,

> *They say that falling in love is wonderful,*
> *It's wonderful—so they say.*
> *And with a moon up above, it's wonderful,*
> *It's wonderful—so they tell me.*
> *I can't recall who said it,*
> *I know I never read it.*

Annie's innocence in such matters is evident in the tags in the second and fourth lines, "so they say" and "so they tell me." Integration emerges with a vengeance in the last line, which harks back to the very first scene, when Annie and her siblings were exposed as illiterate. Also notable here is that only the final two lines rhyme; indeed, there are but three rhymes in the entire song, the second being an internal one of adjacent words, "grand/ And," and the third coming in the last two lines of the chorus, which pair "every way" with "So they say."

Annie's rival and true love Frank Butler sings a true waltz, "The Girl That I Marry," describing anyone but Miss Oakley. Later, in the robust "My Defenses Are Down," he admits that she has caught him. In the duet "They Say It's Wonderful," he shares his wealth of experience with the smitten Annie ("Ev'rything you've heard is really so/ I've been there once or twice and I should know").

Another duet was an unexpected bonus and provided one of the most amusing moments in the show. It came out of a preproduction progress meeting. Logan felt strongly that Merman and Middleton needed to sing a song together in the second act, to balance "They Say It's Wonderful" in the first. He whispered this to Hammerstein, who whispered back, "Another song?"

"Another song?" was echoed in a whisper by Berlin, who had materialized out of nowhere. Logan then made his case. Berlin reminded him that in the second act, Annie and Frank are estranged (he has left the circus and joined the competition because Annie has proved to be a better shot) and not speaking to each other. How, the logical Berlin asked, could they sing together if they weren't even talking?

"Could they do a quarrel song or a challenge song?" Rodgers asked. Berlin liked the latter idea; he had written a few such numbers for the Astaire-Rogers films. The production meeting broke up not long after that, and all went their separate ways. When Logan got back to his apartment, the phone was ringing. It was Berlin.

"Hello, Josh? How's this?" and he sang:

> *Anything you can do, I can do better,*
> *I can do anything better than you.*

And so on through three choruses of challenges, including a masterful affront:

> HE: *I can live on bread and cheese.*
> SHE: *And only on that?*
> HE: *Yes.*
> SHE: *So can a rat.*

After hearing a few lines, a thunderstruck Logan demanded, "When in hell did you write that?"

"In the taxicab. I had to, didn't I? We go into rehearsal Monday."

"Anything You Can Do" is the show's penultimate song, preceding a reprise of the show-biz anthem by the cast of "There's No Business like Show Business." "Anything You Can Do" sets the scene for the Annie-Frank reconciliation that will follow, after she intentionally loses a shooting match to him. This salving of his ego brings Frank into Annie's arms, the two circuses merge, and the curtain falls on a happy ending.

The score is remarkable for its variety of songs, comprising comic numbers, obvious dance tunes ("I'll Share It All with You"), memorable ballads, character definers ("Doin' What Comes Natur'lly" and Frank's "I'm a Bad, Bad Man"), and even a quasi-Indian song to mark Annie's adoption by Sitting Bull and her initiation into the Sioux tribe. Despite the musical's spectacular success, however, theater historians have tended to dismiss it as insufficiently innovative, comparing it unfavorably with *Oklahoma!* and *Carousel,* for example (both with Hammerstein librettos).

If *Annie*'s book did not break new ground, it was nonetheless both literate and functional. The script by Dorothy and Herbert Fields, with flourishes added by Joshua Logan, made for a fine show, and star Ethel Merman, capering practically every moment she was on stage, contributed greatly to turning it into a hit. But in the end it was Berlin's score, with one outstanding song after another keeping the slight plot in motion, that ensured the musical's wide and continuing popularity.

The composer was content with his accomplishment—even a little cocky about it. When a friend, envious as was habitual in the business, remarked that *Annie Get Your Gun* was "old-fashioned," Berlin retorted. "Yeah. A good old-fashioned smash."

THERE'S NO BUSINESS . . .

T O CELEBRATE the truly smashing success of *Annie Get Your Gun* and, belatedly, the twentieth anniversary of their marriage, the Berlins rented a house on a hill in Bermuda in the summer of 1946 for several weeks of sun, swimming, and entertaining, often with the host himself preparing steaks flown in from Dinty Moore's in Manhattan.

While he found the vacation restful and rejuvenating, Berlin was more in his element doing *Annie* business: keeping tabs on sheet-music sales, arranging for the Decca album, and, that summer, tracking the songs on "Your Hit Parade," to which he listened weekly. He was "very grateful," as he wrote to Harry Ruby, though that same old anxiety always fluttered just below the surface: "At my age, 'over twenty-one,' this seems like a second helping. Every time I start with a show I wonder if this time I'll reach for it and find it isn't there."

The year was personally notable for the Berlins' acquisition of a five-story town house on fashionably "exclusive" (meaning that affluence was a requirement) Beekman Place. Number 17 abutted the East River and faced East Fifty-first Street.

Their Bermuda summer interlude over, the Berlins returned to Manhattan, the girls to start school and Ellin to see to their new home. Berlin himself spent most of September in England, checking on the workings of his London office. He was back in time for the release of *Blue Skies* in mid-October.

Even though the critical reception was not particularly favorable, the film was a hit, which success may have given Berlin the idea for his next venture. Later that same month, he was singularly honored by the (Theodore) Roosevelt Memorial Association: of all the recipients of that organization's annual medal, he was the sole civilian, in the good military company of Generals Eisenhower and Douglas MacArthur and Admirals William Halsey and Chester Halsey.

Upon receiving his citation, Berlin made a (characteristically) brief speech conveying his humble thanks and pride and avowing that he "really [didn't] know how to express [him]self"—whereupon he moved, as usual, to the piano to sing and play a medley of his songs, concluding with "God Bless America." The evening capped off an especially heady time for him: the night before, one of the new songs from *Blue Skies,* "You Keep Coming Back like a Song," had been performed on "Your Hit Parade." And of course, *Annie Get Your Gun* was riding high at the Imperial.

Early the next year, 1947, he went to California to meet with Joe Schenck, who since his run-in with the IRS had been kicked downstairs a few flights in the running of Twentieth Century-Fox, though he could still claim the title of producer. Perhaps, Berlin suggested, in light of the popularity of *Blue Skies,* they could do another film, to be called *Easter Parade,* using the same formula: write a script around a collection of songs from the Berlin catalog, with a few new ones added, tailored to the specific talent available to the star. Schenck liked the idea, and they agreed that the studio would pay for the rights to the title, the older songs, and any new creations. But this time Berlin also expected something more: a percentage of the film's earnings.

Schenck's bosses at Fox balked at this demand; they preferred to pay a writer for his or her work and be done with it. Not even the lure of the Berlin name was enough to tempt them out of their resolve. A humbled Joe Schenck had to inform his old friend of the change to their personal agreement. Now it was Berlin who balked, and the deal was canceled.

Such news moves quickly in Hollywood, preceded only by gossip and rumor (in that order); the next voice heard was that of Metro-Goldwyn-Mayer's Louis B. Mayer (whose superior in Loew's New York office was Joe Schenck's brother, Nicholas). He put in a bid for Berlin's services, offering him a flat fee of half a million dollars. Berlin refused him, too.

Mayer was anxious to feature Judy Garland and Gene Kelly in a musical with songs by Irving Berlin. Garland and Kelly had already worked together on *For Me and My Gal* (Kelly's film debut) and the forthcoming *The Pirate.* Separately, Garland had, beginning with *The Wizard of Oz* in 1939, graced several more Metro hits, among them *Meet Me in St. Louis* and *The Harvey Girls,* while Kelly had achieved stardom in *Cover Girl* (on loan to Columbia) and *Anchors Aweigh* back at MGM. The two now-important stars had proved professionally compatible, and their pairing made for good box office. Mayer's plan was to turn the project over to Metro's celebrated Arthur Freed Unit, which had an enviable record of hit musicals to its credit, going back to *The Wizard of Oz,* its debut production. Among the successes that had established this company-within-a-company were *Cabin in the Sky, Best Foot Forward, Good News,* and several Garland pictures, including *Girl Crazy* and *Ziegfeld Follies.*

The studio head's eagerness eventually got the better of him: he consented to pay Berlin $600,000 plus a percentage of the film's profits. The arrangement pleased Berlin, and he was excited by the prospect of writing songs for Judy Garland, who was then wrapping up work on *The Pirate* under the direction of her husband, Vincente Minnelli.

Louella Parsons broke the news of the projected film in a February column, but Production No. 1418 began in earnest in Freed's office on June 5, 1947, when he met with screenwriters (and husband and wife) Frances Goodrich and Albert Hackett. Taking their cue from *The Pirate,* whose script they had rewritten, Goodrich and Hackett imagined their stars in a love-hate relationship, as adversaries who would eventually fall for each other.

The cast that Parsons announced was a formidable one: Garland, Kelly, Frank Sinatra, Kathryn Grayson, and Red Skelton. The original treatment had Kelly being abandoned on Easter by his partner (Grayson, evidently), who leaves him in vaudeville to take a part in the Broadway theater. He, spitefully, vows that he will find a nobody (Garland) and within a year teach her all their routines and make her a star. His attempts to turn Garland into a carbon copy of his ex-partner fail miserably; only when his Galatea is allowed to be herself does she shine. Between Easters, thanks to her, they become major Broadway stars. Freed liked the story and told his screenwriting team to go ahead with the script.

"I worked very closely on the story with the Hacketts," Berlin later told Freed Unit historian Hugh Fordin.

> Remember, this was the period [ca. 1919–25] of the *Ziegfeld Follies* at the New Amsterdam Roof, a period which I knew. . . . I didn't write any of the script, but I was very much involved in how they would develop their scenes. You see, I was anxious to get my songs done in the right atmosphere; the Hacketts were wonderful!

Also for Fordin, Frances Goodrich recalled something of this collaboration from the other side.

> Sometimes, [Berlin] would come in with an idea with a song to illus-
> trate it. For example, he had a new song, "I Love You, You Love
> Him," in which he had envisioned sort of "La Ronde," with a Greek
> vase, etc. And we would say we couldn't work that out . . . and he'd
> answer, "That's all right, I'll use it somewhere else." What we are try-
> ing to say is that he is very flexible.

Berlin's cooperative resilience was likewise called into play when Freed
rejected his newly written "Let's Take an Old-Fashioned Walk": unperturbed,
the composer left, only to return in an hour with a replacement, the amusing
"A Couple of Swells." He would file away the first song and use it elsewhere
two years later.

Other principals from the unit assigned to *Easter Parade* were director
Minnelli (who had done well by his wife in *Meet Me in St. Louis,* the dramatic
nonmusical *The Clock,* and *The Pirate*) and associate producer Roger Edens, in
charge of the music. Edens immediately began picking through the Berlin
cornucopia in search of old songs that could be reused in the film.

In mid-September, Kelly started rehearsing, assisted by choreographer
Robert Alton, who was to direct the big musical numbers; first up was the
new "Drum Crazy." Within days, *Easter Parade* would run into major turbu-
lence. The initial bombshell detonated on September 18, when Minnelli was
summoned to Freed's office.

The director sensed that something was wrong as soon as he saw Freed,
who looked unusually grave. He began, "Vincente, I don't know how to tell
you this. . . ." Minnelli was stunned (his word) to learn that he was being
taken off the picture because his wife's psychiatrist believed that they should
not simultaneously work and live together—and that moreover, Judy herself
wanted him off the film. Freed knew, even if Berlin didn't, that Garland had
had problems during the making of *The Pirate,* and that she felt Minnelli did
not truly understand her talent or pay enough attention to her; she even
resented his rapport with Kelly.

Only recently released from a sanatorium, seemingly cured of her delu-
sions and anxieties, Garland had all too soon succumbed once again to her
chronic dependence on amphetamines. Minnelli realized that their rocky
marriage was coming to an end, despite the cheering presence of their toddler
daughter, Liza. Shocked and bitterly confused, he wondered why Judy

couldn't have given him the news herself. Why from her to her analyst to Freed? Sadly and reluctantly, without fuss, he bowed out of *Easter Parade.* Upon his arrival at home that evening, he was greeted with a kiss and no mention whatsoever of his dismissal.

Minnelli's equally surprised replacement as director was Charles Walters, a Broadway dancer-turned-choreographer who had come to Hollywood to design the dances and to dance himself in Garland's *Presenting Lily Mars* (1943). The two of them had worked together again in *Girl Crazy* and *Meet Me in St. Louis.* When Freed beckoned, Walters had just finished up as choreographer and director of *Good News,* another Freed Unit project, on which he had been teamed with associate producer Roger Edens and associate choreographer Robert Alton.

Before beginning on his new film, Walters read the script by the Hacketts, who had in the meantime left on a European vacation. He was, it soon became known, appalled by the screenplay, which he pronounced "terrible," not least because the "hero is a real heavy." The Hacketts had based Kelly's character on the persona the actor/dancer had brought with him to Hollywood—the manipulative, perfidious heel of *Pal Joey.* It was pretty much the same part he had played in *For Me and My Gal,* but "it's no good," Walters wailed. "It's mean."

He convinced Freed that a rewrite was needed, and Freed protégé Sidney Sheldon (who had written the Oscar-winning screenplay for 1947's *The Bachelor and the Bobby Soxer*) was given the job. Although Sheldon would tell Fordin that he started at page one and did a total revamping, Goodrich and Hackett, when they saw the final film, would disagree. (In any case, it was not Berlin's problem—not *yet,* at any rate.)

In a series of major script and cast changes, Sinatra, Grayson, and Skelton were written out. Singer Grayson was replaced by dancer Cyd Charisse, and Sinatra by nonvocalist Peter Lawford. Kelly's character, meanwhile, was reportedly rendered more lovable—just in time for the production's next big hiccup.

On Columbus Day, less than a month after Minnelli was fired, while participating in a backyard game with some neighborhood youngsters, Gene Kelly broke his ankle. The doctors predicted it would be at least six months before he could begin dancing again.

Kelly later recalled what happened next. First came the phone call: "I told Mayer I'd been rehearsing a rather complicated dance step, because I didn't think he would respond too well to the truth. I said, 'Why don't you give Fred Astaire a ring?' "

Astaire was then on his ranch, once more in "retirement" after finishing *Blue Skies.* Kelly continued his story: "Fred called me back. He said, 'Are you sure you don't want to do this picture? It's a good picture.' I said, 'Fred, you'll be doing me a favor, 'cause they think I'm a bum. L. B. Mayer thinks I broke my leg on purpose. *Please* do it!' "

The fact that the songs and the dance routines had been selected and fashioned especially for Kelly gave Astaire pause, but Kelly assured him that the dances could easily be restyled for him, as could the songs. Then there was the problem of age: Astaire was forty-eight to Garland's twenty-five (Kelly was thirty-four). But even that doubt didn't last long; he had never done a film with Garland and, like Berlin, had always hoped to one day. He agreed to replace Kelly, and rehearsals resumed.

Yet another terpsichorean misadventure befell the second female lead. While filming a dance scene in *On an Island with You,* Cyd Charisse tore some knee ligaments and landed in the hospital; she was forced to join Kelly in several months of enforced retirement. Her replacement was Ann Miller, a veteran of numerous low-budget musicals. Mayer submitted her name to Freed, and, eager to break out of "B" pictures and to appear with Astaire and Garland in a major film, she passed her audition—this despite an injured back that required her to sport a steel brace while offscreen and several yards of tape while on. There was one other requirement: she would have to wear ballet shoes in her dancing scenes with Astaire; in heels, she would have been slightly taller than her partner. She agreed, and the part was hers. Production No. 1418 was back on the track, with filming set to begin on November 25, 1947.

Soon after, the publicity department arranged for production photographs to be taken. Garland later recalled, "The photographer asked us [Garland and Berlin] to stand in a dancing position. I quipped, 'Maybe this will inspire one of the new songs.' Irving laughed and said, 'Maybe.' " As she was leaving, Berlin slipped her a small piece of paper, which he asked her not to show to anyone for the time being. Once off the lot, she got out the slip and read, "It only happens when I dance with you"—a line that would become the title of the film's finest ballad.

The first recording sessions took place before shooting started, and Berlin liked to be on hand for these, sometimes with Freed. He had grown quite fond of Garland, who disguised her insecurity and instability by cracking jokes and making self-deprecating remarks, inquiring, for example, "Did I ever tell you about the first time I went to the nuthouse?" She bantered with everyone on the set in an un-Garlandlike growl. Once, when Walters had just taken over from Minnelli, she reminded him (growling) that she was not the sweet June Allyson type (referring to the star of Walters's previous film, *Good News*).

During one of the recording sessions, Irving Berlin was treated to one of her barbs after offering her a suggestion on the phrasing of one of his songs. Her response tickled him: "Listen, buster. You write 'em, I sing 'em."

All things considered, the rest of the production of *Easter Parade* went fairly smoothly. Although Garland was frequently ill, she loved working with Astaire and "her" Irving. Minnelli, however, saw her at home and witnessed the effort it cost her to get to the studio; he also noted her weight fluctuations. "I welcomed her slight chubbiness," he wrote, "as a sign that she wasn't taking amphetamines. But then she'd lose many pounds in a few short days."

On the set Garland was cheerful, always joking and laughing, but in Minnelli's words, "She delivered for the studio" only "at great personal toll." The studio, for its part, was thrilled when Freed brought in a potential hit at more than $190,000 under budget, even with the elaborate finale, "Easter Parade." The number was shot on a two-block stretch on Lot 3, a reproduction of Fifth Avenue complete with a ten-foot-high segment of the facade of St. Patrick's Cathedral; a full complement of well-dressed extras strolled the avenue and greeted one another as vintage cars and horse-drawn buggies trundled by. The cynosures were an elegantly bonneted (and very slender) Garland and a top-hatted Astaire.

Once Garland got past her fear of her costar's reputation for perfection—his drive to rehearse endlessly and so on—the two worked well together. In fact, she soon proved herself, as Astaire told Minnelli, "just great! Judy's really got it. I go through these very intricate dance steps. She asks me to go through them again. That's all the instruction she needs. She picks it all up so quickly." Later he explained to an interviewer, "Judy's not primarily a dancer. But she's the best of her type—an amazing girl. She could do things—anything—with*out* rehearsing and come off perfectly. She could learn faster, do *every*thing better than most people."

The stars' warm rapport is particularly evident in the comedy number "A Couple of Swells," obviously written for Kelly (the staging replicates that of a Garland-Kelly number from *The Pirate,* "Be a Clown"). For the ever-dapper Astaire, the costuming represented a wild departure: he and Garland are both dressed as tramps for a skit in the show-within-the-show. He was uneasy in the costume, which featured a battered top hat atop an unkempt wig, a patched coat, and worn, ill-fitting shoes. The pair of "swells" put on airs—they have been invited to tea by the Vanderbilts—but lacking the means for a grander conveyance, they must walk up the avenue (foreshadowing the film's finale). Garland evidently loved the number—so much so that in the 1950s she would incorporate it into her stage show.

One solo sequence in which Garland likewise "delivered" for the studio was "Mr. Monotony" (marked "medium jump tempo"; Berlin was keeping up with the times). In ballad fashion, it tells the tale of a trombonist who can play only a single tone, no matter what the song. The one fan who can stand his playing marries him:

> They were happy as could be
> And they raised a family
> Six or seven little Monotonies.

Eventually, however, Mrs. Monotony hears a "snappy clarineter . . . and strange to say, she liked him better." She leaves Mr. Monotony, but not before singing, "Have you got any monotony today?" A unique Berlin song—seventy-six measures long, without verse—it was originally programmed for the revue sequence, which opened with Astaire's big dance number, "Steppin' Out with My Baby," the film's prime rhythm piece (also marked "medium jump tempo"). The tramp getups in the revue's closing segment were designed to provide a comically dramatic contrast to Astaire's top-hatted dance and Garland's skimpy "Mr. Monotony" costume of black silk stockings, shorts, and tuxedo jacket, but this last song was left on the cutting-room floor. (Garland would return a couple of years later in the same costume for her stunning rendition of "Get Happy" in Summer Stock.) "Mr. Monotony" was considered a bravura performance, but as Berlin later explained to Hugh Fordin, "it slowed up the picture. . . . Arthur [Freed] and I were sorry to see it go because we both liked it, a very unusual song based on a phrase. I later used it in the theater." (In fact, he tried to interpolate it twice more, but each time "Mr. Monotony" suffered a similar fate: as Berlin recalled, the song stopped the show, "and everything else," so it had to go.)

Once filming began and all the songs were in, Berlin was free to spend more time with his family, which was feeling some stress. Now deep into her second novel, Lace Curtain, Ellin was also concerned about the restless, rebellious (like her mother) Mary Ellin, who had turned twenty-one on November 25. She sensed that having come of age, her oldest daughter had marriage on her mind, and she was certain she was about to make a mistake. As it turned out, Ellin was right on both counts, though the man whom Mary Ellin refers to in her memoir as "Mr. Wrong" looked like a safe bet at the time: he came from a good family, had been a navy pilot during the war, and had a talent for drawing. In his late twenties when they met, and attending school on the GI Bill, he was raffishly charming with a quick sense of humor. Their romance had begun in New York, as Berlin was commencing work on *Easter Parade*.

In California, the situation continued to make Ellin uncomfortable, and Mary Ellin, taking time off from Barnard, seemed increasingly moody. Ironically, Ellin chose to follow in her own father's footsteps, suggesting that Berlin take their daughter—just the two of them—to Mexico for Christmas. When she explained the plan to her husband, he agreed, but Mary Ellin thought it all a bit peculiar—after all, they had taken a Honolulu holiday only in September, while *Easter Parade* was being reworked after Minnelli's firing. Going on another vacation just four months later seemed illogical, but after some persuading, she gave in.

In Mexico City, Mary Ellin surprised, and delighted, her father with a course in contemporary Mexican art. They visited the studio of one of the modern firebrands, José Clemente Orozco, where Berlin acquired a painting for Ellin and himself and another for Mary Ellin. They also met with another artistic revolutionary, Diego Rivera, who wanted to paint Berlin's portrait— a request the songwriter refused. Berlin had a personal connection with these very original artists whose bold colors and flowing lines celebrated the revolution led by Emiliano Zapata: both had been acquaintances of George Gershwin.

Father and daughter returned to the family's cottage at the Beverly Hills Hotel as filming of *Easter Parade* proceeded into the new year. Judy Garland recorded the rueful "Better Luck Next Time" on January 7, 1948; on the ninth, Ann Miller shot her major sequence, dancing to "Shaking the Blues Away," which Roger Edens had plucked out of the Berlin catalog. Berlin later told Fordin, "In my opinion the one person responsible for the whole musical context of [*Easter Parade*] was Roger Edens. Look, when it came to Ann Miller, Roger dug up 'Shaking the Blues Away.' . . . He knew exactly how to present it and he made the arrangements for her. . . . You can't say enough about Edens where I'm concerned."

Confident that his songs were in very capable hands, Berlin, around the time Judy Garland was rerecording "I Want to Go Back to Michigan (Down on the Farm)," late in February, packed up his family and abandoned Beverly Hills for the Georgian house on Beekman Place.

He had a great deal to catch up on when he checked in at the office. The sharp, wise, and protective Hilda Schneider had replaced the likewise capable Mynna Granat, who had married Dave Dreyer after his divorce; the newlyweds had left Irving Berlin, the year before, wrapping up a long period of what could only be described as faithful yeoman's service. Dreyer wished to form his own publishing company, and he and his wife had departed with Berlin's blessings, plus a generous severance bonus to get the new firm up and running. Schneider served as a buffer, a secretary, a manager who ran a tight ship. Helmy Kresa remained Berlin's number-one musical aide, and other staffers tended to various business matters, such as accounting, shipping, and legalities, but Hilda was the essential rock. During the entire time she worked for Berlin, she invariably addressed him, or spoke of him, as "Mr. Berlin," emphasis on the name's first syllable.

Keeping all of them occupied around this time was the collective headache induced by James Caesar Petrillo, president of the American Federation of Musicans, who had closed down the renascent and flourishing record industry (fortunately not for long). His "boys" would not record any more music—serious or popular.

May 11 marked another milestone for Berlin: he turned sixty. Rodgers and Hammerstein established a scholarship in his name at the Juilliard School of Music, and there was a small family celebration. Two weeks later, *Easter Parade* opened at Loew's State in New York to fine reviews, the gist of which was expressed by *Newsweek*'s critic: "The important thing is that Fred Astaire is back again with Irving Berlin calling the tunes." One publication hailed the film as the "most joyous of the year."

Ann Miller attended the premiere and wired Freed about the film's success and how pleased Berlin was with her dancing (especially gratifying to her after she learned that he had not wanted her cast in the first place; arguably, her "Shaking the Blues Away" is the most exhilarating sequence in the picture). Berlin was in fact so happy with her work, she claimed, that "he is considering a book show with me in mind and other ideas for the future."

In Berlin's more immediate future, however, was his daughter's marriage early in July to her former navy pilot, Dennis Burden, an event that did not gladden her parents' hearts. (Ellin's Christmas-in-Mexico strategy had not been any more successful than Clarence Mackay's similar diversionary tactics almost a quarter of a century before.) The Berlins were resigned to the wedding and even opened the house on Beekman Place for the rather small gathering of relatives and friends. A rabbi blessed the bride- and groom-to-be at breakfast, and a civil ceremony followed at noon. Moments before it, Berlin said to Mary Ellin, "It's not too late. We can still call it off." But it *was* too late, or perhaps too soon: within a year Mary Ellin would be establishing Nevada residency in Lake Tahoe in preparation for a Reno divorce.

In August, once the ill-starred marriage was under way, Berlin, somewhat depressed by recent events (not one song from *Easter* was nominated for an Academy Award, though Johnny Green and Roger Edens would win one for the scoring), traveled to London to look in on his office in Hanover Square. While there, he also went to see Dolores Gray in *Annie Get Your Gun* and met with producer Emile Littler, who broached the subject of doing another Berlin-scored show. Berlin himself had been considering undertaking a musical to be entitled *Stars on My Shoulders,* with a book by Hollywood writer-producer Norman Krasna. (Krasna's *Princess O'Rourke,* which he had also directed, had been a success in 1943, and the previous February, he had had a hit on Broadway with his comedy *John Loves Mary,* produced—like *Annie Get Your Gun*—by Rodgers and Hammerstein.)

Berlin may have been thinking about this new musical early in 1948, when he wrote "What Can You Do with a General?" Krasna's book was to center around a general and the problems he encountered in making the transition from war to peace and finding a new career for himself. Berlin filled a folder with songs, beginning with "It's a Lovely Day for a Walk," a rejected number from *Blue Skies.* Among the other songs in the folder was a fine tune called "Nothing More to Say."

Krasna's libretto was inspired by press speculation about the futures of Generals MacArthur and Eisenhower after the end of the Second World War, when both were being wooed by the major political parties to run for the presidency. Eisenhower would put a temporary end to the second-guessing when, in June 1948, he resigned as Army Chief of Staff to become president not of the United States but of Columbia University. MacArthur had meanwhile returned from Japan, where he was directing the Allied Occupation, to run in the presidential primaries, only to withdraw from the race when he lost in Wisconsin.

Now, in London, when pressed by Littler, who had lined up an English backer, Berlin answered with an ambiguous, "I'll think about it." Somehow a musical about an American general running for high office seemed an unlikely bet for an English audience: while *Annie Get Your Gun,* with its Western setting, its cowboys and Indians, and its circus, might play here, *Stars on My Shoulders,* Berlin felt, would not travel. The whole idea was abandoned shortly thereafter; Krasna returned to Hollywood, and the *Stars* songs went into the file. For Berlin, there was an even more interesting possibility at hand: eminent playwright Robert E. Sherwood had called him with a fascinating idea for a musical.

That year Sherwood would win his fourth Pulitzer Prize, for his book *Roosevelt and Hopkins;* the previous three had been for his work on Broadway, most notably *Abe Lincoln in Illinois.* Two years earlier, he had created the film

The Best Years of Our Lives, winner of multiple Academy Awards, including those for Best Picture and Best Screenplay.

Berlin and Sherwood had known each other since the twenties, when Sherwood had been a charter member of the Algonquin Round Table before leaving that circle, and the editorship of *Vanity Fair,* to devote himself to writing for the theater. Over the intervening years, he and the Berlins had often met socially and at openings.

Sherwood was also close to Harry Hopkins, trusted adviser to President Franklin D. Roosevelt. When war broke out, Hopkins had brought Sherwood into the administration as Director of Overseas Operations in the Office of War Information (predecessor of the Voice of America). In that capacity, beginning in 1940, he had written speeches for Roosevelt and then was sent off to England to prepare press releases. At war's end, he had sailed back to the United States aboard a troopship filled with returning servicemen. As the ship approached New York Harbor, Sherwood had been deeply moved by the GIs' reactions to what was for most their first sight of the Statue of Liberty.

Why not, he now suggested to Berlin, do a musical about the statue—how it came to be where it was, and how it had figured in a newspaper circulation war between news moguls James Gordon Bennett and Joseph Pulitzer? Sherwood outlined his quasi-historical plot: a statue, "Liberty Enlightening the World" by sculptor Frédéric-Auguste Bartholdi, is to be presented to the United States as a symbol of Franco-American friendship, the funds for its design, casting, and shipping having been raised by subscription in France.

The French subscription, however, does not include monies for assembly or installation on Bedloe's Island, New York. The pieces of Liberty thus remain on the docks of Manhattan, in crates, with no place to go. Pulitzer, publisher of the *World,* comes to the rescue . . . to a degree. His newspaper announces a campaign to raise sufficient funds to erect the statue's pedestal. This stratagem not only succeeds in raising $100,000, but also increases the *World*'s circulation. Here Sherwood's libretto began taking a few historical liberties of its own, in having rival newsman Bennett, publisher of the *Herald,* complain of Pulitzer's exploitation of the statue and counter with his own gambit: Bennett offers to bring Bartholdi's model to New York. The French model, a pretty young woman, would introduce the romantic aspect of the plot.

Sherwood had done his research, but Berlin would follow it up with his own. He agreed to do the show, replete with Americana, patriotism, two powerful rivals, and a model on her first trip to America, but he had one major objection. A couple of days into his work, he called Sherwood and said, "Bob, his mother posed for it."

"I know," the playwright replied, "but there must have been younger models who posed for the hands." Berlin found this argument less than convincing; he felt Sherwood must "find some way to get the girl into the picture, to manufacture and make something believable that wasn't true."

Responding to Berlin's exhortation, Sherwood created as his hero a hapless photographer who is fired by his boss, Bennett, for snapping the crated statue instead of the ceremony in which a check for the money raised by the *World* to build the base is presented by Pulitzer to the mayor. Bennett had ordered the green lensman to photograph the event, but to show only Pulitzer's back; however, the crates proved to be more interesting.

The photographer, Horace, has a friend in Maisie, who works for the notorious *Police Gazette.* Feeling like "A Little Fish in a Big Pond" (the title of the apposite Berlin song), he decides to go home to Indiana. But Maisie (who is, of course, in love with him) has a better idea: if he travels to Paris and returns with the girl who posed for Liberty, he'll scoop even the *World,* and Bennett will *have* to rehire him.

Horace arrives at Bartholdi's studio during a model's interview and sees Monique, who needs a job and, in an effort to enchant the sculptor, has costumed herself as the Liberty statue (Bartholdi has already told her that his mother posed for the original). She is reciting the poem that was to be inscribed on the base, "The New Colossus" (another historical anomaly: Emma Lazarus did not in fact write the lines until twenty years after the Statue of Liberty's dedication).

Horace is certain he has found the model he is seeking. Neither he nor Monique fully understands the other, but he nonetheless manages to talk her into coming back to New York with him; they are accompanied by her grandmother the Countess, who lives under a bridge (both women are homeless). Publisher Bennett happily underwrites their passage to America, where they are warmly welcomed.

Only after arriving does Monique learn that she is actually a fraud. She also discovers that she is in love with Horace, thus inadvertently drawing the third leg of a romantic triangle. This geometry makes the ostensibly happy ending—no fraud charges, no problems with immigration—feel incomplete: when Horace decides to marry Monique, the lovable Maisie is necessarily left out in the cold. But no matter: the curtain descends anyway, to a full choral conclusion, as Monique recites the (still-unwritten) Lazarus poem, to one of Berlin's stateliest melodies.

After Sherwood revised his book to eliminate some of its more fanciful historical inaccuracy, Berlin found the libretto acceptable, if not yet totally plausible. He turned to the always reliable Moss Hart, now back in New

York after completing the screenplay for *Gentlemen's Agreement.* Hart's new production, *Light Up the Sky,* had opened in November 1948 to mild success. If he was willing, and free, Berlin wanted to bring him on to *Miss Liberty* as director; his skills and experience with musicals could, Berlin reasoned, help smooth out the book's rough spots. *Miss Liberty* was Sherwood's first musical, and it would be his last.

Once Hart was on board, the final decision was made: he, Sherwood, and Berlin would coproduce the show (according to the *Daily Mirror*'s Robert Coleman, "to the tune of $175,000"). When the production was announced in the press, advance sales of tickets added up to half a million dollars, proving that names counted for something. For his own peace of mind, Berlin made certain that *Annie Get Your Gun*'s Jay Blackton was hired as musical director.

What puzzled Broadway wiseacres was the company. Cast as Horace, the dim-witted photographer, was light comedian and onetime radio singer Eddie Albert, who had last appeared on Broadway in the Rodgers and Hart musical *The Boys from Syracuse,* ten years before; prior to that, Albert's non-musicals had included such comedies as *Brother Rat* and *Room Service.* He had spent the intervening decade in Hollywood, acting in the film versions of *Brother Rat* (and its sequel) and *On Your Toes,* also with a Rodgers and Hart score. His films without music usually employed him as the best friend, the nice guy who rarely gets the girl. He was a deft though undemonstrative comedian with a pleasant enough, if not a big, voice.

The casting of the two women was less mystifying. Monique was portrayed by a beautiful dancer named Allyn McLerie, who sang adequately and danced, in a word, divinely. Broadway rumors suggested that Berlin had spotted her in her role as Amy, opposite Ray Bolger, in Frank Loesser's *Where's Charley?* and that rehearsals had been postponed until she was released from her contract with the still-running Loesser musical.

Mary McCarty, who had a big voice (she had turned down the part of Annie in the touring company of *Annie Get Your Gun,* not wishing to be typecast as another Ethel Merman), was tapped to play Maisie, the smart, sharp *Police Gazette* reporter. Like McLerie, she had made her first indelible impression in a lackluster 1948 revue, in her case entitled *Small Wonder,* in which she belted out "Flaming Youth," nostalgically invoking the twenties. According to her playbill biography, she was the first of the troupe to be signed to appear in *Miss Liberty.*

Another astute casting was that of British actress Ethel Griffies, who had two years earlier, at the age of seventy, announced her retirement but had remained active ever since. She was a veteran of both the London stage and a seventeen-year residence in Hollywood, where she had made one hundred films. After her "retirement," despite her vow to return to England, she was coaxed to appear in several Broadway plays, among them *The Leading Lady* (with Ruth Gordon). When she agreed to take on the part of the raffish Countess in *Miss Liberty,* it marked her first turn in a musical since she had last sung in London, some forty years before. To the Messrs. Berlin, Sherwood, and Hart, Ethel Griffies would prove to be a godsend.

The power of the producers' names was evident in Philadelphia, where a small advertisement in the papers caused the show to sell out for its entire run of three weeks. Its stay was extended an additional week, ostensibly because of the great demand for tickets but in fact because the production was in trouble and needed fixing, especially the muddled second act. The uncredited "fixer"—to the extent that anything could be done—was Moss Hart, who attempted to inject some humor into the show.

One major problem was Sherwood himself: he did not want anyone tampering with his play (which at times he seemed to forget was supposed to be a musical). Part of his inability to work on rewrites may be explained by the fact that he suffered from trigeminal neuralgia (also known as tic douloureux), resulting in flashes of excruciating pain that distorted his face— mostly the chin, cheeks, or lips—for seconds or even minutes. Although medication was available for this condition, Sherwood preferred alcohol, and he spent most of the Philadelphia run in a stupor as his coproducers struggled with the show.

Berlin was experiencing his own headaches as producer, as songwriter (among the road casualties was the recycled "Mr. Monotony" plus seven other numbers, whose loss eliminated a lot of the score's effervescence), and as father. While the show was being "fixed" for New York, Mary Ellin was preparing for her Reno trip. She, her mother, her sisters, her aunt and uncle, and nurse Tenney all left for their Lake Tahoe compound the same week *Miss Liberty* limped through its New York premiere.

Initially the opening had been scheduled for an appropriate date: July 4, 1949. But the addition of the extra "sold-out" Philadelphia week (during which the frantic changes were introduced) pushed it back to Friday, July 15, buying more time for rehearsals.

The Saturday papers on the sixteenth brought little else but grief. The critical consensus of most was voiced in the first sentence of Brooks Atkinson's *Times* review:

> To come right out and say so in public, *Miss Liberty* is a disappointing musical comedy. It is built on an old-fashioned model and is put together without sparkle or originality. This is the Statue of Liberty

antic with songs and lyrics by Irving Berlin, the best-loved songwriter in America, and a book by Robert E. Sherwood, the loftiest
playwright in the country, who has won the Pulitzer Prize so many
times that now he can keep it. . . .

Atkinson followed up his pan a week later with a Sunday essay headlined
"Mediocre Musical."

Concurring with their colleague, Ward Morehouse of the *Sun* pronounced the show a "sharp disappointment," while Richard Watts, Jr., of
the *Post,* an astute judge of musicals, deemed it "only pretty fair." Robert
Sylvester of the *News* admired the efforts of Berlin, Sherwood, and Hart, and
liked several songs, but found the book confusing and believed that the entire
show was carried by Ethel Griffies. He expanded on one observation in his
daily review that Sunday, admitting, "To be fair to the new show, it's likely
that all of us expected too much."

This opinion was echoed in *Variety*'s evaluation a few days after the premiere: "If *Miss Liberty* had been written by a couple of guys named Doakes it
would probably have been considered a promising, even an entertaining
show. But from such eminent authors as Irving Berlin and Robert E. Sherwood, not to mention stager Moss Hart, it is something of a clinker." The
reviewer, Hobe Morrison, suggested that the show had never recovered from
the "original [i.e., Philadelphia tryout] faults of an over-plotty book, undistinguished score, insufficient comedy and merely adequate performance[s]."
Fair enough, perhaps, but that was followed by a curious evaluation of the
score: "Berlin's songs are certainly better than average, though reminiscent
and obviously not up to his best. Probably they'd be better if sung by top
stars." Morrison then provided a list of eight songs that he felt were destined
for popularity. He was right in the cases of "Let's Take an Old-Fashioned
Walk" and "Just One Way to Say I Love You," both introduced by non-top
stars McLerie and Albert.

These two performers were generally, and virtually unanimously, described
as pleasant, though one caddish critic noted that Allyn McLerie sang "like a
dancer." Most, again in concert, condemned the libretto for its lack of wit and
overladen second act. Once Monique and Horace arrive in New York, the plot
thickens into a not-very-smooth blend of the Monique-Maisie-Horace triangle
and the mean-spirited Pulitzer-Bennett feud, leading to the jailing of Horace
and the near-deportation of Monique and her grandmother.

Some revision and tightening of the sprawling plot—though perhaps not
enough—were reflected in the road deletions. Among the first songs to go

was "The Pulitzer Prize," a fitting nod to Sherwood but an undeniable anachronism: *Miss Liberty* was set in 1885, thirty-two years before the prize was established (by which time Joseph Pulitzer himself would be dead). That the newspaper theme was more central to the earlier libretto is evidenced by the omission of three more numbers, "Entrance of the Reporters," "The Hon'rable Profession of the Fourth Estate," and "The Story of Nell and the *Police Gazette.*" All that remained musically of this motif in the New York production was "What Do I Have to Do to Get My Picture Took?," a watered-down version of the cynical "What Do I Have to Do to Get My Picture in the Paper?" The vocalist answers the question: Be a Vanderbilt, bribe the editor, or murder someone.

In "The Hon'rable Profession of the Fourth Estate," Berlin, reflecting on his treatment by that profession, touched on the abuses of yellow journalism, with its "news that's fit and unfit to print," "facts" no sooner invented than published, meddling in politics, and mongering of scandal, true or not. The song may have come down too hard on the press of *Miss Liberty*'s time as well as that of 1949.

Likewise deleted in Philadelphia was a hard-eyed look at life, "Finding Work in Paris," in which Monique tells of an aborted casting-couch experience when she applied for a job in the chorus of the Folies Bergère. When the manager dimmed the lights and asked her to change into tights, she recalls, though she knew business was bad "for a girl who won't unclad," she preferred to keep her clothes on, "[my] above and my belows on." She slapped the manager and found her way to Bartholdi's studio (where she would also have been expected to "unclad," were she not saved by the bumbling Horace).

Another, more satiric deletion was "Sing a Song of Sing Sing," about the criminals' "summer and winter resort" on the Hudson. During the period in which the show was set, and even in more modern times, there was nothing wrong with Sing Sing that a little money couldn't fix: as the song explains, bribing the warden will get you a conjugal visit even if you're not married, or refuge if a rival mobster is out to nail you—just murder your wife and find safety in Sing Sing for life.

It is not entirely clear whether the songs were cut to shorten the evening or because they were considered less than reverently patriotic in their treatment of some aspects of life in the United States (there were casting couches in New York, too, after all). In either event, a good deal of the humor that the critics found lacking in the show was eliminated with these deletions. The single satiric survivor was Ethel Griffies's show-stopping "Only for Americans," in which the Countess saltily warns Horace about Parisian tourist traps, overpriced cafés, French postcards, bordello peepholes, the Folies, and, most of all, *la cuisine:*

> *A Frenchman's food is very plain,*
> *The fancy sauces with ptomaine*
> *Are only for Americans.*
> *A Frenchman seldom eats the snails*
> *With little ulcers on their tails*
> *And all that cheese*
> *Was made to please*
> *Americans from the U.S.A.*

Berlin's lyrics throughout the score are masterly, whether in the witty and satirical (but mostly dropped) political songs or in the fine ballads, written in his customary simple, poetic style. (One ballad especially, "Paris Wakes Up and Smiles," stands out; its arching melody, in 3/4 time, is sung first by a lamplighter, played by Johnny V. R. Thompson, a full-voiced baritone, who is then joined by Monique and the chorus.) The sheer range of his accomplishment went unremarked by the reviewers, though it ran from the philosophical ("A Little Fish in a Big Pond" and "Falling out of Love Can Be Fun"), to the romantic ("Just One Way to Say I Love You," among others), to the poignant (as in the Monique-Maisie duet, "You Can Have Him"). Adding to the mix was "The Policeman's Ball," a metropolitan square dance, replete with folksy imagery, that evolved into the second act's most spectacular dance number (choreographed by Jerome Robbins).

The *New Yorker*'s Wolcott Gibbs pronounced some of the show's songs "pleasant enough musically" but found their lyrics (he excepted "Only for Americans") "strangely deficient in style and wit and originality." Such comments made for unpleasant reading for Berlin.

Turning to the book, Gibbs pointed out what he suspected was a Hart insertion, the first-act curtain line, where an incensed Countess snaps, "And if my granddaughter weren't here, I'd tell you what you could do with that bridge." (She is a flower seller, and a customer has complained about the condition of her stock—the flowers she sold were acquired from a convenient cemetery.) He missed another Hart contribution, spoken by Maisie upon seeing the newly arrived Monique in a Paris gown: "Horace," she observes, "I've got to hand it to you. You certainly spent that money where it shows."

Berlin was upset by all the criticism, but it was Sherwood who, after so many past successes, took the drubbing worst. Among the players, McLerie and Albert were kindly dismissed as "pleasant," and McCarty tut-tutted as "wasted" by the majority of reviewers; only Griffies, in the cast, and Tommy Rall, among the dancers, earned special praise. Also appreciated was the work of choreographer Jerome Robbins, set and lighting designer Oliver Smith, and the costume designer Motley.

Despite the generally ruinous reviews, *Miss Liberty* ran into the next year, closing in April after a fair run of 308 performances, thanks to the pre-premiere advance sale. By that time the resilient Berlin would be at work on another musical.

It took him some months to bounce back, though; in September 1949, he was still miserable. As *Miss Liberty* swam discouragingly against the critical tide, two "blockbusters" dominated the Broadway scene. Cole Porter's *Kiss Me Kate* had commenced its long run in December of the previous year, while Rodgers and Hammerstein's *South Pacific* had started *its* marathon in April, three months before *Miss Liberty* began floundering in Philadelphia. Irving Berlin admittedly liked a hit, and compared to those shows, his Statue of Liberty musical was anything but.

It was clear when he joined his family at Lake Tahoe that he was unhappy with what he now regarded as a failure; nor was he pleased with Mary Ellin's failed marriage. There were no reprimands, no scoldings—only a sorrowful expression and jumpiness. Once the final divorce papers came through, they all returned to Beekman Place. It was of some consolation to Berlin that Columbia Records soon after arranged to record *Miss Liberty*'s score despite the bad reviews; that cast album, along with a set of "demos," or demonstration records, that he and Helmy Kresa made for the actors (on which are preserved several of the deleted songs) survive as validation of the show's musical richness and inventiveness.

One consistent criticism of the *Miss Liberty* score held that it was "reminiscent." Of course it was: it was an Irving Berlin score that *sounded* like Irving Berlin. Porter's songs for *Kiss Me Kate* sound no less Porterish, and the Rodgers and Hammerstein songs from *South Pacific* likewise recall that team's earlier work; the difference lies in the fact that the books for those musicals were captivating, innovative, and compelling (no one, after all, made a point of remarking the relatively unknown stars of the Porter show). Clearly, the overall disappointment in *Miss Liberty* was carried over to, and colored the reception of, its songs.

Still brooding over the criticism of his score and the unfortunate press attention given to Mary Ellin's divorce, Berlin was surprised and heartened one day to get a call from playwright Howard Lindsay and his collaborator,

Russel Crouse (who themselves had a 1946 Pulitzer Prize to their credit, for *State of the Union*). Their most successful effort to date was *Life with Father,* which had opened in 1939 and run for nearly eight years before closing in 1947.

Lindsay and Crouse, the former originally an actor and the latter a publicist for the Theatre Guild, began their collaboration with the Cole Porter musical *Anything Goes,* which starred Ethel Merman (as did their next, *Red Hot and Blue*). Before turning to drama and comedy, they also wrote the book for the 1937 Harold Arlen–E. Y. Harburg antiwar hit, *Hooray for What!*

Their new project had its genesis in Colorado, where Lindsay was resting at a popular resort. From that week's *Life* magazine, he learned that President Harry Truman had appointed celebrated Washington hostess (and generous Democratic party contributor) Perle Mesta to serve as ambassador to Luxembourg, a minuscule European nation triangularly squeezed by Belgium, France, and Germany. He was particularly amused to read that the affluent, inexperienced appointee had taken a wrong turn on her way to her post and got lost. Glancing over toward the pool, Lindsay spotted Ethel Merman sunbathing, fresh from her triumph in *Annie Get Your Gun,* which had closed earlier in the year.

Eureka! Back in New York, the playwright told his partner about the concatenation that had grabbed him in Colorado: Mesta, Merman, and Berlin. In mid-September 1949 he called Berlin and proposed, "We'd like to do a show for Merman about Perle Mesta."

"Who's Perle Mesta?"

Lindsay explained and urged Berlin to have a look at that back issue of *Life,* which he did. He agreed that the idea had possibilities. Soon Leland Hayward, who had produced *State of the Union* as well as *South Pacific,* signed on to produce; he in turn talked RCA Victor Records, which was eager to break into the original-cast-album market then dominated by Columbia and Decca, into putting up $250,000 to stage the show. An oversight on Hayward's part would come back to haunt him (and RCA) after the show opened, to Berlin's fortuitous gain.

When the main elements of the production were set, Berlin sought the warm quiet of Nassau. His work proceeded slowly, as did that of Lindsay and Crouse, who mailed him pieces of their script as they came out of their typewriters. This arrangement was fine with Berlin, whose first songs were crafted for the brash personality of Ethel Merman—and her crystal-clear trumpet voice. Among these were the first act's "The Hostess with the Mostes' on the Ball," a patent identification of the show's inspiration; the pertinent and timely "Can You Use Any Money Today?"; and the romantic "The Best Thing for You Would Be Me." The librettists and their star found the numbers good indeed.

The creation of the show they now called *Call Me Madam* was a painstaking process; Berlin would later say he had worked harder and longer on it than on any other show. The production conceived in September 1949 would not be ready for its New Haven tryout until a year later—at which point it would become obvious that still *more* time was needed. It was then and there that the final work was accomplished. As Berlin saw it, "We were in big trouble. There was a big hole in the second act." And hanging over all their heads was the sword of a million-dollar advance ticket sale.

Hayward had staffed his show wisely. George Abbott, a director, librettist, and producer himself, had directed a number of successful musicals, among them *On Your Toes, Pal Joey, On the Town,* and *Where's Charley?* His distinctive talent lay in his ability to keep a show moving, in which department, on this occasion, he had the aid of Jerome Robbins, who staged the dances as well as the musical numbers. Once again, Berlin saw to it that Jay Blackton conducted the orchestrations (by Don Walker) and did the vocal arrangements.

As *Variety* would later report, *Call Me Madam,* following its New Haven premiere on September 11, 1950, underwent "one of the most brilliant salvage jobs in recent years," to be

> transformed during the tryout. The book was extensively rewritten, with a drastically revised second act. Three tunes, one a dance routine, and one elaborate production number, were scrapped and two replacements inserted. Several numbers were moved around. One new dance number was added. . . . The whole book was tightened and punched up. The performance was speeded and pointed. And the entire show came to life. It was a triumph by real professionals, working under pressure.

The scrapped numbers were the seemingly jinxed "Mr. Monotony," which Merman felt did not reach her audience; it was replaced within hours by the lively "Something to Dance About." The patriotic production number "Free" and the instrumental "Gypsy Dance" were deleted outright, with no replacements.

Meanwhile, there was still that second-act hole. Berlin would credit Abbott with the suggestion that finally filled it in, but in fact, it was a Berlin song that gave Abbott the idea. That fall, it was almost impossible to avoid hearing a duet Bing Crosby had recorded with his son Gary—Berlin's 1914 hit "Play a Simple Melody." One of Crosby's all-time biggest sellers, it was number six on "Your Hit Parade" the week *Call Me Madam* opened in New Haven.

Why not, Abbott suggested, come up with another song like that and have Merman sing it with Russell Nype? (Nype played the shy, brainy, lovesick Harvard graduate who works as an assistant in the embassy and is in love with the Princess of Lichtenburg. A disclaimer in the program, recalling a similar sentence in the *Louisiana Purchase* playbill, stated, "The play is laid in two mythical countries. One is called Lichtenburg, the other the United States of America.")

Berlin's "filler" preceded reprises of three numbers. Like "Play a Simple Melody," it contrapuntally blended two separate songs, in this instance Nype's "I Wonder Why?" and Merman's "You're Just in Love." They finish singing their individual songs together, closing with the line "You're not sick, you're just in love." It was a rare performance at which this inspired display of musical adroitness did not stop the show.

From New Haven the cast and crew moved to Boston before opening at the Imperial in New York on Columbus Day, 1950. The audience was prepared for a politically irreverent evening on reading the playbill's cast listing:

Mrs. Sally Adams . . . . Ethel Merman
(Neither the character of Mrs. Sally Adams, nor Miss Ethel Merman, resembles any other person alive or dead.)

Sally Adams has been appointed ambassador to the Grand Duchy of Lichtenburg by someone she addresses only as Harry. She knows nothing about foreign affairs and has no idea where Lichtenburg is; when she finally finds it, she proceeds to upset protocol by being her earthy, straightforward, friendly, and blunt self—in short, by behaving like Ethel Merman. She immediately falls in love with the minister of foreign affairs (film veteran Paul Lucas), then antagonizes him by offering him all the money his country needs, and more. He sternly informs her that Lichtenburg must get out of its financial predicament on its own, without American aid. The country is so poor that its people can't even buy their own most popular export product, cheese, and the annual fair has just been canceled for lack of money.

Mrs. Adams, naturally (but secretly), finances the fair and endears herself to the minister, Cosmo. (Thanks to the constantly shifting government, his title keeps changing throughout the show.) In the fair scene the villagers dance to "The Ocarina" in colorful ethnic costumes, accompanied by a team called the Potato Bugs, carrying the tune on wooden ocarinas. (A critic or two would note something rather old-fashioned about the production: Lichtenburg itself seems a throwback to the settings of 1920s operettas by Romberg and Friml.)

The not always consistent plot weaves around Sally's attraction to Cosmo (which he, in time, reciprocates) and her meddling in a local election, which leads to Harry's calling and asking for her resignation. Further complications ensue when her assistant, Kenneth, falls in love with the princess (the feeling is mutual). Then there is Sally's disregard for protocol and diplomacy, her propensity for gaffes that raise the Lichtenburgers' hackles. Because the country is a duchy, she thinks the people are Dutch—a misconception that doesn't go over well with the Holland-hating locals. Trailing her long gown ("I don't mind the train, but why do they give me the Superchief?" she muses), she makes her entrance at an important event with a pratfall.

Once back in the States, however, she learns that the Lichtenburgers, even the petty royals, loved her for her honesty and humanity. In appreciation, Cosmo is dispatched to present her with the Order of Philip the First; she is now no longer a Madam but officially a Dame. Cosmo also confesses his love. Meanwhile, her assistant, Kenneth, has chosen to remain in Lichtenburg to build a hydroelectric plant (financed by Sally) and to marry the princess, who, according to local custom, has asked for his hand.

A running gag throughout the show consisted in the series of telephone calls to and from "Harry," with their offhand references to the trouble his daughter was having with the press during a recital tour (President Truman had in fact threatened to punch one Washington critic in the nose for his unfavorable review of a song recital by his daughter Margaret) and his wife's bridge game. The last laugh came after the final curtain, when, during the enthusiastic curtain calls, the last to appear onstage for his bow was—Harry Truman! (in the person of actor Irving Fisher, who uncannily resembled the President).

A curio in *Call Me Madam*'s score is the song "They Like Ike," which predicted that Eisenhower would run for the presidency two years hence and win as a Republican. At the time, though courted by both parties, the former general was reticent; no one knew which party would ultimately win him. Berlin, in his lyric, proved to be more prescient than the political pundits of the day: Eisenhower would declare himself a Republican early in 1952 and win that year's election. In so doing, he would get the votes of both Ellin and Irving Berlin, who had grown disenchanted with the Democratic party after years of active campaigning, particularly on behalf of Franklin D. Roosevelt.

First-nighter Dwight D. Eisenhower, then still at Columbia University, beamed when a chorus of shifty politicians, in song, advised him to run and win. Two years later, as "I Like Ike," this would become his campaign and rally song. It has been implied that Berlin wrote the number to ingratiate himself with the future President, but that is nonsensical conjecture. *Call Me Madam,* though a frothy comedy, was nonetheless politically charged. Besides "Harry," its book employed other political figures in its narration, including Secretary of State Dean Acheson, presidential hopeful and crime-buster Estes Kefauver (who makes an appearance at one of Sally's parties), and professional Red chaser Senator Joseph McCarthy (who can't attend because he is abed with laryngitis).

The slightest song in the score, "They Like Ike," would make for an ideal singsong political chant, repetitious and easy to remember. One stanza states a trenchant truth:

> *They won't take Saltenstall*
> *And Stassen's chance is small,*
> *The same would go for Vandenberg and Taft.*
> *And Dewey's right in line*
> *With William Jennings Bryan,*
> *There isn't anyone that they can draft.*

Drafted Eisenhower would be, in July 1952. Berlin actually had the idea for "They Like Ike" as early as 1948, when rumors first surfaced about the general's running for President; after Eisenhower quashed that notion, Berlin put the song aside until he realized there was a spot for it in *Call Me Madam.* It went over well the first night and got even better as the Broadway run continued. When the show later went on tour, "They Like Ike" was replaced with "Our Day of Independence," but Berlin was not happy with that song's reception; in Chicago, "Ike" was reinstated.

There are better songs in the score, among them "Marrying for Love," "It's a Lovely Day Today," the willowy "The Best Thing for You Would Be Me," and the haunting "Lichtenburg" (which, with its line "Babies and cheese/Are our main industries," was hardly "Hit Parade" material). The rhythm numbers are lively, set with period orchestrations by Don Walker and Joe Glover. Here again, as in *Miss Liberty,* there is a wide range of styles, from folk ("The Ocarina") through contemporary ("Washington Square Dance") and energetic ("Something to Dance About").

But Berlin himself was proudest of "You're Just in Love," proof that even at the age of sixty-two, when a show was in trouble, he could still—literally overnight—come up with a showstopper. The fact that it aired on the "Hit Parade" for three months was icing on the cake.

A funny thing happened to *Call Me Madam* on the way to the recording studio: there was no complete-original-cast album. RCA invested in the show on the understanding that it would record the score, but when producer Hayward signed the agreement and took the money, he was unaware of a serious legal impediment: Ethel Merman had an exclusive contract with Decca Records, and Decca president Dave Kapp refused to release her to work for his rival RCA. So there were two *Call Me Madam* albums. Merman recorded a dozen songs from the show, with Dick Haymes and Eileen Wilson singing the Kenneth and Princess Maria numbers, for the Decca release. For the RCA version, Merman's curious replacement was Dinah Shore, backed by the Mermanless original cast, including Lucas, Nype, Galina Talva (the princess), and others. Neither recording adopted all of the Walker/Glover orchestrations; Decca used none at all, and RCA only a few. The Merman album sold very well, the RCA much less so. RCA Victor advertised its forthcoming "original show album" in the playbill the week of October 30, soon after the premiere; in addition, other recordings of several of the show's songs were made by RCA pop stars Perry Como, the Fontane Sisters, Freddy Martin, and Hugo Winterhalter.

All of this was very good news indeed for Irving Berlin, though a true complete-original-cast album would almost certainly have been a classic, and a best-seller. But Kapp was stubborn. The show would be filmed, virtually intact, in 1953, with Merman starring alongside Donald O'Connor as the Harvard grad, George Sanders in the Paul Lucas role, and dancer Vera-Ellen as the princess (with a dubbed singing voice). Decca's soundtrack album would utilize eight of the original thirteen songs, with two added numbers, "That International Rag" and "What Have I to Do with Love?" The filmed *Call Me Madam* is undoubtedly Merman's finest work on the screen.

It was her show all the way; whatever minor critical carping there was, none was aimed at her. The *News* not only printed John Chapman's review (not especially favorable, except about Merman) but also ran an editorial lauding the book's "shrewd, humorous and deeply penetrating comment on most of the outstanding idiocies of the Fair Dealers." In particular, "The Marshall Plan for shoveling out billions to busted foreign nations comes in for sweet ribbing. So do Washington cocktail orgies, Senators on foreign 'investigation' junkets, Dean Acheson, and Harry Truman himself." The editorialist was certain that Truman must be suffering sleepless nights over "They Like Ike," which he dismissed as an "outwardly trifling ditty" that "sounds like 'Three Blind Mice.' "

Steven Suskin's "Broadway Scorecard" for *Call Me Madam* logs only a single unfavorable newspaper review, no pans, one favorable, and five raves. The *New Yorker, Time, Life* (with a picture spread), *Cue,* and the *Saturday Review* all posted favorable or better notices.

Brooks Atkinson, writing in the *Times,* waxed eloquent about Irving Berlin in his weekly Sunday column—a remarkable reversal of his views of the year before. Berlin can only have smiled when he read,

> After forty-five years on the sidewalks of Tin Pan Alley, Mr. Berlin is entitled to lose some of his rapture and enthusiasm. He doesn't. He has bestowed on *Call Me Madam* one of his most delightful cornucopias of sound. To a theatregoer who first became aware of Mr. Berlin's special brand of genius amid the dismal sandstorms of Yaphank in 1918, his longevity as a composer is not only amazing but gratifying. . . .
>
> No doubt Mr. Berlin keeps fresh from generation to generation by taking an interest in people and maintaining a sympathetic interest in the times. He has long since mastered the American idiom; but instead of exploiting it he serves it sincerely. And like the authors of the book, he represents the best of the liberal American tradition. Note the good taste and warmheartedness of the tender little reverie he has written for "Lichtenburg." For the musical climax of the evening he has composed a counterpoint arrangement for Miss Merman and Russell Nype that is the most triumphant scene in the show. It brings into comic focus the contrast between Miss Merman's jubilee style and Mr. Nype's engaging modesty and wonder.

Leland Hayward's three publicity staffers could not have done better if they had written the piece themselves. Atkinson's pithy appraisal of Berlin's "genius" and his place on the American scene has never been bettered by anyone.

13

GRAY SKIES

BERLIN, with his work on *Call Me Madam* so gratifyingly concluded,
actually mentioned the possibility of taking time out for some sun and
rest; he was visibly spent, looking tired and worn. Ellin suggested a
cruise to Italy—and why not take Mary Ellin along for company? She sensed
that her daughter's new "friendship" with a colleague at *Time* was warming
up. For her part, Mary Ellin, now working as an editor at the magazine (and
with vacation time due her), would have preferred to go to Europe on her
own, or with a girlfriend, but she reluctantly agreed.

Berlin himself would have fancied a slow boat to Bermuda, but after
some wifely urging, he boarded an airliner with Mary Ellin in tow, ready to
squire her on her first trip to France, Italy, and Britain.

In spite of himself, Berlin later had to admit that those three short weeks
were wonderful ones. It was refreshing and invigorating to see and hear his
twenty-four-year-old daughter, now a young woman, express her joy and
wonder. He was proud of the poise and sophistication she displayed when he
introduced her to his friends, including, in Rome, the Leland Haywards.

In Italy, with her father, Mary Ellin saw some of the towns and vistas he
had last seen under very different conditions, during the war. And in Rome,
by pure chance, they encountered none other than Mary Ellin's new "friend"
and *Time* cohort, Marvin Barrett. When Barrett had first visited the Berlin
household, Mary Ellin's father had been too preoccupied with *Call Me*

Madam to take much notice of him, but he had passed muster with the eagle-eyed Ellin, as well as with Linda and Elizabeth and the even sharper-eyed Tenney.

Making his better acquaintance now, Berlin liked this young man who, he learned, had come into the Luce publication empire via Des Moines, Harvard, and the navy. He expressed his approval of Barrett through a typical gesture, supplying the couple with a car so they could see the landmarks of Rome on their own. Although she was not yet aware of it, Mary Ellin had found her Mr. Right.

From Rome, father and daughter flew to London for a brief visit with Alexander Korda, then returned to New York. Berlin barely had a chance to look into his office before boarding another plane—this time with Ellin, Linda, and Elizabeth—for Hawaii, where, on January 4, 1951, the senior Berlins celebrated their silver wedding anniversary. It was a sunny and restful interval, and Berlin, smiling into a camera with Ellin, looked better than he had in a long while. But he was also restless and moody: he missed his Buick.

Since *Madam*'s opening the previous fall, his life had been devoted mostly to travel; sheet-music sales and recordings proliferated, but there would be no new songs published in 1951. There was talk of filming the show, and prospects for a couple of original film scores, but nothing substantial was in the works yet.

Instead, he was on the move again. Ellin, sensing his restlessness, got him to take Mary Ellin to Paris for the June wedding of the son of Albert Willemetz. The senior Willemetz had recently translated the book and lyrics of *Annie Get Your Gun* for its French production; he and Berlin had been friends for decades. After the wedding celebration, Berlin decided to take a detour to the Côte d'Azure, near Nice, for a little time in the sun and, for Mary Ellin, some exciting artistic encounters. Her father informed her that Marc Chagall and Pablo Picasso lived nearby, in small towns near Cannes.

Berlin himself had taken up painting two years before, encouraged by his friend Irving Hoffman, a newspaper columnist, publicist, cartoonist, and fellow artist. During one of Berlin's dry songwriting spells, Hoffman had given him a full set of artist's materials, thereby launching him on an active new pursuit: no mere Sunday painter, he was often consumed by his hobby. Over a long period, his canvases filled up his studio (on the top floor of the Beekman Place house) as well as his office, where they covered walls and jammed closets. If a portrait turned out to look like its subject, Berlin would present said subject—Bing Crosby and Barbra Streisand were two so honored—with the original, after having a full-sized color print made of it.

The Crosby portrait in fact pleased Berlin so much that he sent Harold Arlen, a Sunday painter himself, a copy of it. Arlen, who had a wickedly playful sense of humor, called Berlin after receiving the picture to inform him that he had used a wrong note in the included musical quotation from "White Christmas." Berlin was most upset by this—until a chuckling Arlen reassured him that it was only a joke.

Arlen had several Berlin paintings, both copies and originals, which he placed on the walls alongside works by Dalí, George Gershwin, Henry Botkin, and Gloria Vanderbilt. The imaginative Berlin not only used standard canvases but also sometimes painted directly onto his palettes. In one such memorial painting, he fashioned a bird out of the curve of the board and decorated it with flowers; in the thumb hole, he inserted a photograph of his friend's recently deceased wife. This was the bird's eye.

Berlin had no artistic illusions; he knew that most of his canvases were amateurish, even crude, but except for one interval when he gave up painting for a while, discouraged by that crudeness, he enjoyed his new hobby. Besides painting at home, he liked to take his equipment to the country to paint scenes of rural life. While an occasional effort could be startlingly impressive—one of his most powerful paintings was a haunting portrait of a woman that might have been done at Auschwitz—he managed to keep his newfound occupation in perspective. One afternoon he took a friend to Beekman Place to show him his improvised studio and recent work, recounting as he did so the story of "my first canvas. Because of my ego, I decided to do a self-portrait. This is what it turned out to be," he said, pointing to a painting of a cow in a meadow.

When Hoffman started Berlin on his new pastime, he also introduced him to another dabbler in paints: Pablo Picasso. Now, two years later, when Berlin took Mary Ellin to visit Picasso's studio and Chagall's, his invariably searching mind drove him to ask detailed questions about their work and technique as he viewed their art. The setting of Picasso's studio, on a hill in the town of Vallauris, inspired Berlin to consider doing a musical with sets by the Spaniard, a proposal that amused the painter, if it did not interest him. In the event, that intriguing idea evaporated the moment the Berlins left Vallauris for home.

That summer Berlin relaxed in the Catskills but again wrote no songs. Beyond the on-and-off-and-on-again discussions about the filming of *Call Me Madam,* and some nibbles for catalog-skimming anthologies from Paramount and Twentieth Century-Fox, no new musical project presented itself.

The next year, 1952, began noisily and politically, if not very inspiringly. Early in the year Ellin shifted her allegiance from the Democrats to the

Republicans, who were eager to draft Eisenhower for the presidency. The general had resigned from his position at Columbia and was now serving in Europe as head of the North Atlantic Treaty Organization (NATO). An Eisenhower rally was held on February 8 at Madison Square Garden, with celebrities on hand to entertain what the organizers hoped would be a large gathering (they were not disappointed). Present were Clark Gable (himself a former air force hero), Mary Martin (who sang her *South Pacific* hit about being in love with a wonderful guy), and composer Richard Rodgers (to conduct).

After Ethel Merman declaimed "There's No Business like Show Business," Berlin came on to sing, in his diminutive voice, "I Like Ike." He was joined in the final chorus by President Truman himself, in the person of *Call Me Madam*'s Irving Fisher—a patent touch of Berlin showmanship. The entire event was an enormous success.

Four days after the rally, Berlin's sister Rebecca died after a long bout with cancer, at the age of sixty-seven. She had changed her name to Ruth when she married Abraham Kahn, and moved to Montclair, New Jersey, where she and her husband kept a small shop and ran a newspaper distributorship. Her death left only Irving, Ben, and Gussie out of the eight Beilins who had arrived at Ellis Island almost sixty years before. Ben was now a prosperous furrier in New London, Connecticut; Gussie, long divorced and never remarried, was devoted to Jewish charities and worked as a translator. She had been especially close to her sister.

Rebecca's death, though not unexpected, nonetheless took the edge off the excitement and surge of energy Berlin had felt at the Eisenhower rally. And, too, it was an inevitable reminder of mortality: Rebecca had been less than four years his senior. He distracted himself from such depressive musings by concentrating on work: the London company of *Call Me Madam,* with an English cast, was to open in mid-March, while the American touring company, with Elaine Stritch in the Merman role and Kent Smith as Cosmo, would set out for eleven successful months early in May.

With Eisenhower now in the running for the presidency, it seemed to all concerned that keeping the "Ike" song in the show might be considered a partisan statement on the part of the producers. Berlin conceded the point and quickly wrote a replacement, "Our Day of Independence," but by the time the *Madam* company reached Chicago, "They Like Ike" was back by popular demand.

There was good news around this time from even farther west, where *Call Me Madam* had been acquired for filming by Twentieth Century-Fox; Ethel Merman, though branded as box-office poison by the studios, was signed to reprise her role as as Sally Adams. This was a most welcome development for Berlin, though there would be little for him to do on the film except keep up with its progress. Broadway, in the two years since *Call Me Madam*'s premiere, seemed to have gone cold on him, as the names of a new generation of composers began lighting up the marquees, notably Alan Jay Lerner and Frederick Loewe (*Paint Your Wagon*), Frank Loesser (*Guys and Dolls*), and Harold Rome (*Wish You Were Here*). Among the host of newcomers who wrote the songs for *New Faces of 1952* was yet another very promising lyricist, Sheldon Harnick. Of the old-timers, only Rodgers and Hammerstein remained active; Cole Porter had slowed down—painfully so—because of a fall from and under a horse some years before.

Berlin felt he was ready to try Hollywood again, though the studios now preferred, it seemed, Broadway-proved hits. While Berlin was engaged in preparing *Call Me Madam* for the stage, Metro's Arthur Freed had been struggling with the film version of *Annie Get Your Gun*. Freed's troubles had in fact begun even earlier, during Berlin's unhappy *Miss Liberty* period, and only got worse over time.

It had all started well enough, in the first week of March 1949, with Judy Garland content in her role as Annie Oakley; there were rehearsals, costume fittings, and, after a couple of months, studio recording dates for the star and fellow cast members Howard Keel (as Frank) and Frank Morgan (playing Buffalo Bill).

It soon became apparent, however, that Garland was once again depressed and dependent on drugs and alcohol; sometimes (too often) she simply did not show up for work. Reluctantly, Freed agreed to her suspension in May—and the search for a new Annie was on.

Berlin, in the midst of his own *Miss Liberty* mess, took the news badly, for he was fond of Judy Garland—and who, he wondered, could replace her? The answer came out of the casting office's left field: bouncy, loud, and blond Betty Hutton, on loan from Paramount. Wiser heads questioned the choice, but in fact it was an extraordinarily good one. Meanwhile, during the delay (the refilming of Garland's scenes, with Hutton, would not begin till October), the death of Frank Morgan brought in Louis Calhern, requiring the reshooting of more scenes and the rerecording of "There's No Business like Show Business" as well as all of Garland's/Hutton's numbers. Miraculously, production was virtually complete by December, and a screening was scheduled for Long Beach on January 29, 1950.

When the preview audience-reaction cards were in and read, *Annie Get Your Gun* looked like a surefire hit. Berlin telegrammed Freed his congratulations, only mildly sorry for the cutting of "Let's Go West Again" (preserved on Judy Garland's track recordings). After its general release, in May 1950, *Annie* would go on to become the biggest film musical of the year, outgrossing even Fred Astaire's *Three Little Words* and Gene Kelly and Judy Garland's *Summer Stock* (which endured its own eight-month shooting schedule due to Garland's "health" problems).

Around the time production was beginning on the film version of *Call Me Madam,* two new offers from Fox and Paramount came through. They were, in Somerset Maugham's phrase, the mixture as before. Fox's Darryl F. Zanuck, impressed with Merman's presence in *Madam,* signed her to star in a Berlin musical to be entitled, fittingly, *There's No Business like Show Business.* The score would require only a few original songs, with the rest to be filled in from the Berlin inventory, following the pattern established by *Alexander's Ragtime Band* and *Easter Parade.* A musical cavalcade, the film would tell the story of a show-business family—parents, daughter, and two sons—over a couple of decades, as it rises from vaudeville to Broadway. Period flavor would be musically injected through the use of such songs as "Alexander's Ragtime Band" for the early days, "Heat Wave" for the twenties, and, for the eve of the Second World War, the newly written "A Man Chases a Girl" and "A Sailor's Not a Sailor." One song, "But I Ain't Got a Man," was conceived especially for Marilyn Monroe, cast as a showgirl who causes friction, and a breakup of the family, when she takes up with one of the sons (Donald O'Connor). The number was later dropped; instead, Monroe slithered through the provocative "Heat Wave."

The Paramount film, to be written simultaneously with the Fox one, was a shameless replication of *Holiday Inn* and *Blue Skies,* entitled *White Christmas.* It would reunite Astaire and Crosby in their usual roles as affectionate rivals; the script even went so far as to feature the canonical inn.

In the summer of 1952 the Berlins spent some time in California so that Berlin could get a better conception of what he needed to do for the two productions. By the end of August, writing from the Catskills, he was pleased to inform his friend Irving Hoffman that he had written his first *White Christmas* song, "Sittin' in the Sun" (intended for Crosby but unfortunately, for some reason, not used). This good beginning, and the country air, moderated his chronic insomnia—but only to a degree. In *A Daughter's Memoir,* Mary Ellin Barrett reveals the inside story of how one of the best of the new songs was born.

Even as songs began to come more easily to him—"faster and better"— Berlin would have bad, sleepless nights. One day, exhausted, he called his

A new phase in Berlin's film career commenced with *Alexander's Ragtime Band,* a musical anthology compiled from the Berlin catalog with the addition of a couple of new songs. Here Berlin accompanies stars Alice Faye, Tyrone Power, and Don Ameche. *Photofest.*

The Berlins celebrate at the Starlight Roof of the Waldorf-Astoria following the radio broadcast tribute that marked the release of *Alexander's Ragtime Band* in May 1938. *Photofest.*

Victor Moore, mustachioed William Gaxton, and ballerina Vera Zorina in a scene from *Louisiana Purchase* (1940). Corrupt politician Gaxton is attempting to place Moore, a crusading senator, in a compromising position, a tactic that ultimately backfires. The musical, a hit, was graced with one of Berlin's finest scores. *Photofest.*

Berlin with assistant Staff Sergeant Ezra Stone at a dress rehearsal of *This Is the Army,* shortly before the show's July 4 premiere. After a successful Broadway run, the show was to go on the road in the United States before being filmed and traveling overseas to tour war zones from Britain to the Pacific. *Photofest.*

This Is the Army curtain call. In its three-year run the show raised close to ten million dollars for the Army Emergency Relief Fund. *ASCAP.*

Berlin re-creates his famous number "Oh! How I Hate to Get Up in the Morning" from *Yip! Yip! Yaphank* for the filmed version of *This Is the Army*, released in 1943. *ASCAP.*

Jerome Kern and Dorothy Fields in Hollywood, circa 1936. The well-matched songwriting team would be reunited briefly nine years later, when Rodgers and Hammerstein tried to coax Kern to score their first musical production, a show based on the career of Annie Oakley, with a book by Fields and her brother Herbert. Kern's sudden death initiated a frantic search for a replacement; once Berlin agreed to the assignment, Fields was out as lyricist but remained as colibrettist of what became *Annie Get Your Gun. Gershwin Archive.*

(*Left*) "**A**nything You Can Do, I Can Do Better": Ray Middleton as Frank and Ethel Merman as Annie, in a typical confrontational duet before true love dawns. *Photofest.*

The *Miss Liberty* creative team. Standing behind Berlin are director Moss Hart and librettist Robert E. Sherwood. *Photofest.*

(*Facing page, lower right*) Back in Hollywood as *Annie Get Your Gun* broke records in New York: with Judy Garland and Fred Astaire on the sound stage of *Easter Parade,* another compendium of Berliniana, featuring vintage as well as new songs. *ASCAP.*

Choreographer Jerome Robbins directs Allyn McLerie and Tommy Rall in *Miss Liberty*'s second act's "Follow the Leader Jig" at the Policeman's Ball. The cast called this dance the "Washing Machine Ballet" or the "Bonecrusher." *Photofest.*

Finale: *Miss Liberty*'s "Give Me Your Tired, Your Poor." In the front row are principals Allyn McLerie, Eddie Albert, Mary McCarty, Charles Dingle, Maria Karnilova, and Tommy Rall. *Photofest.*

Showstopper: Ethel Merman and Russell Nype in the contrapuntal "You're Just in Love" from *Call Me Madam,* the show that gave Berlin a welcome hit after the tepid reception of *Miss Liberty. Photofest.*

President Dwight D. Eisenhower informs the Berlins that he has signed a congressional bill, dated July 16, 1954, approving the striking of a medal for Berlin. The medal is to commemorate the writing of "God Bless America." *ASCAP.*

(Right) Late July 1962: Berlin teaching First Lady Nanette Fabray a song for *Mr. President* during a rehearsal. *Photofest.*

During an informal dance at the White House, the First Lady and President Robert Ryan glide to the strains of "Let's Go Back to the Waltz." *Friedman-Abeles Photo.*

Beverly Hilton Hotel, March 3, 1963: "Irving Berlin Day" is officially declared in Los Angeles. At the dinner that evening Berlin received the Laurel Award, presented by the Screen Producers Guild. With Berlin are Arthur Freed (then planning the luckless *Say It with Music*), Frank Sinatra (who sang a Berlin medley), and Ira Gershwin, who rarely ventured from his house on North Roxbury Drive if he could help it. *Courtesy of Ira and Leonore Gershwin Trusts. Used by permission.*

Berlin's last public appearance, at the White House in May 1973, celebrated the return of prisoners of war from Vietnam (and coincided with the beginning of Nixon's Watergate anxieties). A rather skeptical-looking Joey Heatherton joins the President and Berlin for "God Bless America." *Photofest.*

doctor, who drove over and listened with some impatience as the songwriter complained about the night before. (Berlin himself admitted that his recitation was laced with "a lot of self-pity.") Finally the doctor offered his prescription: Why not count your blessings instead of sheep? Berlin at once perked up—what an idea for a song! "Count Your Blessings Instead of Sheep" was decidedly worth the price of a house call.

As was the practice, there were several interpolations—"Blue Skies," "Mandy," the title song—but beyond those, Berlin composed a substantially new score for *White Christmas*. Three songs—"The Old Man," "Gee, I Wish I Was Back in the Army," and "What Can You Do with a General?"—were probably extracted from the abandoned *Stars on My Shoulder* (no coincidence, since one of the screenplay writers was Norman Krasna, with whom Berlin had worked on that short-lived idea for a musical). "Free," a *Call Me Madam* reject, was revised and inserted as "Snow." Among the signal new compositions were "Love You Didn't Do Right by Me" and "The Best Things Happen While You're Dancing."

While Berlin's work went well, the production itself suffered some early setbacks. Fred Astaire was ill when *White Christmas* was ready to start up, so the producers had to go looking for a replacement. Donald O'Connor, who had shone in *Call Me Madam* and all but stolen *Singin' in the Rain* from Gene Kelly, turned out to be on the sick list as well; Kelly himself was under contract to Metro and in any case busy with the filming of *Brigadoon*. Danny Kaye, however, was both available and in good health, and took the part of Crosby's veteran army buddy and postwar partner in a theater team. This time around, Crosby played the workaholic of the two; Kaye's character, tired of moving constantly from one club to another, decides to become a matchmaker and get his friend married off and settled down. That way, Kaye will be free to gad about town, a fun-loving ladies' man with an aversion to marriage (his own, at least). The two men soon become involved with a sister act they spot in a club, Rosemary Clooney and Vera-Ellen. Kaye selects Clooney as the bride-to-be, but (of course) she and Crosby do not hit it off very well at first. Not to worry: the film's end will see them all in a final, happy clinch.

Of the Crosby-Berlin trilogy, *White Christmas* has the best script, by Krasna and comedy specialists Norman Panama and Melvin Frank. The dialogue is literate and amusing, and the film itself, despite a few forgivable clichés, well directed by Michael Curtiz. The script opens with Crosby, circa 1944, singing "White Christmas" in a bombed-out building somewhere in Europe, joined by a chorus of GIs and their beloved general, who is being relieved of his command (he has a convincing limp). It closes, in neat symmetry, with Crosby's singing the song again, this time with chorus and children dancing against a backdrop of snowy mountains. The new-fallen snow—a white Christmas— and a special Christmas Eve show produced by Crosby, and attended by scores of former comrades in arms, have saved the general's Vermont inn from bankruptcy.

In between, there are the predictable Kaye-Crosby shenanigans, as well as a serious misunderstanding that threatens the Crosby-Clooney romance. When the four leads first arrive at the inn (by train from sunnier climes), the sisters have been booked to sing, but they find no snow and, naturally enough, no skiers—they are the only ones at the place, and Crosby and Kaye the sole paying guests.

When they learn that the general is about to lose his inn, Crosby and Kaye summon their theater company, dispersed on vacation, to come up and put on a show. Crosby also appeals to the men of their old army company: a full house for the show will save the day, snow or no snow.

The moment of conflict comes when Clooney's character mistakenly believes that the entire evening is to be a mere publicity stunt designed to advertise Crosby's troupe. She leaves the enterprise and finds work in a club, where she sings the affecting "Love You Didn't Do Right by Me." Christmas Eve, however, brings her back to the general's—just in time to lend her voice to the "White Christmas" reprise, and to reunite with her not-such-a-bad-guy-after-all.

An earlier number, "Count Your Blessings," is openly autobiographical and typically Berlinesque in its simple, to-the-point allusions to insomnia and leaner times. The most personal lines go back to the nursery:

> *I picture curly heads*
> *And one by one I count them as they slumber in their beds.*

Since Crosby sings this in the film, and his character is a childless bachelor, the image of the wakeful songwriter-father, following his doctor's orders, seems all the clearer, and all the more poignant.

By October Berlin was finished with his latest stint in Hollywood and back in Beekman Place. *White Christmas* would not be released for another two years, but then it would become the top money-maker of 1954, grossing $12 million. On October 30 of that year "Count Your Blessings" would make the "Hit Parade" and go on to be recorded by Eddie Fisher, for whom it would be a hit. It would be joined on the "Parade," on the Christmas Day 1954 broadcast, by the evergreen "White Christmas."

On his return to New York in 1952, Berlin set his staff in motion, arranging for the publication of the *White Christmas* songs "The Old Man" and "Count Your Blessings," even though the film's release was still a long way off. He also liked the rejected "Sittin' in the Sun" enough to publish it without film accreditation. The activity eased his tensions, and soon there was more busy work: it was time to begin shipping copies of "White Christmas" to arrive in the stores before Thanksgiving.

He was at home one day in mid-October, and Ellin out at lunch with a friend, when the phone rang. It was Mary Ellin calling from Mexico, Linda told her father. He took the phone and learned that his headstrong, adventurous oldest daughter had married Marvin Barrett the day before, in a private, unpublicized ceremony in a small Mexican town—a blessing Berlin himself could only envy and admire. This was indeed good news; as soon as he hung up, he called his wife at the Colony Club. She, too, was delighted.

Their combined pleasure in this not-unexpected event would flower soon after, when the Barretts returned to New York, quit their jobs at *Time,* and left for Sicily with their luggage and a "large wedding check." They settled in Taormina, at the foot of Mount Etna, overlooking the Ionian Sea; in this beautiful, spectacular setting, the young newlyweds planned to launch twin writing careers.

Taormina, a popular resort town, was and is noted for its gentle climate and its centuries-old ruins—Greek, Roman, and Arab. The incipient writers had barely begun typing their respective manuscripts when a message came from New York: Would it be convenient for them to receive visitors during the holidays? The Berlins—Ellin, Linda, and Irving—arrived, accompanied by the matchless Tenney, in time to celebrate Christmas 1952. (Hilda Schneider could report, on their return, that "White Christmas" had remained on the "Hit Parade" throughout their absence and into January.)

Presents had been carried all the way from New York; family celebrations were matched by one or two in public, including a tribute to the famed American songwriter (word spread quickly through the little town) by an indigenous mandolin band, performed in the town hall. The stock of the newly arrived writers-to-be rose loftily in Sicily. But in Mary Ellin's recollections, the loveliest gift she received was her father's simple statement, "You've done fine."

Unfortunately, he was not always so sure of himself. The weather, and the sun, were perfect; their hotel, once a picturesque convent with a vine-covered cloister, was ideal, and the people were wonderful. But Berlin's moods switched on and off without warning, and a sense of foreboding, of depression, would descend over him. Counting his blessings helped—a loving family, a happily married daughter, a beautiful wife whose mind was as sharp as her tongue, a successful career—but what, he wondered, did he have to return to in the New York of 1953? He would reach the conventional retirement age that May, and he knew he couldn't spend all of his time painting. An inexorable, miserable nervousness and irritability began to overtake him.

After returning from Taormina in early 1953, he suffered through a protracted "dry spell," as he termed it, during which the few songs he published were mostly years-old, ones written for the movies, or for musicals begun but never completed. It was largely a lost year, with a sorrowful ending bracketed by two happier beginnings, one professional, the other personal.

In March, *Call Me Madam* was released on celluloid, putting Ethel Merman finally (if only temporarily) on the Hollywood map. Ever a realist, Berlin was forced to acknowledge that the star was more responsible for the film's success than were the songs.

In May he turned sixty-five, and his brother Ben died of cancer in New London, a loss that deepened his gloomy outlook. Now there were but two Beilins left alive.

November brought the major joyous event of that most disheartening and unproductive year of 1953: the birth, in New York, of Elizabeth Esther Barrett, the Berlins' first grandchild. (Others would follow in the years to come: Elizabeth was just the first of the Barretts' four children, to be joined in due time by five Emmet and Peters cousins.)

The next year was only slightly more active for Berlin: he published just two original songs, one of them the political salute "I Still Like Ike." In July, President Eisenhower invited the Berlins to the White House, where he announced that Congress had approved, and funded, a Congressional Medal honoring Berlin's contribution to American song and, especially, his establishment of the "God Bless America" and *This Is the Army* funds. (The medal would be struck and presented in February 1955.)

There's No Business like Show Business was finally released that December, in time to run in tandem with *White Christmas* over the holidays. The film was a success, but for Berlin there was no excitement in this rather conventional, albeit well-produced, musical: the cast was fine, particularly Ethel Merman, vaudeville veteran Dan Dailey (as her husband), and Donald O'Connor (as their wayward son), but the score contained only two new songs amid a litany of old hits. Admittedly, however, the presence of Marilyn Monroe, fresh from her sex spoof *Gentlemen Prefer Blondes,* made for lively viewing: her performance, full of jiggle and bounce, of the 1920s number "After You

Get What You Want, You Don't Want It" so unnerved one censor, in fact, that the sequence was deleted from the film's Canadian prints.

One curious bit of casting was that of Johnnie Ray, then a million-record-selling pop star (reason enough, perhaps) whose overwrought performances of his major songs, "The Little White Cloud That Cried" and "Cry," packed nightclubs in 1952–53. In the film, he portrayed Merman and Dailey's elder son, who leaves the family troupe for the priesthood, much to the dismay of his parents (an unusual twist for a musical). His going-away party provides the occasion to revive a tune Berlin had written in 1940, "If You Believe," which the terminally emotional Ray, joined by his family and friends, converts into a gospel song.

Show Business (Merman's last film) did not do as well at the box office as *White Christmas*. For one thing, the family's show-biz saga clutters up the song flow; the long tale begins in 1919 and ends with the coming of the Second World War, its quasi-happy denouement featuring a father-son reconciliation, wedding bells, and the two boys in uniform (Father Donahue is an army chaplain, and his brother a common sailor, set to marry the not-so-common Monroe). The ambiguous ending cannot have helped the picture's popularity: all are happily together, and all is forgiven, but the two young men are going off to war. Worst of all, as far as Berlin was concerned, was the fact that *Show Business* produced no hit numbers.

After the two films' previews, the Berlins left New York's winter for the warmth of Haiti, where one evening they found an old friend, Noël Coward, wittily holding forth for an appreciative group that included designer Ginette Spanier. Spanier once professed that Coward was the Beatles of his day (the twenties) and that he had initiated the practice of addressing everyone, of whatever sex, as "darling"; her sharp eye now saw Berlin as a "little old man who was feeling very, very sad."

The congenitally bubbly Coward went to the piano in the bar to entertain the company with a medley of Berlin songs, spreading cheer and delight. Ellin Berlin was especially touched by this thoughtful and selfless gesture; Coward refused to play any Coward that night.

Then it was back to the States in time for Berlin to receive his Congressional Medal, only to see its luster tarnished by an annoying lawsuit the following month. An amateur aspiring songwriter, appositely named Smith, accused Berlin of plagiarizing "I Fell in Love," a song he claimed to have written in 1947. (This form of lawsuit was, and remains, common in the popular-music business—one good argument for publishers' sending unsolicited manuscripts back to hopefuls in their original, unopened envelopes.) Smith charged that Berlin had stolen his tune and used it in *Call Me Madam* under the title "You're Just in Love." The question arose, If the song had been submitted to someone (a person who, it turned out, did not exist) at the Berlin office in 1947, and had gone on to become one of the most popular hits (combined with "I Wonder Why?") of 1950–51, why had Mr. Smith waited until 1955 to sue?

There was another, even more indefensible hitch in Smith's case: the two songs, written to be sung as a duet, had been suggested by George Abbott and practically written in public during the show's New Haven tryout—in the theater and in Berlin's hotel suite, with Helmy Kresa present. Members of the company had actually heard it being worked out; it was not a song Berlin had retrieved from the trunk.

If nothing else, the otherwise pointless trial took Berlin's mind off his lack of work. One day he testified in court himself, using a piano to demonstrate how the "I Wonder Why?"/"You're Just in Love" duet had taken its inspiration from "Play a Simple Melody." His convincing performance made the following day's *Times,* in an item trumpeting the news that Berlin played with all ten fingers, not just one, as legend had it.

At the end of April, Justice Martin Frank ruled in favor of Irving Berlin, leaving him, ironically, at loose ends once again. Later in the year, or perhaps early in 1956, he was cheered to learn that playwrights George S. Kaufman and S. N. Behrman were working up an idea for a musical and wanted him to score it. The subject had been suggested by Max Gordon, a producer who counted among his successes *The Band Wagon, The Cat and the Fiddle,* and *Roberta* (and among his flops *Very Warm for May* and *The Firebrand of Florence*). Highly regarded as an astute man of the theater, Gordon was confident enough in this project to commit to producing it.

He believed that a good musical, with songs by Irving Berlin, could be fashioned out of the stories of Wilson and Addison Mizner, as told in a recently published book by Alva Johnston, *The Legendary Mizners.* Kaufman and Behrman were amenable and brought the notion to Berlin, who, anxious for something to do, at once signed on.

Berlin had known Wilson as early as 1914 as a playwright, man-about-town, devoted gambler, and inveterate trickster (Wilson had given him the fake "Last Will and Testament" that he had transformed into the hit song "When I Leave the World Behind"). His brother, Addison, had been a con man turned architect. During the Florida land boom of the midtwenties, the latter had traveled south to try his hand at real estate, some acreage of which eventually proved to be more water than land (a situation recalling that depicted in *The Cocoanuts*).

As he pondered his position, Addison realized that all those who acquired the boom land would sooner or later require costly housing. Addison reportedly taught himself his new profession—architecture—in about two weeks. In short order he was designing million-dollar mansions and supposedly established the city of Boca Raton.

Berlin had last seen the brothers when he, Ellin, and Mary Ellin visited Palm Beach in 1927. By then the land boom was over, and the Mizners themselves faded. Wilson's plays remained unperformed; today his most famous piece of cynical advice is much better known than its author: "Never give a sucker an even break." Berlin remembered him and Addison as colorful, witty, a bit slippery but nonetheless likable. The period during which they had flourished, from roughly 1910 to the depression, their lives and loves— all seemed ideal fodder for a musical.

Kaufman and Behrman had had recent musicals on Broadway. With his wife, Leueen McGrath, Kaufman had written the book for Cole Porter's last show, *Silk Stockings*. It had required some fixing, however, and Abe Burrows had been called in to punch it up (a sad irony, for it had always been *Kaufman* who was called in as a show doctor in the past). Behrman had been more fortunate: he and Joshua Logan had written the book for Harold Rome's *Fanny* early in 1954.

When the Berlin-Kaufman-Behrman collaboration began, the Mizner musical's provisional title, incongruously, was *Sentimental Guy;* accordingly, late in 1956, Berlin completed a song named "You're a Sentimental Guy," in which one of the brothers' girlfriends speculates that though he may prowl along Broadway from dusk till dawn (as Berlin himself had done, many years before), he would be happier living in Yonkers with a garden and a lawn.

More incisive is Berlin's "You're a Sucker for a Dame," a biographically accurate description of Wilson; one especially racy line refers to Mizner's weakness for a woman "in a sweater and a shelf along her chest." Another number is much tougher: the mistress of one of the brothers tells him, after ending their affair (and as he carries on pathetically), to "Go Home and Tell It to Your Wife." Likewise bitter is "Love Leads to Marriage," one of the best songs in the unfinished score. Before the project was, sadly, abandoned, the show's title was changed to *Wise Guy*.

After months of work, the librettists finally gave up, explaining that their book lacked substance. Kaufman sensed—borrowing a phase from Behrman—that he himself belonged among those "writers who mask sterility with incessant productivity"; after this, he produced nothing more of significance for the theater. His collaborator, meanwhile, would go on to write a play and several volumes of memoirs.

Berlin, for his part, returned to his office and his easel, though he did write one song in time for the August 1956 Republican National Convention in San Francisco: "Ike for Four More Years." Eisenhower would win a landslide victory that November, becoming the first Republican in the twentieth century to serve two successive terms.

At sixty-eight, Berlin was only a couple of years older than the President, and he bristled at the word *retirement.* Some time later he would vent his feelings in an interview with Herbert Kretzmer of the London *Daily Express.*

"Retirement," Berlin asserted when Kretzmer raised the question,

> made me sick. I mean that. I got really sick. I suffered severe bouts of depression. I worried about everything when, really, I had nothing to worry about. . . . It takes a very rare person to retire gracefully if he has been a success.
>
> I tried to take up painting, but I was no good at it. I felt, you see, I had to be as good a painter as I was a songwriter. I hope that doesn't sound conceited, but it's the truth. I had no hobbies. . . . My only hobby is songwriting. So I went back to work.

(He also returned to painting, though he would dismiss his hobby with the self-deprecating line, "As a painter I'm a pretty good songwriter.")

During their time together Kretzmer noted Berlin's "beaming good will and benevolence in all directions. He is a happy and chatty man, giving the lie to the reputation for extreme reticence that has preceded him to Britain." And, Kretzmer might have added, a remarkably frank as well as happy man, given that he had only recently passed through a protracted period of hell on earth.

"I am a ham," Berlin admitted. "I think to be a good songwriter you've got to be a kind of ham. The same with actors. You must *like* to show off what you can do. You must like to be a success. It's not ego . . . wait a minute . . . it *is* ego. It's the same in my business."

Kretzmer informed his readers that Berlin "talks in a hoarse, throaty voice, each word sounding like an egg softly cracked. His conversation is as simple as his songs. Irving Berlin is an ordinary man with a God-given talent and does not seek to disguise that fact by trying to be cute or quotable." Overcoming the latter obstacle, he then went on to quote him:

> The reason I write simply is that I just wasn't clever when I started. I have never been a Smart Aleck. I could not read music and I couldn't play the piano in any key except F. Matter of fact, I still can't.

By the time I sharpened the tools of my trade, I found I wrote simple songs because that's how they came out of my head. I didn't try to change anything. A certain emotional something went into the songs and I never tried to analyze it too much. It is often the unself-conscious thing that makes a hit. You can be *too* clever.

Reporter Kretzmer had the last word: "Irving Berlin, I report with pleasure, looked very healthy to me." At the time of this unique interview, the songwriter had another quarter of a century of life ahead of him. They would not be easy years.

14

SWAN SONGS?

AT THE TIME of the London interview in which Berlin fairly glowed with self-assurance, he was seventy-five. Professionally and personally, things were going well. He and Ellin were in England for the wedding of their youngest daughter, Elizabeth, to editor Edmund Fisher, son of eminent ornithologist James Fisher; back in the States, the promise of an important film project awaited his return.

That signal birthday on May 11, 1963, which Berlin claimed not to have celebrated at all, had indeed been largely ignored, save for a quiet family gathering in the Catskills: "I didn't have to prove anything to myself anymore," he explained. And as for age, "So who is counting? I don't think of myself as any age. . . . There are a lot of old guys writing songs. You've got to stay healthy. That's all."

But "staying healthy" had not, for him, proved possible. Soon after *Wise Guy* went into limbo, some seven years before, he had gone into a deep depression. That he fretted over the change in the popular-music scene is indicated by his defensive comment about "old guys writing songs": the music world was now dominated by "young guys" writing something called rock and roll, or just "rock." To the veterans of Tin Pan Alley, it seemed loud, primitive, and pounding—only the kids could stand it. But it would shake up the market for sheet music and records. The new darlings of the "youth market" included Bob Dylan, Brian Wilson of the Beach Boys (specializing

in California "surfer" tunes), and, from 1956, a southern boy named Elvis
Presley, who had initiated a craze for what would become known as rocka-
billy, a fusion of rock and southern folk music.

The young people who swooned over Elvis did not, needless to say, purchase original-cast or soundtrack albums. Nor did their parents, who instead
of buying sheet music now collected recordings by the few traditionalists
who persisted in singing old-fashioned songs—Frank Sinatra, Doris Day,
Tony Bennett, and others. The tenants of the Brill Building, successor to Tin
Pan Alley, panicked as publishers realized that an unrecorded song wasn't
worth publishing.

Then, too, fewer musicals were being produced on Broadway, and therefore in Hollywood, since the bulk of the Hollywood product consisted of
filmed Broadway hits. Original film musicals were now a breed apart: the
first of the surfer movies, *Gidget,* a celluloid equivalent of a Beach Boys song,
would be released in 1959, while Presley had made his own film debut three
years before, in *Love Me Tender.* The studio heads, like the recording-industry
executives, were quick to recognize the youth market as a major source of
potential profit.

In this musical climate, Irving Berlin felt frozen out. With little to do
after the demise of *Wise Guy,* in despair, irritably nerve-racked, he came down
with shingles (Herpes zoster), a viral disease related to chicken pox. Most
often afflicting individuals past middle age, it is characterized by a rash, blis-
ters, and severe pain in the affected nerve centers, generally the abdomen and
lower chest. Miserable and ill, Berlin retreated to his rooms on the top floors
of the town house, preferring not to be seen by anyone; his wife respected that
wish and remained in another part of the house. Berlin did his own cooking
and stayed indoors until after nightfall, when he might go out for a walk.
When he felt a bit better, he would see Ellin, who finally encouraged him to
seek hospitalization (his own doctors had not been much help).

And so Irving Berlin "retired"—to a hospital—and slipped out of sight.
He missed his seventieth-birthday celebrations in 1958, marked by radio and
television tributes and even new recordings, despite the rock influx. One of
the best albums of the several released was a two-LP set conducted by Berlin
favorite Jay Blackton. A well-produced and -sung survey, it begins with his
first song, "Marie from Sunny Italy," and closes with one of his then most
recent, 1957's "You Can't Lose the Blues with Colors."

In 1959 Berlin published his first new song in two years, in honor of a
new nation whose history and future greatly concerned him: the song was
"Israel." He himself was celebrated that same year in a broadcast aired on the

State Department's Voice of America network, featuring some of the stars for whom he had written songs, including Rogers and Astaire, Ethel Merman, Eddie Cantor, and Bing Crosby. President Eisenhower came on to sum up the presentation: "I can think of no one more deserving of today's tribute than Irving Berlin," he said. "He has contributed conscientiously of his time and talent in peace and war to bring joy and entertainment to Americans everywhere."

By early 1960 Berlin was back in his office, painting again and tending to business, looking well and fully recovered from his "retirement." Three days before his seventy-second birthday, he granted an interview to a writer planning a piece on a friend of his, composer Harold Arlen. "In a nutshell," he began, "I have a deep affection for Harold Arlen as a person. He has great courage, not shown by all of us, and he kept on going, kept on working"—a veiled reference to Arlen's troubled marriage and recent near-fatal illness.

Berlin has often been drawn as highly competitive, envious of others, but his admiration for Arlen the songwriter is clear from his testimony here. "In my opinion no one has written greater songs," he asserted. "That goes for me, too. Quantity doesn't mean a damn thing—it's quality." As for his own early songs, Berlin said, "I call 'em bad. They were not only bad, they were amateurish."

He was especially impressed with the Arlen-Harburg film score for *The Wizard of Oz* (1939), which he believed "could have been a great [Broadway] show—one of a handful [of such films]." He turned practical at this point, adding a fellow songwriter's fiduciary lament: "It was just a great misfortune that [Arlen] and Yip [Harburg] didn't own the rights to *The Wizard.*" Metro had a so-called work-for-hire contract with the collaborators on *The Wizard of Oz:* the writers were paid a fixed fee for their score, and that was it. Thanks to ASCAP, they retained the rights to the songs—sheet music, recordings, performances—but they had no rights in the film itself, nor in any of its future showings. The advent of television and the movie's popular and lucrative annual airings thus brought them no additional income. (Berlin himself, in contrast, had wisely sewn up the rights to his musicals before television was even dreamed of, controlling them to the degree that he could have prevented such broadcasts from airing at all if he had been so inclined.)

"Harold's taste," he continued, "is reflected in his [choice of] collaborators," among whom he singled out E. Y. Harburg and the cosmopolitan-folksy Johnny Mercer. Berlin praised Harburg's adroit way with words, though he disagreed heartily with his leftish politics; his favorite Mercer-Arlen song was "Blues in the Night."

He concluded with a last thought: "Harold has never written a cheap song; he has good talent, good taste, good feeling and no commercialism."

As was customary, Berlin subsequently fretted over what he had said in the interview. A month later, in June, after reading over his comments, he called the writer with revisions that were virtually identical to his original statements. He did, however, choose to eliminate his own view on the composer-versus-songwriter question: "Maybe Harold prefers to be called a composer. He is also a great songwriter. I am a songwriter. George Gershwin is the only songwriter I know who became a composer."

In the summer of 1960 he shortened his time in the Catskills to make himself available for further interviews. The next year would mark the fiftieth anniversary of "Alexander's Ragtime Band," and Helmy Kresa was put to work phoning musical-theater writers to arrange for coverage. Berlin enjoyed reminiscing about his Bowery days, about the personalities he had known, particularly the "Mayor of Chinatown," Chuck Connors. His memory for names, dates, and places was remarkably precise, and his office files could supply any other facts he needed.

He was quick and sharp, speaking, as always, in succinct, almost staccato sentences. At seventy-two, he was dapper and had taken on a little weight; his tightly combed hair was black. The "Alexander" anniversary came and went, but still the interviews continued, through the summer of 1961. On August 25, a writer noticed that he seemed livelier than ever, excited by something unmentioned.

Soon enough, the secret was out. In the Friday *Times* for September 1, 1961, Sam Zolotow published his scoop:

> *Mr. President* is the title of a new musical that is being written to Irving Berlin's songs by Howard Lindsay and Russel Crouse.
>
> The pivotal character is a President of the United States as he is finishing his second term and after he has left office. Those concerned insist the concept is not related to any President, living or dead, or to the family of a President.

The same team that had created *Call Me Madam,* including producer Leland Hayward, would work on *Mr. President.* When Zolotow asked why it had taken him so long—a decade—to return to Broadway, Berlin hedged a little, saying, "Most of the intervening time I have been waiting for an idea that excited me. Lindsay and Crouse have come up with that idea. And I am excited." He expected it would require about eight months to get the show to Broadway. And no, no actors had yet been chosen for the leads.

The enterprise had, in fact, been initiated by Berlin himself, as he told William Ewald in an interview before *Mr. President* opened in New York:

If you'll pardon me for quoting my own line, there's no business like show business—Broadway show business. Writing movie musicals is for the birds. They're just rehashes of old tripe cut to a formula. I needed the stimulation of doing something new for the theater, but I was scared to death to tackle it.

Several scripts that turned out to be big hits were submitted to me, but I told producers I was too old to commit myself to a project. I was using age as an excuse for my fear of failure, and you know what? I practically talked myself into a wheelchair.

But finally the need to feel vital again overcame my fear. I went to Leland Hayward, who produced *Call Me Madam,* and told him I wanted to do another show with Howard Lindsay and Russel Crouse, the great old pros who had written *Madam.*

In the deluge of articles that followed the announcement of the show's conception, the issue of Berlin's age was inevitably raised, as was that of the lofty degree of professionalism of all concerned. The latter would later be used as a stick to beat them with.

After Berlin spoke to him, Hayward arranged for a meeting with Lindsay and Crouse, then at work on a new play. "[We] told Irving about an idea we'd been kicking around a few years," Crouse confided to Ewald. "It dealt with the personal problems facing a President ending his second term and his daughter's love affair with a Secret Service man assigned to guard her. The story was so vague in our minds we didn't know if it would add up to anything."

The plot as it finally evolved was not so much vague as flaccid. It chronicles the final White House days, and some days after, of an outgoing president, Stephen Decatur Henderson, his young vivacious wife, Nell, and their frisky daughter, who eventually falls in love with a Secret Service operative. There is a troublesome son, who turns out well in the end. Out of office, the former President refuses a political appointment because of the attached strings. He does make a trip, promoting peace, around the world and even lands his plane in the Soviet Union without permission. The show ends on a happy, patriotic note.

Three days after the meeting Berlin came around with two comic songs, as he called them, one of which was unquestionably the future showstopper "The Secret Service."

"They were great songs," Crouse recalled, "as good as anything he's ever done. They hooked Lindsay and me into shelving the play [in favor of] the musical." They now had to fashion a book out of their admittedly "vague" story.

When there was enough to work from, Berlin climbed back into harness with youthful zest, writing songs, as he put it, "to the idea"—that is, with an eye to where the song fitted into the script and who sang it. He felt it was a good omen that Hayward had signed Joshua Logan to direct. The team of Berlin, Hayward, Lindsay, Crouse, and Logan arrived at a curious decision about their cast album (perhaps, at least in part, in deference to the *Call Me Madam* debacle). Cast-album sales could make millions for the record companies, which often moved to secure those rights by backing the musical itself. To retain full control, the *Mr. President* quintet resolved to back the show itself (to the tune of $400,000 to $500,000) rather than depend on financing from RCA Victor or Columbia, the most active players in the genre. The three companies were then asked to bid against each other for the recording rights. Goddard Lieberson, of Columbia, won by offering a 17 percent royalty on each album.

Being back at work was exhilarating that winter of 1961, the planning, the talks, new ideas for songs popping out of nowhere. Berlin at work was a happy Berlin. Then came the distressing news from Palm Springs, California; his longtime friend and happy collaborator, Moss Hart, died of a heart attack on December 20, at the age of fifty-seven.

As librettists and composer worked, excitement ran high, but by February of 1962, Hayward had little to report to the press beyond the dates for the Boston and Washington, D.C., tryouts and the tentative opening (on October 15) at an as-yet-unbooked theater in New York. He could not release the names of the leads because no one had been signed. In January, Nanette Fabray, en route to Rome from her home in Hollywood, had spent an hour with Lindsay, Crouse, and Berlin. The authors, she recounted to writer William Ewald, "began reading jokes and bits of the show off paper napkins, menus, envelopes, all sorts of things. And Irving hummed a couple of tunes—he doesn't hum very well. I was undecided. . . ."

The writers had hoped to cast Fabray in the role of the First Lady, but for the moment she chose to defer her decision and fly on to Italy. There was a touch of Jacqueline Kennedy in her demeanor, though the point was regularly made that no character in the show represented any real person. The actress had first garnered high praise in a major role in the 1947 period piece *High Button Shoes;* her most recent Broadway musical, *Make a Wish,* in which she had starred in 1951, had been a failure. Deserting the stage, she had made a second career for herself in television, notably on Sid Caesar's show. She also completed a film role in *The Band Wagon* as a librettist collaborating with her husband, played by Oscar Levant; released in the summer of 1953, the picture had been a huge hit.

Fabray would be a vivacious forty by the time *Mr. President* finally opened in New York (she also told Ewald that she decided to take the part of the President's wife only two days before rehearsals began). Remarkably, considering the demands of her profession—the dependence on sound cues, the need to synchronize with an orchestral backing—she overcame the obstacle of a major hearing loss, performing with a hearing aid hidden by her coiffure and never missing a cue.

By mid-February, Lindsay and Crouse had assembled more than a few fragments on odd bits of paper: they had completed seven scenes for the first act. Berlin, working from that, had finished several songs. Press frenzy over what seemed a monumental resurrection of a man over seventy, returning to work after a ten-year hiatus, generated constant interest, curiosity, and requests for interviews. Berlin agreed to participate in this publicity barrage, meeting interviewers in his office. Those granted access ranged from *Variety*'s Abel Green to the *Herald Tribune*'s John Crosby, who had not seen Berlin in years but found him "absolutely unchanged, still full of that galvanic energy, that gushing eager boyish charm."

Berlin was consistent in these encounters, easy enough since most reporters began with the same query: How did it feel to return to work after a ten-year layoff? In March he informed one interviewer, "I'll tell you better after I see the show. I feel very satisfied and gratified that I've been able to do it. I didn't dig into the trunk." By the end of that month, working at his estate in the Catskills, he would be able to tell a friend that he had written fifteen songs for the show.

Recurring themes ran through all the interviews: the return (inevitably; he confided to Crosby that initially, he "got awfully nervous"), his age, integrated shows, honest patriotism (he was sensitive to the student protests of the American role in Vietnam), and the massive advance ticket sales for *Mr. President.*

This last subject made him very uneasy. By April, even before auditions were scheduled, ticket sales were in excess of a million dollars (thanks primarily to theater parties, though box-office sales added to the take). Such sales would keep the show running until May of 1963, whatever the critics thought of it.

Since none of the leads' names had yet been announced, the sales had to be attributed to the involvement of Irving Berlin, Lindsay and Crouse, and Joshua Logan, professionals all. Berlin's reaction to the advance was typical: "I wouldn't pay a million dollars for something I haven't seen." As time went on, the figure mounted; by opening night in New York it was up to $2,500,000.

As for the age question, Berlin told Louis Calta of the *Times* that "age has nothing to do with it. The only thing that counts is how good the show will be when it opens in Boston. Twenty-four, sixty-four, or seventy-four makes no difference." Calta noted that the songwriter was "reluctant to discuss his appearance—not that he has any [thing to be ashamed of in that department]. But, he said that his weight was between 140 and 145 pounds and that it had been that way for 'many years.' He also admits that he has been 'pretty lucky with my hair.' "

This interview was conducted via telephone on Berlin's seventy-fourth birthday, just as he and his wife were leaving for the Catskills, where they planned to spend a few quiet days with the family at Livingston Manor (formerly Lewbeach), away from work and incommunicado. Calta was impressed by Berlin's graciousness. Despite his hurry, he told the reporter, "It's very kind of you to notice my birthday. I feel fine and am particularly pleased that I can keep going and that I'm working." His one complaint was insomnia, about which he spoke freely, confessing that since he had given up painting, fishing, and golfing, "the only thing I [have] to do [is] just liv[e] with a warm family—eating well, sleeping badly." He quipped that even when he managed to fall asleep one night, "I kept dreaming that I couldn't sleep."

The musical theater had changed drastically during Berlin's absence, a revolution often laid at the doorstep of Rodgers and Hammerstein's *Oklahoma!*, the quintessential "integrated" show, which had married song and music (and ballet) to plot and character all the way back in 1943. In fact, the trend had its origins in an even earlier production, Gershwin, Kaufman, and Ryskind's *Of Thee I Sing*, of 1931. And, too, in January 1941, Moss Hart's *Lady in the Dark*, a play with music (by Kurt Weill and Ira Gershwin), had boasted an intricately integrated score.

When reporter John Crosby brought up the subject in their interview, Berlin dismissed the notion of integration, a concept that annoyed him. "This time," he explained, "I've tried to write a little closer to the book. [But] I hate that term 'integrated score.' "

As he told a friend, "We tried to integrate the score. Everybody integrates. . . . All the ballads are woven into the score. . . . I tried to make them a part of the script—general songs that fit the situation. If you have a good song, you can integrate it into any show." He reiterated this point to Crosby, supplying an example from a familiar score: "It wouldn't be hard to integrate any of the songs from *My Fair Lady* in another show. One of the characters gets the urge to dance all night, and there you are." He did not want his songs to be so firmly threaded into the plot that they could not be sung, and enjoyed, outside the theater. And he hoped they would be popular, too: "Certainly I want hits. Hits represent that the song is good. What do you think scientists are trying to do, trying to be a failure?"

He was even more defensive on the topic of patriotism (and would be still more so after *Mr. President* opened). When Herbert Mitgang, interviewing him for the *New York Times Magazine,* asked, "Do [you] consider *Mr. President* a patriotic musical?" Berlin replied, a bit evasively, "We are showmen after all. . . . There is no special message except what may be an extra to the entertainment, and what comes through because of the sort of people we are."

Warming up to the subject, he reminded Mitgang that Lindsay and Crouse's Pulitzer Prize–winning *State of the Union* had itself been a political play, "and they are men with something to say. *Mr. President* is all about America. But put it this way: while we take a lot of things lightly, we take America seriously. . . .

"You can't sell patriotism unless people feel patriotic. For that matter, you can't sell people anything they don't want." He did not set out to write patriotic songs, he said; they just came to him. "I have the normal pride of any American when I see a [John] Glenn shooting up there in space; of course I'm proud and I'm rooting for him. But I don't think you can write songs about that—almost anything but, though some writers have tried."

Berlin deplored cynicism and felt that some recent musicals, not to mention popular songs, were short on love. "Perhaps," he suggested to John Chapman, an old acquaintance who was then writing for the *News,* "they [the songwriters] have become cynical in this cynical age. Or maybe they think love is too corny to write about. Sure, the words 'I love you' are corny, but there is no other way of saying it. You've got to say 'I love you.' . . . Songwriters are either ashamed of writing about love or incapable of it."

Early on in the writing of *Mr. President* he observed, "There is a cynicism about flag-waving and patriotism until something happens. 'God Bless America' for instance. It is simple, honest—a patriotic statement. It's an emotion, not just words and music." He enlarged on that idea: "A patriotic song *is* an emotion, and you must not embarrass an audience with it, or they'll hate your guts. It has to be right, and the time for it has to be right."

By March he had completed one such song, to be used as the show's finale. "Hats Off to America, It's a Great Country" (its title then) ends with the lines "If this be flag-waving,/ Do you know of a better flag to wave?" The word *flag-waving*—and the concept of corniness—would echo uncomfortably later in the year.

The April auditions filled in the cast, though neither a President nor a First Lady was announced; the initial concentration was upon the chorus and dancers. In Berlin's view, one of the major changes the American musical had undergone consisted in the greater emphasis on dancing, due largely to the influence of George Balanchine and Agnes de Mille. "When Sam Harris and I were auditioning dancers for a musical in the old days," he reminisced, "we didn't care if the kids could dance or not. We'd just line up a bunch of girls on the stage and ask each other, 'Which twelve are the best-looking?' It's incredible. We were auditioning dozens of dancers for *Mr. President* and the things those kids could do were unbelievable." One of those selected was the Hawaiian-born Wisa D'Orso, a former Aloha Airlines employee who had also been a professional hula dancer before winning a scholarship to study ballet. She would lead *Mr. President*'s corps de ballet (women's division) in a belly dance.

By the time the scheduled rehearsals began, on July 23, 1962, the cast was complete: Robert Ryan, not at all known for his singing, would play President Stephen Decatur Henderson, and Nanette Fabray would be Nell, his wife. Their daughter, Leslie, was to be portrayed by Anita Gillette, who had costarred with Ray Bolger in the previous season's *All American.* The part of the First Son, young, troublesome Larry, went to a newcomer named Jerry Strickler, who hailed from Goose Creek, Texas. Appearing as the Secret Service overseer of the President's daughter was radio and television personality Jack Haskell, in his Broadway debut.

When Ryan auditioned for Berlin and company in Hayward's office, he sang Kurt Weill and Maxwell Anderson's "September Song" (originally written for John Huston, himself not vaunted for his musical talents) in what was described as "a clean but tremulous baritone." In fact, his was a most pleasant voice, if not a powerful one.

"Berlin listened," Ryan later recalled, "and advised me not to take any singing lessons. He said, 'If you were any better, you'd be lousy.' "

On the appointed afternoon, the cast assembled to hear the score of *Mr. President* for the first time. An obviously anxious and tense Berlin emerged from the wings and removed his jacket, revealing a short-sleeved white shirt set off by a dark tie. Helmy Kresa took his place at the piano.

Crouse recalled that taut moment: "Boy, what a dramatic scene when the cast heard the score at the first rehearsal! Irving was as nervous as a cat up a tree, but after he had sung a score or more of numbers in that high, cracked voice, everybody broke into spontaneous applause."

And so the race was on. In early June, the book had still been "in work," though Crouse could report that "we've finished what we call a rehearsal script. . . . We'll continue writing all summer, which I assure you is no time for any sensible adult to be trying to write a play." He and Lindsay promised to have a fully realized libretto ready for the Boston tryout premiere on August 27. This did not bode well.

The first reviews made for dispiriting reading on August 28, a grim Wednesday. The collaborators' collective reaction was best encapsulated in a remark made by Crouse. They were all housed in Boston's Ritz-Carlton, Lindsay and Crouse on the eleventh floor and Berlin on the fifth. The librettists, after a stroll across the street in the Public Garden, went up to Berlin's suite, where they found him seated on the window ledge, posing for a photographer.

"Don't jump, Irving!" Crouse shouted. "Not yet!"

Of the major reviewers, only Elinor Hughes of the *Boston Herald* detected a measure of good in the show, remarking that if "it was not the unqualified smash hit that had been hoped for, it has a lot of good qualities." While conceding that the musical was "amusing in part," the *Globe*'s Cyrus Durgin also found it "to my taste sometimes cornily dull," though he admired Fabray, Ryan, and most of all Anita Gillette, with her show-stopping rendition of "The Secret Service."

The town's most powerful critic, Elliot Norton of the *Record American,* admitted that the score featured "at least three or four songs with the authentic lilt and magic of Irving Berlin at his magic best," but he felt (and rightly so) that the evening got bogged down in the second act. His fatal final word was, "*Mr. President* is in dreadful shape at the present time."

Producer Hayward quickly announced that rewriting was already under way. New lines, new jokes, and a couple of new songs were added. Berlin's contributions were "You Need a Hobby" and "Empty Pockets Filled with Love," the former inspired by a phrase he had heard frequently during his "retirement," and the latter a contrapuntal duet, the likes of which had perked up *Call Me Madam* in New Haven a dozen years before. Three other songs were jettisoned. There was no panic, just a sense of getting down to work. After averring that the critical reception, rather than knocking everyone for a loop, "only confirms what we, ourselves, thought we had to work on," Hayward concluded with *his* final word: "Critics don't know anything about musicals."

The evening after the show's premiere, director Joshua Logan crossed swords with critic Elliot Norton on the latter's television interview show. Logan was especially incensed by Norton's characterization of some of the Berlin songs as "corny."

Norton opened with a question: "Where were you last night? Were you in front or out back watching the show?"

"Well," Logan retorted, "it was obviously a different seat than yours." He then started right in on the subject of corn, saying, "Now the very [songs] you picked out as corny, I think you're going to find, are going to bore you to death because you're going to be hearing them for the rest of your life and the rest of your son's life! Because—because nobody dares to judge an Irving Berlin song on the first hearing. . . . He's a genius." To prove his point that Berlin was "a poet . . . a primitive poet," he recited the lyric to "Is He the Only Man in the World?," a simple, engaging waltz.

Norton rebutted with, "Well, what would you think of the circumstances? Now what I mean by 'corny' in that case is easy to define. I mean something that's embarrassingly sentimental and a little bit out of date." He reminded Logan that in his review, "I said that there were four or five of the best Berlin songs, [and] this is one."

Logan allowed that on this particular opening night, the show had not been ready, nor had the performers or even the audience itself. Nonetheless, "I just plain don't think you're right about [Mr. President]. I think our play is not in proper shape. I think we're overserious at times, but that is partly my fault, you know, for hitting too hard."

Here Norton broke in, "Directors make mistakes, too!"

"Well," Logan countered, "you know me! I've made some beauts. But oh, sure, we all make mistakes. Irving Berlin has thrown three songs out of the show that he didn't like."

Afterward, Logan stated that "there will be no radical changes made. Just the jiggering that happens constantly with every show out of town. If it's only ninety percent as good as it can be, this will be a great show."

Berlin himself was more laconic, musing, "What are Boston, New Haven, and Philadelphia for?"

Still, the "corny" tag irked him. Late in September, after the show had been "frozen" for the Washington opening—meaning that no more changes or additions could be made—Berlin spoke with Abel Green of *Variety*. He praised Lindsay and Crouse, pronounced himself pleased with the songs, and insisted that

we all feel it's a hit musical.

You read about Ethel Kennedy being in the [Boston] audience and liking the "First Lady" number and everything in general. Sure, we have kept changing since the opening night. I've punched up some comedy lyrics to make sure I get the laughs even stronger. Bits and pieces all throughout have been switched. . . .

[We] feel the show is timely, entertaining, emotional without being heavy. . . . If some of [my] songs are corny, then it's because they're simple, and all I know [is] that some of the corniest and simplest songs have lasted, be they "White Christmas" and "Easter Parade" or "My Old Kentucky Home."

He had been less upbeat earlier that month, in the middle of the tryout run, when he called a friend in New York to say in a strained, tired voice, "Come to Boston and see a show in trouble." But now, as the show settled into the National in Washington, his optimism returned. "The work we're doing may mean the difference between a two-year run and maybe a four-year run," he predicted. Despite the freeze, small changes were introduced, though it was important, he realized, "to know when to stop. It's better to come in with something ninety percent perfect than to fool around and spoil what we have."

The entire two-and-a-half-week Washington run of *Mr. President* was sold out (including standing room) before they left Boston. Opening night, September 25, was described by Marjorie Hunter, writing in the *New York Times,* as "one of the gayest . . . in Washington's history," a "Gala Benefit," according to the subhead of her article. The premiere performance was a benefit for the Lieutenant Joseph P. Kennedy, Jr. Institute and the Kennedy Child Study Center, a facility devoted to the study of mental retardation.

A hundred-dollar ticket entitled the purchaser to a pre-theater dinner party at one of various locations, including the home of Vice President and Mrs. Johnson, the Averell Harrimans' (the secretary of state served ham), or Chief of Protocol Angier Biddle Duke's (beef Stroganoff). After the final curtain, the ticket holders could enjoy a champagne supper dance under the Queen's Tent at the British Embassy. *Mr. President* was as conspicuous in the society pages of the *Washington Post* as in its entertainment section.

Berlin found it all "flattering, but . . . crazy." *Mr. President* had accumulated the greatest advance sale in the history of the theater (up to that time) and was more closely followed, both in the press and by theater people, than any production in years.

David Wise, in the *Post,* reported that on this second opening night

the real show was outside, under the marquee of the National [Theater], as each new political celebrity arrived Hollywood-style, stepping out of black limousines while bobby-soxers, held back by police barricades, squealed.

They squealed for Lyndon. They squealed for Lady Bird. They squealed for Ethel. And when Jackie stepped out onto the sidewalk they squealed with an abandon that would have turned Darryl F. Zanuck green with envy.

There was a show inside, too, before the curtain rose. In the Kennedy box, besides the real First Lady, were the President's sisters Jean and Pat and their respective husbands, Stephen Smith and Peter Lawford. Absent for the first act was the President himself, who would arrive during intermission.

The house glittered with generals, diplomats, politicians, and assorted Secretaries. Even a few New Yorkers attended, noted the *Times:* the Laurence Rockefellers, the Alfred Gwynn Vanderbilts, and the William Paleys. The knowledgeable audience enjoyed the quite gentle political barbs, tittering appropriately at lines such as, "In Washington the twist is a way of life." Berlin's "The Washington Twist" expands on this theme; the songwriter's nod to the present (in October 1961 a young Chubby Checker had swept the nation with his rock-and-roll hit/dance craze, "The Twist"), it is emblematic of the musical's new, younger President, newly installed, like Kennedy, in the White House. The show's outgoing administration, more Eisenhowerishly sedate, has a very different anthem: "Let's Go Back to the Waltz."

While it was virtually impossible to confuse Robert Ryan with John Kennedy, in a couple of scenes Nanette Fabray came close to suggesting his wife, Jacqueline—when she appeared in a very Jackie-like wig, for example, only to doff it onto a bust of George Washington, or when she took a turn atop an elephant on a goodwill tour (ignoring a "Yankee Go Home" sign in the background), as the real First Lady had done the previous March in India. Then, too, Fabray's song "They Love Me" was one Mrs. Kennedy herself might have sung after her return from Pakistan later in the month.

Washingtonians, and just about everyone else, tried to identify the characters in this musical roman à clef (the opening number, sung by the Manager, disclaims that any of them is based on anyone—the Trumans, the Eisenhowers, or the Kennedys—but who wanted to believe *that*?). The audience, according to reporter Hunter of the *Times,* showed its appreciation "with spontaneous applause. But many first-nighters agreed that the show dragged in spots." So now *everyone* was a critic—but the paid practitioners of that profession had to concur, in this instance, with the amateurs. It was becoming unanimous.

After the Washington reviews were in, the New York box office nonetheless managed to take in an additional $50,000. Berlin, besides deploring his sleep habits and the "fuss" made about his age, remained sanguine. He believed that "all the hoopla" early on had placed them at a disadvantage, since audiences, he told John Keating of the *New York Times* while the show was still in Washington, expected "nothing less than a miracle."

> Now, the news that we weren't received so warmly by the critics out of town may work to our advantage. The New York audiences may not expect the miraculous. And instead of a built-in resentment that any pre-sold show is bound to run into, they may be willing to come and judge us on our own merits.
>
> Maybe I shouldn't say this. Maybe my colleagues wouldn't agree with me. But speaking for myself, I don't think we have a Pulitzer Prize show, or a Critics Circle Award show. I do think we have a show that audiences will love. Of course, it would be nice if the critics liked us, too.

Then he added, somewhat ruefully, "And I wouldn't turn down a Pulitzer Prize or a Critics Award."

At the British Embassy party after the Washington premiere, he was sitting quietly with Ellin when Crouse's daughter Lindsay, then about fourteen (and later to become well known in her own right, as an actress), invited him to dance. He did well enough until the beat switched to a favorite of the current residents of the White House, "The Twist." He might be able to write 'em, but he couldn't dance 'em; he took Miss Crouse back to her table.

The next day, a gloomy Berlin read the latest reviews. Although the dreaded adjective *corny* appeared more than once, the score fared better than the book. Crouse entered his suite and had the final word in Washington: "Well, Irving, *you* can't complain."

Then it was back to Beekman Place, where, at least, when he couldn't sleep, he could not sleep in his own bed. Besides, during one of those wakeful nights in Washington, he had begun thinking about the *next* show, "a germ of an idea for Ethel Merman."

Still, he couldn't help but be apprehensive about New York, and *Mr. President*'s *real* premiere. "It's going to be a rough weekend," he admitted to interviewer William Ewald. "The opening is on a Saturday night. So we'll have to wait an extra day for the reviews. . . . In the old days I used to go crazy over the weekend until I got reports on a new show. I'm still getting butterflies waiting for the verdict on this one."

That verdict, principally, would be "guilty."

Variety's appraiser summed up the trade consensus in two sentences, his first, "There are no miracles," and his last, "It's a disappointing show." Some of the gentle, even kind words between those critical pillars ultimately damned *Mr. President* as an "undistinguished show by distinguished people." As for the songs, "it remains to be seen whether there's anything in this new show with the stature or durable appeal of past top Berlin songs."

John McClain began his review for the *Journal-American* with the damaging declaration, "There is just no way to be charitable about *Mr. President*." Its top talents had joined forces to create, "quite simply, an old-fashioned dud." McClain conceded, however, that some of the songs harked back "to the old Berlin genius: 'In Our Hide-Away' is sweet and compelling; 'Meat and Potatoes' is singable[?] and 'The Secret Service' is cute." The list continued: " 'Is He the Only Man in the World?' is a pleasant waltz; 'Empty Pockets Filled with Love' is danceable[?] and 'You Need a Hobby' is a charming novelty." He did not much care for the patriotic (or "chauvinistic," as one critic called it) "This Is a Great Country"; few did. In a final insult-upon-injury that must have galled Berlin no end, McClain charged, "They [Berlin, Lindsay, Crouse, and Logan] give corn a bad name."

Walter Kerr, writing in the *Herald Tribune,* hated to do it but nevertheless panned the show in his daily review and followed that up with a Sunday essay on how *not* to write a musical, using *Mr. President* as a case study. (He had learned the lesson himself in 1958 with *Goldilocks,* written in collaboration with his wife, Jean, and scored by Leroy Anderson and Joan Ford. After that flop, he concentrated on criticism, most of it both perceptive and literate.)

In his "Broadway Scorecard" for the show, historian Steven Suskin tabulated no raves, no favorable reviews, one mixed, one unfavorable, and five pans—enough to kill *two* shows. And that was just the dailies.

The weekly magazines, which reached beyond New York to vast hinterlands where the *Times,* the *Herald Tribune,* and the *Journal-American* were rarely read, joined in the doleful chorus. *Time,* the most powerful, likened *Mr. President*'s premiere to the "maiden voyage of the S.S. *Titanic*" and twisted the knife in its weekly capsule listings by labeling it the "worst musical on Broadway."

Several reviewers employed the ubiquitous *corn,* though it was not always clear whether this starchy vegetable described the songs or the book. Once again, Lindsay and Crouse took the brunt of the abuse: their libretto was savaged in every review, while the critics tended to give Berlin the benefit of the doubt. If the songs were not from the composer's top drawer, they allowed, at least a song here, a song there, or a funny lyric line raised the score above the hapless book.

The second act, where the book did fall apart, was musically enlivened by "The Washington Twist" and "The Only Dance I Know (Song for Belly Dancer)," the latter a Logan touch that, as McClain noted, featured a "belly dancer . . . and some of the most frightening companions this side of Minsky [the raunchy old burlesque-house proprietor]." One of the act's five reprises (filling musical holes big enough to drive a motorcade through) was the show's outstanding ballad, "Don't Be Afraid of Romance." The finale was the flag-waver "This Is a Great Country," an almost defensive and seemingly personal statement that alienated a number of critics even as it made for a stirring conclusion to the show.

Some problems, though, even a Berlin song couldn't cure—not even a reprised one. Of a particularly baffling plot device, Walter Kerr asked, "Why the belly dancer?" He reviewed the librettists' strategy: "Have the President's son bring one to a Washington party and introduce her as a princess; have five more [dancers] appear at a small-town fair, while prizes are being awarded for jellies and jams." The sheer aimlessness of it all appalled him, as did the unlikely coincidence. The writers, he charged, despite their patent skills, "vacillate nervously [between] the desperately obvious and the desperately fantastic."

Why all this fuss about a simple musical that did not quite work? It had its bright moments, and a capable cast (Nanette Fabray was its most admired member; Howard Taubman of the *Times* called her the show's "savior"). Had the advance ticket sale not climbed to a record-breaking $2,700,000, would such microscopic critical scrutiny have been applied? Probably not. The watch fires had been lighted the previous September, when Berlin came out of retirement after ten years; and then there was his age, seventy-four. Lindsay was almost his exact contemporary, and Crouse, at sixty-nine, not much younger; Logan was only fifty-four, but everyone knew *he* went off the deep end from time to time. *Mr. President* was the most talked-about, speculated-about musical since the problematic *Camelot* in 1960, and for many of the same reasons. Could they do it again? First Lerner and Loewe, now Berlin and company.

In retrospect, after nearly four decades, is the score of *Mr. President* as substandard as the majority of critics claimed? Based on its cast album (available on compact disk), minus the book, the answer is a qualified no. Nanette Fabray is effervescent; Ryan's inoffensive baritone is well miked; Anita Gillette comes across effectively as a spirited, headstrong young woman; and Jack

Haskell is unfortunate enough to get stuck, for want of a better word, with a pair of folksy, I'm-just-a-regular-guy numbers, "Pigtails and Freckles" and "Meat and Potatoes" (not one of Berlin's better titles). These two, and perhaps Ryan's "It Gets Lonely in the White House," along with "This Is a Great Country," were undoubtedly among the songs that some regarded as corny. On the whole, however, *Mr. President* offers up a typical Irving Berlin score, at once sentimental ("Let's Go Back to the Waltz"), lively ("The First Lady"), and, yes, at a time when the new styles of popular song were invading the music industry and the theater, even old-fashioned. Berlin would have been the first to admit that.

He was not happy with the critical reception, of course, but he did not, despite intimations to the contrary, slip into a deep depression, give up, and retreat into curmudgeonly isolation.

The show creaked along for 265 performances (less than the run of *Miss Liberty*), to close in June of 1963, a month after Berlin's seventy-fifth birthday. He and Ellin quietly went to the country for May 11, "not to celebrate," as he put it, but to escape the appeals for interviews and the phone in general. Back at the office, Hilda Schneider fielded and put off all callers. The occasion was marked with music on radio and television, but to Berlin it was by now just a date.

He had already begun his next assignment, initiated late in 1962, after *Mr. President* opened, by Arthur Freed. As past president of the Screen Producers Guild, Freed had been appointed chairman of the Milestone Award dinner at the Beverly Hilton Hotel, and in that capacity he had convinced the committee to present Berlin with the Guild's most prestigious Laurel Award, on March 3, 1963. In tribute, Los Angeles Mayor Sam Yorty declared it "Irving Berlin Day." Professional toastmaster George Jessel was to introduce the speakers for the evening—Stanley Adams (president of ASCAP), Samuel Goldwyn, Jack Warner, and Adolph Zukor—and Frank Sinatra had promised to sing.

This was an impressive honor indeed (it was heralded by the Guild as the "Greatest Milestone Award Ever"), but as Freed's biographer Hugh Fordin noted, the producer "had a difficult time persuading [Berlin] to come out [west] for the dinner." In time he relented, however, and flew out with Ellin to attend the big event. On Irving Berlin Day, Los Angeles radio stations broadcast twenty-four hours of his songs. The evening itself came off well, bringing a reunion with Ginger Rogers followed by a gathering around an upright piano with Dinah Shore and other Hollywood lights, among them Rosalind Russell and Yvette Mimieux, a new Metro/Freed Unit star.

"Arthur produced the affair very beautifully," Berlin told Fordin, admitting, "It was very emotional." But Freed had more than nostalgia on his mind. He came to the point later in the evening: he wished to produce an Irving Berlin film biography, an idea that Berlin himself, despite the emotional atmosphere, dismissed out of hand. He had seen other such movies distort the lives and careers of his friends—Gershwin, Kern, Porter—beyond all recognition; the only "biopic" of a songwriter he had ever approved of was *Yankee Doodle Dandy,* devoted to the career and songs of another friend, George M. Cohan.

No, he said, there would be no film biography (in fact, he decreed, no biography at all) while he was still around. Undeterred, Freed took another tack: How about a musical spanning decades, in which the songs would serve to define the time frame? That sounded better—if not terribly original—to Berlin; it would be almost a form of artificial integration. He knew that Freed would assemble a top cast and crew of writer, musical director, and all-important film director. For the latter two, he could call on the best in the business: Vincente Minnelli to direct, and Roger Edens to tend to the music.

Berlin proposed *Say It with Music* as a title; if the details could be worked out, he would place his catalog at Freed's disposal and also supply a few new songs. Contract negotiations would, as always, be a time-consuming process; Freed once half joked that it took longer for him to sew up a Berlin contract than it did for Berlin himself to write the score.

Sadly, the project that began with such high hopes (at least on Freed's part) would ultimately come to nothing. If *Mr. President* had been a prolonged ordeal with a fretful conclusion, the *Say It with Music* experience would prove an interminable study in frustration, with a fruitless ending.

Soon after the Guild's dinner, Berlin turned over the negotiations with Metro's legal staff to his attorney, George Cohen, though he himself would remain close by to keep a wary eye on things and offer tactical advice. Cohen initially informed Freed that Berlin wanted a million dollars to work on the film. Freed took his terms to Metro's new president, Robert O'Brien, who had come from the New York headquarters of M-G-M's parent company, Loew's, Inc. Unbeknownst to Berlin, and even, for a time, to Freed, O'Brien's arrival had ushered in the era of the bookkeeper: innocent (or ignorant) of *how* movies were made, the neophyte studio head was concerned with what they cost and, more important, what they took in at the box office.

When Freed submitted Cohen's offer, O'Brien responded with the equivalent of "I'll get back to you." Then, instead of dealing with the matter personally, he handed it off to the studio's legal department, which made Berlin a counteroffer: 25 percent of the profits. That was quickly rejected, Cohen being well versed in what was known as creative bookkeeping, where profits began being totaled up only *after* all the costs were wiped out—something that might never happen, even if the film was a hit.

And so it went, back and forth, through the rest of March and into April, with Berlin reiterating that he would make his catalog available and come up with six new songs. In exchange, Cohen asked for 10 percent of the *gross,* with no advance. Berlin envisioned a major film, with a budget of six million dollars (as he would later reveal to Hugh Fordin); waiving his customary advance would, he knew, make it easier on Freed's bottom line, then a critical concern at Metro.

Agent Irving P. Lazar (best known as Swifty, and for very good reason, though Shifty might have done as well) was in Freed's office one day when Berlin arrived with a package in hand. "It was obvious that he had a portfolio of music," Lazar recalled.

"What's that?" Freed asked. Some songs for *Say It with Music,* he was told.

"I've got to hear them," Freed insisted.

When Berlin demurred, saying he did not want anyone to hear the songs yet, Lazar assumed that the real reason for his reticence was something other than modesty: Freed's office had a standard piano, without a shifting keyboard, so the untutored songwriter could not (so thought Swifty) play for them. (In fact, he could have done fine using just the black keys.) Finally, however, more pleading by Freed induced Berlin to take a song from the envelope and sing it for the audience of two to his own accompaniment.

"The way Berlin sold a song was unique," Lazar remembered. "He would lean his face within an inch of yours and sing it to you. Well, he sang the song and some others and Freed bought the score for a million dollars. He was the first to sell a score for a million."

Later, over lunch at Romanoff's, Lazar upbraided Berlin. "Why do you go around selling your own stuff?" he demanded. "Why don't you have me as your agent—it's more dignified. . . . [The way you're going about it is] so cheap, so second-rate."

Berlin studied his face for a moment. "Listen," he said, "if you were me, would you hire you to be my agent?"

"No," Lazar admitted.

"So what are you bothering me for?" Subject closed. Lazar did well enough representing Ira Gershwin, Burton Lane, and Harold Arlen, among others.

Near the end of April, the various lawyers at last reached an agreement: Berlin was promised the million dollars he had asked for in the first place. On the thirtieth, Metro announced that *Say It with Music* would be undertaken by the Freed Unit at some future date. Optimistically, Berlin had begun writing songs that he believed would work in any picture they might make, among them the enticingly titled "The Ten Best Undressed Women in the World." He, Freed, and Minnelli met with O'Brien and production chief Robert Weitman, and he performed some of the songs; Weitman's take on "Undressed Women" was that it could not be used because the censors would object to it. (Historian Fordin's parenthetical reaction to this was a disbelieving "This was 1963!" In 1962, *Lawrence of Arabia* had won the Academy Award for Best Picture despite its containing, among other things, a scene implying homosexual rape; in 1963 *Tom Jones,* a very rakish romp, would take home the prize.)

However dubiously, and however haltingly, the old team was nonetheless on its way again. Late in June Arthur Laurents, the first of the film's several eventual writers, was assigned to turn out a screenplay of his own design. Although Laurents was better known on Broadway, for such dramas as *Home of the Brave* and *Time of the Cuckoo* and the librettos for *Gypsy* and *West Side Story,* he had also done the film adaptation of Leonard Bernstein's modern retelling of *Romeo and Juliet.* Released in 1961, the movie version of *West Side Story* had been a major money-maker and an Academy Award winner.

With work under way on the script, and some of his score already finished, Berlin left Hollywood for New York, and in September he and Ellin flew to London to see their daughter Elizabeth marry Edmund Fisher. During his spirited interview with the *Daily Express*'s Herbert Kretzmer, Berlin confirmed the making of *Say It with Music* and revealed that he was in the process of writing ten new songs for the film.

The Berlins were back in New York by the time Laurents submitted his screenplay, as recorded in Fordin's files, on November 26, 1963. His plot had male lead Robert Goulet—then noted only for his nightclub vocalizing and his turn as Lancelot in the troubled (but hit) musical *Camelot*—romancing a series of beautiful women in various countries: Sophia Loren in Italy, Brigitte Bardot in France, Julie Andrews in England, and Ann-Margret in the United States.

The questions at once arose: Was Irving Berlin expected to supply indigenously suitable songs for each nationality? Would the film be shot on location (expensive) or on Metro's lot? These concerns were rendered academic when Laurents's script was rejected and the film put on hold while the search for a new writer began.

Freed returned to *Say It with Music* the next year, after he himself received the 1964 Milestone Award and his contract with M-G-M was renewed. During the hiatus, in March, Berlin became involved in a lawsuit against the irreverent, often sophomoric *Mad* magazine, which had published the following lyric:

> *Louella Schwartz*
> *Describes her malady*
> *To anyone in sight.*
> *She will complain*
> *Dramatize every pain.*
> *And then she'll wail*
> *How doctors fail*
> *To help her sleep at night.*

The words fitted the tune of "A Pretty Girl Is like a Melody" perfectly, and Berlin (or his attorneys, notably Simon Rifkind) branded it the "worst kind of piracy"—to wit, "piracy on the high C's." It was, from the beginning, a hopeless case. *Mad* was guilty only of parody, not plagiarism: neither the music nor Berlin's lyric was published in the magazine. Judge Irving R. Kaufman ruled that the parody had merely borrowed from the original, "a tribute to feminine beauty," and modified it "into a burlesque of a feminine hypochondriac" (was it only a coincidence that Louella's malady was insomnia?). Kaufman concluded, "We doubt that even so eminent a composer as Irving Berlin should be permitted to claim a propietary interest in iambic pentameter."

Unsatisfied, Rifkind and company would take the case all the way to the state supreme court, which would finally deny their appeal in October 1964.

Meanwhile, Arthur Freed had found a new writer for *Say It with Music:* Leonard Gershe, a friend, and collaborator, of the Freed Unit's musical stalwart Roger Edens (they had together concocted the "Born in a Trunk" sequence that was inserted into Judy Garland's *A Star Is Born,* much to the dismay of the score's authors, Harold Arlen and Ira Gershwin). A playwright and lyricist, Gershe had written the screenplay for Fred Astaire and Audrey Hepburn's 1957 success, *Funny Face,* and had even doctored some of Ira Gershwin's lyrics from the original (more dismay). He and Edens had also composed several quite good songs that were added to the Gershwin score.

Gershe delivered his script to Freed late in May 1965; two years had now slipped by since the project's launch. According to Fordin, Berlin liked Gershe's draft and was inspired to add another original tune to the score. One day, deciding to demonstrate the new number for a visitor, he called Helmy

Kresa into his office, a spacious room whose walls were covered with his paintings and photographs of his family. He had taken his original, battered Buick out of storage and kept it in repair and tuned (as he explained, "I like to keep it around the office; I love working on it"), but Kresa went to the other, more recent piano, also equipped with a special movable keyboard.

Strangely, Berlin was unaware that his musical assistant's right hand was hampered by arthritis (why he did not know this is a mystery). When Kresa began the introduction of "I Used to Play It by Ear," Berlin cupped his hands in the direction of his guest, then said, "Helmy, stop; you left a note out of that chord." Obviously he was not the musical ignoramus of legend.

Kresa explained his predicament, revealing his curled fingers. Berlin sympathized, "Oh, too bad," and then Kresa continued, as best he could. Berlin sang what was probably the last song written for *Say It with Music.*

Meanwhile, back at Metro, O'Brien rejected the Gershe screenplay and demanded another. Next up was the brilliant team of Betty Comden and Adolph Green, primarily lyricists but also scriptwriters (*Singin' in the Rain* and *The Band Wagon*). Their screenplay—the third in as many years—was written with Fred Astaire and Julie Andrews in mind for the leads; it was turned in on February 17, 1966. Berlin soon pronounced it *the* one.

Taking Berlin's musical output as its inspiration, their story ranged over half a century. "Three stories were told simultaneously," Hugh Fordin recorded, "jumping back and forth from one to the other, 1911 [the year of "Alexander's Ragtime Band"], 1925 [the Music Box Revues] and 1965, carrying out the thesis that no matter how times change, human relationships and the need for love remain."

Times might have changed in the larger world, but not, it seemed, at Robert O'Brien's Metro-Goldwyn-Mayer: the Comden-Green screenplay was rejected, and a new script undertaken by George Wells, a Metro veteran and specialist in musicals and comedies. *His* attempt was submitted on Irving Berlin's seventy-eighth birthday, by which time Berlin was preoccupied with a revival of *Annie Get Your Gun,* set to open at Lincoln Center's New York State Theater on May 31, 1966. In this presentation, produced by the theater's president, Richard Rodgers, Ethel Merman would portray an Annie twenty years older than in the original production. At fifty-seven, she proved amazingly sprightly; Rodgers marveled that she had "possibly more energy than ever."

Berlin, in his by-now-mandatory birthday interview, told a *Times* reporter, "For a guy who keeps having birthdays it becomes damn boring." Of Merman's reprise of her role as Annie Oakley, he said, "She can play it till she's ninety, and I hope she does." He made a special point of reminding his interviewer that he was working on a musical for Metro.

The revived *Annie* was once again a smash. For this new production, Berlin had written two new songs, "Take It in Your Stride" (a casualty of the six-week Toronto tryout) and "An Old-Fashioned Wedding," sung by Merman and her latest Frank Butler, Bruce Yarnell. Yet another Berlin contrapuntal duet, it served the usual function—as a "showstopper," in Rodgers's estimation. The show was greeted in New York by one reviewer's hailing, "Welcome back Annie. Goodbye Dolly. Move over Mame. From now on, it's every girl for herself." Berlin was especially pleased to read the *Times*'s verdict: "It's Tin Pan Alley all right but out of the top drawer."

For the songwriter, it was a happy reunion. Merman was as snappy and raunchy as ever as they exchanged quips and stories. One evening after a rehearsal Berlin gleefully called Harold Arlen, a steady confidant, to tell him of one bit of raillery that had turned bawdy when Merman told him, "If you can get it up, Irving, I can get it in."

With *Say It with Music* back in rewrite, he had been pondering a new Broadway musical to be entitled *East River*, conceived as a quasi-autobiographical show. As he had explained to the *Times* reporter covering his birthday, "Most of my life I've lived near the East River downtown. I'm a little farther uptown, but we see the same tugboats and ships." The plot would probably have traced his alter ego's rise from the Bowery to a town house in, say, Beekman Place. He completed one fine idiomatic song with Hebraic touches, "Wait Until You're Married," but never got much further.

Encouraging word now came from the Coast. With the Wells screenplay in hand, Freed informed the *Hollywood Reporter* that the film, presently in its final planning stages, would be the "greatest physical [*sic*] musical ever made. It will cover all of Irving Berlin's career with his songs to be used in medley, ballet, . . . vocal and imaginative forms." With Astaire still penciled in as the star-to-be, the extravaganza (now budgeted at a whopping $10 million) was scheduled to begin production "late in 1967."

Needless to say, that did not occur.

There was another letdown that year. Despite the inroads made into the music and recording businesses by rock and roll, the more traditional record producers continued to release albums by the classic greats of American popular song—Kern, Gershwin, Porter—often in lush orchestrations conducted by Kostelanetz, Percy Faith, Melachrino, and others. The smaller independent companies meanwhile made a cottage industry of producing collections comprising these songwriters' lesser-known efforts.

Soon after the *Annie Get Your Gun* revival opened, with Berlin now back in the news with a hit show and song, Goddard Lieberson of Columbia Records expressed an interest in producing a set of four or five long-playing disks of Berlin's best work, sumptuously boxed. The package would include a hardcover book and a bonus recording featuring an interview with the composer as well as a couple of vocals, among them "God Bless America" (on which Berlin was to be accompanied by a chorus of Girl and Boy Scouts). Lieberson's plan was to cover the entire Berlin oeuvre with a hundred songs interpreted by various stars, many associated in one way or another with the songs.

To be titled either . . . *The Melody Lingers On* . . . or *Always,* followed by a facsimile of Berlin's signature, the collection was to have been a typical Lieberson production. The past master of the original-cast album, he had also initiated the concept of recording the complete Bartók string quartets, Stravinsky conducting his own works, and a survey of the compositions of Arnold Schönberg.

It was around this time that rock and roll finally caught up with Irving Berlin. In June 1967 the Beatles' album *Sergeant Pepper's Lonely Hearts Club Band* dominated the charts, along with other rock and rhythm-and-blues LPs. Columbia had serious second thoughts about "Project X," as the Berlin enterprise was known around his office (for reasons unknown, its planning and, particularly, his participation were a deep secret). Lieberson was kicked upstairs to the board of CBS, and a new executive was put in charge of Artists and Repertory at Columbia, with instructions to tap into the youth market and tighten up on the classical end and the traditional songs of the past. Project X was summarily canceled.

The *Say It with Music* saga dragged on. On January 22, 1968, the *Los Angeles Times* published a statement attributed to Robert H. O'Brien, announcing that "one of the biggest and most important musicals in the history of M-G-M, Irving Berlin's *Say It with Music,* will star Julie Andrews under the direction of Blake Edwards [her husband]." To be filmed in 70-millimeter format, in Super Panavision, it would be a reservation-only release. The press item contained an ominous sentence: "The spectacular musical will be coproduced by Arthur Freed and Blake Edwards" (Roger Edens, who had in the past frequently served as coproducer on Freed's films, had left Metro). O'Brien's final word was that the film would "go before the cameras at M-G-M's Culver City studios in early 1969 [a year hence!] with an all-star cast—one of the largest array of musical talents assembled for one motion picture."

Later that year, in May, a *fifth* screenplay was prepared by George Axelrod, a comedy specialist (*The Seven-Year Itch, Will Success Spoil Rock Hunter?*) who had also written the dramatic *Manchurian Candidate.* By then Berlin was extremely busy.

He would turn eighty on May 11 and had agreed to cooperate with television producer Ed Sullivan on a birthday tribute to air on Sunday, May 5, 1968. The elaborate show would bring together Bing Crosby, Ethel Merman, the Peter Gennaro Dancers, Robert Goulet, and Diana Ross and her Supremes (the up-to-the-minute touch of Motown was no doubt intended to appeal to the "youth market").

Sullivan's Sunday-night program was the most popular on television. A remarkable showman, he effectively brought back vaudeville with a variety hour whose acts ranged from Maria Callas to Elvis Presley, from Harry Belafonte to the Beatles, from acrobats to comics to magicians. For the Berlin salute, his usual hour was extended to ninety minutes.

Berlin agreed to help promote the event by doing interviews. In speaking with Phyllis Battelle, he plugged the still-in-the-works *Say It with Music* and then turned once again to the subject of patriotism. He insisted that the success of "God Bless America" owed more to the timing of its introduction than to its sentiment: "It was a very ordinary patriotic song that any child could have written . . . 'Land that I love'—what child couldn't write that? It was the timing that counted."

"White Christmas," his biggest hit, was, he told Battelle, "a publishing business in itself." He debunked "this legendary stuff about great inspirations in popular song writing. If you're a professional, you sit down and write, and you've got to be realistic and recognize how good you are and how bad you can be." He admitted that he himself had produced some bad songs along with the good, but he prided himself on being able to recognize which was which. He wrote only Irving Berlin songs, not necessarily following the latest fad, which might come and go so quickly (or, all too often, not quickly enough). He recounted an apposite anecdote: an unnamed producer (who cannot have been Freed) once listened to some songs he had written and was dissatisfied with all of them. Considering Berlin's always high fee, he asked, "Don't you have something fresh?"

"What am I," Berlin snapped, "a baker?"

Promotion accomplished, the Sullivan evening was an enormous success. It opened with a taped introduction by President Lyndon Johnson, who proclaimed America the "richer for [Berlin's] presence"; then Crosby proceeded to sing young Izzy's first published song, "Marie from Sunny Italy," and a few others, among them "White Christmas." There were clips from several films, and the Supremes did a half dozen or more Berlin tunes in their mechanical, gesturing Motown fashion. Robert Goulet, once touted to star in *Say It with Music,* appeared to croon one of the numbers from that score, "I Used to Play It by Ear," and the Gennaro Dancers treated the audience, including Ellin and Irving Berlin, to an athletic interpretation of "This Is the Army, Mr. Jones."

Saved for last—the "evening's showstopper," in the opinion of the *Times*'s George Gent—was Merman, "who once again brought down the house with a medley from *Annie Get Your Gun.*" But the real climax was yet to come: Berlin himself was coaxed onstage to sing "God Bless America," accompanied by a large chorus of Girl and Boy Scouts (whose organizations were supported in part by the song's royalties). Sullivan brought out a huge cake ablaze with eighty candles, to waves of applause for the smiling honoree. "Schmaltz?" Gent asked, and answered, "Certainly. But it was a marvelous party."

The celebration was not yet over, however. On his actual birthday, with Ellin beside him, Berlin was driven in an open convertible to the Sheep Meadow in Central Park, preceded by the Silver Beach Fife and Drum Corps, a children's marching band from the Bronx. In attendance at a special Field Day hosted by the Girl Scout Council of Greater New York were some eight thousand Scouts, who, the *Times* reported, waved miniature American flags and "cheered and squealed" when the songwriter arrived. Kitty Carlisle Hart, widow of Moss, and herself an old friend of Berlin's, led the girls in singing "Happy Birthday."

A stage had been erected in the meadow, and after the birthday song, Berlin mounted the stairs and took the microphone to say, "There have been many high spots, but this is it!" The Girl Scouts then joined him in a rendition of "God Bless America." When Mayor John Lindsay turned up later to greet the Scouts, the eight thousand voices welcomed him with another chorus of the song.

This latest round of excitement finally over, the Berlins left for the Catskills for a month.

Early 1969 came and went, but nothing happened on *Say It with Music.* Metro began the year in upheaval: Edgar M. Bronfman, of the Seagrams Distilleries in Canada, managed to acquire control of M-G-M, and O'Brien was appointed chairman of the board. The president of the studio was now Lewis F. Polk, whose qualifications for the job seem to have consisted in his having once worked in Minneapolis for General Mills. By mid-1969 Metro was in deep financial trouble and suffering heavy losses. Millionaire Kirk Kerkorian (a Las Vegas real estate tycoon) moved in and acquired large amounts of stock; by autumn he succeeded in gaining control of the studio. Soon Polk was out and John T. Aubrey, Jr. (once head of production at CBS), in as president. Aubrey at once set about dismantling Metro-Goldwyn-Mayer, and one of the first properties to go was *Say It with Music.* Freed himself would leave the following year.

Berlin was paid his million dollars; he had furnished a complete score. But as he told Fordin, he would much rather "they had made the picture. And they could have. It was to be Arthur's and my swan song in motion pictures. But those civilians, as I call them—the guys in New York—making decisions that should have been made by Arthur Freed. They were stupid!"

The songs that Aubrey let get away were good Berlin, a far cry from the typically hedonistic pop tunes of the sixties (though one song the songwriter did like at the time was the Beatles' "Michelle," with its decidedly Kernish melody). Berlin never followed the crowd but always remained true to himself. The stylish "Is He the Only Man in the World?" (from 1962's *Mr. President*) could just as well have been written by the Irving Berlin of the midtwenties, reigning Waltz King of the Jazz Age, though in fact it was written in 1954 and probably intended for *White Christmas.*

Of the dozen or so songs composed for *Say It with Music,* "I Used to Play It by Ear," "Outside of Loving You, I Like You" (an ingenious sentiment), and the lovely "Whisper It" are most worthy of him. Their lyrics are simple, never self-consciously clever, and their melodies graceful, as always.

"They" *were* stupid: Metro ceased to exist. But Berlin's songs live on.

CODA:

A HUNDRED AND ONE

IN THE TWO DECADES following the protracted scuttling of *Say It with Music,* Irving Berlin's life unfolded as a succession of birthdays, awards, tributes, obscurity, and even neglect. As May elevenths inexorably accumulated, once each year a volley of attention would be directed his way; even if he dodged it, columnists would invariably mark the date. As he moved into his high nineties, they became punctual to a fault, their readers often expressing surprise at learning that Irving Berlin was still alive.

Every year around birthday time—until 1983, when her health became more precarious and he turned ninety-five—the Berlins would slip away to their estate in the Catskills for a quiet few days, often with their daughters and grandchildren. In 1969, however, he chose to remain at home a great deal, painting, though he did not stay away from the office, coming in several times a week. He met friends and colleagues there since it was more central than his home on the East River. He was, it must be noted, not nearly as reclusive, inactive, or bad-tempered as some writers, rejected and disgruntled, portrayed him at the time.

Under the sharp eye of the faithful, tough Hilda Schneider, the office functioned smoothly. While batteries of attorneys and accountants attended to permissions requests, contracts, and Berlin's real estate holdings, his good friend A. L. Berman, a show-business veteran and sometime representative for Harold Arlen and Ethel Merman, among others, handled the "God Bless

America" Fund and oversaw his interest in the Music Box, held in partnership with the Shubert Organization (the founding brothers were by now long gone).

From Beekman Place, Berlin was in daily contact with Hilda on business matters and available when needed. She also served as a sort of switchboard operator for his friends. Although he was out of the limelight, his name surfaced regularly with the revival of the Astaire-Rogers films and others—*Holiday Inn* especially—on television. Then, too, Easter and Christmas were always bustling times at the Irving Berlin Music Corporation, whose offices occupied a large suite and a storage-cum-shipping room on the Avenue of the Americas (Sixth Avenue to New Yorkers), near Rockefeller Center. If a letter required the boss's signature, an employee would carry it up to Beekman Place; when he was in the Catskills, he would dictate his letters to Hilda Schneider over the phone, and she would sign them in his stead.

He and Ellin spent the 1969–70 holidays in Paris, visiting their daughter Linda and her family. Once intent on making a career for herself in the theater (she had studied at the prestigious American Academy of Dramatic Arts in New York), she had instead married banker and later artist Edouard Emmet, moved to France, and had three children. Berlin enjoyed the liveliness of his grandchildren, and they in turn adored him.

The Berlins returned to Manhattan in early January 1970. On March 9, Anya Arlen, wife of composer Harold, died following surgery for a brain tumor, and Berlin, like an affectionate uncle (he was seventeen years older), did his best to console his devastated friend. Once he had gotten over the worst of it, they went to the movies together, often accompanied by A. L. Berman. Arlen wrote down the jokes Berlin told him and shared them with other friends; some of these jests were risqué.

Later, when Arlen was housebound with Parkinson's disease and Berlin himself had trouble getting around, the two men spent a great deal of time chatting by phone. They discussed songs, art, books, the state of the world—Israel's fortunes, Watergate—and more personal matters; the one bit of advice Arlen did not follow was Berlin's suggestion that he remarry. Over the ensuing years, through Arlen's final, decade-long illness, right up to his death, in 1986, it was a rare day when Berlin did not call his younger, ailing friend.

In the spring of 1970, Berlin took pride in the success of Ellin's fourth novel, *The Best of Families.* He had read the work in progress and made a critical comment here and there, sometimes appreciated and sometimes provoking sharp words. As for himself, he found some solace in his painting and in schmoozing with the "boys"—Arlen, Stanley Adams, and, later, Morton Gould, Adams's successor as president of ASCAP. He liked to hear about the goings-on at the society, but he had no wish to participate any longer.

Berlin did take part in the celebration of the fiftieth anniversary of the Music Box the following year, even going so far as to pose for a photographer in front of the theater, then housing the successful *Sleuth*. His smile in the photo is slightly pinched, his hair thinner. He had vetoed the idea of a Salute to Berlin day, on which West Forty-fifth Street would have been closed off, and speeches given by friends and performances by musical stars from stage and screen.

"I'm not up to it," he said simply. He did offer up the statistics on *Sleuth* (written by Anthony Shaffer), the most profitable play ever to open at the Music Box, then grossing around $56,000 a week, with steady sold-out performances. (About $9,000 of that went directly into the Music Box treasury.) He informed *Times* reporter Mel Gussow that he and Sam Harris had almost lost the theater during the depression but had been saved by Gershwin's *Of Thee I Sing* in 1931.

He had considered doing a fiftieth-anniversary edition of the Music Box Revue, he told Gussow, using some of the original numbers and adding new ones, along with a few new sketches. But, he explained, "I have songwriter's stomach, and at eighty-three, it makes me worry. I worried so about [doing an] anniversary show." Still, he added, maybe he would get around to it "someday, before I die."

This was to be his final public interview; his last public appearance would come two years later. Nineteen seventy-three was a crucial year for President Richard M. Nixon, who was inaugurated for his second term on January 20, after a landslide election victory the previous November over Democrat George McGovern. An estimated crowd of 100,000 jammed the capital for the event, among them vociferous protesters of the Vietnam War. A peace agreement with Hanoi was finally signed a week later; by mid-February, released American prisoners of war began coming home.

In March, entertainer Sammy Davis, Jr., a great Nixon admirer, suggested that the President host an "Evening at the White House," at which he and others would entertain without compensation, with the funds raised going to the widows and families of Vietnam veterans. This notion came at a good time: Nixon, despite his electoral victory, was suffering through the slow destruction of his administration as a result of Watergate.

The event took place that spring. Irving Berlin was among those invited to perform; he entertained Nixon and the audience of POWs, their families, and other guests with a heartfelt delivery of "God Bless America." This was, at last, and truly, his swan song: now in his eighty-fifth year, he believed it was time to leave the limelight to others.

In a letter of thanks to friends who sent flowers on his birthday that May, he reflected on the question of age, saying, "Incidentally, eighty-five is no different from eighty-four, and I'm sure if I'm around at eighty-six it will still be the same." He was, and it was—though he spent most of his time that year painting.

The fiftieth wedding anniversary of Ellin and Irving Berlin was celebrated simply on January 4, 1976; his special gift to her was a gold band from Cartier. His next birthday slipped by unnoticed except by a few close friends, among them Harold Arlen, who, as he had for several years, wrote him a special song, recorded it, and had it delivered to Beekman Place. An earlier Arlen ditty, composed in 1965, saluted Berlin the artist:

A SUNNY SEVENTY-SEVEN
(Pablo B.)

Burthen—Brightly—With Proud Reverence
A sunny seventy-seven
No more nights of ennui
A heap of heavenly-heaven
Is due to thee, Pablo B.

The boys can w{h}ine,
They can pine—
'Svet gornisht helfin {"It's no use"}
The music "box" you are in
You got yourself in

The starlit songs will stay on
Thumb their nose at reviewers
With your paint and crayon
Immortality's yours

Second chorus
There's no curtailin'
The F sharp scalin'
Of Izzy Baline
The mighty B.

(A piano quotation from "God Bless America")
So to sum it up
Fee-fi-fo-fum it up
Music'lly
Happy days
Full of joie d'esprit
A jolly seventy-seven
Pablo B.

    Chaim

Years later, when Arlen's illness precluded his playing and singing, and curtailed his sense of fun, Berlin would relieve him of the annual effort by writing his own birthday song. More years later, after seeing songwriter Sammy Cahn present a theatrical evening of his work, accompanied by a few professional vocalists, Berlin insisted that Arlen could do even better—he was a superior singer, he argued, and a fine pianist in his own right. The modest Arlen disagreed.

On February 28, 1977 (a week or so after Arlen's seventy-second birthday and the performance of several songs in celebration), the persistent Berlin tried again:

Dear Harold:
    When I seriously suggested that you consider doing a one-man "and then I wrote" show with your wonderful catalogue, your answer was, "I've shot my wad."
    Following is the verse I wrote about it . . .

              "I've Shot My Wad"

A nightingale looked up to God
And said, "Dear God, I've shot my wad,
No longer can I do my thing,
Dear God, no longer can I sing."
And He replied, "Don't be a schmuck,
No nightingale has had such luck,
Your songs have built a golden nest
For Stanley Adams and the rest.
They're praying for the moment when
You get off your ass and sing again."

Arlen's response was an appreciative, hearty laugh and a request for copies to send to a few friends.

In January 1978, Berlin lost his sister Gussie, leaving him, at eighty-nine, the last survivor of the bewildered and distressed Beilins who had descended the *Rhynland*'s gangplank at Ellis Island more than eighty-four years before. His birthday, despite its newsworthy high round number, went generally unnoticed, as would a few more in the years to come.

In his ninety-second year, he executed a special painting for a friend and pronounced himself "pleased with [his] reaction." He added a favorite comment: "As a painter I'm *still* a pretty good songwriter. . . ."

A few months later there was a small crisis at Irving Berlin Music that Berlin himself would eventually resolve in characteristic fashion. October 1979 saw the release of a documentary film entitled *Best Boy;* a critical success, it was nominated for an Academy Award the next year. Filmed and written by Ira Wohl, it told the story of Wohl's retarded cousin, aged sixty or so, whose elderly parents were confronting the problem of what would become of him when both of them were dead. Wohl finally convinced his aunt to place her son in a home. The film took viewers through the discussions with the actual family and then showed the mother placing her son in an institution. As she left the building in tears, with the door closing behind her on her son, she spontaneously sang, "What'll I do when you are far away . . . ?"

The song was not mentioned in the script, though others were. Wohl, having cleared those other songs, belatedly applied to Berlin Music for a license—but only *after Best Boy* was released. Berlin's law firm, evidently miffed by the oversight, refused to grant the request. Wohl's chances for an Academy Award were now in jeopardy: if there was a legal problem, the film would be out of the running. In a panic, the filmmaker called his friend Emily Paley, Ira Gershwin's sister-in-law, hoping that a good word from Gershwin might get Berlin's lawyers to change their minds. Gershwin was then in frail health and unable to intervene, so Paley asked another friend to talk to Berlin directly.

After the caller explained the situation, the exchange went something like this:

BERLIN: They should have taken out the license, they got them for the other songs.
CALLER: But the mother sang the song unconsciously, it wasn't in the script.
BERLIN: I let my lawyers make the decisions, and they made it.

CALLER: If there is any hint of litigation, the Academy Award will be out the window.

BERLIN: Then they can take [the song] out.

CALLER: That would ruin one of the most touching scenes in the movie.

BERLIN: You stay out of this.

A disappointed Emily Paley put off calling Wohl for the time being. Her hesitation was rewarded: the next day, circumventing his attorneys, Berlin called back and said, "They will get the license." *Best Boy* went on to win the Academy Award for Best Documentary Feature.

As Berlin had frequently predicted and claimed, retirement ill became him. In September of 1982, returning to an idea he had been toying with for some time, he engaged a researcher to dig into the lives and times of some of the colorful characters he had known so many years before on the Bowery, beginning with Chuck Connors, the "Mayor of Chinatown." His plan was to produce a quasi-autobiographical musical, tentatively entitled *The Story of the Music Box,* tracing the origin and subsequent history of his still-flourishing theater. In outlining his concept for the researcher, he explained that the score would consist of highlights from the original revues plus some new numbers. "I've got ten, fifteen songs," he said, "enough for two shows." Then, clearly excited by the prospect, he added, "I'm not conceited, but I know what a goddamn good songwriter I am!"

The research began, but the production was not to be; while Irving Berlin could elude the press, there was no escaping the calendar. He abandoned the Music Box musical in 1983, as Ellin's health began to decline. They gave up their Catskills estate to be closer to her physician (and his), and spent more time together, often watching television. That year, his ninety-sixth and her eighty-first, their Christmas was brightened when a neighborhood musician named John Wallowitch gathered a group of friends in Beekman Place on Christmas Eve to serenade the couple with Berlin songs, including "White Christmas." Touched, and wanting to thank them all, Berlin invited them in to warm themselves, inadvertently initiating an annual event that would become a burden as Ellin's condition worsened. In March 1988 she suffered a stroke and was under constant care, and Berlin himself was in no mood for song.

He was also ninety-nine, a formidable number. Since he continued to dodge interviews—what did he have to say that he hadn't said before?—the enterprising Jeremy Gerard of the *Times* instead talked to some of his friends and a colleague or two.

Composer Jule Styne, who had begun in Hollywood as a vocal superviser on *On the Avenue,* recalled a little-known side of Irving Berlin. "You know," he began,

> he was out there alone—his wife had stayed in New York. I was there with my wife, but I probably didn't eat at home for three months.
>
> He was a great Chinese chef. We'd go into a Chinese restaurant and he'd pay the chef $50 or $100 to let him cook the meal. . . . I think Irving Berlin was an even greater showman than George M. Cohan. He's the one-of-kind man of all time.

A few years earlier, another friend, Oscar Levant, speaking on the subject of tributes, had wisely observed of Berlin, "I know of no man who needs [them] less and deserves [them] more." Another said, "He doesn't need the money and doesn't need to be any more immortal than he already is."

Theater historian Stanley Green, once a regular on Berlin's phone, touched on the topic of the songwriter's physical condition. "He doesn't see very well," he told Gerard—Berlin was then afflicted with cataracts—"and things have to be read to him. He always says, 'My health is wonderful from the neck up.' But his memory! I haven't seen him in some time, but we chatted about a year ago, and he recalled details of a musical he had written in the teens."

The headline of Gerard's article was "Berlin, at 99, a Reclusive Immortal." The description helped solidify the legend of the curmudgeonly loner who no longer went on long walks around his neighborhood, once "a daily ritual; the walks have grown briefer and less regular. . . ." Unaware of the weakened state of Berlin's legs, the writer also failed to mention that he took his walks, when he was able, accompanied by a male nurse (not a bodyguard, as some believed).

The "recluse" himself complained to a friend about that ninety-ninth birthday, "I can't take a walk without being chased by photographers."

"Wait'll next year," came the reply.

"I'm not kidding myself."

Toward the end of the year, Ellin's condition worsened. Her daughters gathered around her, and she made a slight recovery. Still, it made for a bleak Christmas.

Earlier, in September, ASCAP's Morton Gould had announced that Berlin's "next year" would begin early, in time for the centennial event in May 1988. Gould made public the fact that with Berlin's "agreement and blessing," a gala celebration of his hundredth birthday would be staged at, and for the benefit of, Carnegie Hall (ticket prices would go as high as $1,000), with the whole evening to be telecast at the end of the month by CBS. Also benefiting would be the ASCAP Foundation, an organization dedicated to bringing music to children and assisting young musical talent. Berlin had made two stipulations, both readily met: he would not participate in person, and only published songs would be used.

The celebratory year began in January at the 92nd Street Y, where Maurice Levine devoted the entire five programs of his "Lyrics and Lyricists" series, running until June, to the songs of Irving Berlin. Three days later, the Library and Museum for the Performing Arts at Lincoln Center gave over its Amsterdam Avenue gallery to an exhibition of Berliniana, including a Buick, sheet music, photographs, and documents. Berlin did not attend the opening, but Hilda Schneider did, characteristically remaining self-effacingly in the background.

An unusual tribute was mounted at the Arena Stage in Washington, D.C. The small but prestigious theater, noted for its extraordinary and beautifully directed productions of classics, revivals, and adventurous works for the theater, managed a coup: Berlin, and his attorneys, granted the company the right to produce a revival of the 1925 Marx Brothers musical *The Cocoanuts,* which had not been staged in more than sixty years. Director Douglas A. Wager and musical director Rob Fisher, after a good deal of research, reconstructed the score from various sources, including the 1929 film version, the New York State Archives, the Princeton Library, and the Library of Congress. One lost song, "The Bellhops," was used instrumentally but not sung in the movie; a close viewing confirmed that it fitted the lyrics that had survived.

The Cocoanuts premiered on April 20, 1988, and was booked to run through June 5. The reception was close to ecstatic. The *New York Times* dispatched its veteran observer of the musical theater to cover the event, and he echoed the local high opinion, noting that the score featured "Berlin spoofs of the tango, and of Bizet; a tongue-in-cheek toast to afternoon tea that could have been brewed by Noël Coward; several hummable tunes, including 'We Should Care,' and 'Florida by the Sea,' which deserves and receives a reprise." He concluded admiringly, "After seeing and savoring *The Cocoanuts,* one wonders why it took so long for revival."

Berlin was pleased with the notices, and with the praise accorded a number of songs that he had not thought significant, but that had somehow stood the test and survived, to sparkle with bright and witty lyrics (with the possible exception of the expendable "The Monkey Doodle-Doo," one of the more grotesque sequences retained for the film). The run of the show was extended, and the cast played consistently to standing-room-only audiences.

Delighted though he was with this outcome, Berlin soon had to deal with a rights complication that it occasioned.

In light of *The Cocoanuts'* critical and commercial success, as well as its historical significance, staff at the Library and Museum for the Performing Arts at Lincoln Center suggested that a performance of the show be filmed for the library's archive. The cast and all concerned were thrilled, and a formal request was immediately submitted to the Berlin office. The answer arrived all too soon: no. Understandably distressed at being denied the chance to preserve its work for future reference and study (the video would not be sold or shown in public), the company was willing to grasp at any straw. Cast member Judith Bardi, a former New Yorker and gifted soprano, knew a friend of Berlin's in Manhattan, and she came up with an idea.

Early in June, an envelope was slipped under Bardi's friend's door by another New Yorker who happened to live nearby; inside was a note from Mitchell Greenberg, who played Chico in the show. He had composed a letter to Berlin, asking for his permission to tape a performance of *The Cocoanuts,* but he hoped that "rather than go through channels & red tape, you [i.e., Bardi and Berlin's mutual friend] might be able to get the letter into Mr. Berlin's hands. This might get us further than dealing with 'his people.' "

Greenberg's long, affectionate letter to Berlin read, in part:

Dear Mr. Berlin,

Let us be the 287,000th to wish you Mazel Tov and Happy Birthday—albeit somewhat belatedly. Actually, on the day itself we had a party in your honor following the performance of *The Cocoanuts.* The cast and audience all sang and had some birthday cake. It was good, too. Thanks!

We'd love to have some record of our achievement and success [i.e., the reviews, the several extensions of the run, the SRO's] with *The Cocoanuts.* The Lincoln Center Library is ready, willing and able to videotape us in performance—strictly for archival and research purposes. . . . The cast and creative personnel have all signed waivers allowing our work to be recorded for posterity without recompense, just for a small taste of immorality.

The second page was signed by the entire company, "with love and gratitude." The letter was forwarded to Beekman Place and read to Berlin, who then called Hilda Schneider and dictated a letter granting permission for the filming of *The Cocoanuts.* (A poignant note: some months later, Judith Bardi, who had conceived the tactic and the approach, died of cancer. Happily, her vibrant performance has been preserved on the videotape that Berlin gave, in a sense, to the company.)

The gala hundredth came around soon enough. The big week dawned on Sunday, with nearly two pages of the *Times*'s Arts & Leisure section being devoted to Berlin; the coverage began on page 1 with a lead article by Marilyn Berger and ran to all of page 14, sidebarred by an especially perceptive appreciation of Berlin and his work by British songwriter Rupert Holmes.

Berger's piece was a well-crafted and well-organized mixture of biography, anecdote (some questionable), and brief factual excursion. Among the anecdotes was one curiously malicious quote attributed to songwriter Harry Warren, who in March 1944, after an American air force attack of the German capital, had muttered, "They bombed the wrong Berlin." The statement had undoubtedly been inspired by the popularity of "White Christmas," at a time when Warren's own Hollywood career was in decline; the musical king of movies in the thirties, he had boasted an output and record as a composer of hits that had made him, for a while, Berlin's nearest rival. Noted for his caustic wit and competitive resentment of others' success, Warren was a good friend but a formidable antagonist.

If Berlin ever responded to his colleague's remark, or if he harbored any reciprocal (or similar) resentment, there is no record of it. He rarely spoke ill of another's character or work—to the extent, in fact, that one of the worst things he is known to have said about anyone is that he "did not admire" the lyrics of Richard Rodgers, the composer having recently written music and words for the musical *No Strings.* Then he added, with a twinkle in his eye, Ira's [Gershwin] a pretty good lyric writer."

Because the Carnegie celebration later that week was to be a fund-raising event, Ms. Berger reminded her readers that the *This Is the Army* Fund had raised nearly $10 million for the Army Emergency Relief Fund. When that fund was no longer needed, all further royalties from the show's songs had been redirected into the "God Bless America" Fund for the Girl and Boy Scouts, which in 1982 had gleaned $110,000 and in 1985, $90,000. She noted, too, that this was Berlin's only publicized charitable contribution; any other gifts he made were anonymous. (In a conversation with a friend, he once offhandedly revealed that after Harold Arlen's death, in 1986, he had set up a scholarship in his name at the Juilliard School of Music.)

Holmes, in his essay, took a longer view. "American popular music," he asserted,

> continues to sprawl across the decades, embracing every musical cult
> form like an amoeba, sometimes diluting it, sometimes reflexively

snapping back to things old or borrowed. But through it all, for well over half the century of years he has lived, Irving Berlin has anchored American popular music, influenced it and defined it. Songwriters can only measure up to the standards he has set, and follow his principles of clarity, of honest sentiment fully felt and simply but memorably expressed, of melody that lingers in the room after the fiddlers have fled.

Three days later, Carnegie Hall was packed with a sell-out audience and stars of every magnitude and aptitude. Berlin chose to remain at home with Ellin and have dinner in a flower-filled library; they were represented at the concert by their three daughters, who sat in the fourth row of the hall with their husbands and children.

Walter Cronkite began the evening by listing some of Berlin's greatest songs:

"Anything You Can Do, I Can Do Better." "Blue Skies." "Cheek to Cheek." "God Bless America." His words could never be simpler, yet with them, Irving Berlin helped write the story of this country by capturing the best of who we are and the dreams that shape our lives. Wander through his music, and you stand in wide-eyed amazement, that from the hand of one man could have glowed so much that is dear to us.

The roster of those who appeared that night (some of whom indeed "wandered") began with Beatrice Arthur and ended with a herd of Boy and Girl Scouts, the U.S. Army Chorus, and a company of soldiers from Fort Dix, New Jersey. These last entered marching down the aisles with the Scouts, while the chorus massed onstage.

It was a long, tuneful (if at times out-of-tune) evening, and at its best, it glittered. Among the more memorable highlights were Madeline Kahn's wickedly suggestive "You'd Be Surprised," Ray Charles's husky-voiced, bluesy "How Deep Is the Ocean?," Michael Feinstein's snappy "I Love a Piano," Nell Carter's robust "Alexander's Ragtime Band," Rosemary Clooney's rich "White Christmas," and Tony Bennett's moody "Let's Face the Music and Dance." Dressed all in white in tribute to Fred Astaire (who had died the year before), Tommy Tune tapped his way through "Puttin' On the Ritz."

There were a couple of curiosities: Willie Nelson, in full formal western regalia, black tie below cowboy hat, covered "Blue Skies" on solo guitar; the less musical but more affecting Garrison Keillor, after declaring that Berlin had taken "common American talk, our talk, and turned it into poetry," recited the lyric to "All Alone" to prove his point. At least Keillor refrained from making a speech, unlike Morton Gould of ASCAP, Isaac Stern (the president and savior of Carnegie Hall), and host Cronkite.

In an evening as long and celebrity-cluttered as this, there was bound to be a gaffe or two. The most embarrassing moments came from unexpected sources: glitterati Frank Sinatra and Leonard Bernstein.

Sinatra, inexplicably, whether by some unhappy attempt at biographical juxtaposition or through simple ignorance, was selected to sing a pair of songs closely associated with Berlin's two marriages—one a poignant reminder of the long-dead Dorothy, the other a reflection of the complicated early days with Ellin. Tim Page, writing in *Newsday,* missed the emotional significance but couldn't help noticing that "Sinatra's under-rehearsed run-throughs of 'Always' and 'When I Lost You" [were] so sloppily performed that somebody decreed that they [must] be repeated." The members of the audience were caught quite thoroughly off guard by this; what they, and Page, did not know was that because the show was being filmed for television, a second take was required. The reshooting was supposed to be done *after* the show, but since there was no certainty that Sinatra and his party would stick around that long, the mystified patrons got a little extra Frank for their (high) price of admission.

"Then," Page lamented,

there was the sad spectacle of Leonard Bernstein. Who else would have had the audacity to sing one of his *own* compositions in a concert devoted to America's greatest songwriter? Bernstein began by playing fragments of Berlin's "Russian Lullaby," interrupting the song several times to tell us how this was one of *his* favorites, and how this was *his* Carnegie Hall singing debut, and a host of other personal irrelevancies. Then he broke into "Twelve-Tone Lullaby," which aside from its dedication and the repeated invocation of Berlin's name, seemed addressed to Bernstein's own esthetic concerns, rather than anything to do with the composer of "Alexander's Ragtime Band." "Irving Berlin, I'm sorry!" Bernstein sang ["in a hilariously distressed baritone," Lee Jeske reported in the *Post*], again and again. So, one gathered from the embarrassed tittering in Carnegie Hall, was the audience.

Bernstein had obviously fortified himself alcoholically for his debut.

The protracted evening closed with opera star Marilyn Horne, accompanied by the army chorus and all others present, singing "God Bless America."

The finale was introduced by actress Shirley MacLaine, who announced, "We can't sing 'Happy Birthday' because that's one of the few songs that [Irving Berlin] didn't write." Instead, the entire company crowded onstage to render "There's No Business like Show Business." Then the birthday celebration— finally—ended.

For Irving Berlin it had truly been a very long day. Just before midnight on May 10, Berlin devotee John Wallowitch had assembled a motley group at the entrance to 17 Beekman Place. *Daily News* reporter Patricia O'Haire put their number at more than forty, all told: "There were actors and bag ladies, people walking dogs in the pleasant night, a few pedestrians attracted by the crowd. They stood quietly, whispering to each other, clutching the music, watching the clock."

At the stroke of midnight, all sang "Happy Birthday" to Berlin. All the while, according to O'Haire, "the house was as silent as the Williamsburg Bridge. Every shade was drawn, but there were lights on behind them, and several windows open on the top floor."

As the crowd grew, some waved photographs of the new centenarian and shouted greetings (did they expect autographs?). They saw a fluttering shade: "[A] light went out, the shade was raised, someone looked out. But who? No one knew. . . ."

Nor did anyone realize that the house sheltered, besides one extremely tired hundred-year-old man, a very frail Ellin Berlin. The well-wishers forged ahead with a chorus of "Always" and a reprise of "Happy Birthday."

From above, they heard a voice (probably that of a nurse) shout, "He's coming down." Expectantly, Wallowitch and his serenaders (one a ten-year-old boy) waited and waited. Then came the voice again, saying, "Sorry. He looked out and decided it was too cold. But he thanks you very much."

Within twenty-four hours, the Carnegie Hall tribute would be over, and Ellin and Irving Berlin, together always, would be awaiting the coming of the long night.

The centennial frenzy subsided soon after, and Berlin heard what had been written about the Carnegie Hall event and got a fuller, often amusing report from his daughters. He called a writer who had contributed an essay to the ASCAP program to tell him how much he liked it.

About a week later he suffered what his nurse called an episode, as she described it to Mary Ellin Barrett. He was feverish, but more concerned about Ellin than about anything else. He asked Mary Ellin to tell her mother that he was away on a business trip and that she shouldn't worry, adding, "Be sure to give her my love."

Late in July, Ellin Berlin had another stroke and was taken to Doctors Hospital. She died there on the morning of July 29, 1988, at the age of eighty-five. Mary Ellin and Elizabeth brought the unhappy news to Berlin as he lay in bed; Linda had not yet arrived from Paris. The services, with all the family present except Berlin, were held on Tuesday, August 2, in the Lady's Chapel of St. Patrick's Cathedral, where Ellin had worshiped since being rebaptized in the midthirties.

The ceremony was an elaborate one, with several priests in attendance. The cathedral's rector, the Reverend Anthony Dalla Valla, spoke directly to Ellin's daughters, saying, "The song is not ended and it will continue into eternity. To use your father's words, 'Always, always.' Someone whose life was so meaningful, so creative, so elegant has touched us. . . ."

The mourners that day included in their number former mayor John Lindsay; the Berlins' good friend (and head of the New York State Arts Council) Kitty Carlisle Hart; opera singer Robert Merrill; Douglas MacArthur's widow, Jean; editor Helen Gurley Brown and her husband, producer David Brown; and Hilda Schneider, representing, in a sense, her boss, who was not strong enough to attend.

Jessie Mangaliman, reporting for *Newsday,* noted that among the several hundred people present in the cathedral were "scores of sweaty tourists in wrinkled cotton shirts and shorts [who] milled up and down the cathedral aisle, taking polite glimpses at the mourners in black."

Cardinal John O'Connor appeared near the end of the Mass and declared that he could not resist delivering a blessing: "No man could have given the joy to the world that Irving Berlin gave had he not had the love and support of a wonderful woman. I came today to thank her for his great contribution to the world."

Berlin was infirm and bedridden most of the time now, his days and nights fused together, monotonously similar, interrupted only by regular visits from the doctor and nurses' round-the-clock ministrations. Time was a vacuum.

Despite the bleakness of his life, Berlin rallied long enough to salute his old associate Johnny Green, a songwriter, pianist, and former head of the music department at M-G-M.

In October of 1988, Green was very ill, but his family was planning to celebrate his eightieth birthday, if he lived to see it, by renting a small theater for an evening devoted to his musical achievements in Hollywood. His daughter Kim, who regarded Berlin as her father's mentor, called in hopes of getting a statement from him that could be read at the event. Berlin generously composed a kind greeting, which Green was present to hear (he would die on May 15, 1989, four days after Berlin's hundred-and-first birthday).

During the holiday season, two months later, and six months after the death of his wife, Berlin suffered a stroke and briefly slipped into a coma. After New Year's—1989—he began to recover, and slowly regained some strength. Miraculously, May 11 came around once again. There was no press flurry that year—just "a quiet day with the family," as Hilda Schneider told a reporter from the Associated Press. "That he always has. He never had any big to-dos." Hilda was now virtually in charge of the Irving Berlin Music Corporation. Helmy Kresa, himself in poor health and hearing-impaired, had retired the year before. The offices had meanwhile been moved from the expansive Avenue of the Americas location to a building that Berlin had owned since 1921: 29 West Forty-sixth Street, the town house where he and Ellin had begun their marriage.

The entire building, which appeared deserted from the sidewalk, was now devoted to Irving Berlin Music—all seven floors of it. The seventh story, formerly the upper floor of Berlin's duplex, had become a storeroom, and Hilda's office overflowed with cartons filled with hundredth-birthday wishes—cards, letters, and children's drawings, telegrams and gifts that Berlin himself never saw—all systematically, as always, acknowledged. On the hundred-and-first birthday, the office was as quiet as the house on Beekman Place.

Berlin still had his moments of awareness; when a friend who had not heard from him for a long time called in mid-September, for example, the nurse, Ellen Duncan, said he was having lunch. Informed of the caller's identity, Berlin was heard to say, in a strong voice, "Tell him I'll call him back."

About a week after that, when Mary Ellin came by to see him, she found him quite weak, but he seemed to perk up when she told him that his great-grandchild Peter, then two, loved dancing to "Alexander's Ragtime Band," and that a friend's production, set to open soon at the Music Box, promised to be a hit.

Berlin responded "Good" to both pieces of news.

The next day, September 22, 1989, late in the afternoon, he died. When word got out, both the office phones and the Beekman Place line (supposedly unlisted, a constant myth) began ringing incessantly. At the Berlin home, the songwriter's son-in-law Alton Peters (Elizabeth's husband) picked up the receiver and told the AP reporter on the other end that yes, Irving Berlin had died, at around five-thirty.

"Was he ill?" the reporter wondered.

"No," Peters replied. "He was a hundred and one. . . . He just fell asleep."

Alone except for the nurse, he had died at home, in the once-happy house that his incomparable gifts had built. By six o'clock, 17 Beekman Place was filled with grief and loss.

An onslaught of attention followed. At 9:55 P.M. the UPI issued a terse, two-line "Bulletin Preced": "Songwriter Irving Berlin died in his sleep Friday at his Manhattan home at the age of 101." Reuters soon after released an "Urgent," expanding the flash to "Irving Berlin, who never learned to read music but became one of the world's best-known and best-loved composers, died in his sleep Friday at the age of 101, his son-in-law said." At her desk at CBS News, Elizabeth Dribble accumulated paper as the evening wore on. Reuter's three lines had grown to three pages, and dispatches kept coming from the other wire services as well: biography, accomplishments, comments by colleagues and friends (but no family). Peters had had the final word when he stated that the funeral would be private.

Testimonials were gathered from Bobby Short, Ginger Rogers (working with Irving Berlin was "like heaven," she said after singing the first line of "Cheek to Cheek"), Morton Gould (Berlin's songs had "become part of our language, part of our heartbeat, part of our soul"), and songwriters Burt Bacharach, Jule Styne, and Sammy Cahn.

The Berlin friend most frequently quoted in the press had been dead for more than forty years already: Jerome Kern. Printed in Woollcott's biography, a letter written by Kern in 1925 yielded a choice excerpt that by 1988 had become virtually a cliché: "Irving Berlin has *no* place in American music. HE *IS* AMERICAN MUSIC."

Kern's original, witty letter made other perceptive points as well. "I once delivered myself of a nifty," he wrote.

It was at a dinner in London, and I was asked, in my opinion, what were the chief characteristics of the American nation. I replied that the average citizen was perfectly epitomized in Irving Berlin's music. I remember I got this off quite glibly, just as if I had thought of it on the spur of the moment. Of course, I enlarged upon the notion and went on to explain that both the typical Yankee and a Berlin tune had humor, originality, pace and popularity; both were wide-awake, and both, sometimes, a little loud,—but what might unsympathetically be mistaken for brass, was really gold.

Before his grand, capitalized statement, Kern had fashioned an even richer evaluation: "[Berlin] doesn't attempt to stuff the public's ears with pseudo-original ultra modernism, but he honestly absorbs the vibrations emanating from the people, manners and life of his time, and in turn, gives these impressions back to the world,—simplified,—clarified,—glorified."

Was Berlin American music? No; no more so than George Gershwin, Charles Ives, Aaron Copland, or Harold Arlen. But all were great American musicians. Berlin was an influential innovator, especially in his lyrics. Lacking the formal education of his peers in this art (a fact of which he was frequently overly conscious), he sang in the voice of the average man and woman, as other folk singers before him had been doing for centuries.

He and Kern both changed the direction of American popular song and the theater musical by influencing other American giants who came after them—men such as Gershwin, Rodgers, and Arlen, to cite only three. Had Berlin and Kern not existed, would those three have been the great songwriters they became? Probably so, for all were naturals. But Berlin and Kern set examples for them and led the way.

As a lyricist, Berlin did not attempt to write like Lorenz Hart, whose rueful wit was characterized by intricate rhymes; nor did he share Ira Gershwin's quiet, satirical take on life and love. E. Y. Harburg, another lyricist Berlin admired, loved wordplay and songs of social significance, but neither was for Berlin. Neither did his dear friend Cole Porter's "sophistication" (a categorization Porter himself came to abhor) speak to his own experience. Yet he loved the words written by all these poets, and in fact he often equaled them with his own, without trying.

He once said, in an excess of modesty, "All good songwriters have no more than half a dozen songs in their systems, and if they have that many, they're liberally blessed." When George Abbott once expressed his admiration for a particular Berlin song, saying that he really liked it, Berlin replied, "I do too. I've used it lots of times."

If it is true that he ultimately based thousands of songs on a mere six models, all the while working within the confines of the octave, Berlin did a remarkable job of concealing his limitations. His seam-bursting catalog reveals his versatility, his imagination, his humor, and his sense of fellowship toward the people for whom he wrote. His language was theirs, the vernacular of the middle class, except when a song's function called for slang or for dialect.

If he rarely wrote a lyric that expressed a personal emotion—he admitted to doing this only in "When I Lost You," "Always," "Count Your Blessings," and "God Bless America"—he was nonetheless a sharp observer with a fine ear.

His unerring craftsmanship is everywhere evident in the rightness, the seeming inevitability, of his songs. While it is true that he could produce a song, when necessary, in a rehearsal hall or riding home in a cab, much more often Irving Berlin worked hard, even painfully so, over his compositions. Perhaps the fact that he created both words and music—and who knows which came first?—gave his songs that oneness (for want of a better word), that cohesive quality that made them seem born from his Buick all of a piece, or sprung from nowhere or everywhere, as if they had always simply *been* there. As Rupert Holmes wrote for the songwriter's one hundredth, "Certain songs like 'God Bless America,' 'There's No Business like Show Business' and 'White Christmas' weren't actually *written* by anyone at all; they just appeared on the Fifth Day shortly after 'every winged bird according to its kind.' "

Irving Berlin was a singer of songs—a songwriter, not a composer, by his own definition. He began and ended, too, as a seller of songs, and a Bowery bard who unconsciously created art—simplified, clarified, glorified art, the art of a streetwise poet or, more aptly, a wise street-poet. His songs belong to everyone, but they are his alone.

APPENDIX

1. THE SONGS OF IRVING BERLIN

The listing that follows includes all the Berlin songs, published and unpublished, known to me as of this writing. More titles will probably surface over time, particularly with the publication of *The Lyrics of Irving Berlin,* edited by Robert Kimball, an imposing and important undertaking. Although my compilation is chronological, precise dating has frequently been a problem. Early in his career Berlin appears to have filed for copyright as soon as a song was completed—a wise move in Tin Pan Alley, where the walls had ears, especially if another songwriter occupied the adjoining room. Later on, songs were filed and copyrighted only when actually used in a film or a show, though often as not, movie songs were written months before the film's release. Dates for stage musicals have been collected from the original programs and from reference works by Steven Suskin—*Show Tunes* and *Opening Night on Broadway*—as well as from Tommy Krasker and Robert Kimball's scholarly *Catalog of the American Musical.*

Names of Berlin's collaborators are enclosed in brackets, as are some other explanatory details, such as original dates of composition and the like. Within each year, songs are listed alphabetically where they were not part of a stage or film score; within entries for shows or movies, they are listed in order of presentation in the production.

1907
Marie from Sunny Italy [*lyric only; music by M. Nicholson*]

1908

The Best of Friends Must Part
Queenie, My Own [*with Maurice Abrahams*]

1909

Christmas-Time Seems Years and Years Away [*with Ted Snyder*]
Dorando
Do Your Duty, Doctor [*with Ted Snyder*]
Goodbye Girlie, and Remember Me [*with George W. Meyer*]
I Didn't Go Home at All [*with Edgar Leslie*]
If I Thought You Wouldn't Tell [*with Ted Snyder*]
I Just Came Back to Say Goodbye
I Wish You Was My Gal, Molly [*with Ted Snyder*]
Just like the Rose [*with Al Piantadosi*]
My Wife's Gone to the Country, Hurrah! Hurrah! [*with George Whiting and Ted Snyder*]
Next to Your Mother Who Do You Love? [*with Ted Snyder*]
No One Could Do It like My Father [*with Ted Snyder*]
Oh, Where Is My Wife Tonight? [*with Ted Snyder*]
Sadie Salome, Go Home [*with Edgar Leslie*]
She Was a Dear Little Girl [*with Ted Snyder; interpolation:* The Boys and Betty]
Some Little Something about You [*with Ted Snyder*]
Someone Just like You, Dear [*with Ted Snyder*]
Someone's Waiting for Me [*with Edgar Leslie*]
Stop That Rag (Keep On Playing, Honey) [*with Ted Snyder; interpolation:* The Jolly Bachelors]
Sweet Marie, Make a Rag-a-Time-a Dance with Me [*with Ted Snyder; interpolation:* The Jolly Bachelors]
That Mesmerizing Mendelssohn Tune
Wild Cherries Rag [*with Ted Snyder*]
Yiddle on Your Fiddle Play Some Ragtime

1910

Alexander and His Clarinet [*with Ted Snyder*]
Before I Go and Marry I Will Have a Talk with You
Bring Back My Lena to Me [*with Ted Snyder*]
Call Me Up Some Rainy Afternoon
Colored Romeo [*with Ted Snyder*]
Dat Draggy Rag
Dear Mayme, I Love You [*with Ted Snyder*]
Dreams, Just Dreams [*with Ted Snyder*]
Goodbye, Becky Cohen
Grizzly Bear [*with George Botsford; interpolation:* Ziegfeld Follies of 1910]
Herman, Let's Dance That Beautiful Waltz [*with Ted Snyder; interpolation:* Two Men and a Girl]

If the Managers Only Thought the Same as Mother [*with Ted Snyder; interpolation:* The Jolly Bachelors]

I Love You More Each Day [*with Ted Snyder*]

I'm a Happy Married Man [*with Ted Snyder*]

I'm Going on a Long Vacation [*with Ted Snyder*]

Innocent Bessie Brown

Is There Anything Else That I Can Do for You? [*with Ted Snyder*]

Kiss Me, My Honey, Kiss Me [*with Ted Snyder*]

Oh, How That German Could Love [*with Ted Snyder; interpolation:* The Girl and the Wizard]

Oh, That Beautiful Rag [*with Ted Snyder; interpolation:* Up and Down Broadway]

Piano Man [*with Ted Snyder*]

Stop! Stop! Stop! Come Over and Love Me Some More

Sweet Italian Love [*with Ted Snyder; interpolation:* Up and Down Broadway]

Telling Lies [*with Henrietta Blanke Belcher*]

Thank You Kind Sir, Said She [*with Ted Snyder; interpolation:* Jumping Jupiter]

That Kazzatsky Dance

That Opera Rag [*with Ted Snyder*]

Try It on Your Piano

When I Hear You Play That Piano, Bill [*with Ted Snyder*]

Wishing [*with Ted Snyder; interpolation:* Two Men and a Girl]

Yiddisha Eyes

1911

After the Honeymoon [*with Ted Snyder*]

Alexander's Ragtime Band

Bring Back My Lovin' Man

Bring Me a Ring in the Spring

Business Is Business, Rosey Cohen

Cuddle Up [*interpolation:* A Real Girl]

Dat's-a My Gal

Doggone That Chilly Man [*interpolation:* Ziegfeld Follies of 1911]

Don't Put Out the Light [*with Edgar Leslie*]

Don't Take Your Beau to the Seashore [*with E. Ray Goetz; interpolation:* Fascinating Widow]

Down to the Folies Bergère [*with Vincent Bryan and Ted Snyder; interpolation:* Folies Bergère]

Ephraham Played upon the Piano [*with Vincent Bryan; interpolation:* Ziegfeld Follies of 1911]

Everybody's Doin' It Now

He Promised Me

How Do You Do It, Mabel, on Twenty Dollars a Week?

I Beg Your Pardon, Dear Old Broadway [*interpolation:* Folies Bergère]

Meet Me Tonight

Molly O! Oh Molly!

My Melody Dream

One O'Clock in the Morning I Get Lonesome [*with Ted Snyder; interpolation:* A Real Girl]

Ragtime Violin

Run Home and Tell Your Mother

Sombrero Land [*with E. Ray Goetz and Ted Snyder; interpolation: Winter Garden show*]

Spanish Love [*with Vincent Bryan and Ted Snyder; interpolation:* Folies Bergère]

That Dying Rag [*with Bernie Adler*]

That Monkey Tune

That Mysterious Rag [*with Ted Snyder; interpolation:* A Real Girl]

There's a Girl in Havana [*with E. Ray Goetz and Ted Snyder; interpolation:* The Never Homes]

Virginia Lou [*with Earl Taylor*]

When I'm Alone I'm Lonesome

When It Rains, Sweetheart, When It Rains

When You Kiss an Italian Girl

When You're in Town (in My Home Town) [*interpolation:* A Real Girl]

Whistling Rag

Woodman, Woodman, Spare That Tree [*with Vincent Bryan: interpolation:* Ziegfeld Follies of 1911]

Yankee Love [*with E. Ray Goetz*]

Yiddisha Nightingale

You've Built a Fire in My Heart [*interpolation:* Ziegfeld Follies of 1911]

You've Got Me Hypnotized

1912

Alexander's Bag-Pipe Band [*with E. Ray Goetz and A. B. Sloane; interpolation:* Hokey-Pokey]

Antonio, You'd Better Come Home

Becky's Got a Job in a Musical Show

Call Again

Come Back to Me, My Melody [*with Ted Snyder*]

Do It Again

Don't Leave Your Wife Alone

Down in My Heart [*interpolation:* The Little Millionaire]

Follow Me Around [*interpolation:* My Best Girl]

Goody, Goody, Goody, Goody, Good

He Played It on His Fid, Fid, Fiddle-Dee-Dee [*with E. Ray Goetz*]

Hiram's Band [*with E. Ray Goetz; interpolation:* The Sun Dodgers]

If All the Girls I Knew Were like You

I'm Afraid, Pretty Maid, I'm Afraid

I'm Going Back to Dixie [*with Ted Snyder; interpolation:* She Knows Better Now]

I've Got to Have Some Lovin' Now

Keep Away from the Fellow Who Owns an Automobile
Lead Me to That Beautiful Band [*with E. Ray Goetz*]
A Little Bit of Everything
The Million-Dollar Ball [*with E. Ray Goetz; interpolation:* Hanky Panky]
My Sweet Italian Man
Opera Burlesque *based on the Sextette from* Lucia di Lammermoor [*interpolation:* Hanky Panky]
Pick, Pick, Pick on the Mandolin, Antonio
The Ragtime Jockey Man
Ragtime Mocking Bird
Ragtime Soldier Man
Spring and Fall
Take a Little Tip from Father [*with Ted Snyder*]
That's How I Love You
That Society Bear [*interpolation: Winter Garden show*]
A True Born Soldier Man
Wait Until Your Daddy Comes Home
When I Lost You
When I'm Thinking of You, I'm Thinking of a Wonderful Love
When Johnson's Quartet Harmonize
When the Midnight Choo-Choo Leaves for Alabam'
The Yiddisha Professor

1913

Anna Liza's Wedding Day
The Apple Tree and the Bumble Bee
At the Devil's Ball
At the Picture Show [*with E. Ray Goetz; interpolation:* The Sun Dodgers]
Daddy Come Home
Down in Chattanooga
Happy Little Country Girl
He's So Good to Me
If You Don't Want Me (Why Do You Hang Around?)
In My Harem
I Was Aviating Around [*with Vincent Bryan*]
Jake! Jake! The Yiddisher Ball Player [*with Blanche Merrill*]
Keep On Walking
The Ki-I-Youdling Dog [*with Jean Schwartz*]
Kiss Your Sailor Boy Goodbye
The Monkey Doodle-Doo [*interpolation: All Aboard*]
The Old Maids' Ball
The Pullman Porters on Parade [*with Maurice Abrahams*]
San Francisco Bound
Snookey Ookums

Somebody's Coming to My House
Take Me Back [*interpolation:* All Aboard]
That International Rag
There's a Girl in Arizona [*with Grant Clarke and Edgar Leslie*]
They've Got Me Doin' It Now
Tra-La-La-La
We Have Much to Be Thankful For
Welcome Home
You Picked a Bad Day to Say Goodbye
You've Got Your Mother's Big Blue Eyes

1914

Along Came Ruth
Always Treat Her like a Baby
Follow the Crowd [*interpolation:* Queen of the Movies]
Furnishing a Home for Two [*interpolation:* The Society Buds]
God Gave You to Me
He's a Devil in His Own Home Town [*with Grant Clarke*]
He's a Rag Picker
If I Had You
If That's Your Idea of a Wonderful Time (Take Me Home)
If You Don't Want My Peaches (You'd Better Stop Shaking the Tree)
I Love to Quarrel with You
It Isn't What He Said, But the Way He Said It
I Want to Go Back to Michigan (Down on the Farm)
Morning Exercise
Stay Down Here Where You Belong
That's My Idea of Paradise [*interpolation:* The Society Buds]
They're on Their Way to Mexico
This Is the Life

WATCH YOUR STEP

Book by Harry B. Smith, based on Augustin Daly's play *Round the Clock;* directed by R. H. Burnside. Produced by Charles B. Dillingham at the New Amsterdam Theatre, December 8, 1914; 175 performances. Cast: Vernon and Irene Castle, Frank Tinney, Charles King, Elizabeth Brice, Harry Kelly, Sallie Fisher, and others.

Overture

ACT 1

Office Hours
What Is Love?
I'm a Dancing Teacher Now
The Minstrel Parade
Let's Go Round the Town
They Always Follow Me Around

Show Us How to Do the Fox Trot
When I Discovered You [*with E. Ray Goetz*]
The Syncopated Walk
Entr'acte 1
ACT 2
Metropolitan Nights
I Love to Have the Boys around Me
Settle Down in a One-Horse Town
Polka [*instrumental*]
Chatter Chatter
Ragtime Opera Medley
Entr'acte 2
ACT 3
Homeward Bound
Move Over
High Stepper's March [*instrumental, De Witt C. Coolman*]
Play a Simple Melody
Ann Eliza's Tango Tea
Look at Them Doing It
Come to the Land of the Argentine
When It's Night Time in Dixie Land
I Hate You
Lock Me in Your Harem and Throw Away the Key
Town Hall Tonight
Lead Me to Love [*with Ted Snyder*]
I've Gotta Go Back to Texas
Watch Your Step
[*deleted:* He's a Rag Picker]

1915
Araby
Cohen Owes Me Ninety-seven Dollars
I Love to Stay at Home
I'm Going Back to the Farm
My Bird of Paradise
Si's Been Drinking Cider
Until I Fell in Love with You
The Voice of Belgium
When I Leave the World Behind
When You're Down in Louisville (Call on Me)
While the Band Played an American Rag
STOP! LOOK! LISTEN!
Book by Harry B. Smith; directed by R. H. Burnside. Produced by Charles B. Dillingham at the Globe Theatre, December 25, 1915; 105 performances.

Cast: Gaby Deslys, Harry Fox, Justine Johnson, Blossom Seeley, Marion Davies, and Marion Sunshine.

Overture

ACT 1

Opening: These Are the Costumes (Mirror Specialty)
Blow Your Horn
Why Don't They Give Us a Chance?
I Love to Dance
And Father Wanted Me to Learn a Trade
The Girl on the Magazine Cover
I Love a Piano
Finale: I Love to Sit by the Fire
Entr'acte 1

ACT 2

Opening: Oh, What a Place Is Dreamy Honolulu
That Hula Hula
A Pair of Ordinary Coons
When I'm Out with You
Oozums
Take Off a Little Bit
Teach Me How to Love
The Law Must Be Obeyed
Finale: Ragtime Melodrama
Entr'acte 2
When I Get Back to the U.S.A.
Stop! Look! Listen!
I'll Be Coming Home with a Skate On
Everything in America Is Ragtime
[*deleted:* Sailor Song; Until I Fell in Love with You; Hunting for a Star; Poor Mary]

1916

The Friars' Parade [*written for the Friars Club Frolic*]
He's Getting Too Darn Big for a One-Horse Town
Hurry Back to My Bamboo Shack
I'm Down in Honolulu Looking Them Over
I'm Not Prepared
In Florida among the Palms [*interpolation:* Ziegfeld Follies of 1916]
I've Got a Sweet Tooth Bothering Me [*interpolation:* Step This Way]
Santa Claus: A Syncopated Christmas Song [*published in the* New York World]
When the Black Sheep Returns to the Fold

THE CENTURY GIRL

A revue, with no book attribution, produced by Charles Dillingham and Florenz Ziegfeld at the Century Theatre, November 6, 1916; 200 performances.

With Elsie Janis, Hazel Dawn, Frank Tinney, and Sam Bernard. Songs also by Victor Herbert, lyrics by Henry Blossom. Herbert also composed a great deal of instrumental music for the show.

Alice in Wonderland

The Chicken Walk

It Takes an Irishman to Make Love [*with Elsie Janis*]

The Music Lesson

On the Train of a Wedding Gown

You've Got Me Doing It

1917

Dance and Grow Thin [*with George W. Meyer; interpolation:* Dance and Grow Thin]

For Your Country and My Country

From Here to Shanghai

How Can I Forget?

If I Had My Way I'd Live with the Gypsies

I'll Take You Back to Italy

It Takes an Irishman to Make Love

Let's All Be Americans Now [*with Edgar Leslie and George W. Meyer*]

Mr. Jazz Himself

My Sweetie

Poor Little Rich Girl's Song [*interpolation:* The Rambler Rose]

The Road That Leads to Love

Smile and Show Your Dimple

Someone Else May Be There

There Are Two Eyes in Dixie

There's Something Nice about the South

Wasn't It Yesterday?

Whose Little Heart Are You Breaking Now?

1918

The Blue Devils of France [*interpolation:* Ziegfeld Follies of 1918]

The Circus Is Coming to Town [*interpolation:* Everything]

Come Along to Toy Town [*interpolation:* Going Up]

The Devil Has Bought Up All the Coal

Down Where the Jack'o'Lanterns Grow [*interpolation:* The Cohan Revue]

Goodbye France

I Have Just One Heart for Just One Boy [*interpolation:* The Canary]

I'm Gonna Pin My Medal on the Girl I Left Behind [*interpolation:* Ziegfeld Follies of 1918]

It's the Little Bit of Irish [*interpolation:* The Canary]

I Wouldn't Give That for the Man Who Couldn't Dance [*interpolation:* The Canary]

Over the Sea, Boys

Polly Pretty Polly [*with George M. Cohan; interpolation:* The Cohan Revue of 1918]

They Were All out of Step but Jim

When the Curtain Falls [*interpolation:* Going Up]

YIP! YIP! YAPHANK

Conceived by Irving Berlin; staged by Will H. Smith. Presented by "Uncle Sam" at the Century Theatre, August 19, 1918; 32 performances. All-soldier cast.

Opening Chorus: Hello, Hello, Hello

Silver Threads

What a Difference a Uniform Will Make

Sterling Silver Moon [*later titled "Mandy"*]

Ding Dong [*originally written for* The Canary]

Come Along, Come Along, Come Along

Oh! How I Hate to Get Up in the Morning

Kitchen Police (Poor Little Me, I'm on K.P.)

Dream On, Little Soldier Boy [*with Jean Havez*]

I Can Always Find a Little Sunshine in the Y.M.C.A.

Send a Lot of Jazz Bands over There

We're on Our Way to France

[*deleted:* God Bless America (*revised and published 1939*)]

1919

Everything Is Rosy Now for Rosie [*with Grant Clarke*]

Eyes of Youth

The Hand That Rocked My Cradle Rules My Heart

I Left My Door Open and My Daddy Walked Out

I Lost My Heart in Dixieland

I Never Knew [*with Elsie Janis*]

I've Got My Captain Working for Me Now

I Wonder

The New Moon [*interpolation:* The New Moon]

Nobody Knows (and Nobody Seems to Care)

Sweeter than Sugar (Is My Sweetie)

That Revolutionary Rag

Was There Ever a Pal like You?

When My Baby Smiles

You'd Be Surprised

You're So Beautiful [*interpolation:* The Canary]

ZIEGFELD FOLLIES OF 1919

Sketches by Rennold Wolf, Eddie Cantor, Gene Buck, and David Stamper. Directed by Ned Wayburn. Produced by Florenz Ziegfeld at the New Amsterdam Theatre, June 16, 1919; 171 performances. Cast: Eddie Dowling, Bert Williams, Eddie Cantor, John Steel, Ray Dooley, the Fairbanks Twins, and others. Additional songs by others.

Bevo
Harem Life
I'd Rather See a Minstrel Show
I'm the Guy Who Guards the Harem
Look Out for the Bolsheviki Man
Mandy [*formerly "Sterling Silver Moon"*]
My Tambourine Girl
The Near Future
A Pretty Girl Is like a Melody
Prohibition
Syncopated Cocktail
We Made the Doughnuts over There
You Cannot Make Your Shimmy Shake on Tea [*with Rennold Wolf*]

1920

After You Get What You Want, You Don't Want It
Beautiful Faces Need Beautiful Clothes [interpolation: *Broadway Brevities*]
But! She's Just a Little Bit Crazy
(I'll See You in) Cuba
Lindy

**INTERPOLATED INTO THE SCORE OF THE *ZIEGFELD FOLLIES
OF 1920,* WITH SONGS BY OTHER WRITERS:**

Bells
Chinese Firecrackers
Come Along Sextette
The Girls of My Dreams
The Leg of Nations
Metropolitan Ladies
The Syncopated Vamp [*with Harry Ruby and Bert Kalmar*]
Tell Me, Little Gypsy

1921

All by Myself
Drowsy Head [*with Vaughan DeLeath*]
Home Again Blues [*with Harry Akst*]
I Like It
The Passion Flower
Pickaninny Mose
There's a Corner up in Heaven

MUSIC BOX REVUE

Sketches by William Collier, George V. Hobart, and others; directed by William
Collier and Hassard Short. Produced by Sam H. Harris at the Music Box Theatre, September 22, 1921; 440 performances. Cast: William Collier, Sam Bernard,
the Brox Sisters, Emma Haig, Irving Berlin, and others.

At the Court around the Corner
Behind the Fan
Everybody Step
I'm a Dumbbell
In a Cozy Kitchenette Apartment
Legend of the Pearls
My Ben Ali Haggin Girl
My Little Book of Poetry
Say It with Music
The Schoolhouse Blues
Tell Me with a Melody [*written for the London production, May 1923*]
They Call It Dancing

1922

Homesick
Some Sunny Day

MUSIC BOX REVUE

Sketches by George V. Hobart, Walter Catlett, and others; directed by Hassard Short. Produced by Sam H. Harris at the Music Box Theatre, October 23, 1922; 330 performances. Cast: Charlotte Greenwood, Grace LaRue, William Gaxton, John Steel, Bobby Clark and Paul McCullough, the Fairbanks Twins, and others.

Bring On the Red Pepper
Crinoline Days
Dancing Honeymoon
Diamond Horseshoe
I'm Looking for a Daddy Long Legs
Lady of the Evening
The Little Red Lacquer Cage
Montmartre
Pack Up Your Sins and Go to the Devil
Porcelain Maid
Take a Little Wife
Three Cheers for the Red, White and Blue
Will She Come from the East? (East-North-West or South)

1923

Tell All the Folks in Kentucky (I'm Coming Home)
Too Many Sweethearts
When You Walked Out, Someone Else Walked In

MUSIC BOX REVUE

Sketches by George S. Kaufman, Edwin Burke, Robert Benchley, Stanley Rauh, and others; directed by Hassard Short and Sam Forrest. Produced by Sam H. Harris at the Music Box Theatre, September 22, 1923; 273 performances. Cast:

Frank Tinney, John Steel, Grace Moore, Phil Baker, the Brox Sisters, Robert Benchley, and others.
Climbing the Scale
Learn to Do the Strut
Little Butterfly
Maid of Mesh
One Girl
An Orange Grove in California
Tell Me a Bedtime Story
The Waltz of Long Ago
[*interpolation:* What'll I Do?]

1924

The Happy New Year Blues
Lazy
We'll All Go Voting for Al

MUSIC BOX REVUE

Sketches by Bert Kalmar and Harry Ruby, Bobby Clark and Paul McCullough, Ralph Bunker, and others; directed by John Murray Anderson and Sam H. Harris. Produced by Harris at the Music Box Theatre, December 1, 1924; 184 performances. Cast: Fanny Brice, Clark and McCullough, Oscar Shaw, the Brox Sisters, Claire Luce, and others.
Alice in Wonderland
All Alone
The Call of the South
Don't Send Me Back to Petrograd
Don't Wait Too Long
In the Shade of a Sheltering Tree
Listening
Rock-a-Bye Baby
Tell Her in the Springtime
Tokio Blues
Unlucky in Love
Where Is My Little Old New York?
Who

1925

Always
He Doesn't Know What It's All About
It's a Walk-in with Walker
Remember
Venetian Isles

THE COCOANUTS
  Book by George S. Kaufman; directed by Oscar Eagle. Produced by Sam H.
  Harris at the Lyric Theatre, December 8, 1925; 276 performances. Cast: Grou-
  cho, Harpo, Chico, and Zeppo Marx, Margaret Dumont, Janet Velie, Basil
  Ruysdael, Frances Williams, Georgie Hale, and others.
  Overture
ACT 1
  Opening: The Guests (So This Is Florida)
  The Bellhops
  The Family Reputation
  Lucky Boy
  Why Am I a Hit with the Ladies?
  A Little Bungalow
  Florida by the Sea
  The Monkey Doodle-Doo
  Entr'acte
ACT 2
  Opening: Five O'Clock Tea
  They're Blaming the Charleston
  We Should Care
  Minstrel Days
  Tango Melody (Spain)
  The Tale of the Shirt (Bizet)
  Why Do You Want to Know Why?
  When We're Running a Little Hotel of Our Own
  What's There about Me?

1926
  At Peace with the World
  Because I Love You
  Everyone in the World Is Doing the Charleston [*for summer edition of* The Cocoa-
    nuts]
  Gentlemen Prefer Blondes [*for summer edition of* The Cocoanuts]
  How Many Times?
  I'm on My Way Home
  Just a Little Longer
  That's a Good Girl
  Ting-A-Ling, the Bells'll Ring [*for summer edition of* The Cocoanuts]
  To My Mammy [*for film* Mammy]
  We'll Never Know
  Why Do You Want to Know Why? [*for summer edition of* The Cocoanuts]

1927
  Blue Skies [*interpolation: Rodgers and Hart's* Betsy]
  Russian Lullaby

The Song Is Ended
Together We Two
What Does It Matter?

ZIEGFELD FOLLIES (TWENTY-FIRST EDITION)

Sketches by Harold Atteridge and Eddie Cantor; directed by Zeke Colvan. Produced by Florenz Ziegfeld, Jr., and A. L. Erlanger at the New Amsterdam Theatre, August 16, 1927; 167 performances. Cast: Eddie Cantor, Ruth Etting,
Andrew Tombes, Franklyn Baur, Cliff Edwards, Paulette Goddard, the Brox Sisters, Edgar Fairchild and Ralph Rainger (piano duo), and others.

It All Belongs to Me
It's Up to the Band
I Want to Be Glorified
Jimmy
Jungle Jingle
Learn to Sing a Love Song
My New York
Ooh! Maybe It's You
Rainbow of Girls
Ribbons and Bows
Shaking the Blues Away
Ticklin' the Ivories
What Makes Me Love You?

1928

Better Times with Al
Coquette [*for film* Coquette]
How about Me?
I Can't Do without You
Let Me Sing and I'm Happy [*for film* Mammy]
Marie [*for film* The Awakening]
Roses of Yesterday
Sunshine
To Be Forgotten
Where Is the Song of Songs for Me? [*for film* Lady of the Pavements]
Yascha Michaeloffsky's Melody

1929

In the Morning
Looking at You across the Breakfast Table [*for film* Mammy]
My Little Feller [*for film* The Singing Fool; *not used*]
Puttin' On the Ritz [*for film* Puttin' On the Ritz]
Swanee Shuffle [*for film* Hallelujah!]
Waiting at the End of the Road [*for film* Hallelujah!]
When My Dreams Come True [*for film version of* The Cocoanuts]
With You [*for film* Puttin' On the Ritz]

1930

Just a Little While
The Little Things in Life
Reaching for the Moon [*for film* Reaching for the Moon]

1931

Begging for Love
Do You Believe Your Eyes, or Do You Believe Your Baby? [*for film* Reaching for the Moon; *not used*]
I Want You for Myself
Me
When the Folks High Up Do the Mean Low-down [*for film* Reaching for the Moon]

1932

How Deep Is the Ocean?
I'll Miss You in the Evening
I'm Playing with Fire
Say It Isn't So

FACE THE MUSIC

Book by Moss Hart; directed by Hassard Short (music) and George S. Kaufman (book). Produced by Sam H. Harris at the New Amsterdam Theatre, February 17, 1932; 165 performances. Cast: Mary Boland, Hugh O'Connell, J. Harold Murray, Katherine Carrington, Andrew Tombes, David Burns, and others.
Overture

ACT 1

Opening: Lunching at the Automat
Let's Have Another Cup of Coffee
Reisman's Doing a Show
Torch Song
You Must Be Born with It
On a Roof in Manhattan
My Rhinestone Girl
Soft Lights and Sweet Music
Entr'acte

ACT 2

Opening: Well, of All the Rotten Shows
I Say It's Spinach (and the Hell with It)
Drinking Song
Dear Old Crinoline Days
I Don't Want to Be Married (I Just Wanna Be Friends)
Manhattan Madness
Investigation
How Can I Change My Luck?
[*deleted:* Two Cheers Instead of Three]

1933
 I Can't Remember
 Maybe It's Because I Love You Too Much
AS THOUSANDS CHEER
 Sketches by Moss Hart; directed by Hassard Short. Produced by Sam H. Harris
 at the Music Box Theatre, September 30, 1933; 400 performances. Cast: Mari-
 lyn Miller, Clifton Webb, Helen Broderick, Ethel Waters, Hamtree Harrington,
 Jerome Cowan, and others.
 Prologue: Man Bites Dog
ACT 1
 How's Chances?
 Heat Wave
 Lonely Heart
 The Funnies
 Easter Parade
ACT 2
 Supper Time
 Revolt in Cuba
 Our Wedding Day
 Harlem on My Mind
 Not for All the Rice in China

1934
 Butter Fingers
 I Never Had a Chance
 Moon over Napoli [*written for unproduced revue* More Cheers]
 So Help Me

1935
TOP HAT
 Screenplay by Dwight Taylor and Allan Scott; directed by Mark Sandrich. Pro-
 duced by Pandro S. Berman for RKO-Radio; released August 1935. Cast: Fred
 Astaire, Ginger Rogers, Edward Everett Horton, Helen Broderick, Erik Rhodes,
 and Eric Blore.
 No Strings
 Isn't This a Lovely Day (to Be Caught in the Rain)?
 Top Hat, White Tie and Tails
 Cheek to Cheek
 The Piccolino
 [*deleted:* Get Thee behind Me, Satan; Wild about You; You're the Cause]

1936
FOLLOW THE FLEET
 Screenplay by Dwight Taylor and Allan Scott, based on the play *Shore Leave;*
 directed by Mark Sandrich. Produced by Pandro S. Berman for RKO-Radio;

released February 1936. Cast: Fred Astaire, Ginger Rogers, Randolph Scott, Harriet Hilliard, Astrid Allwyn, Lucille Ball, Tony Martin, and Frank Jenks.
We Saw the Sea
Let Yourself Go
Get Thee behind Me, Satan
I'd Rather Lead a Band
But Where Are You?
I'm Putting All My Eggs in One Basket
Let's Face the Music and Dance
[*deleted:* Moonlight Maneuvers; With a Smile on My Face]

1937
ON THE AVENUE

Screenplay by Gene Markey and William Conselman; directed by Roy Del Ruth. Produced by Markey for Twentieth Century-Fox; released February 1937. Cast: Dick Powell, Madeleine Carroll, Alice Faye, George Barbier, Alan Mowbray, Cora Witherspoon, Walter Catlett, Joan Davis, Stepin Fetchit, and the Ritz Brothers.
He Ain't Got Rhythm
The Girl on the *Police Gazette*
You're Laughing at Me
This Year's Kisses
I've Got My Love to Keep Me Warm
Slumming on Park Avenue
[*deleted:* On the Avenue; On the Steps of Grant's Tomb; Swing Sister]

1938
ALEXANDER'S RAGTIME BAND

Screenplay by Kathryn Scola and Lamar Trotti; directed by Henry King. Produced by Darryl F. Zanuck and Harry Joe Brown for Twentieth Century-Fox; released May 1938. Cast: Tyrone Power, Alice Faye, Don Ameche, Ethel Merman, Jack Haley, Helen Westley, Jean Hersholt, John Carradine, Wally Vernon, Dixie Dunbar, Grady Sutton, Chick Chandler, and others.

INTERPOLATIONS:

Alexander's Ragtime Band; The Ragtime Violin; That International Rag; Everybody's Doin' It Now; This Is the Life; When the Midnight Choo-Choo Leaves for Alabam'; For Your Country and My Country; I Can Always Find a Little Sunshine in the Y.M.C.A.; Oh! How I Hate to Get Up in the Morning; We're on Our Way to France; Say It with Music; A Pretty Girl Is like a Melody; Blue Skies; Pack Up Your Sins and Go to the Devil; What'll I Do?; Remember; Everybody Step; All Alone; Easter Parade; Heat Wave

NEW SONGS:

Now It Can Be Told
My Walking Stick

CAREFREE

Screenplay by Ernest Pagano and Allan Scott; directed by Mark Sandrich. Produced by Pandro S. Berman for RKO-Radio; released September 1938. Cast: Fred Astaire, Ginger Rogers, Ralph Bellamy, Luella Gear, Jack Carson, Clarence Kolb, Franklin Pangborn, and Hattie McDaniel.

Since They Turned "Loch Lomond" into Swing [*instrumental*]

I Used to Be Color-Blind

The Yam

Change Partners

The Night Is Filled with Music

1939

God Bless America [*1918; revised*]

It's a Lovely Day Tomorrow [*interpolation:* Louisiana Purchase, *1940*]

SECOND FIDDLE

Screenplay by Harry Tugend, based on a story by George Bradshaw; directed by Sidney Lanfield. Produced by Gene Markey for Twentieth Century–Fox; released July 1939. Cast: Sonja Henie, Tyrone Power, Rudy Vallee, Edna Mae Oliver, Mary Healy, Lyle Talbot, Alan Dinehart, Minna Gombell, and Spencer Charters.

An Old-Fashioned Tune Always Is New

The Song of the Metronome

Back to Back

When Winter Comes

I Poured My Heart into a Song

I'm Sorry for Myself

1940

I Believe

LOUISIANA PURCHASE

Book by Morrie Ryskind, based on a story by B. G. DeSylva; directed by Edgar MacGregor. Produced by DeSylva at the Imperial Theatre, May 28, 1940; 444 performances. Cast: William Gaxton, Victor Moore, Vera Zorina, Irene Bordini, Carol Bruce, Robert Pitkin, Ray Mayer, Ralph Riggs, and others.

Overture

ACT 1

Apologia (Opening Letter)

Sex Marches On

Louisiana Purchase

It's a Lovely Day Tomorrow [*1939*]

Outside of That I Love You

You're Lonely and I'm Lonely

Dance with Me Tonight (at the Mardi Gras)

Finale: What's This We Hear?

Entr'acte

ACT 2

    Latins Know How

    What Chance Have I with Love?

    The Lord Done Fixed Up My Soul

    Fools Fall in Love

    Old Man's Darling, Young Man's Slave

    You Can't Brush Me Off

    Finale: Somebody Handed Us a Ticket to Picket

    [*deleted during tryout:* I'd Love to Be Shot from a Cannon with You; It'll Come to
        You; Wild about You (*from* Top Hat)]

1941

    Angels of Mercy

    Any Bonds Today?

    Arms for the Love of America

    A Little Old Church in England

    When That Man Is Dead and Gone

    When This Crazy World Is Sane Again

1942

    I Paid My Income Tax Today

    I Threw a Kiss in the Ocean

    Me and My Melinda

THIS IS THE ARMY

    Conceived by Irving Berlin; directed by Ezra Stone and Joshua Logan. Presented
    by "Uncle Sam" at the Broadway Theatre, July 4, 1942; 113 performances. Cast:
    Ezra Stone, Julie Oshins, Philip Truex, Fred Kelly, Burl Ives, Earl Oxford, Joe
    Cook, Jr., Stuart Churchill, Irving Berlin, and others.

ACT 1

1. **A Military Minstrel Show**

    Opening chorus: You Thought That Many, Many Years Ago . . .

    This Is the Army, Mr. Jones

    I'm Getting Tired So I Can Sleep

    My Sergeant and I Are Buddies

    I Left My Heart at the Stage Door Canteen

    The Army's Made a Man out of Me

    Mandy [*1918, from* Yip! Yip! Yaphank, *as* Sterling Silver Moon]

2. **A Military Vaudeville Show**

    Ladies of the Chorus [*1918, from* Yip! Yip! Yaphank]

    That Russian Winter

    That's What the Well-Dressed Man in Harlem Will Wear

    Finale: This Is the Army; How about a Cheer for the Navy

ACT 2

    American Eagles

    With My Head in the Clouds

Aryans under the Skin (Jap-German Sextette)
A Soldier's Dream
Oh! How I Hate to Get Up in the Morning [*1918, from* Yip! Yip! Yaphank]
This Time
Dressed Up to Win

HOLIDAY INN

Screenplay by Claude Binyon, based on a story by Elmer Rice; directed by Mark
Sandrich. Produced by Sandrich for Paramount; released August 1942. Cast:
Bing Crosby, Fred Astaire, Marjorie Reynolds (vocals by Martha Mears), Virginia
Dale, Walter Abel, Louise Beavers, Harry Barris, and the Bob Crosby Bob Cats.
I'll Capture Your Heart Singing
You're Easy to Dance With
White Christmas
Happy Holiday
Holiday Inn
Let's Start the New Year Right
Abraham
Be Careful, It's My Heart
I Can't Tell a Lie
Let's Say It with Firecrackers
Song of Freedom
Plenty to Be Thankful For
[*interpolations:* Lazy; Easter Parade]
[*deleted:* It's a Great Country]

1943

The Kick in the Pants [*written for* This Is the Army *tour*]
My British Buddy [*written for* This Is the Army *tour*]
Ve Don't Like It [*written for* This Is the Army *tour*]
What Does He Look Like? [*for film version of* This Is the Army]
[*interpolated in film version of* This Is the Army: My Sweetie (*1917*); Goodbye
France (*1918*)]

1944

All of My Life
The Fifth Army Is Where My Heart Is [*written for* This Is the Army *tour*]
There Are No Wings on a Foxhole [*written for* This Is the Army *tour*]
What Are We Gonna Do with All the Jeeps? [*written for* This Is the Army *tour*]

1945

Everybody Knew but Me
Heaven Watch the Philippines [*written for* This Is the Army *tour*]
I Get Along with the Aussies [*written for* This Is the Army *tour*]
I'll Dance Rings around You

Just a Blue Serge Suit

Oh, to Be Home Again [*written for* This Is the Army *tour*]

1946

BLUE SKIES

Screenplay by Arthur Sheekman; directed by Stuart Heisler. Produced by Sol C. Siegel for Paramount; released October 1946 (delayed). Cast: Bing Crosby, Fred Astaire, Joan Caulfield, Billy DeWolfe, Olga San Juan, Jimmy Conlin, Cliff Nazarro, and others.

INTERPOLATIONS:

A Pretty Girl Is like a Melody; I've Got My Captain Working for Me Now; You'd Be Surprised; All by Myself; Puttin' On the Ritz; (I'll See You in) Cuba; Always; Blue Skies; The Little Things in Life; Not for All the Rice in China; Russian Lullaby; Everybody Step; How Deep Is the Ocean?; Heat Wave; Any Bonds Today?; This Is the Army, Mr. Jones; White Christmas

NEW SONGS:

You Keep Coming Back like a Song [*1943*]

A Couple of Song and Dance Men [*1945*]

Getting Nowhere (Running Around in Circles) [*1945*]

Serenade to an Old-Fashioned Girl

[*deleted:* It's a Lovely Day for a Walk]

ANNIE GET YOUR GUN

Book by Herbert and Dorothy Fields; directed by Joshua Logan. Produced by Richard Rodgers and Oscar Hammerstein at the Imperial Theatre, May 16, 1946; 1,147 performances. Cast: Ethel Merman, Ray Middleton, Marty May, Kenny Bowers, Betty Anne Nyman, William O'Neal, Ellen Hanley, Harry Bellaver, and others.

Overture

ACT 1

Colonel Buffalo Bill

I'm a Bad, Bad Man

Doin' What Comes Natur'lly

The Girl That I Marry

You Can't Get a Man with a Gun

There's No Business like Show Business

They Say It's Wonderful

Moonshine Lullaby

I'll Share It All with You

My Defenses Are Down

I'm an Indian Too

Entr'acte

ACT 2

I Got Lost in His Arms

Who Do You Love I Hope

I Got the Sun in the Morning
Anything You Can Do
Finale: There's No Business . . . *[reprise]*
[deleted during tryout: Let's Go West Again; Take It in Your Stride; With Music]

1947

The Freedom Train
Help Me Help My Neighbor
Kate
Love and the Weather

1948
EASTER PARADE

Screenplay by Sidney Sheldon, Frances Goodrich, and Albert Hackett; directed by Charles Walters. Produced by Arthur Freed for M-G-M; released May 1948. Cast: Judy Garland, Fred Astaire, Peter Lawford, Ann Miller, Jules Munshin, Benay Venuta, Lola Albright, and others.

INTERPOLATIONS:

Everybody's Doin' It Now; I Want to Go Back to Michigan (Down on the Farm); Beautiful Faces Need Beautiful Clothes; I Love a Piano, Snookey Ookums; The Ragtime Violin; When the Midnight Choo-Choo Leaves for Alabam'; Shaking the Blues Away; The Girl on the Magazine Cover; Easter Parade

NEW SONGS:

Happy Easter [*1948*]
Drum Crazy [*1947*]
It Only Happens When I Dance with You [*1947*]
A Fella with an Umbrella [*1947*]
Steppin' Out with My Baby [*1947*]
A Couple of Swells [*1947*]
Better Luck Next Time [*1947*]
[deleted: Mr. Monotony]

1948

In Acapulco
Let's Keep in Touch While We're Dancing
What Can You Do with a General? *[interpolation:* White Christmas, *1954*]

1949

I'm Beginning to Miss You
MISS LIBERTY

Book by Robert E. Sherwood; directed by Moss Hart. Produced by Berlin, Sherwood, and Hart at the Imperial Theatre, July 15, 1949; 308 performances. Cast: Eddie Albert, Allyn McLerie, Mary McCarty, Charles Dingle, Philip Bourneuf,

Ethel Griffies, Herbert Berghof, Tommy Rall, Eddie Phillips, Johnny V. R. Thompson, and Maria Karnilova.

Overture

ACT 1

Extra! Extra!

What Do I Have to Do to Get My Picture Took?

The Most Expensive Statue in the World

A Little Fish in a Big Pond

Let's Take an Old-Fashioned Walk

Homework

Paris Wakes Up and Smiles

Only for Americans

Just One Way to Say I Love You

Entr'acte

ACT 2

Miss Liberty

The Train [*instrumental*]

You Can Have Him

The Policeman's Ball

Me an' My Bundle

Falling out of Love Can Be Fun

Give Me Your Tired, Your Poor [*words by Emma Lazarus*]

[*deleted on the road:* The Hon'rable Profession of the Fourth Estate; The Next Time I Fall in Love; What Do I Have to Do to Get My Picture in the Paper?; Mr. Monotony; Finding Work in Paris; The Pulitzer Prize; Entrance of the Reporters; Sing a Song of Sing Sing; The Story of Nell and the *Police Gazette*]

1950

CALL ME MADAM

Book by Howard Lindsay and Russel Crouse; directed by George Abbott. Produced by Leland Hayward at the Imperial Theatre, October 12, 1950; 644 performances. Cast: Ethel Merman, Paul Lukas, Alan Hewitt, Russell Nype, Galina Talva, Tommy Rall, Pat Harrington, and others.

Overture

ACT 1

Mrs. Sally Adams

The Hostess with the Mostes' on the Ball

Washington Square Dance

Lichtenburg

Can You Use Any Money Today?

Marrying for Love

The Ocarina

It's a Lovely Day Today

The Best Thing for You Would Be Me

Entr'acte

ACT 2

Something to Dance About
Once Upon a Time Today
They Like Ike
You're Just in Love/I Wonder Why?
Finale: You're Just in Love [*reprise*]
[*deleted during tryouts:* Free; Mr. Monotony]

1952

Anthem for Presentation Scene [*for film version of* Call Me Madam]
For the Very First Time
I Like Ike
Our Day of Independence [*for* Call Me Madam *tour; later deleted*]

1953

[*See 1954:* White Christmas]

1954

I'm Not Afraid
I Still Like Ike

WHITE CHRISTMAS

Screenplay by Norman Krasna, Norman Panama, and Melvin Frank; directed by Michael Curtiz. Produced by Robert Dolan for Paramount; released August 1954. Cast: Bing Crosby, Danny Kaye, Rosemary Clooney, Vera-Ellen (vocals dubbed by Trudy Ewen), Dean Jagger, Grady Sutton, Sig Ruman, Barrie Chase, and George Chakiris.

INTERPOLATIONS:

White Christmas; Blue Skies; Mandy; What Can You Do with a General? [1948]

NEW SONGS:

The Old Man [*1952*]
Sisters [*1953*]
The Best Things Happen While You're Dancing [*1953*]
Snow [*1953; revised version of* Free (*1950*) *from* Call Me Madam]
Count Your Blessings Instead of Sheep [*1952*]
Choreography [*1953*]
Love You Didn't Do Right by Me [*1953*]
Gee, I Wish I Was Back in the Army [*1954*]
[*deleted:* Sittin' in the Sun]

THERE'S NO BUSINESS LIKE SHOW BUSINESS

Screenplay by Henry and Phoebe Ephron; directed by Walter Lang. Produced by Sol C. Siegel for Twentieth Century–Fox; released December 1954. Cast: Ethel Merman, Dan Dailey, Donald O'Connor, Marilyn Monroe, Johnnie Ray, Mitzi Gaynor, Hugh O'Brian, Frank McHugh, Lee Patrick, Chick Chandler, and Lyle Talbot.

INTERPOLATIONS:

When the Midnight Choo-Choo Leaves for Alabam'; Play a Simple Melody; After You Get What You Want, You Don't Want It; You'd Be Surprised; Heat Wave; Alexander's Ragtime Band; If You Believe; There's No Business like Show Business

NEW SONGS:

A Sailor's Not a Sailor

A Man Chases a Girl

[*deleted:* But I Ain't Got a Man; I Can Make You Laugh (but I Wish I Could Make You Cry]

1955

Please Let Me Come Back to You

1956

Ike for Four More Years

1957

I Keep Running Away from You

Sayonara [*title song for film*]

You Can't Lose the Blues with Colors

1959

Israel

1962

MR. PRESIDENT

Book by Howard Lindsay and Russel Crouse; directed by Joshua Logan. Produced by Leland Hayward at the St. James Theatre, October 20, 1962; 265 performances. Cast: Robert Ryan, Nanette Fabray, Anita Gillette, Jack Haskell, Jack Washburn, Stanley Grover, Jerry Strickler, Charlotte Fairchild, Wisa D'Orso, John Cecil Holm, and David Brooks.

Overture

ACT 1

Opening: Just Someone Doing the Best Job . . .

Let's Go Back to the Waltz

In Our Hide-Away

The First Lady

Meat and Potatoes

I've Got to Be Around

The Secret Service

It Gets Lonely in the White House

Is He the Only Man in the World?

They Love Me

Pigtails and Freckles

Don't Be Afraid of Romance
Laugh It Up
Empty Pockets Filled with Love
Entr'acte

ACT 2

Glad to Be Home
You Need a Hobby
The Washington Twist
The Only Dance I Know (Song for Belly Dancer)
I'm Gonna Get Him
This Is a Great Country
[*deleted during tryouts:* Once Every Four Years; Anybody Can Write; Poor Joe]

1966

An Old-Fashioned Wedding [written for *Annie Get Your Gun* revival]

ADDENDA
SONGS FOR NEVER-PRODUCED SCORES
STARS ON MY SHOULDERS (1948)

A Beautiful Day in Brooklyn
It's a Lovely Day for a Walk [*for film* Blue Skies]
Let's Keep in Touch While We're Dancing
Nothing More to Say
When a One-Star General's Daughter Meets a Four-Star General's Son

WISE GUY (CA. 1952–56)

Go Home and Tell It to Your Wife
Love Leads to Marriage
You're a Sentimental Guy
You're a Sucker for a Dame

SAY IT WITH MUSIC (1963–65, ARTHUR FREED FILM FOR M-G-M, NEVER MADE)

A Guy on Monday
(It's) Always the Same
I Used to Play It by Ear
Long as I Can Take You Home
A Man to Cook For
One-Man Woman
Outside of Loving You, I Like You
The P.X.
The Ten Best Undressed Women in the World
Whisper It
Who Needs the Birds and the Bees?

MISCELLANEOUS

Aesop, That Able Fable Man
I'll Know Better Next Time
I Never Want to See You Again

It Takes More than Love to Keep a Lady Warm
Klondike Kate
Out of This World into Your Arms
Please Let Me Come Back to You
Smiling Geisha
Wait Until You're Married [*for a proposed musical,* East River, *1966*]
When Love Was All
You Got to Be Way Out to Be In [*for unproduced TV version of* Call Me Madam]

2. REPRESENTATIVE RECORDINGS

"Selected" is probably the more precise description here, for like all American popular songwriters, Berlin is widely represented on records spanning the course of his
long career. With a few notable exceptions, only recordings devoted solely to Berlin
songs are included below. So many popular singers have recorded the songs that
identifying them all would be impossible. Since the long-playing record has now all
but vanished (save as a collector's item), only currently (one hopes) available compact disks are listed here. Also, I have provided only the album title, the performers, and the company label, in the firm belief that CD numbers are designed for use
by computers, not by human beings. Major chain stores such as Tower Records and
HMV stock these selections, conveniently categorized by composer and show or
film title.

A. COLLECTIONS

i. **Come On and Hear!** *Early Songs by Irving Berlin 1909–1915.*

ii. **Keep On Smiling** *Songs by Irving Berlin 1915–1918.*
Oakton Recordings, 70 Allston Street, Boston, Massachusetts 02134. Featuring Benjamin Sears and Bradford Conner, voice and piano. Two priceless intro-
ductions to the young Berlin, comprising nearly fifty songs altogether,
including first recordings and alternate versions (e.g., in the first set, a solo
piano version of "Alexander's Ragtime Band" as well as the song proper). A
good example of Berlin's way with dialect, and humor, is "Cohen Owes Me
Nintey-seven Dollars" (in the second set; it may upset some, but it is decidedly of its time). Then there is the lovely ballad "Dream On, Little Soldier
Boy" from *Yip! Yip! Yaphank,* and, as an added treat, "Smile and Show Your
Dimple" before it became "Easter Parade." Scholarly? Yes, but presented with
a light touch, free of condescension, beautifully sung and with accompaniment
to match. Pianist Conner sometimes assists vocally, and others also contribute,
among them Julie Collins, Elbert Oxley, and Charles Ricker. The annotations
are exemplary.

iii. **Irving Berlin**   *Smithsonian American Songbook Series.*
Featuring Fred Astaire, Connee Boswell, Kate Smith, Irving Berlin, Bing Crosby, Dinah Shore, Judy Garland, Mary Martin, Ethel Merman, Donald O'Connor, Max Morath, Barbara Cook, Michael Feinstein, and others.

This release could be advertised as a "cornucopia," a collection ranging from the historical through the fairly recent: Astaire's "Cheek to Cheek," Kate Smith's "God Bless America," Berlin's "Oh! How I Hate to Get Up in the Morning," Mel Tormé's "Let's Face the Music and Dance," Dinah Shore's duet (with herself) "Play a Simple Melody," and Johnny Mathis's "What'll I Do?" Including two dozen tracks in all, it is available on CD and cassette, though not all record shops carry it. Write to Smithsonian Recordings, Washington, DC 20560.

iv. **An Irving Berlin Showcase**   *Produced by Pearl Flapper.*
Primarily a British compilation, this title nonetheless features some familiar performers, such as Rudy Vallee with his Connecticut Yankees (doing "Say It Isn't So," a song he introduced on the air in 1932), the Brox Sisters (singing "How Many Times?"), and Mantovani ("The Piccolino"). All are vintage period recordings excellently transcribed from 78rpm shellac discs. Also included are some fine but little-known songs such as "I Can't Remember," "Tango Melody," and "I'm Playing with Fire"; especially interesting are a medley from *The Cocoanuts* and another from *Mammy* (the latter even preserves "To My Mammy," which was dropped from the film but contained the germ of the later hit "How Deep Is the Ocean?"). Pearl Records, an import, may be difficult to find; it is stocked by the chains and can be ordered by mail.

v. **Irving Berlin Revisited**   *Painted Smiles Records.*
Featuring Richard Chamberlain, Blossom Dearie, Dorothy Loudon, Bobby Short, Ann Hampton Callaway, Arthur Siegel, Sandy Stewart, and William Cantor. Arrangements by Norman Paris.

A good mix of rarities and not-so-rare songs, generally well sung. Richard Chamberlain's "Lonely Heart," for example, is exemplary, and Dorothy Loudon manages "Mr. Monotony" with her usual wit. She and Bobby Short revive "Waiting at the End of the Road" (from *Hallelujah!*). Less well known, and unavailable elsewhere, are "He's a Rag Picker," "Listening," and "Lead Me to Love." Producer Ben Bagley's annotations are best ignored.

vi. **Unsung Irving Berlin**
Varese Sarabande (two compact disks).

Indispensable is the word for this compilation of thirty-one songs, sung with affection, understanding, and no vocal posturing by more than two dozen talented vocalists. The selections range in time from 1909's "That Mesmerizing Mendelssohn Tune" to some of the late songs written for *Stars on My Shoulders, Wise Guy,* and *Say It with Music.* They encompass Berlin's wide range of creativity, his versatility, and his humanity. To single out this or that performance for special praise would be difficult as well as unfair; in every case it is the song that is served, not the singer. The program is directed, arranged, and orchestrated by Lanny Meyers. The annotations, by Isaiah Sheffer (who produced the twelve-hour marathon "Wall-to-Wall Irving Berlin," at Symphony Space in New York in March 1994) are informative, wise, and quite simply excellent.

vii. **Remember: Michael Feinstein Sings Irving Berlin** *Elektra Records.*
With Michael Feinstein and Liza Minnelli. Feinstein, David Ross, and Stan Freeman, piano; Jim Hughart, bass; Dennis Budmir, guitar and banjo.

A typically well chosen and sensitively sung Feinstein collection, offering up early songs, ballads, rhythm numbers, film and show tunes, and comic songs. Filling the cup are a lovely trio of duets with Liza Minnelli, with Stan Freeman (who also arranged) at the piano.

viii. **Starring Fred Astaire** *Columbia Records (two compact disks).*
Fred Astaire, vocals, accompanied by Leo Reisman and his orchestra, Johnny Green and his orchestra, Ray Noble and his orchestra, Benny Goodman and his orchestra, and Perry Botkin and his orchestra.

Although not soundtrack takes, the songs included in this set come from *Top Hat, Follow the Fleet,* and *Carefree.* These are some of the finest recordings Astaire made; the Johnny Green accompaniments are especially good. In addition to the Berlin tunes, the CDs also feature songs from Gershwin's *Shall We Dance?* and *A Damsel in Distress* and Kern's *Swing Time.* Rounding out the selection are the Gershwins' "Who Cares?" (with Goodman), a couple of songs written by Johnny Mercer, and a number by Astaire himself.

ix. **That's Entertainment 3** *Angel Records.*
Featuring Judy Garland and numerous M-G-M stars.

A rich selection from Metro's so-called Golden Age, during the Arthur Freed years. Berlin songs featured include the filmed but never used "I'm an Indian Too" and "Doin' What Comes Natur'lly" by Judy Garland; she also does the (perpetually) unused "Mr. Monotony." Betty Hutton joins Howard Keel on "Anything You Can Do I Can Do Better," and Ann Miller does "Shaking the Blues Away." Other fine songs and interpretations round out the disk.

x. **Judy Garland:** *Collector's Gems from M-G-M Films* *Turner Classic Movies (two compact disks).*
Judy Garland and many others.

A retrospective covering Judy Garland's career at Metro from beginning (*Every Sunday,* 1936) to end (*Annie Get Your Gun,* 1949). For the latter, this collection presents the soundtrack recordings she made before her suspension: "You Can't Get a Man with a Gun," "There's No Business like Show Business,"

"They Say It's Wonderful," "The Girl That I Marry," "I Got the Sun in the Morning," "Anything You Can Do," and the deleted "Let's Go West Again." The compendium contains outtakes, alternate takes, and reprises from several of her films.

B. SOUNDTRACKS

i.   **Ginger and Fred: *Follow the Fleet/Swing Time*** *Chansons Cinéma.*
Complete from the title music to the finale, except for the unfortunate omission of "Get Thee behind Me, Satan," this well-engineered transcription from a French source makes for good listening. (The "Satan" song was dropped because the film from which the disk was made had a mutilated soundtrack: the word *Satan* was eliminated each time it was sung by Harriet Hilliard.) An added bonus is the inclusion of the songs from Jerome Kern and Dorothy Fields's *Swing Time.* This disk is labeled as the second in the "Ginger and Fred" series; no doubt the first contains the *Top Hat* songs. Issued by the French firm Chansons Cinéma, the CD may be difficult to find.

ii. **Ginger and Fred: *Shall We Dance?/Carefree*** *Chansons Cinéma.*
The third in the series mentioned above, and a good combination, though "The Night Is Filled with Music" is absent from the Berlin score and the "Walking the Dog" instrumental from the Gershwin.

iii. **Flying Down to Rio/Carefree** *Sandy Hook Records.*
With Fred Astaire, Ginger Rogers, Raul Roulien, and Etta Moten.
     The Vincent Youmans/Gus Kahn–scored *Flying Down to Rio* introduced the Astaire-Rogers team. The *Carefree* selections duplicate those on the Chansons Cinéma disk; both releases include the instrumental "Since They Turned 'Loch Lomond' into Swing."

iv. **Bing Crosby Sings Irving Berlin and Rodgers and Hart** *Conifer Records.*
Although not soundtrack recordings, the twenty-two tracks on this disk nonetheless include most of Crosby's songs from *Holiday Inn.* Additional Berlin songs of note herein are "Soft Lights and Sweet Music," "On a Roof in Manhattan," "How Deep Is the Ocean?," and "I'm Playing with Fire," all recorded in the early thirties. Also "Alexander's Ragtime Band" (with Connee Boswell), "Now It Can Be Told," and such patriotic statements as "God Bless America" and "Angels of Mercy." Besides Rodgers and Hart's wartime "The Bombardier Song," three songs from Crosby's 1935 film *Mississippi* are provided, chief among them the memorable "It's Easy to Remember." Conifer Records is an English firm that issues "nostalgia" under the rubric of its Happy Days series; its releases should be reasonably easily available.

v. **Blue Skies**   *Sandy Hook Records.*
With Bing Crosby, Fred Astaire, Olga San Juan, Billy DeWolfe, and Joan Caulfield.
The virtually complete soundtrack released by Sandy Hook Radiola Records.

vi. **Easter Parade**   *Rhino Records Movie Music.*
With Judy Garland, Fred Astaire, Peter Lawford, and Dick Beavers.
No stinting here: Rhino has reissued the complete soundtrack, including instrumentals, reprises, and the out-taken "Mr. Monotony." The package includes an excellent booklet, fully annotated (with recording dates) and illustrated, with an informative essay by the conscientious film historian John Fricke.

C. STAGE MUSICALS

i. **Louisiana Purchase**   *DRG Records.*
With Judy Blazer, Tania Elg, Debbie Gravitte, George S. Irving, Michael McGrath, New York Voices, and many others; musical direction by Rob Fisher.
Herein the complete score, including such rarities as "I'd Love to Be Shot from a Cannon with You," "Wild about You," and the ballet "Old Man's Darling, Young Man's Slave," with original orchestrations by Robert Russell Bennett and N. Lang Van Cleve and an addition by a master restorer of vintage scores, Russell Warner. The original vocal arrangements by Hugh Martin and Ralph Blane are also heard. The large cast of nineteen sings beautifully under the expert direction of Rob Fisher, himself a master of restoration.

ii. **Annie Get Your Gun**   *MCA Broadway Classics.*
With Ethel Merman, Ray Middleton, Robert Lenn, and Kathleen Carnes; chorus and orchestra conducted by Jay Blackton.
This original-cast recording, made in 1946, is not complete, but it contains a generous portion of the show's score, capturing Merman at her best.
The 1966 revival, in which Merman costarred with Bruce Yarnell, Benay Venuta, Jerry Orbach, and others, is preserved on an RCA CD that provides the complete score, including "An Old-Fashioned Wedding," especially written for that production. The orchestration is by Robert Russell Bennett, with chorus and orchestra under the direction of Franz Allers.
A Mary Martin–John Raitt *Annie,* taken from a 1957 television broadcast, is also available in Angel Records' Broadway Classics series. Mary Martin was not the belter Merman was, but her softer, prettier voice is well suited to the lovely "They Say It's Wonderful" and "Moonshine Lullaby." Raitt's Frank Butler is fine.
Finally, there are two studio productions of the complete *Annie Get Your Gun.* The first, which stars the superb Kim Criswell and Thomas Hampson

along with an extended singing cast, accompanied by a full chorus and the London Sinfonietta conducted by John McGlinn, may be found on the EMI Classics label. The second, starring another extraordinary Annie, Judy Kaye, opposite the fine Barry Bostwick, is available on two CDs (comprising all the songs and more orchestral music) issued by TER, with orchestra and chorus under the direction of John Owen Edwards.

iii. **Miss Liberty**   *Sony Broadway.*
With Eddie Albert, Allyn McLerie, Mary McCarty, and other members of the original cast; chorus and orchestra under the direction of Jay Blackton.

A fortunate recording of a charmingly scored musical, in a new master made from the original mono release.

iv. **Ethel Merman: Twelve Songs from *Call Me Madam* (with Selections from *Panama Hattie*)**   *MCA Classics, Broadway Gold series.*
Ethel Merman with Dick Haymes, Eileen Wilson, and Joan Carroll.

This is the non-original-cast album made at the time of *Madam*'s Broadway run (another, with the original cast plus Dinah Shore—substituting for the contractually unavailable Ethel Merman—was released by RCA Victor). "Lichtenburg," Paul Lukas's opening number, is sung by a chorus with Gordon Jenkins conducting; Haymes, as usual, is in good voice here.

The complete score of *Call Me Madam* is available on a DRG Theater release, with Tyne Daly's singing the Merman songs in a concert adaptation staged at New York's City Center, in its estimable Encores! series. Walter Charles appears in the Lukas part, Melissa Errico sings the Princess Maria songs, and Lewis Cleale is the lovesick Kenneth Gibson. This formidable cast, plus chorus and the nifty Coffee Club Orchestra under Rob Fisher, treats the music right.

v. **Mr. President**   *Sony Broadway.*
With Robert Ryan, Nanette Fabray, Anita Gillette, Jack Haskell, Wisa D'Orso, Jack Washburn, and others from the original cast; chorus and orchestra conducted by Jay Blackton.

Happily, despite the show's carping critical reception, Columbia Records producer Goddard Lieberson agreed to make this original-cast recording (newly available in the Sony Broadway series). Unburdened by the less-than-sparkling plot, the score proves a treasurable song collection.

3. IRVING BERLIN FILMS ON VIDEOCASSETTE

i. **The Cocoanuts**   *(1929) MCA Home Video.*
An early, and primitive, example of a filmed stage musical: the first Marx Brothers movie, shot (on New York sound stages, not in Hollywood) before the advent

of the flexible camera and before directors quite understood the art of filming musicals. Most of the Berlin score survived the transition from stage to screen, but like the stage production, the movie is primarily a Marx Brothers vehicle.

ii. **Hallelujah!** *(1929) M-G-M/UA Home Video.*
A drama with music, strongly directed by King Vidor with a unique (for Hollywood at that time) all-black cast. The score draws on traditional spirituals, with two Berlin songs. A beautiful film.

iii. **Reaching for the Moon** *(1930) VHS HMV-8061.*
Included here only for completeness's sake, since the score was mutilated and most of Berlin's songs were jettisoned. Interesting largely for Fairbanks's athletic performance and for Bing Crosby in an early appearance on film, singing one of Berlin's survivors, "When the Folks High Up Do the Mean Low-down." Otherwise a dud.

iv. **Top Hat** *(1935) Turner VC.*

v. **Follow the Fleet** *(1936) Turner VC.*

vi. **Carefree** *(1938) Turner VC.*
The Astaire-Rogers RKO trilogy from the first golden era of the film musical. The towering *Top Hat* was the team's first starring production, and *Carefree* its last appearance in this type of musical (it was followed by the stars' final film together, the biographical *Story of Vernon and Irene Castle*). Wonderful fun, with delightful songs.

vii. **On the Avenue** *(1937) Fox Video.*
A change of scene for Berlin, working at Twentieth Century–Fox with Dick Powell and Alice Faye and producing such songs as "This Year's Kisses," "I've Got My Love to Keep Me Warm," and "You're Laughing at Me." Berlin's smooth transition from Astaire-Rogers to Powell-Faye reveals his versatility and adaptability; the songs are specially tailored to the vocalists, always with unerring craftsmanship.

viii. **Alexander's Ragtime Band** *(1938) Fox Video.*
The first of the musical film anthologies, drawing upon the Berlin catalog with the addition of, in this instance, two new songs. Ethel Merman revives the older songs, and Alice Faye does a fine job on, among others, the haunting "Now It Can Be Told."

ix. **Second Fiddle** *(1939) Fox Video.*
Stars Sonja Henie and Tyrone Powers leave most of the singing to Mary Healy and Rudy Vallee, though Henie does the winning "The Song of the Metronome,"

accompanied by a children's chorus. Vallee is particularly good on the romantic "I Poured My Heart into a Song" and the rhythm-ballad "When Winter Comes."

x. **Louisiana Purchase**   *(1941) MCA Universal.*
A reasonably faithful transfer from stage to screen, brightened by the casting of Vera Zorina, Irene Bordoni, and Victor Moore in their original roles; Bob Hope appears in the William Gaxton part. A smart, lavish production, and an outstanding score.

xi. **Holiday Inn**   *(1942) MCA Home Video.*
This legendary musical counts the long-lived "White Christmas" among its abundant score. The plot may be a bit thin, but the songs and dances are nourishing fare.

xii. **This Is the Army**   *(1943) Vintage Video or Video Yesteryear.*
The film adds a few characters and a plot of sorts but otherwise leaves the stage production intact. The GI cast is great, as are Irving Berlin's rendition of "Oh! How I Hate to Get Up in the Morning" and Kate Smith's "God Bless America."

xiii. **Blue Skies**   *(1946) MCA Universal.*
The second in the Astaire-Crosby-Berlin musical anthology series, inspired by the success of *Holiday Inn.* The score consists of seventeen old songs and four new ones, sung by Crosby, Astaire, Billy DeWolfe, and Olga San Juan.

xiv. **Easter Parade**   *(1948) M-G-M/UA Home Video.*
A lushly filmed period piece with fine performances by Judy Garland, Fred Astaire, and Ann Miller. Another Berlin parade of ten old hits and seven new songs. One of Arthur Freed's most ambitious, and most successful, productions.

xv. **There's No Business like Show Business**   *(1954) Fox Video.*
Plenty of songs, including two new ones, given glowing interpretations by Ethel Merman, Donald O'Connor, Mitzi Gaynor, and Marilyn Monroe. The plot occasionally gets in the way of the musical numbers, but not insurmountably so.

xvi. **White Christmas**   *(1954) Paramount Home Video.*
Another variation on the *Holiday Inn* formula, combining vintage Berlin with new (nine songs), and with Danny Kaye substituting for Fred Astaire. A well-plotted screenplay makes this one of the best of the Berlin film musicals.

SOURCES

In addition to those people I have interviewed and queried, and the volumes enumerated in the bibliography, my sources include several newspapers and magazines, many contemporaneous with the events in Irving Berlin's career. Often as not, the same anecdote flourishes in several variations, each with a different cast and/or a different outcome; Berlin engendered tales precisely *because* of his uniqueness, his untutored quality, and his wild success. Early in his career, obviously ghostwritten (or well-edited) articles attributed to him appeared in print; they made his points well enough—whether on ragtime, jazz, opera, or how to write a popular song—but they are not in his voice. Happily, later attributions sound more authentic. Still, I have had to exercise discretion. Plenty of documentation exists (I have two bulging notebooks), for despite his later reclusiveness, his professional life was always public. His private family life was his, however, and theirs, and rightly so.

PRELUDE: GOLDEN SHORE

The bulk of the story of life in czarist Russia and the route of escape to the New World is gleaned from the studies by Howe and Sanders, both of whom quote liberally from original sources and documents ranging from Mary Antin's *From Plotzk to Boston* to the (London) *Times* of May 12, 1881. The spelling of variable Russian place-names is lifted from *The Times Atlas of the World* (London: Times Books, 1977). Widgoder's *Encyclopedic Dictionary of Judaica* was a most useful reference for spellings, definitions, and biographies. The treatment of newcomers to Ellis Island is covered in Howe and Sanders, and in the *Newsday Magazine* for September 2, 1990. Life on the Lower East Side at the time of the Balines' arrival is documented, once again, by Howe and Sanders and, more romantically if perhaps less accurately, by Woollcott in his biography.

1. THE BOW'RY

The bulk of the story of Berlin's early life emanated from Woollcott and published interviews. The story of the piece-by-piece selling of the Balines' samovar comes from a Berlin interview that appeared in the *New York Sun* on February 24, 1947. The identification of Bill Schultz as the musician who took down Berlin's improvised-on-the-spot tune to "Sadie Salome" is from a Berlin interview on August 21, 1961.

2. WANDERING MINSTREL

Much here comes from Woollcott. The story about the writing of "Alexander's Ragtime Band" is based on interviews with Berlin; the "We'd go out plugging till around one or two . . ." dates from August 21, 1961, and other information from March of the same year. The results of the interviews and phone conversations appear in an article by me, "Alexander and Irving" (not my title), published in *Listen: A Music Monthly,* September–October 1964. Berlin commented on Mike Salter in an article by Walter Davenport, printed in the *New York Herald* on December 18, 1922.

3. UP AND DOWN BROADWAY

Woollcott again, including George M. Cohan's tribute and Berlin's Friars speech. The materials involving Berlin and Victor Herbert come from Waters's excellent biography, and some others from an interview with Berlin on May 19, 1949. The early Gershwin-Berlin encounters are chronicled in Goldberg's *George Gershwin.* Information about Berlin's early songs is derived from the annotations for the Sears-Conner compact disk collections. The same enterprising team managed to discover a previously unknown Berlin number entitled "Santa Claus: A Syncopated Christmas Song," published in the Christmas Eve 1916 edition of the *New York World.*

4. THIS IS THE ARMY, MR. B

An oft-told tale, beginning with Woollcott; the recollections of Harry Ruby, who worked with Berlin at Camp Upton, were reproduced in Max Wilk's collection of firsthand interviews. General Bell's reaction to the demand that Berlin change his name comes from an interview with Berlin on April 4, 1961. The *Yip! Yip! Yaphank* review appeared in the *Times* on August 20, 1918; Bell's introductory comments were reprinted in *Variety* three days later.

5. THE MUSIC BOXES

The genesis of the Music Box and its revues comes from Woollcott; the *Times* published Berlin's own recollections on September 23, 1982. Berlin on John

Golden and Sam Bernard's reaction is from a Mel Gussow interview in the *Times*, September 23, 1971. Stanley Green on the *Ziegfeld Follies of 1919* is derived from the liner notes of a long-playing album from the Smithsonian American Theatre Series, released in 1977. The description of Neysa McMein's salon is taken from Gallagher's history of the Algonquin and biography of McMein, *Anything Goes*. The formation of ASCAP and the early legal actions initiated by Victor Herbert are covered in the Waters biography.

6. FACING THE MUSIC

Much of the background on the Ellin Mackay–Irving Berlin romance appears, most personally, in Mary Ellin Barrett's *A Daughter's Memoir*, as well as in contemporary newspapers, interviews, and subsequent biographies. The story of the making of *The Cocoanuts* is told in Scott Meredith's biography of George S. Kaufman; Kaufman on music appeared in *Stage* magazine, August 1938.

7. CROSS-COUNTRY TRAUMA

Berlin's initial problems with Hollywood were part of the gossip of the period and are corroborated by his daughter in her *A Daughter's Memoir*. Berlin only hinted at his unhappiness there in a few interviews and tended to dismiss the songs. The genesis of *Hallelujah!* (omitting mention of Berlin) is told in Vidor's autobiography.

8. COMEBACK

Franklin P. Adams covered the comings and goings of the Berlins in his columns in the *Evening Mail*, the *Tribune*, and the *World*, entitled "The Diary of Our Own Samuel Pepys" (collected in two volumes and published by Simon and Schuster in 1935). Berlin's interview about *Face the Music* with Percy N. Stone appeared in the *Herald Tribune* on February 23, 1932; Hart's recollections were published in *Stage* in August 1938. Ethel Waters on "Supper Time" is from her autobiography, written with Charles Samuels (Garden City, N.Y.: Doubleday, 1951). The genesis of "Easter Parade" is corroborated in Stanley Green's *Ring Bells! Sing Songs!*

9. NEW DEAL

The situation in Hollywood circa 1933–34 is documented in *Show Biz: Vaude to Video* by Abel Green and Joe Laurie, Jr. (New York: Henry Holt & Co., 1951). The ins and outs of the making of the Astaire films are recounted in Arlene Croce's *The Fred Astaire & Ginger Rogers Book* (Outerbridge & Lazard, distributed by E. P. Dutton, 1972), as well as the Green/Goldblatt and John Mueller books. The position of various Berlin songs on "Your Hit Parade" is documented in John R. Williams, *This Was Your Hit Parade*, published by the author in Camden, Maine, in 1973. The Berlins' social life during a portion of their Hollywood residence is chronicled in *The Hollywood Reporter* by Tichi Wilkerson and

Marcia Bori (New York: Coward-McCann, 1984). Berlin's statement "I feel slow in Hollywood . . ." is taken from an interview that appeared in the *Journal-American* on September 4, 1938.

10. **TWICE IN A LIFETIME**

The bulk of the material on *This Is the Army* was gleaned from contemporary newspapers, *Variety,* and Logan's *Josh.* Cole Porter's letter to Berlin is quoted in George Eells, *The Life That He Led* (New York: G. P. Putnam's Sons, 1967). Berlin's observation "In 1918 the boys . . ." was quoted in the *New York Times* in August 1944. The chapter's title is borrowed from Berlin himself, who sometime in the 1960s thought about writing a book by that name about his two war musicals.

11. **OLD-FASHIONED SMASH**

The creation of *Annie Get Your Gun* is covered by Barrett, Fordin, Logan, and Rodgers. Some material is also drawn from my Time/Life Records annotation for *Annie Get Your Gun,* based on talks with Berlin. Miles Krueger's interviews are published in the brochure for the EMI Records CD *Annie Get Your Gun* (1991). Berlin's description of Oscar Hammerstein as a "genius" appears in Fordin, *World of Entertainment,* page 244.

12. **THERE'S NO BUSINESS . . .**

Hugh Fordin's *The World of Entertainment* gives a thorough account of Berlin's experiences at Metro-Goldwyn-Mayer. Vincente Minnelli's dismissal from *Easter Parade* is recounted by the director himself in *I Remember It Well* (Garden City, N.Y.: Doubleday, 1974). John Fricke furthered the narrative in his brochure notes for the Rhino Movie Music CD of the *Easter Parade* score. Most of the *Miss Liberty* and *Call Me Madam* annotations for Time/Life Records' American Musicals series are based on interviews granted by Irving Berlin sometime in 1981.

13. **GRAY SKIES**

Leonard Lyons on Berlin's introduction to painting appeared in the *New York Post* in May 1972. Ginette Spanier on Noël Coward is taken from *Noël* by Charles Castle (Garden City, N.Y.: Doubleday, 1973). The "You're Just in Love" litigation was covered in the *Times* on March 31 and April 1, 1955; Judge Smith's decision was published and is in the court records. The interview in which Berlin stated, "Retirement made me sick . . . ," was printed in the (London) *Daily Express* on September 13, 1963.

14. **SWAN SONGS?**

Berlin endured countless interviews in connection with *Mr. President.* These were published in newspapers and magazines (*The Saturday Evening Post, Colliers, Look*) and broadcast on radio. An especially pertinent example of this latter format is an interview recorded by Paul Bermann in 1962 and aired on the "Robert Sherman Hour" on December 24, 1988. Berlin was consistent throughout these talks, inevitably touching on patriotism, integrated scores, and old age. The Joshua Logan–Elliot Norton encounter on Boston's WGBH-TV was reported at length in *Variety* on September 5, 1982. Hugh Fordin tells the sad tale of *Say It with Music* in his *World of Entertainment,* while Richard Rodgers covers the *Annie Get Your Gun* revival in his autobiography. Berlin's "it gets damn boring . . ." statement appeared in the *New York Times* on May 15, 1966.

CODA: A HUNDRED AND ONE

Virtually all of the quotations from Berlin's colleagues appeared in the *Times, Newsday,* or the *Washington Post.* Press coverage of the hundredth-birthday celebrations may be found in *Newsday* and the *Post* for May 12, 1988. Berlin's final year is touchingly recalled in Barrett's *A Daughter's Memoir.* The various news-agency reports came to me courtesy of Elizabeth Dribble.

BIBLIOGRAPHY

Barrett, Mary Ellin. *Irving Berlin: A Daughter's Memoir.* New York: Simon & Schuster, 1994.

Bergreen, Laurence. *As Thousands Cheer.* New York: Viking, 1990.

Bordman, Gerald. *American Musical Theatre.* New York: Oxford University Press, 1978.

————. *Jerome Kern: His Life and Music.* New York: Oxford University Press, 1980.

Burton, Jack. *The Blue Book of Tin Pan Alley.* Watkins Glen, N.Y.: Century House, 1950.

Case, Frank. *Tales of a Wayward Inn.* New York: Garden City Publishing, 1940.

Fordin, Hugh. *The World of Entertainment.* Garden City, N.Y.: Doubleday, 1975.

————. *Getting to Know Him.* New York: Random House, 1977.

Gallagher, Brian. *Anything Goes.* New York: Times Books, 1987.

Goldberg, Isaac. *Tin Pan Alley.* New York: Simon & Schuster, 1930.

————. *George Gershwin.* New York: Simon & Schuster, 1931.

Green, Stanley. *Ring Bells! Sing Songs!* New Rochelle, N.Y.: Arlington House, 1971.

————. *Encyclopedia of the Musical Theatre.* New York: Dodd, Mead, 1976.

————. *The World of Musical Comedy.* New York: A. S. Barnes, 1980.

————. *Encyclopedia of the Musical Film.* New York: Oxford University Press, 1981.

Green, Stanley, and Burt Goldblatt. *Starring Fred Astaire.* New York: Dodd, Mead, 1973.

Harriman, Margaret Case. *The Vicious Circle.* New York: Reinhart, 1951.

Howe, Irving, with Kenneth Libo. *The World of Our Fathers.* New York: Simon & Schuster, 1983.

Jones, Maldwyn A. *Destination America.* New York: Holt, Reinhart & Winston, 1976.

Krasker, Tommy, and Robert Kimball. *Catalog of the American Musical.* New York: National Institute for Opera and Musical Theater, 1988.

Krueger, Miles. *The Movie Musical from Vitaphone to* Forty-second Street. New York: Dover, 1975.

Logan, Joshua. *Josh.* New York: Delacorte Press, 1976.

Loos, Anita. *The Talmadge Girls.* New York: Viking, 1978.

McCabe, John. *George M. Cohan: The Man Who Owned Broadway.* Garden City, N.Y.: Doubleday, 1973.

Mattfield, Julius. *Variety Music Cavalcade.* New York: Prentice-Hall, 1952.

Meredith, Scott. *George S. Kaufman and His Friends.* Garden City, N.Y.: Doubleday, 1974.

Mueller, John. *Astaire Dancing: The Musical Films.* New York: Knopf, 1985.

Oliver, Donald, ed. *By George: A Kaufman Collection.* New York: St. Martin's, 1979.

Osgood, Henry O. *So This Is Jazz.* Boston: Little, Brown, 1926.

Rodgers, Richard. *Musical Stages.* New York: Random House, 1975.

Sanders, Ronald. *Shores of Refuge.* New York: Schocken, 1988.

Sante, Luc. *Low Life.* New York: Farrar, Straus & Giroux, 1991.

Spaeth, Sigmund. *A History of Popular Music in America.* New York: Random House, 1948.

Suskin, Steven. *Show Tunes 1905–1985.* New York: Dodd, Mead, 1986.

———. *Opening Night on Broadway.* New York: Schirmer Books, 1990.

Vidor, King. *A Tree Is a Tree.* New York: Harcourt, Brace, 1952.

Waters, Edward N. *Victor Herbert: A Life in Music.* New York: Macmillan, 1955.

Widgoder, Geoffrey. *Encyclopedic Dictionary of Judaica.* New York and Paris: Leon Amiel, 1974.

Wilder, Alec. *American Popular Song.* New York: Oxford University Press, 1972.

Wilk, Max. *They're Playing Our Song.* New York: Atheneum, 1973.

Woollcott, Alexander. *The Story of Irving Berlin.* New York: G. P. Putnam's Sons, 1925.

ACKNOWLEDGMENTS

Over a long period of time—decades, in fact—as a student of American music, popular and unpopular, for the concert hall, film, and theater, I've encountered many gifted individuals—giants, some of them—who have each contributed to this work. As a writer-reviewer I met with music publishers, record producers, radio and television people, and theater personalities. I made notes and even, briefly, kept a diary. During that time, Irving Berlin was discussed, his work appraised, and anecdotes (always suspect) accumulated. I frequently wrote about him in music publications and record-liner notes.

Aware of his attitude, his uneasiness, in regard to a biography, I never broached the matter with him. (Others did, however, including the late Ken McCormick, one of my Doubleday editors, and Berlin's friend the attorney A. L. Berman; but Berlin always prevailed.) I went on to produce biographies of the Gershwins and Harold Arlen, all the while hoping one day to present my view of Irving Berlin and his work. The opportunity came recently when Ray Roberts, of Henry Holt, asked me to do just that.

Although I know, and have met with and spoken to, Mary Ellin Barrett, I did not interview her for this work. This, in short, is not an "authorized" biography (whatever that is; I've never written one, so far as I know, not even the one Lowell Thomas and I did of Jimmy Doolittle: though he cooperated, his advice was, If it's true, print it). But I am deeply grateful to have been able to read Mrs. Barrett's honest, straightforward, and beautifully crafted (very Berlinish) *Irving Berlin: A Daughter's Memoir.* It provided me with much information, some of it new to me, and corroboration of Irving Berlin the human being, the man I knew. Her lovely book should be widely read; it is an impressive work. Her suggestions—and corrections—on portions of the manuscript were invaluable.

Others who contributed to this biography are Toni Ausnit, New York, for rare Berlin sheet music; Rose Charon, New York, who shared the story of her brief encounter with a stranger on a plane; Kevin Cole, Chicago and elsewhere, pianist (a Berlin favorite), who went through so much of the music for me and who has a wonderful piano collection of Berliniana that really ought to be reissued on compact disk; Bradford Conner, Cambridge, Massachusetts, who provided information on, not to mention performances of, early Berlin songs. Many thanks as well to Elizabeth L. Dribble, New York, for information over the years; Linda Emmet, Paris, on Russian geography; Mark Trent Goldberg, Beverly Hills (the Ira and Leonore Gershwin Trusts), for his kind friendship and rare photographs; Michael Kerker, New York (American Society of Composers, Authors and Publishers), for too much to go into; Maurice I. Kessler, National Archives, Northeastern Region, New York; Marie Lampard for a very good lead and years of friendship; Dorothy Lewis-Griffith, New York; Howard and Ronald Mandelbaum, Photofest, New York, godsends; Walter Rappeport, head of the All State Café literary section, for discussions, suggestions, insight, and laughs; Robin Rupli, Washington, D.C., the Voice of America's authority on American popular music; Berthe Schuchat, New York, for research and her vast knowledge of American song; Benjamin Sears, Cambridge, Massachusetts, for aid in the discovery of some wonderful songs; Karen Sherry, New York (ASCAP), for her aid over the years; James Steinblatt, New York (ASCAP), for taking time out from his work on *ASCAP Playback* to search out some valuable photographs; Lawrence D. Stewart, Beverly Hills, for insight and information gleaned during his association with Ira Gershwin and his work on films; Michael Strunsky, San Francisco (the Ira and Leonore Gershwin Trusts); Janet Tempel, Upton, New York (Brookhaven National Laboratory) for invaluable *Yip! Yip! Yaphank* materials; Kevin Winkler, New York, Theatre Collection of the New York Public Library; and Joan Young, National Archives, Northeastern Region, New York.

Sadly, a number of others who helped me over the years are no longer alive. To Harold Arlen, Ira Gershwin, and Burton Lane I owe a great debt of thanks for observations, biographical notes, recollections, and views of Berlin and his work. Arlen kept notes on many of his conversations with his fellow songwriter, and Gershwin's greatest thrill in his later years was to get a birthday call from Irving Berlin; Lane, of course, had Berlin to thank for dispatching him to Hollywood, where his career truly began.

Of Berlin's office staff, Hilda Schneider, his secretary for several decades, was not only sharp but kind; a good friend, she permitted me access, to a point, to files and photographs. Helmy Kresa, too, was a longtime associate and friend. Finally, A. L.

Berman, while he did not actually work in the Berlin office, was an important member of the organization, and another good friend.

Stanley Green is special. We worked pretty much in the same field as writers but were never competitors. Instead we shared information, photographs, and a friendship of several years. His meticulous histories and dictionaries devoted to theater and film music are constantly at my side, always ready to provide or verify a date, a title, or some arcane fact.

William Sweigert, before leaving New York, presented me with his extensive collection of playbills. He probably saw every musical that opened in New York after the Second World War, and not only dated the programs but also preserved the reviews from several sources, an effort that saved me numerous trips to the library.

Last of all, or first, Irving Berlin treated me to discussions, visits, and a beautifully thoughtful painting, and touched me with his deep well of concern for the ailing Harold Arlen. He invariably asked about my children and my work, which seemed to interest him no less when in the fields of aviation or history than in music. His was an impressive intelligence, belonging to, in my personal experience, a kindly if diffident man. He was honest, edgy, apparently never still—and thoughtful, generous, and considerate. He was, of course, tough in certain matters; he had to be. But informally he was astute, curious, and gentle.

I am especially grateful to my family for their generous encouragement, suggestions, perceptive questions, and enthusiasm for my work. Without going into tedious detail, they are, in order of appearance, David and his wife, Susan Kidwell, University of Chicago; Carla, of New York and Edinburgh (a singer of songs); Emily and her husband, Richard Ahlberg; and, most delightfully, Michelle and Matthew. Stalwart supporters all.

And, finally, I owe special thanks to my editor, Ray Roberts; astute copy editor, Dorothy Straight; and indexer, Elaine Luthy. Bless you all.

INDEX

Titles followed by a date are stage productions unless otherwise noted. Parenthetical names for musicals are those of the composer and lyricist. **Boldface** page numbers refer to the main appendix listing for a stage show or film; individual songs listed in the appendix are indexed only when the song is also mentioned in the text.

DATE DUE

JAN 3 1 2001			

Demco, Inc. 38-293